THE 1988 GUINNESS BOOK OF OLYMPIC RECORDS

* Viewer's Guide to 1988's Winter and Summer Games

* New Photos of Winners in Action

*Dramatic and Fascinating Facts, Information, and History

* 1988 Schedule of Events

Inside are more answers than you have questions!
Track and Field, Skiing, Hockey, Skating,
Basketball, Judo, Weightlifting, Boxing,
Wrestling, Swimming, Fencing, Cycling,
Yachting, and many, many more!
—PLUS—
A COMPLETE ROLL OF OLYMPIC MEDAL
WINNERS FROM 1896 THROUGH 1984!

Bantam Books in the Guinness Series

GUINNESS BOOK OF WORLD RECORDS
GUINNESS BOOK OF OLYMPIC RECORDS

GUINNESS
BOOK OF
OLYMPIC RECORDS

COMPLETE ROLL OF
OLYMPIC MEDAL WINNERS (1896–1980,
including 1906) FOR THE SPORTS (7 WINTER
and SUMMER) CONTESTED IN THE
1984 CELEBRATIONS AND OTHER
USEFUL INFORMATION

Editors and Compilers

**STAN GREENBERG, editor-in-chief
PETER MATTHEWS
NORRIS McWHIRTER
DAVID A. BOEHM**

BANTAM BOOKS
TORONTO • NEW YORK • LONDON • SYDNEY • AUCKLAND

GUINNESS BOOK OF OLYMPIC RECORDS

*A Bantam Book / published by arrangement with
Sterling Publishing Co., Inc.*

PRINTING HISTORY

*Original Sterling edition published May 1964
2nd printing ... August 1964
Revised edition / October 1975
Revised Bantam edition / June 1967
New Revised Bantam edition / December 1971
New Revised Bantam edition / February 1976
New Revised Bantam edition / November 1979
New Revised Bantam edition / December 1983
New Revised Bantam edition / February 1988*

ISBN 0-553-27194-6

Published simultaneously in the United States and Canada

PRINTED IN THE UNITED STATES OF AMERICA

O   0 9 8 7 6 5 4 3

TABLE OF SUPERLATIVES

Most gold medals (men)	10	Ray Ewry (USA)	1900–1908
Most gold medals (women)	9	Larissa Latynina (URS)	1956–1964
Most medals (men)	15	Nikolai Andrianov (URS)	1972–1980
Most medals (women)	18	Larissa Latynina (URS)	1956–1964
Oldest gold medalist (men)	64 yr 258 days	Oscar Swahn (SWE)	1912
Oldest gold medalist (women)	45 yr 13 days	Liselott Linsenhoff (GER)	1972
Oldest medalist (men)	72 yr 280 days	Oscar Swahn (SWE)	1920
Oldest medalist (women)	46 yr 258 days	Maud Van Rosen (SWE)	1972
Youngest gold medalist (men)	7–10 yr	Unknown French boy	1900
Youngest gold medalist (women)	13 yr 267 days	Marjorie Gestring (USA)	1936
Youngest medalist (men)	7–10 yr	Unknown French boy	1900
Youngest medalist (women)	12 yr 24 days	Inge Sörensen (DEN)	1936
Most gold medals in one Games (men)	7	Mark Spitz (USA)	1972
Most gold medals in one Games (women)	4	Six women	
Most medals in one Games (men)	8	Alexandr Ditiatin (URS)	1980
Most medals in one Games (women)	7	Maria Gorochowskaya (URS)	1952
Most Games attended (men)	8	Raimondo d'Inzeo (ITA)	1948–1976
Most Games attended (women)	6	Janice York-Romary (USA)	1948–1968
	6	Lia Manoliu (ROM)	1952–1972
Longest span (men)	40 yr	Ivan Osiier (DEN)	1908–1948
	40 yr	Magnus Konow (NOR)	1908–1948
Longest span (women)	24 yr	Ellen Müller-Preis (AUT)	1932–1956
Oldest competitor (men)	72 yr 280 days	Oscar Swahn (SWE)	1920
Oldest competitor (women)	70 yr 5 days	Lorna Johnstone (GBR)	1972
Youngest competitor (men)	7–10 yr	Unknown French boy	1920
Youngest competitor (women)	11 yr 73 days	Cecilia Colledge (GBR)	1932

TABLE OF CONTENTS

TABLE OF MEDAL WINNERS
BY NATIONS 1896 TO 1980

Note: These totals include all first, second and third places including those in events no longer on the current schedule. (Not included are medals for the official Olympic art competitions of 1912 to 1948.) The 1906 Games which were officially staged by the International Olympic Committee have been included.

OLYMPIC GAMES (Summer)

	GOLD	SILVER	BRONZE	TOTAL
1. U.S.A.	710	529	448	1,687
2. U.S.S.R.	340	292	253	885
3. Great Britain	168	212	197	577
4. France	147	163	171	481
5. Germany[1]	146	193	192	631
6. Italy	141	117	120	378
7. Sweden	131	135	162	428
8. East Germany[2]	116	94	97	307
9. Hungary	113	106	130	349
10. Finland	96	74	108	278
11. Japan	83	72	75	230
12. Australia	68	61	82	211
13. Romania	48	53	76	177
14. Czechoslovakia	42	45	47	134
15. Netherlands	41	45	58	144
16. Switzerland	40	63	56	159
17. Norway	40	30	33	103
18. Poland	38	51	86	175
19. Canada	36	60	68	164
20. Belgium	35	48	40	123

1. Germany 1896–1964, West Germany from 1968
2. East Germany (GDR) from 1968

Development of the Olympic Games

These figures relate to the Summer Games and exclude Demonstration Sports.

	Countries Represented	Number of Sports	Number of Competitors Male	Female
1896	13	9	311	0
1900	22	17	1,319	11
1904	13	14	617	8
1906	20	11	877	7
1908	22	21	1,999	36
1912	28	14	2,490	57
1920	29	22	2,543	64
1924	44	18	2,956	136
1928	46	15	2,724	290
1932	37	15	1,281	127
1936	49	20	3,738	328
1948	59	18	3,714	385
1952	69	17	4,407	518
1956	71	17	2,958	384
1960	83	17	4,738	610
1964	93	19	4,457	683
1968	112	18	4,750	781
1972	122	21	6,077	1,070
1976	92	21	4,834	1,251
1980	81	21	4,265	1,088
1984	140	21	5,458	1,620

For the Winter Olympics see tables on page 220

PREFACE

Students of the modern Olympic Games movement seem to be offered in existing books either a bare Roll of Champions since 1896, or else a highly detailed and expensive (and in the case of the earlier Games, very rare) report of a single celebration. We have attempted, in an inexpensive form and in as much detail as space permits, to set out *all* the medal winners of all time—that is, the holders of the gold, silver, and bronze awards for every event on the 1988 program.

The Olympics have many fascinations to those who follow them round the world for television, radio, or the press, but there are two peculiarities perhaps above all others.

First, the competitors themselves make friendships that will last for the rest of their lives. This happens despite the tendencies of some commentators to overemphasize any disagreement that inevitably occurs in such a highly charged competitive atmosphere. Occasionally there are even Olympic marriages. Olympic friendships, particularly notable since the custom started in 1932 of lodging the participants in an Olympic village, transcend the mere difficulties of conflicting language, race and creed. The Olympic spirit of common interest in the techniques of sport makes rather light of nationalistic differences, which so often leave professional diplomats in deadlock.

Secondly, especially in those sports that enjoy a dependence on absolute measurement of either time, distance, or weight to determine their results—such as track and field athletics, swimming, and weightlifting—the continuous urge to improve on previous high-water marks is most evident. It is practically a law of the Olympics that every record set in previous Games will be in great jeopardy when the next celebration takes place four years later.

This work has been again revised in the light of continuing research, including attention to the earlier Games. The leading authority is Erich Kamper whose *Enzyklopädie der Olympischen Spiele* (Römer, 1972) and *Lexikon der Olympischen Winter Spiele* (Union Verlag Stuttgart, 1964) should be recognized as the most complete text of Olympic results yet compiled of the first 18 Games.

NORRIS McWHIRTER

Celebrations of the
Modern Olympic Games

I	1896	Athens	April 6–15
II	1900	Paris	May 20–Oct. 28
III	1904	St. Louis	July 1–Nov. 23
*	1906	Athens	April 22–May 2
IV	1908	London	April 27–Oct. 31
V	1912	Stockholm	May 5–July 22
VI	1916	Berlin	not celebrated owing to war
VII	1920	Antwerp	April 20–Sept. 12
VIII	1924	Paris	May 4–July 27
IX	1928	Amsterdam	May 17–Aug. 12
X	1932	Los Angeles	July 30–Aug. 14
XI	1936	Berlin	Aug. 1–16
XII	1940	Tokyo, then Helsinki	not celebrated owing to war
XIII	1944	London	not celebrated owing to war
XIV	1948	London	July 29–Aug. 14
XV	1952	Helsinki	July 19–Aug. 3
XVI	1956	Melbourne[1]	Nov. 22–Dec. 8
XVII	1960	Rome	Aug. 25–Sept. 11
XVIII	1964	Tokyo	Oct. 10–24
XIX	1968	Mexico	Oct. 12–27
XX	1972	Munich	Aug. 26–Sept. 10
XXI	1976	Montreal	July 17–Aug. 1
XXII	1980	Moscow	July 19–Aug. 3
XXIII	1984	Los Angeles	July 28–Aug. 12
XXIV	1988	Seoul	Sept. 17–Oct. 2

* *This celebration (to mark the 10th anniversary of the modern Games) was officially intercalated but is not numbered.*
[1] *The equestrian events were held in Stockholm June 10–17, 1956.*

The Winter Olympic Games

I	1924	Chamonix, France	Jan. 25–Feb. 4
II	1928	St. Moritz, Switzerland	Feb. 11–19
III	1932	Lake Placid, U.S.A.	Feb. 4–15
IV	1936	Garmisch-Partenkirchen, Germany	Feb. 6–16
V	1948	St. Moritz, Switzerland	Jan. 30–Feb. 8
VI	1952	Oslo, Norway	Feb. 14–25
VII	1956	Cortina d'Ampezzo, Italy	Jan. 26–Feb. 5
VIII	1960	Squaw Valley, California	Feb. 18–28
IX	1964	Innsbrück, Austria	Jan. 29–Feb. 9
X	1968	Grenoble, France	Feb. 6–18
XI	1972	Sapporo, Japan	Feb. 3–13
XII	1976	Innsbrück, Austria[2]	Feb. 4–15
XIII	1980	Lake Placid, U.S.A.	Feb. 14–23
XIV	1984	Sarajevo, Yugoslavia	Feb. 8–19
XV	1988	Calgary, Canada	Feb. 13–28

[2] *Originally awarded to Denver, U.S.A.*

HISTORY OF THE OLYMPIC GAMES

1. THE ANCIENT GAMES

Few human institutions can even remotely approach the antiquity of the Olympic Games. Though precise records of the Ancient Games began only in 776 B.C., there is abundant evidence of their occasional celebration up to six centuries earlier. A date conservatively attributed to the Games at Olympia sponsored by Pelops is 1370 B.C. This date is, of course, subject to adjustment in the light of evidence of new archeological techniques. All the signs are, however, that Olympic history spans some thirty-three centuries.

The Olympic Games faded away about the middle of the 9th Century B.C., but were reputedly revived by King Iphitos of Elis. During this period came the idea of a temporary truce among all the warring factions in Greece: the Olympic peace or *ekecheiria* was proclaimed to last for about three months before the Games (which themselves lasted for five days) and long enough after them for the competitors to enjoy a safe passage back to their homes.

The Games of 776 B.C.—the first of which there is an actual record of the name of a champion—seem to have consisted of merely one event: the stadium race (about 170 meters or 186 yd.), won by Coroibos of Elis. But the Games rapidly expanded in scope—with longer races, plus a penthathlon of running, discus throwing (about 9lb *4kg* in weight), long jump with weights, javelin throwing with a lever, and wrestling; as well as boxing and wrestling. Moreover, the Greeks had to compete soon against the challenge of both Sicilians and Cretans.

Even in those days each celebration had its hero. There were winners of what would now be called the sprint double, there were heats for the shorter events, and eventually women had their own Games.

A famous champion, Chionis, in the middle of the 7th century B.C. is credited by modern researchers to have long jumped, almost certainly with the aid of dumb-bell weights, *7 m 05 cm* or 23 feet 1½ in.

From this time onwards, the names and feats of many champions are recorded and competitions in the fine arts were added.

The original prizes were only olive wreaths, but gradually the champions began to acquire valuable rewards and the Games became corrupted. The long Roll of Champions ends in A.D. 369, and in 393 the Emperor Theodosius decreed from Milan the end of the Olympic Games. So the Olympic torch went out for 1,503 summers.

2. THE MODERN (OR REVIVED) GAMES

The gérm of the idea of reviving the Ancient Olympic Games was born in Germany. J. C. F. Guts-Muths (1759–1839), the founder of

Pierre, Baron de Coubertin (1863–1937), the founder of the Olympic movement, stated the ideals of the Modern Olympic Games that have inspired succeeding generations.

the notable German gymnastics movement, put forward the idea. Ernst Curtius (1814–96) gave a lecture on the Ancient Games in Berlin on January 10, 1852. His researches aroused interest in Greece where the wealthy Major Euangelis Zappas organized the first "Pan-Hellenic Games," in 1859 watched by 20,000 spectators. These games—a purely national affair—were repeated in 1870, 1875, 1888 and 1889. They at least kindled a spark of interest in other countries.

It is Baron Pierre de Coubertin (1863–1937) of France who is, however, rightly styled the "Founder of the Modern Olympic Games." This wealthy young nobleman was commissioned by the French Government in 1889 to study physical culture throughout the civilized world. His inquiries produced a disquieting picture of feuding and dissension between sport and sport, nation and nation, and the already apparent commercial spirit in sport.

On November 25, 1892, de Coubertin in a lecture at the Sorbonne in Paris for the first time publicly advanced his conviction that there should be a modern revival of the Ancient Games. His lecture was received with an ovation. In 1893, de Coubertin convened an international conference at the Hall of Sciences at the Sorbonne from June 16–23, 1894. Thirteen countries sent representatives and 21 others sent messages of support. On the last day a resolution was passed that "sport competitions should be held every fourth year on the lines of the Greek Olympic Games and every nation should be invited to participate."

De Coubertin envisaged the first Games being in Paris at the beginning of the century, but a Greek motion was passed giving the Greeks the privilege of holding the First Celebration at Athens in 1896. Accordingly, the International Olympic Committee (IOC)—then 12 strong—was formed.

1896—The Ist Games at Athens

On April 6, after a gap of 1,503 years 80,000 Athenians witnessed the revival of the Olympics.

Despite the support of 34 nations at the Paris Conference only 13 sent representatives to Athens. The white marble stadium was a splendid sight, but too long and narrow for track events. The small American team won 9 out of the 12 track and field events, while the Germans dominated the gymnastics, and the French the cycling. The Greeks became depressed as the titles, even those which they regarded as their national specialties, such as the discus throw, were won by foreigners. Happily, the last event—the Marathon—(24 miles 1503 yd *40 km*) was dramatically won by Spyridon Louis, a post office messenger from Marusi near Athens, one of 21 Greek starters.

1900—The IInd Games at Paris

It was feared that the Second Games would rival the World Exhibition in Paris in the same year, so de Coubertin was subdued and the Games were allowed to be nothing more than a sideshow. Another factor that reduced interest was that the Games in the Bois de Boulogne, Paris, were spread over more than five months. Despite these drawbacks, the standards shot up and quite a few world best performances were set. The hero of the Games was Alvin Kraenzlein (U.S.A.) who won the 60 meters, 100 meters hurdles, 200 meters hurdles, and long jump.

1904—The IIIrd Games at St. Louis

Again the Olympics were organized as a mere sideshow to a World's Fair. Because of the distance and expense of travel, only seven European and five other countries were represented. Interest in the 85 Olympic events was minimal: the record crowd was 2,000.

Despite the rather crude facilities, mostly at Washington University, the competitive spirit and advancing skill of the contestants—the golden thread of the whole Olympic tapestry—was undiminished. There was a major scandal in the Marathon when an American (Lorz) got a clandestine 10 mile lift in a car in the middle section of the race and naturally arrived in the Stadium first. When the truth dawned, wild applause soon thinned to vituperative abuse and immediate expulsion.

1906—The Intercalated Games at Athens

These Games were to mark the tenth anniversary of the Ist Games at Athens in 1896.

They were in no sense unofficial—the International Olympic Committee sanctioned them—but they were unnumbered because they did not conform to the regular Olympic four-year cycle.

The Games were far more successful than the Exhibition sideshow type of Games in 1900 or 1904. Twenty nations were represented by 884 competitors. Great crowds, including a galaxy of royalty, thronged to the marble stadium.

There were 11 sports including 22 track and field, 16 shooting and 8 fencing events.

The individual hero was Paul H. Pilgrim (U.S.A.) who financed his own journey to Athens and won the 400 and 800 meters double.

Reginald Walker turned in a time under 11 seconds in the 100 meters event at the 1908 Games.

1908—The IVth Games at London

Italy was originally awarded the IVth Games but resigned them and London took on the job. With the White City Stadium that could hold 100,000, full royal patronage, a vast schedule, good publicity, and 2,035 competitors from 22 nations, the Olympics at last broke through as a world event.

The two most memorable incidents were in the track and field athletics, and both sadly involved disqualification. There was an unfortunate rumpus over the 400 meters final in which the U.S. runner Carpenter was disqualified for obstruction. His compatriots Robbin and Taylor then scratched in protest, so the only remaining competitor, Lt. Wyndham Halswell (G.B.), had a 50.0 sec. walk-over for the gold medal.

The marathon from Windsor to the Stadium was watched by the then world's largest recorded sports crowd—an estimated 250,000 people. The leader, a frail looking little Italian, Dorando Pietri, tottered into the Stadium in the last stages of exhaustion. Harassed officials aided him when he fell for a second time, so he had to be disqualified for receiving aid, and the race went to the U.S. runner Johnny Hayes, who took the gold medal while Pietri got a gold cup from a sympathetic Queen Alexandra.

1912—The Vth Games at Stockholm

Following the success of the London Games, this celebration at Stockholm confirmed and cemented worldwide interest in the Olympics. The number of participants rose to 2,547, drawn from 28 countries. The hero of the Games was the American Indian, Jim Thorpe, who won both the pentathlon and the decathlon. Thorpe was later discovered by the A.A.U. to have rather thoughtlessly transgressed their amateur rules by earlier acceptance of payment for some minor baseball appearances. Inevitably he was struck off the Roll of Champions and his two gold medals were re-awarded to his runners-up. But he was reinstated as an amateur in 1973 by the A.A.U. twenty years after his death.

1916—The VIth Games, awarded to Berlin

Owing to the World War which developed following Germany's invasion of Belgium and part of France, in August, 1914, the Games inevitably had to be cancelled.

1920—The VIIth Games at Antwerp

The Olympics were resumed at Antwerp but were without any representation from the defeated central European countries or the Russians, who remained absent until 1952. The Games were highly successful, with the Finns challenging even the Americans in the track events.

Forty years elapsed between the appearance of Czarist Russia's last Olympic team in 1912, shown above, and the first Soviet team in 1952.

1924—The VIIIth Games at Paris

The Olympic Games again leapt forward in growth—44 countries entered 3,092 competitors. The Finn, Paavo Nurmi, won 5 gold medals—for the 1,500 meters, 5,000 meters, 10,000 meters cross-country race (both team and individual), and the 3,000 meters team event. The American, Johnny Weissmuller, later to be the most famous of Hollywood's dynasty of Tarzans, won 3 gold medals for sprint swimming.

1928—The IXth Games at Amsterdam

At Amsterdam the Germans reappeared. Olympic medals tended to be more widely distributed among the nations. The Finns were again dominant in distance running, but this time Nurmi won only the 10,000 meters. Weissmuller won two more swimming gold medals. Women's events were successfully introduced in track and field with world records being set in all five events.

1932—The Xth Games at Los Angeles
Under the famous sunny California climatic conditions a profusion of Olympic and world records were set. Every single track and field Olympic record, except the long jump, was improved. America's black sprinters and jumpers excelled while the Japanese collected five gold medals in the men's swimming events. It was wrongly predicted that records made under these "freak California conditions" would remain unbroken for years.

1936—The XIth Games at Berlin
At Berlin the Nazi government of Germany disgracefully attempted to turn the Olympic movement into a propaganda vehicle for the glorification of their creed. The strong internationalism of the Games prevented complete subversion. The levels of performance in most events left many of the 1932 "super-records" well behind, against all prediction. The hero of the Games was the modest American Jesse Owens, who won the 100 meters, 200 meters, 4 × 100 meters relay, and the long jump. The Japanese marathon runners (gold and bronze medals) and the Dutch women swimmers made a strong impression.

Paavo Nurmi, the Flying Finn, is the most successful medal winner in Olympic track and field history, with 9 gold and 3 silver medals in the 1920, 1924, and 1928 Games.

Jim Thorpe, the American Indian (US), shown here in the pole vault, won the gold medal in the 1912 decathlon with 6,845 points, but was disqualified later when it was discovered that he had received $25 once for playing semipro baseball. In 1982, after 70 years, his medals (2 golds) were restored post-mortem.

1940–44—The XIIth Games, awarded to Tokyo and then Helsinki; the XIIIth Games awarded to London

Neither of these two celebrations could be held because of the World War. The 1940 Games were originally awarded to Tokyo but when the Japanese became involved in war with China, they were re-awarded to Helsinki. The 1944 Games were hopefully given to London but the war still had a year to run.

1948—The XIVth Games at London

London and the Wembley Stadium attracted 4,099 competitors from 59 countries. For the first time a woman became the Victrix Ludorum and Mvr. Fanny Blankers-Koen, the mother of two children, won the 100 meters, 200 meters, 80 meter hurdles, and the 4 × 100 meters relay for the Netherlands. Other athletes who attracted great interest were Harrison Dillard (U.S.) in the 100 meters and 4 × 100 meters relay; Emil Zatopek (Czechoslovakia) in the 10,000 meters; Bob Mathias (U.S.) in the decathlon; and Willi Grut (Sweden) in the modern pentathlon.

1952—The XVth Games at Helsinki

Sixty-nine nations and 4,925 competitors came to the Finnish capital city, Helsinki (population 350,000) in 1952. The Games were notable for the reappearance of the Russians after an absence of 40 years. The undoubted heroes of the Games were the Zatopeks of Czechoslovakia. Emil won the unprecedented triple—the 5,000 meters, 10,000 meters, and the marathon—all in Olympic record time. On the day he won the 5,000 meters, his wife, Dana, won the women's javelin throwing title, also with an Olympic record.

1956—The XVIth Games at Melbourne

The Games were celebrated in the Southern Hemisphere for the first and so far only time. Inevitably, the difficulties of season, distances, and expense reduced the entries, but only slightly. The equestrian events had to be held separately in Stockholm because of rigid horse quarantine laws in Australia. Outstanding on the track was Vladimir Kuts (U.S.S.R.) with a great 5,000 meters and 10,000 meters double victory; and the sprinters Bobby-Joe Morrow (U.S.) and Miss Betty Cuthbert of Australia, each of whom won three gold medals in the 100 meters, 200 meters and 4 × 100 meters relay. The Australians dominated the swimming, winning 8 out of 13 events.

1960—The XVIIth Games at Rome
Rome, which missed its opportunity of staging the Games in 1908, made a magnificent setting for the XVIIth Games. Eighty-three nations contributed 5,348 competitors to a fortnight of the most intense competition, for the most part in exceptionally hot conditions. Awards were widely spread with 23 countries gaining at least one gold medal. Outstanding achievements were the 1,500 meters world record by the Australian, Herbert Elliott, and the unexpected marathon success of the Ethiopian, Abebe Bikila. In the women's events, Miss Wilma Rudolph, a black American runner, dominated the sprints and won three gold medals. The Australians in equestrianism and the Russian girl gymnasts left a great impression.

1964—The XVIIIth Games at Tokyo
The first celebration in Asia was the organizational high-water mark of the Games, thanks to meticulous attention to detail by the Japanese. A conservative estimate is that the cost of all the public works and other expenses with a direct bearing on the Games was $560,000,000.

Vast crowds, undeterred by frequent rain, added atmosphere to a celebration in which Olympic records again fell wholesale, though, perhaps significantly, the number of world records set was fewer than in past Games. The highlights included the unique marathon double by Abebe Bikila (Ethiopia); a blazing finish in the 10,000 meters by Billy Mills (U.S.) with less than 1½ seconds between the three medalists; the four swimming gold medals won by Don Schollander (U.S.); and the third successive win in the 100 meters free-style by Dawn Fraser (Australia).

1968—XIXth Games at Mexico City
A record 5,531 competitors from one hundred and twelve nations did battle at nearly seven and a half thousand feet above sea level: these are the two salient figures to remember for the first Games in Latin America—the size and the height.

The technical organization in Mexico was excellent, while the brilliantly colorful fiesta atmosphere excused the few flaws in the ancillary arrangements for programs, information to the public, and transport.

Because nobody dropped dead it did not mean that the altitude problem was insignificant. Just as predicted the performances in the "explosive" events—memorably Bob Beamon's incredible long jump of 29 ft 2½ in (*8,90 m*)—were records, while those involving more than three minutes' continuous effort were in some cases back to standards achieved as long ago as 1948.

Bob Mathias (U.S.A) won the decathlon title in 1948 when he was only 17 years old. He successfully defended his crown at Helsinki in 1952—the only man ever to retain this championship.

Up 90 steps to the Olympic flame cauldron in 1968 in Mexico City ran the first woman to take the final pass of the torch and to light the Olympic flame.

Olga Korbut was the darling of the spectators at the Munich Games in 1972. The elfin Russian gymnast won a silver and 3 gold medals.

1972—XXth Games at Munich

West Germany's massive effort to provide perfect and efficient Olympic conditions was cruelly marred by the callous murder of 11 members of the Israeli team by Palestinian terrorists on September 5th.

The great show stumbled, some commentators mistakenly predicted the death of the whole Olympic movement. After a stunned 24-hour pause the Games started off again and the entire program was fulfilled.

The Olympics, which attracted over 4,000 "media men" and an estimated 1,000,000,000 world television viewership, had become an irresistible stage for murderous protesters. Obviously the Olympics were becoming too large but the IOC was finding it very difficult to hold the program to its present size.

The heroine of the Games was the diminutive Russian gymnast, Olga Korbut, who was the darling of the crowds and the despair of the judges. The male hero was the swimmer Mark Spitz (U.S.A) who won 7 gold medals each in a world record time.

In the stadium there were two sprint doubles by Valeriy Borzov (U.S.S.R.) and East Germany's Renate Stecher, but the greatest acclaim went rightly to Finland's Lasse Viren who won the 5,000 and 10,000 meters double. The almost traditional United States dominance suffered a partial eclipse and the termination of its famous pole-vault monopoly.

The Soviet team won ten more medals than the United States including 17 more golds than their traditional rivals. The efficiency of the U.S.S.R.'s deployment of their strength over the entire Olympic program certainly produced handsome dividends.

1976—XXIst Games at Montreal

The 1976 Games, the first in Canada, saw some substantial changes in the program but all attempts to reduce the number of events from the 1972 record of 195 were frustrated and in fact there were 198 Olympic titles open for competition.

The program changes included the elimination of the 50 kilometer walk, the tandem event, the slalom canoeing events, the free rifle event and three swimming events.

But the pruning was more than cancelled by the introduction of women's basketball, four canoeing events over 500 meters, women's handball and no less than seven new rowing events, six of them for women.

The run-up to the Games was beset by financial, constructional and political disputes. The excessive costs of the facilities, the industrial problems, and then the withdrawal of 22 Third World countries, mainly African, seemed destined to diminish the Games. However, once they were underway, the quality of performance was exceptionally high and provided, in the petite form of gymnast Nadia Comaneci of Romania, and the powerful Cuban runner, Alberto Juantorena, two athletes whose deeds will far outlive a single Olympiad.

1980—XXIInd Games at Moscow

There had been only a little dissent in 1974 when the IOC voted by a substantial majority to award the 1980 Games to Moscow. Tsarist Russia had competed in 1900 and from 1906 to 1912. Athletes from Estonia and Latvia, which had been provinces of Russia prior to 1918 and were taken over by the Soviet Union in 1940, had competed independently from 1920 to 1936. The Soviet Union had entered the Games in force in 1952 and was now the second highest medal scorer of all time.

In December 1979 the Soviet Union invaded Afghanistan, and much of the non-Communist world, led by the United States, tried to impose a boycott on the Games—but not, it should be noted, on trade and other economic activity. Not all countries supported the boycott, although sports within those countries sometimes did. It is difficult to finalize a list of those who did not go to Moscow in support of the boycott, as a number of those previously included were unlikely to attend anyway for other, usually financial, reasons. The most reliable estimate is 45–50, of which the most important in sporting terms were the United States, the Federal Republic of (West) Germany, and Japan. When the Games were officially opened by Leonid Brezhnev, President of the U.S.S.R., there were eight first time entries to the Games, not including Zimbabwe which had previously been at the Olympics as Rhodesia.

Facilities, including the 103,000 capacity Lenin Stadium, were excellent and large crowds attended most sports. New competitions such as women's hockey, two extra judo classes, one extra weightlifting class, and reintroduced events brought the total of gold medals available to a record 203 (barring ties).

The heroine of Montreal, Nadia Comaneci (ROM) returned but was not the force she had been, and the star of the gymnastics was a male, Alexandr Ditiatin (URS). By winning three golds, four silvers and one bronze he set a record for the most medals ever won by a competitor, of any sport, in a single Games. He also was awarded a maximum 10.00 in the horse vault, the first such score ever to a man in the Olympics. His teammate Nikolai Andrianov brought his total of medals to a men's record 15, comprising seven golds, five silvers and three bronze, in three Games. This total has only ever been exceeded in Olympic history by Larissa Latynina (URS), also a gymnast.

1984—XXIIIrd Games at Los Angeles

The IOC awarded the Games of 1984 to Los Angeles only after involved negotiations about the financial guarantees usually required from a host city. Various innovations to protect Los Angeles from a Montreal-like deficit proved highly successful. These included widespread sponsorship by private corporations. Television rights amounted to some $287 million, of which the major part came from the ABC network for US rights.

Against current thinking the program was expanded to 221 events, including an extra 12 events for women, while tennis and baseball were demonstration sports.

The Memorial Coliseum, main site of the 1932 Games, was refurbished, and many other venues, famous in their own right, were utilized. There were complaints that some of these venues were too far-flung, but the overall good weather and the enthusiasm, at times overwhelming, of the American crowds offset most problems. Smog and traffic congestion did not materialize to anything like the degree predicted. One unfortunate phenomenon, however, was the orgy of American chauvinism displayed—especially by the media. Attendances at all sports were quite remarkable with the highest single figure 101,799 for the final of the soccer tournament at the famed Rose Bowl. The one, albeit major, disaster of these Games was the last-minute boycott by the Soviet Union and other Socialist countries, although of 159 official invitations sent out, a record 140 countries accepted and competed—notably including Romania. Nevertheless standards in most sports were generally high.

Aided enormously by the absence of Soviet and East German opposition, the U.S. gained the lion's share of the medals. Leading the gold rush were sprinter/jumper Carl Lewis, who equaled the feat of Jesse Owens in 1936, with four golds, and another track star, Valerie Brisco-Hooks, and five swimmers who all won three golds each.

At the end of the Games the organizers reported a profit of $215 million.

1988—XXIVth Games at Seoul, Korea

The capital of Korea, Seoul, has one of the largest populations of any city on earth—an estimated 9,000,000. Nearly all facilities for the Games were in place by the end of 1986 when the Asian Games were held there. Most major installations are part of the sports complex on the bank of the Han River, and include a 100,000-capacity stadium.

Once again the program has been expanded, with the reintroduction of tennis (for the first time since 1924), the addition of table tennis, and the inclusion of extra events which will bring the total to a record 237. Badminton, tae-kwon-do and women's judo will be demonstration sports. American television companies offered incredible sums (up to $750 million) for the USA rights, provided that major sports finals take place during American prime-time viewing. This would require that track and field finals take place 9.00–11.00 AM Korean time. This was opposed by the International Amateur Athletic Federation and the IOC, although some compromise was reached. Television income will still be immense. Though there have been threats of possible boycotts, the most tenacious problem, still unsolved at time of writing, has been the claim of North Korea to host half of the Games. Against IOC rules, but with their blessing, some sports have been offered to them, but they continue to be intransigent. However, it seems unlikely that the major countries of the Communist bloc would miss the Games again on their behalf.

Official Olympic International
Abbreviations of Names of Countries

AFG — Afghanistan
AHO — Netherlands Antilles
ALB — Albania
ALG — Algeria
AND — Andorra
ANG — Angola
ANT — Antigua
ARG — Argentina
ARS — Saudi Arabia (now SAV)
AUS — Australia
AUT — Austria
BAH — Bahamas
BAN — Bangladesh
BAR — Barbados
BEL — Belgium
BEN — Benin
BER — Bermuda
BHU — Bhutan
BIR — Burma
BIZ — Belize
BOH — Bohemia
BOL — Bolivia
BOT — Botswana
BRA — Brazil
BRN — Bahrain
BRU — Brunei
BUL — Bulgaria
BWI — British West Indies
CAF — Central Africa
CAN — Canada
CAY — Cayman Islands
CEY — Ceylon (now Sri Lanka)
CGO — Congo
CHA — Chad
CHI — Chile
CHN — China
CIV — Ivory Coast
CMR — Cameroun
COL — Columbia
CRC — Costa Rica
CUB — Cuba
CYP — Cyprus
DAH — Dahomey
DEN — Denmark
DOM — Dominican Republic
ECU — Ecuador
EGY — Egypt
ESA — El Salvador
ESP — Spain
EST — Estonia
ETH — Ethiopia
FIJ — Fiji Islands
FIN — Finland
FRA — France
FRG — Federal Republic of Germany
GAB — Gabon
GAM — Gambia
GBR — United Kingdom
GDR — German Democratic Republic
GEQ — Equatorial Guinea
GER — Germany (but West Germany only from 1968)
GHA — Ghana

GRE — Greece
GRN — Grenada
GUA — Guatemala
GUI — Guinea
GUY — Guyana
HAI — Haiti
HBR — British Honduras (now BIZ)
HKG — Hong Kong
HOL — Netherlands
HON — Honduras
HUN — Hungary
INA — Indonesia
IND — India
IRL — Ireland
IRN — Iran
IRQ — Iraq
ISL — Iceland
ISR — Israel
ISV — Virgin Islands
ITA — Italy
IVB — British Virgin Islands
JAM — Jamaica
JOR — Jordan
JPN — Japan
KEN — Kenya
KHM — Cambodia
KOR — Korea
KUW — Kuwait
LAO — Laos
LAT — Latvia
LBA — Libya
LBR — Liberia
LES — Lesotho
LIB — Lebanon
LIE — Liechtenstein
LIT — Lithuania
LUX — Luxembourg
MAD — Madagascar
MAL — Malaysia
MAR — Morocco
MAW— Malawi
MEX — Mexico
MGL — Mongolia
MLI — Mali
MLT — Malta
MON — Monaco
MOZ — Mozambique
MRI — Mauritius
MTN — Mauritania
NCA — Nicaragua
NEP — Nepal
NGR — Nigeria
NGU — Papua New Guinea
NIG — Niger
NOR — Norway
NZL — New Zealand
OMA — Oman
PAK — Pakistan
PAN — Panama
PAR — Paraguay
PER — Peru
PHI — Philippines
POL — Poland

POR — Portugal
PRK — Dem. People's Rep. of Korea
PUR — Puerto Rico
QAT — Qatar
RHO — Rhodesia (now Zimbabwe)
ROC — Republic of China
ROM — Romania
SAF — South Africa
SAM — Western Samoa
SAU — Saudi Arabia
SEN — Senegal
SEY — Seychelles
SIN — Singapore
SLE — Sierra Leone
SMR — San Marino
SOM — Somali Republic
SRI — Sri Lanka
SUD — Sudan
SUI — Switzerland
SUR — Surinam
SWE — Sweden
SWZ — Swaziland
SYR — Syria

TAN — Tanzania
TCH — Czechoslovakia
THA — Thailand
TOG — Togo
TON — Tonga
TPE — Taiwan
TRI — Trinidad and Tobago
TUN — Tunisia
TUR — Turkey
UAE — United Arab Emirates
UGA — Uganda
URS — U.S.S.R.
URU — Uruguay
USA — United States of America
VEN — Venezuela
VIE — Vietnam
VOL — Upper Volta
YAR — Yemen Arab Republic
YMD — Yemen Democratic Republic
YUG — Yugoslavia
ZAI — Zaire
ZAM — Zambia
ZIM — Zimbabwe

ROLL OF OLYMPIC MEDAL WINNERS SINCE 1896 IN THE 21 CURRENT SPORTS

*throughout indicates an Olympic record or best performance.
d.n.a. indicates data not available.

1. Archery

MEN'S DOUBLE F.I.T.A. ROUND

(2 × 36 arrows at 90, 70, 50 and 30 meters. Possible is 2,880 points.)

	GOLD	SILVER	BRONZE
1972	John C. Williams (USA) 2,528	Gunnar Jarvil (SWE) 2,481	Kyoesti Laasonen (FIN) 2,467
1976	Darrell Pace (USA) 2,571	Hiroshi Michinaga (JPN) 2,502	Giancarlo Ferrari (ITA) 2,495
1980	Tomi Polkolainen (FIN) 2,455	Boris Isachenko (URS) 2,452	Giancarlo Ferrari (ITA) 2,449
1984	Darrell Pace (USA) 2,616*	Richard McKinney (USA) 2,564	Hiroshi Yamamoto (JPN) 2,563

WOMEN'S DOUBLE F.I.T.A. ROUND

(2 × 36 arrows at 70, 60, 50 and 30 meters. Possible is 2,880 points)

	GOLD	SILVER	BRONZE
1972	Doreen Wilbur (USA) 2,424	Irena Szydlwska (POL) 2,407	Emma Gapchenko (URS) 2,403
1976	Luann Ryon (USA) 2,499	Valentina Kovpan (URS) 2,460	Zebiniso Rustamova (URS) 2,407
1980	Keto Losaberidze (URS) 2,491	Natalya Butuzova (URS) 2,477	Paivi Meriluoto (FIN) 2,449
1984	Hyang-Soon Seo (KOR) 2,568*	Lingjuan Li (CHN) 2,559	Jin-Ho Kim (KOR) 2,555

(Archery was included in the Games of 1900, 1904, 1908 and 1920. But none of the events in those celebrations compare with the championship events of 1972–80.)

Action in the 1948 basketball finals between the United States (in white) and France. From the introduction of the sport in the Olympic program in 1936 to the disputed title of 1972, the U.S.A. never lost a single Olympic match.

2. Basketball (Men)

GOLD	SILVER	BRONZE
1896–1932 Event not held[1]		
1936 UNITED STATES	CANADA	MEXICO
Francis Johnson	James Stewart	Carlos Borja Morco
Carl S. Knowles	Jan Allison	Victor H. Borja Morco
Joe Fortenberry	Charles Chapman	Luis I. de la Vega Leija
William Wheatly	Malcolm Wiseman	José Pamplona
Jack W. Ragland	Gordon Aitchison	Lecuanda
Ralph Bishop	Douglas Peden	Rodolfo Choperanna
Carl Shy	Arthur Chapman	Irizarri
Duane A. Swanson	Irving Meretsky	Jesus Olmos Moreno
Samuel Balter	Edward J. Dawson	Raul Fernández Robert
John H. Gibbons		Greer Skousen
Frank J. Lubin		Spilsbury
Arthur O. Mollner		Francisco Martinez
Donald A. Piper		Cordero
Willard Schmidt		Silvio Hernandez del
		Valle
		Andrés Gómez
		Domingues

---

[1] There were basketball competitions in the 1904 and 1928 Games, but they were only demonstration events.

	GOLD	SILVER	BRONZE
1948	**UNITED STATES** Clifford Barker Donald Barksdale Ralph Beard Louis Beck Vincent Boryla Gordon Carpenter Alexander Groza Wallace Jones Robert Kurland Raymond Lumpp Robert C. Pitts Jesse Renick R. Jackie Robinson Kenneth Rollins	**FRANCE** André Barrais Michel Bonnevie André Buffière René Chocat René Dérency Maurice Desaymonnet André Even Fernand Guillou Maurice Girardot Raymond Offner Jacques Perrier Yvan Quénin Lucien Rebuffic Pierre Thiolon	**BRAZIL** Zenny de Azevedo João F. Braz Marcus V. Dias Alfonso A. Evora Ruy de Freitas Alexandre Gemignani Alberto Marson Alfredo R. da Mota Nilton P. de Oliveira Massinet Sorcinelli
1952	**UNITED STATES** Charles Hoag William Hougland John Keller M. Dean Kelley Robert Kenney William Lienhard Clyde Lovelette Marcus Frieberger V. Wayne Glasgow Frank McCabe Daniel Pippin Howard Williams Ronald Bontemps Robert Kurland	**U.S.S.R.** Viktor Vlassov Styapas Butautas Yvan Lysov Kazis Petkyavitschus Nodar Dzhordzhikiya Anatoliy Konyev Otar Korkiya Ilmar Kullam Yuriy Ozerov Aleksandr Moiseyev Heino Kruus Yustinas Lagunavichus Maigonis Valdmanis Stassis Stonkus	**URUGUAY** Martin Acosta y Lara Enrique Boliño Victorio Cieslinkas Héctor Costa Nelson Demarco Héctor Garcia Otero Tabaré Larre Borges Adesio Lombardo Roberto Lovera Sergio Matto Wilfredo Pelaez Carlos Roselló
1956	**UNITED STATES** Carl C. Cain William Hougland K. C. Jones William Russell James P. Walsh William Evans Burdette Haldorson Ronald Tomsic Richard J. Boushka Gilbert Ford Robert E. Jeangerard Charles F. Darling	**U.S.S.R.** Valdis Muizhnieks Maigonis Valdmanis Vladimir Torban Stassis Stonkus Kazis Petkyavitschus Arkhadiy Bochkaryev Yanis Kruminsch Mikhail Semyonov Alguirdas Lauritenas Yuriy Ozerov Viktor Zoubkov Mikhail Studenetskiy	**URUGUAY** Carlos Blixen Ramiro Cortes Héctor Costa Nelson Chelle Nelson Demarco Héctor Garcia Otero Carlos Gonzalez Sergio Matto Oscar Moglia Raúl Mera Ariel Olascoaga Milton Scarón

1960	**UNITED STATES**
	Jerry West
	Walter Bellamy
	Robert Boozer
	Terry Dischinger
	Burdette Haldorson
	Darrall Imhoff
	Allen Kelley
	Lester Lane
	Jerry Lucas
	Adrian Smith
	Jay Arnette
	Oscar Robertson
		U.S.S.R.
		Valdis Muizhnieks
		Maigonis Valdmanis
		Tsezars Ozers
		Guram Minashvili
		Viktor Zoubkov
		Vladimir Ugrekhelidze
		Yanis Kruminsch
		Mikhail Semyonov
		Yuriy Korneyev
		Aleksandr Petrov
		Albert Valtin
		Gennady Volnov
			BRAZIL
			Zenny de Azevedo
			Amaury A. Pasos
			Wlamir Marques
			Moyses Blas
			Carlos Domingos
			          Massoni
			Fernando Pereira
			          de Freitas
			Carmo de Souza
			Jatyr E. Schall
			Edson Bispo dos Santos
			Antônio Salvador Sucar
			Waldyr Geraldo
			          Boccardo
			Waldemar Blatkauskas

GOLD	SILVER	BRONZE
1964 UNITED STATES	**U.S.S.R.**	**BRAZIL**
Jim Barnes	Valdis Muizhnieks	Amaury A. Pasos
William Bradley	Nikolay Bagley	Wlamir Marques
Lawrence Brown	Armenak Alachachian	Ubiratan P. Maciel
Joe Caldwell	Aleksandr Travin	Carlos Domingos
Mel Counts	Vyacheslav Khrynin	Massoni
Richard Davies	Yanis Kruminsch	Friedrich Wilhelm Brauň
Walter Hazzard	Levan Mosheshvili	Carmo de Souza
Lucius Jackson	Yuriy Korneyev	Jatyr E. Schall
John McCaffrey	Aleksandr Petrov	Edson Bispo dos Santos
Jeffrey Mullins	Gennady Volnov	Antônio Salvador Sucar
Jerry Shipp	Yaak Lipso	Victor Mirshawka
George Wilson	Yuris Kalninsh	Sergio de Toledo
		Machado
		José Edvar Simões
1968 UNITED STATES	**YUGOSLAVIA**	**U.S.S.R.**
Michael Barrett	Dragutin Čermac	Vladimir Andreyev
John Clawson	Krešimir Ćosič	Sergei Belov
Donald Dee	Vladimir Cvetkovič	Vadim Kapranov
Calvin Fowler	Ivo Daneu	Sergei Kovalenko
Spencer Haywood	Radivoje Korač	Anatoly Krikun
William Hoskett	Zoran Maroevič	Yaak Lipso
James King	Nikola Plečas	Anatoly Polivoda
Glynn Saulters	Trajko Rajkovič	Modestas Paulauskas
Charles Scott	Dragoslav Raznatovič	Zurab Sakandelidze
Michael Silliman	Petar Skansi	Yuri Selikhov
Kenneth Spain	Damir Šolman	Priit Tomson
Joseph White	Aljoša Zorga	Gennady Volnov
1972 U.S.S.R.	**UNITED STATES**	**CUBA**
Anatoli Polivoda	Kenneth Davis	Juan Domecq
Modestas Paulauskas	Douglas Collins	Ruperto Herrera
Zurab Sakandelidze	Thomas Henderson	Juan Roca
Alshan	Michael Bantom	Pedro Chappe
Sharmukhamedov	Robert Jones	José M. Alvarez
Aleksander Boloshev	Dwight Jones	Rafael Camizares
Ivan Edeshko	James Forbes	Conrado Perez
Sergei Belov	James Brewer	Miguel Calderon
Mishako Korkia	Tommy Burleson	Tomas Herrera
Yvan Dvorni	Thomas McMillen	Oscar Varona
Gennadi Volnov	Kevin Joyce	Alejandro Urgelles
Aleksander Belov	Ed Ratleff	Franklin Standard
Sergei Kovalenko	Henry Iba	Juan C. Ortega
Vladimir Kondrashin		
1976 UNITED STATES	**YUGOSLAVIA**	**U.S.S.R.**
Phil Ford	Blagoye Georgijevski	Vladimir Arzamaskov
Steve Sheppard	Dragan Kicanovic	Alexandr Salnikov
Adrian Dantley	Vinko Jelovac	Valeriy Miloserdov
Walter Davis	Rajko Zizic	Alshan Shamukhamedov
William Buckner	Zeljko Jerkov	Andrei Makeyev
Ernie Grunfeld	Andro Knego	Ivan Edeshko
Kenneth Carr	Zoran Slavnic	Sergei Belov
Scott May	Kresimir Cosic	Vladimir Tkachenko
Michel Armstrong	Damir Solman	Anatoli Mychkin
Thomas La Garde	Zarko Varajic	Mikhail Korkiya
Philip Hubbard	Drazen Dalipagic	Aleksander Belov
Mitchell Kupchak	Mirza Delibasic	Vladimir Zhigiliy

The 1972 U.S. basketball squad (dark uniforms), seen here against Brazil, lost to the U.S.S.R. in a highly controversial final match.

	GOLD	SILVER	BRONZE
1980	**YUGOSLAVIA**	**ITALY**	**U.S.S.R.**
	Andro Knego	Romeo Sacchetti	Stanislav Yeremin
	Dragan Kicanovic	Roberto Brunamonti	Valeriy Miloserdov
	Rajko Zizic	Michael Sylvester	Sergey Tarakanov
	Minovil Nakic	Enrico Gilardi	Aleksandr Salnikov
	Zeljko Jerkov	Fabizio Della Fiori	Andrei Lopatov
	Branko Skroce	Marco Solfrini	Nikolai Deryugin
	Zoran Slavnic	Marco Bonamico	Sergei Belov
	Kresimir Cosic	Dino Meneghin	Vladimir Tkachenko
	Ratko Radovanovic	Renato Villalta	Anatoliy Mishkin
	Duje Krstulovic	Renzo Vecchaito	Sergey Yovaysha
	Drazen Dalipagic	Pier Luigi Marzorati	Aleksandr Belostenny
	Mirza Delibasic	Pietro Generali	Vladimir Shigili
1984	**USA**	**SPAIN**	**YUGOSLAVIA**
	Steve Alford	Jose Manuel Beiran	Drazen Petrovic
	Leon Wood	Jose Luis Llorente	Aleksandar Petrovic
	Patrick Ewing	Fernando Arcega	Nebojsa Zorkic
	Vern Fleming	Jose Maria Margall	Rajko Zizic
	Alvin Robertson	Andres Jiminez	Ian Sunara
	Michael Jordan	Fernando Romay	Emir Mutapcic
	Joseph Kleine	Fernando Martin	Saabit Hadzic
	Jon Koncak	Juan Antonio Corbalan	Andro Knego
	Wayman Tisdale	Ignacio Solozabal	Ratko Radovanovic
	Chris Mullin	Juan Domingo de la Cruz	Mihovil Nakic-Vojnovic
	Samuel Perkins	Juan Maria Lopez	Drazen Dalipagic
	Jeffrey Turner	Juan Antonio San Epifanio	Branko Vukicevic

Basketball (Women)

1896–1972 Event not held

	GOLD	SILVER	BRONZE
1976	**U.S.S.R.**	**UNITED STATES**	**BULGARIA**
	Angele Rupshene	Cindy Brogdon	Nadka Goltcheva
	Tatyana Zakharova	Susan Rojcewicz	Penka Methodieva
	Raisa Kurvyakova	Ann Meyers	Petkana Makaveyeva
	Olga Barisheva	Lusia Harris	Snejana Mikhailova
	Tatyana Ovetchkina	Nancy Dunkle	Krassim Guiourova
	Nadyezhda Shuvayeva	Charlotte Lewis	Krassim Bogdanova
	Iuliyana Semenova	Nancy Lieberman	Todorka Yardanova
	Nadyezhda Zakharova	Gail Marquis	Diana Dilova
	Nelli Feryabnikova	Patricia Roberts	Margari Shtarkelova
	Olga Sukharnova	Mary Anne O'Connor	Maria Stoyanova
	Tamara Daunene	Patricia Head	Guirgui Skerlatova
	Natalia Klimova	Juliene Simpson	Penka Stoyanova

GOLD	SILVER	BRONZE
1980 U.S.S.R.	BULGARIA	YUGOSLAVIA
Angele Rupshene	Nadka Goltcheva	Vera Djuraskovic
Lubov Sharmay	Penka Methodieva	Mersada Berhirspahic
Vida Besselene	Petkana Makaveyeva	Jelica Komnenovic
Olga Korosteleva	Snejana Mikhailova	Mir Bjedov
Tatiana Ovechkina	Vania Dermenoyieva	Vukica Mitic
Nadezda Olkhova	Krassim Bogdanova	Sanja Ozegovic
Iuliana Semenova	Angelina Mikhailova	Sofija Pekic
Ludmila Rogozina	Diana Brainova	Marija Tonkovic
Nelly Feriabnikova	Evladia Slavcheva	Zorica Djurkovic
Olga Sukharnova	Kostadinka Radkova	Vesna Despotovic
Tatiana Nadyrova	Silvia Ghermanova	Biljana Majstorovic
Tatiana Ivinskaya	Penka Stoyanova	Jasmina Perazic
1984 USA	KOREA	CHINA
Teresa Edwards	Aei-Young Choi	Yuefang Chen
Lea Henry	Yang-Gae Park	Xiaoqin Li
Lynette Woodard	Eun-Sook Kim	Yan Ba
Anne Donovan	Hyung-Sook Lee	Xiaobo Song
Cathy Boswell	Kyung-Hee Choi	Chen Qiu
Cheryl Miller	Mi-Ja Lee	Jun Wang
Janice Lawrence	Kyung-Ja Moon	Lijuan Xiu
Cindy Noble	Hwa-Soon Kim	Haixia Zheng
Kim Mulkey	Myung-Hee Jeong	Xuedi Cong
Denise Curry	Young-Hee Kim	Hui Zhang
Pamela McGee	Jung-A Sung	Qing Liu
Carol Menken-Schaudt	Chan-Sook Park	Yueqin Zhang

---

3. Boxing

From 1952 each losing semi-finalist was awarded a bronze medal.

LIGHT FLYWEIGHT
Weight up to *48 kg* 105.8 lb

1896–1964 Event not held		
1968 Francisco Rodriguez (VEN)	Yong-ju jee (KOR)	Harlan Marbley (USA)
		Hubert Skrzypczak (POL)
1972 Gyoergy Gedo (HUN)	U. Gil Kim (PRK)	Ralph Evans (GBR)
		Enrique Rodriguez (ESP)
1976 Jorge Hernandez (CUB)	Byong Uk Li (PRK)	Payao Pooltarat (THA)
1980 Shamil Sabyrov (URS)	Hipolito Ramos (CUB)	Byong Uk Li (PRK)
		Ismail Moustafov (BUL)
1984 Paul Gonzales (USA)	Salvatore Todisco (ITA)	Keith Mwila (ZAM)
		Jose Marcelino Bolivar (VEN)

FLYWEIGHT

From 1948 the weight limit has been *51 kg* 112½ lb. In 1904 it was 105 lb *47,6 kg*. From 1920–1936 it was 112 lb *50,8 kg*.

GOLD	SILVER	BRONZE
1896–1900 Event not held		
1904 George Finnegan (USA)	Miles Burke (USA)	d.n.a.
1906–1912 Event not held		
1920 Frank De Genaro (USA)	Anders Petersen (DEN)	William Cuthbertson (GBR)
1924 Fidel LaBarba (USA)	James McKenzie (GBR)	Raymond Fee (USA)
1928 Antal Kocsis (HUN)	Armand Appel (FRA)	Carlo Cavagnoli (ITA)
1932 István Énekes (HUN)	Francisco Cabañas (MEX)	Louis Salica (USA)
1936 Willi Kaiser (GER)	Gavino Matta (ITA)	Louis D. Laurie (USA)
1948 Pascual Perez (ARG)	Spartaco Bandinelli (ITA)	Soo-Ann Han (KOR)
1952 Nathan Brooks (USA)	Edgar Basel (GER)	Anatoliy Bulakov (URS) William Toweel (SAF)
1956 Terence Spinks (GBR)	Mircea Dobrescu (ROM)	John Caldwell (IRL) René Libeer (FRA)
1960 Gyula Török (HUN)	Sergey Sivko (URS)	Kiyoshi Tanabe (JPN) Abdelmoneim Elguindi (EGY)
1964 Fernando Atzori (ITA)	Artur Olech (POL)	Robert Carmody (USA) Stanislav Sorokin (URS)
1968 Ricardo Delgado (MEX)	Artur Olech (POL)	Servilio Oliveira (BRA) Leo Rwabwogo (UGA)
1972 Gheorghi Kostadinov (BUL)	Leo Rwabwogo (UGA)	Leszek Blazynski (POL) Douglas Rodriguez (CUB)

Willi Kaiser (GER), the winner of the flyweight championship at the Berlin Games in 1936, rests in his corner between rounds.

1976	Leo Randolph (USA)	Ramon Duvalon (CUB)	Leszek Blazynski (POL) David Torosyan (URS)
1980	Petar Lessov (BUL)	Viktor Miroshnickenko (URS)	Hugh Russell (IRL) Janos Varadi (HUN)
1984	Steven McCrory (USA)	Redzep Redzerovski (YUG)	Eyup Can (TUR) Ibrahim Bilali (KEN)

BANTAMWEIGHT

From 1948 the weight limit has been *54 kg* 119 lb. In 1904 it was 115 lb *52,16 kg*. In 1908 it was 116 lb *52,62 kg*. From 1920 to 1936 118 lb *53,52 kg*.

	GOLD	SILVER	BRONZE
1896–1900	Event not held		
1904	Oliver L. Kirk (USA)	George Finnegan (USA)	d.n.a.
1906	Event not held		
1908	A. H. Thomas (GBR)	John Condon (GBR)	W. Webb (GBR)
1912	Event not held		
1920	Clarence Walker (SAF)	Christopher J. Graham (CAN)	James McKenzie (GBR)
1924	William Smith (SAF)	Salvatore Tripoli (USA)	Jean Ces (FRA)
1928	Vittorio Tamagnini (ITA)	John Daley (USA)	Harry Isaacs (SAF)
1932	Horace Gwynne (CAN)	Hans Ziglarski (GER)	José Villanueva (PHI)
1936	Ulderico Sergo (ITA)	Jack Wilson (USA)	Fidel Ortiz (MEX)
1948	Tibor Csik (HUN)	Giovanni B. Zuddas (ITA)	Juan Venegas (PUR)
1952	Pentti Hämäläinen (FIN)	John McNally (IRL)	Gennadiy Garbuzov (URS) Joon-Ho Kang (KOR)
1956	Wolfgang Behrendt (GER)	Soon-Chun Song (KOR)	Frederick Gilroy (IRL) Claudio Barrientos (CHI)
1960	Olyeg Grigoryev (URS)	Primo Zamparini (ITA)	Brunoh Bendig (POL) Oliver Taylor (AUS)
1964	Takao Sakurai (JPN)	Shin Cho Chung (KOR)	Juan Fabila Mendoza (MEX) Washington Rodriguez (URU)
1968	Valeriy Sokolov (URS)	Eridadi Mukwanga (UGA)	Eiji Morioka (JPN) Kyou-Chull Chang (KOR)
1972	Orlando Martinez (CUB)	Alfonso Zamora (MEX)	George Turpin (GBR) Ricardo Carreras (USA)
1976	Yong Jo Gu (PRK)	Charles Mooney (USA)	Patrick Cowdell (GBR) Chulsoon Hwang (KOR)

1980	Juan Hernandez (CUB)	Bernardo Pinango (VEN)	Michael Anthony (GUY) Dumitru Cipere (ROM)
1984	Maurizio Stecca (ITA)	Hector Lopez (MEX)	Dale Walters (CAN) Pedro Nolasco (DOM)

FEATHERWEIGHT

From 1952 the weight limit has been *57 kg* 126 lb. In 1904 it was 125 lb *56,70 kg*. From 1908 to 1936 it was 126 lb *57,15 kg*. In 1948 it was *58 kg* 127¾ lb.

	GOLD	SILVER	BRONZE
1896–1900	Event not held		
1904	Oliver L. Kirk (USA)	Frank Haller (USA)	d.n.a.
1906	Event not held		
1908	Richard Gunn (GBR)	C. W. Morris (GBR)	Hugh Roddin (GBR)
1912	Event not held		
1920	Paul Fritsch (FRA)	Jean Gachet (FRA)	Edoardo Garzena (ITA)
1924	John Fields (USA)	Joseph Salas (USA)	Pedro Quartucci (ARG)
1928	Lambertus van Klaveren (HOL)	Victor Peralta (ARG)	Harold Devine (USA)
1932	Carmelo Robledo (ARG)	Josef Schleinkofer (GER)	Carl Carlsson (SWE)
1936	Oscar Casanovas (ARG)	Charles Catterall (SAF)	Josef Miner (GER)
1948	Ernesto Formenti (ITA)	Denis Shepherd (SAF)	Aleksey Antkiewicz (POL)
1952	Jan Zachara (TCH)	Sergio Caprari (ITA)	Joseph Ventaja (FRA) Leonard Leisching (SAF)
1956	Vladimir Safronov (URS)	Thomas Nicholls (GBR)	Henryk Niedzwiedzki (POL) Pentti Hämäläinen (FIN)
1960	Francesco Musso (ITA)	Jerzy Adamski (POL)	William Meyers (SAF) Jorma Limmonen (FIN)
1964	Stanislav Stepashkin (URS)	Antony Villanueva (PHI)	Charles Brown (USA) Heinz Schultz (GER)
1968	Antonio Roldan (MEX)	Albert Robinson (USA)	Philip Waruinge (KEN) Ivan Michailov (BUL)
1972	Boris Kousnetsov (URS)	Philip Waruinge (KEN)	Clemente Rojas (COL) András Botos (HUN)
1976	Angel Herrera (CUB)	Richard Nowakowski (GDR)	Juan Paredes (MEX) Leszek Kosedowski (POL)
1980	Rudi Fink (GDR)	Adolfo Horta (CUB)	Viktor Rybakov (URS) Krzysztof Kosedowski (POL)

1984 Meldrick Taylor (USA)	Peter Konyegwachie (NGR)	Turgut Aykac (TUR)
		Omar Catari Peraza (VEN)

LIGHTWEIGHT

From 1952 the weight has been *60 kg* 132 lb. In 1904 and from 1920 to 1936 it was 135 lb *61,24 kg*. In 1908 it was 140 lb *63,50 kg*. In 1948 it was *62 kg*. 136½ lb.

GOLD	SILVER	BRONZE
1896–1900 Event not held		
1904 Harry J. Spanger (USA)	James Eagan (USA)	Russel Van Horn (USA)
1906 Event not held		
1908 Frederick Grace (GBR)	Frederick Spiller (GBR)	H. H. Johnson (GBR)
1912 Event not held		
1920 Samuel Mosberg (USA)	Gotfred Johansen (DEN)	Clarence Newton (CAN)
1924 Hans Nielsen (DEN)	Alfredo Coppello (ARG)	Frederick Boylstein (USA)
1928 Carlo Orlandi (ITA)	Stephen M. Halaiko (USA)	Gunnar Berggren (SWE)
1932 Lawrence Stevens (SAF)	Thure Ahlqvist (SWE)	Nathan Bor (USA)
1936 Imre Harangi (HUN)	Nikolai Stepulov (EST)	Erik Agren (SWE)
1948 Gerald Dreyer (SAF)	Joseph Vissers (BEL)	Svend Wad (DEN)
1952 Aureliano Bolognesi (ITA)	Aleksey Antkiewicz (POL)	Gheorghe Fiat (ROM)
		Erkki Pakkanen (FIN)
1956 Richard McTaggart (GBR)	Harry Kurschat (GER)	Anthony Byrne (IRL)
		Anatoliy Lagetko (URS)
1960 Kazimierz Pazdzior (POL)	Sandro Lopopoli (ITA)	Richard McTaggart (GBR)
		Abel Laudonio (ARG)
1964 Józef Grudzien (POL)	Vellikton Barannikov (URS)	Ronald Harris (USA)
		James McCourt (IRL)
1968 Ronald Harris (USA)	Józef Grudzien (POL)	Calistrat Cutov (ROM)
		Zvonimir Vujin (YUG)
1972 Jan Szczepanski (POL)	László Orban (HUN)	Samuel Mbugua (KEN)
		Alfonso Perez (COL)
1976 Howard Davis (USA)	Simion Cutov (ROM)	Ace Rusevski (YUG)
		Vasiliy Solomin (URS)
1980 Angel Herrera (CUB)	Viktor Demianenko (URS)	Kazimierz Adach (POL)
		Richard Nowakowski (GDR)

LIGHT-WELTERWEIGHT
Weight up to *63,5 kg* 140 lb

	GOLD	SILVER	BRONZE
1896–1948	Event not held		
1952	Charles Adkins (USA)	Viktor Mednov (URS)	Erkki Mallenius (FIN)
			Bruno Visintin (ITA)
1956	Vladimir Yengibaryan (URS)	Franco Nenci (ITA)	Henry Loubscher (SAF)
			Constantin Dumitrescu (ROM)
1960	Bohumil Němeček (TCH)	Clement Quartey (GHA)	Quincy Daniels (USA)
			Marian Kasprzyk (POL)
1964	Jerzy Kulej (POL)	Yvgeniy Frolov (URS)	Eddie Blay (GHA)
			Habib Galhia (TUN)
1968	Jerzy Kulej (POL)	Enrique Regueiferos (CUB)	Arto Nilsson (FIN)
			James Wallington (USA)
1972	Ray Seales (USA)	Anghel Anghelov (BUL)	Zvonimir Vujin (YUG)
			Issaaka Daborg (NIG)
1976	Ray Leonard (USA)	Andres Aldama (CUB)	Vladimir Kolev (BUL)
			Kazimier Szczerba (POL)
1980	Patrizio Oliva (ITA)	Serik Konakbaev (URS)	Anthony Willis (GBR)
			Jose Aguilar (CUB)
1984	Jerry Page (USA)	Dhawee Umponmaha (THA)	Mircea Fulger (ROM)
			Mirko Puzovic (YUG)

WELTERWEIGHT

From 1948 the weight limit has been *67 kg* 148 lb. In 1904 it was 143¾ lb *65,27 kg*. From 1920 to 1936 it was 147 lb *66,68* kg.

	GOLD	SILVER	BRONZE
1896–1900	Event not held		
1904	Albert Young (USA)	Harry J. Spanger (USA)	Joseph Lydon (USA)
1906–1912	Event not held		
1920	Albert Schneider (CAN)	Alexander Ireland (GBR)	Frederick Colberg (USA)
1924	Jean Delarge (BEL)	Héctor Mendez (ARG)	Douglas Lewis (CAN)
1928	Edward Morgan (NZL)	Raul Landini (ARG)	Raymond Smillie (CAN)
1932	Edward Flynn (USA)	Erich Campe (GER)	Bruno Ahlberg (FIN)
1936	Sten Suvio (FIN)	Michael Murach (GER)	Gerhard Petersen (DEN)
1948	Julius Torma (TCH)	Horace Herring (USA)	Alessandro D'Ottavio (ITA)
1952	Zygmunt Chychla (POL)	Sergey Schtscherbakov (URS)	Victor Jörgensen (DEN)

	GOLD	SILVER	BRONZE
1956	Nicholae Linca (ROM)	Frederick Tiedt (IRL)	Günther Heidemann (GER) Kevin J. Hogarth (AUS) Nicholas Gargano (GBR)
1960	Giovanni Benvenuti (ITA)	Yuriy Radonyak (URS)	Leszek Drogosz (POL) James Lloyd (GBR)
1964	Marian Kasprzyk (POL)	Ritschardas Tamulis (URS)	Pertti Purhonen (FIN) Silvano Bertini (ITA)
1968	Manfred Wolke (GDR)	Joseph Bessala (CMR)	Vladimir Musalinov (URS) Mario Guilloti (ARG)
1972	Emilio Correa (CUB)	Janos Kajdi (HUN)	Dick T. Murunga (KEN) Jesse Valdez (USA)
1976	Jochen Bachfeld (GDR)	Pedro J. Gamarro (VEN)	Reinhard Skricek (GER) Victor Zilberman (ROM)
1980	Andres Aldama (CUB)	John Mugabi (UGA)	Karl-Heinz Kruger (GDR) Kazimierz Szcezerba (POL)
1984	Mark Breland (USA)	Young-Su An (KOR)	Joni Nyman (FIN) Luciano Bruno (ITA)

LIGHT-MIDDLEWEIGHT

Weight up to *71 kg* 157 lb

	GOLD	SILVER	BRONZE
1896–1948 Event not held			
1952	László Papp (HUN)	Theunis van Schalkwyk (SAF)	Boris Tishin (URS) Eladio Herrera (ARG)
1956	László Papp (HUN)	José Torres (USA)	John McCormack (GBR) Zbigniew Pietrzykowski (POL)
1960	Wilbert McClure (USA)	Carmelo Bossi (ITA)	Boris Lagutin (URS) William Fisher (GBR)
1964	Boris Lagutin (URS)	Josef Gonzales (FRA)	Nojim Maiyegun (NGR) Jozef Grzesiak (POL)
1968	Boris Lagutin (URS)	Rolando Garbey (CUB)	John Baldwin (USA) Günther Meier (GER)
1972	Dieter Kottysch (GER)	Wieslaw Rudkowski (POL)	Alan Minter (GBR) Peter Tiepold (GDR)
1976	Jerzy Rybicki (POL)	Tadija Kacar (YUG)	Rolando Garbey (CUB) Victor Savchenko (URS)

1980 Armando Martinez (CUB)	Aleksandr Koshkin (URS)	Jan Franek (TCH) Detlef Kastner (GDR)
1984 Frank Tate (USA)	Shawn O'Sullivan (CAN)	Manfred Zielonka (FRG) Christophe Tiozzo (FRA)

MIDDLEWEIGHT

From 1952 the weight limit has been *75 kg* 165 lb. From 1904 to 1908 it was 158 lb *71,68 kg*. From 1920 to 1936 it was 160 lb *72,57 kg*. In 1948 it was *73 kg* 161 lb.

GOLD	SILVER	BRONZE
1896–1900 Event not held		
1904 Charles Mayer (USA)	Benjamin Spradley (USA)	d.n.a.
1906 Event not held		
1908 John Douglas (GBR)	Reginald Baker (AUS/NZL)	W. Philo (GBR)
1912 Event not held		
1920 Harry W. Mallin (GBR)	Georges A. Prud'homme (CAN)	Moe H. Herscovitch (CAN)
1924 Harry W. Mallin (GBR)	John Elliott (GBR)	Joseph Beecken (BEL)
1928 Piero Toscani (ITA)	Jan Hermánek (TCH)	Léonard Steyaert (BEL)
1932 Carmen Barth (USA)	Amado Azar (ARG)	Ernest Pierce (SAF)
1936 Jean Despeaux (FRA)	Henry Tiller (NOR)	Raúl Villareal (ARG)
1948 László Papp (HUN)	John Wright (GBR)	Ivano Fontana (ITA)
1952 Floyd Patterson (USA)	Vasile Tita (ROM)	Boris Nikolov (BUL) Stig Sjölin (SWE)
1956 Genadiy Schatkov (URS)	Ramón Tapia (CHI)	Gilbert Chapron (FRA) Victor Zalazar (ARG)

Laszlo Papp (HUN), a southpaw, is the first of two boxers to win three gold medals. He took the middleweight title in 1948, and the light-middleweight title in 1952 and 1956.

	GOLD	SILVER	BRONZE
1960	Edward Crook (USA)	Tadeusz Walasek (POL)	Iona Monea (ROM)
			Evgeniy Feofanov (URS)
1964	Valeriy Popentschenko (URS)	Emil Schultz (GER)	Franco Valle (ITA)
			Tadeusz Walasek (POL)
1968	Christopher Finnegan (GBR)	Aleksey Kisselyov (URS)	Agustin Zaragoza (MEX)
			Alfred Jones (USA)
1972	Viatcheslav Lemechev (URS)	Reima Virtanen (FIN)	Prince Amartey (GHA)
			Marvin Johnson (USA)
1976	Michael Spinks (USA)	Rufat Riskiev (URS)	Alec Nastac (ROM)
			Luis Martinez (CUB)
1980	Jose Gomez (CUB)	Viktor Savchenko (URS)	Valentin Silaghi (ROM)
			Jerzy Rybicki (POL)
1984	Joon-Sup Shin (KOR)	Virgil Hill (USA)	Mohamed Zaoui (ALG)
			Aristides Gonzalez (PUR)

The future professional champion Floyd Patterson (USA) captured the middleweight title at Helsinki in 1952.

LIGHT-HEAVYWEIGHT

From 1952 the weight limit has been *81 kg* 178½ lb. From 1920 to 1936 it was 175 lb. *79,38 kg*. In 1948 it was *80 kg* 176¼ lb.

	GOLD	SILVER	BRONZE
1896–1912	Event not held		
1920	Edward Eagen (USA)	Sverre Sörsdal (NOR)	H. Franks (GBR)
1924	Harry Mitchell (GBR)	Thyge Petersen (DEN)	Sverre Sörsdal (NOR)
1928	Victor Avendaño (ARG)	Ernst Pistulla (GER)	Karel L. Miljon (HOL)
1932	David Carstens (SAF)	Gino Rossi (ITA)	Peter Jörgensen (DEN)
1936	Roger Michelot (FRA)	Richard Vogt (GER)	Francisco Risiglione (ARG)
1948	George Hunter (SAF)	Donald Scott (GBR)	Maurio Cia (ARG)
1952	Norvel Lee (USA)	Antonio Pacenza (ARG)	Anotiliy Perov (URS) Harri Siljander (FIN)
1956	James F. Boyd (USA)	Gheorghe Negrea (ROM)	Carlos Lucas (CHI) Romualdas Murauskas (URS)
1960	Cassius Clay (USA)	Zbigniew Pietrzykowski (POL)	Anthony Madigan (AUS) Giulio Saraudi (ITA)
1964	Cosimo Pinto (ITA)	Aleksey Kisselyov (URS)	Aleksandar Nikolov (BUL) Zbigniew Pietrzykowski (POL)

Cassius M. Clay (USA), then an 18-year-old schoolboy, and later three-time heavyweight champion of the world, is shown on the way to his 1960 Olympic lightheavyweight gold medal, bouncing a right off the head of Tony Madigan (AUS), the bronze-medal winner.

GOLD	SILVER	BRONZE
1968 Dan Poznyak (URS)	Ion Monea (ROM)	Georgy Stankov (BUL) Stanislav Dragan (POL)
1972 Mate Parlov (YUG)	Gilberto Carrillo (CUB)	Isaac Ikhouria (NGR) Janusz Gortat (POL)
1976 Leon Spinks (USA)	Sixto Soria (CUB)	Costica Dafinoiu (ROM) Janusz Gortat (POL)
1980 Slobodan Kacar (YUG)	Pawel Skrzecz (POL)	Herbert Bauch (GDR) Ricardo Rojas (CUB)
1984 Anton Josipovic (YUG)	Kevin Barry (NZL)	Mustapha Moussa (ALG) Evander Holyfield (USA)

HEAVYWEIGHT

From 1952 the class has been for those over *81 kg* 178½ lb. From 1904 to 1908 it was over 158 lb *71,67 kg*. From 1920 to 1936 it was over 175 lb *79,38 kg*. In 1948 it was over *80 kg* 176¼ lb.

1896–1900 Event not held		
1904 Samuel Berger (USA)	Charles Mayer (USA)	d.n.a.
1906 Event not held		
1908 A. L. Oldhan (GBR)	S. C. H. Evans (GBR)	Frederick Parks (GBR)
1912 Event not held		
1920 Ronald Rawson (GBR)	Sören Petersen (DEN)	Xavier Eluère (FRA)
1924 Otto von Porat (NOR)	Sören Petersen (DEN)	Alfredo Porzio (ARG)
1928 Arturo Rodriguez Jurado (ARG)	Nils Ramm (SWE)	M. Jacob Michaelsen (DEN)
1932 Santiago Lovell (ARG)	Luigi Rovati (ITA)	Frederick Feary (USA)
1936 Herbert Runge (GER)	Guillermo Lovell (ARG)	Erling Nilsen (NOR)
1948 Rafael Iglesias (ARG)	Gunnar Nilsson (SWE)	John Arthur (SAF)
1952 Hayes Edward Sanders (USA)	Ingemar Johansson (SWE)*	Andries Nieman (SAF) Ilkka Koski (FIN)
1956 T. Peter Rademacher (USA)	Lev Mukhin (URS)	Daniel Bekker (SAF) Giacomo Bozzano (ITA)
1960 Franco de Piccoli (ITA)	Daniel Bekker (SAF)	Josef Nemec (TCH) Günter Siegmund (GER)
1964 Joe Frazier (USA)	Hans Huber (GER)	Giuseppe Ros (ITA) Vadim Yemelyanov (URS)

*Medal awarded in October 1981 after initial disqualification

GOLD	SILVER	BRONZE
1968 George Foreman (USA)	Ionas Tschepulis (URS)	Giorgio Bambini (ITA) Joaquin Rocha (MEX)
1972 Teofilo Stevenson (CUB)	Ion Alexe (ROM)	Peter Hussing (GER) Hasse Thomsen (SWE)
1976 Teofilo Stevenson (CUB)	Mircea Simon (ROM)	Johnny Tate (USA) Clarence Hill (BER)
1980 Teofilo Stevenson (CUB)	Pyotr Zaev (URS)	Istvan Levai (HUN) Jurgen Fanghanel (GDR)
1984 Henry Tillman (USA)	Willie Dewit (CAN)	Angelo Musone (ITA) Arnold Vanderlijde (HOL)

Teofilo Stevenson (CUB) won the heavyweight title three times. No other heavyweight ever successfully defended the title even once.

SUPER-HEAVYWEIGHT

| 1984 Tyrell Biggs (USA) | Francesco Damiani (ITA) | Robert Wells (GBR) Salihu Azis (YUG) |

Nine canoes run head-to-head during one of the 1,000 meters K-2 preliminary heats at Munich in 1972.

4. Canoeing (Men)

500 METERS KAYAK SINGLES (K-1)

GOLD	SILVER	BRONZE
1896–1972 Event not held		
1976 Vasile Diba (ROM) 1:46.41	Zoltan Szytanity (HUN) 1:46.95	Rudiger Helm (GDR) 1:48.30
1980 Vladimir Parfenovich (URS) 1:43.43	John Sumegi (AUS) 1:44.12	Vasile Diba (ROM) 1:44.90
1984 Ian Ferguson (NZL) 1:47.84	Lars-Erik Moberg (SWE) 1:48.18	Bernard Bregeon (FRA) 1:48.41

1,000 METERS KAYAK SINGLES (K-1)

1896–1932 Event not held		
1936 Gregor Hradetzky (AUT) 4:22.9	Helmut Cämmerer (GER) 4:25.6	Jacob Kraaier (HOL) 4:35.1
1948 Gert Fredriksson (SWE) 4:33.2	Johan F. Kobberup (DEN) 4:39.9	Henri Eberhardt (FRA) 4:41.4
1952 Gert Fredriksson (SWE) 4:07.9	Thorvald Strömberg (FIN) 4:09.7	Louis Gantois (FRA) 4:20.1
1956 Gert Fredriksson (SWE) 4:12.8	Igor Pissaryev (URS) 4:15.3	Lajos Kiss (HUN) 4:16.2
1960 Erik Hansen (DEN) 3:53.00	Imre Szöllösi (HUN) 3:54.02	Gert Fredriksson (SWE) 3:55.89
1964 Rolf Peterson (SWE) 3:57.13	Mihály Hesz (HUN) 3:57.28	Aurel Vernescu (ROM) 4:00.77

	GOLD	SILVER	BRONZE
1968	Mihály Hesz (HUN) 4:02.63	Aleksandr Shaparenko (URS) 4:03.58	Erik Hansen (DEN) 4:04.39
1972	Aleksandr Shaparenko (URS) 3:48.06	Rolf Peterson (SWE) 3:48.35	Geza Csapo (HUN) 3:49.38
1976	Rudiger Helm (GDR) 3:48.20	Geza Csapo (HUN) 3:48.84	Vassile Diba (ROM) 3:49.65
1980	Rudiger Helm (GDR) 3:48.77	Alain Lebas (FRA) 3:50.20	Ion Birladeanu (ROM) 3:50.49
1984	Alan Thompson (NZL) 3:45.73	Milan Janic (YUG) 3:46.88	Greg Barton (USA) 3:47.38

500 METERS KAYAK PAIRS (K-2)

1896–1972 Event not held

	GOLD	SILVER	BRONZE
1976	EAST GERMANY 1:35.87	U.S.S.R. 1:36.81	RUMANIA 1:37.43
	Joachim Mattern Bernd Olbricht	Sergei Nagorny Vladimir Romanovski	Larion Serghei Policarp Malihin
1980	U.S.S.R. 1:32.38	SPAIN 1:33.65	EAST GERMANY 1:34.00
	Vladimir Parfenovich Sergey Chukhrai	Herminio Menendez Guillermo Del Riego	Bernd Olbricht Rudiger Helm
1984	NEW ZEALAND 1:34.21	SWEDEN 1:35.26	CANADA 1:35.41
	Ian Ferguson Paul MacDonald	Per-Inge Bengtsson Lars-Erik Moberg	Hugh Fisher Alwyn Morris

1,000 METERS KAYAK PAIRS (K-2)

1896–1932 Event not held

	GOLD	SILVER	BRONZE
1936	AUSTRIA 4:03.8	GERMANY 4:08.9	NETHERLANDS 4:12.2
	Adolf Kainz Alfons Dorfner	Ewald Tilker Fritz Bondroit	Nicolaas Tates Willem van der Kroft
1948	SWEDEN 4:07.3	DENMARK 4:07.5	FINLAND 4:08.7
	Hans Berglund Lennart Klingström	Ejvind Hansen Bernhard Jensen	Thor Axelsson Nils Björklöf
1952	FINLAND 3:51.1	SWEDEN 3:51.1	AUSTRIA 3:51.4
	Kurt Wires Yrjö Hietanen	Lars Glassér Ingemar Hedberg	Max Raub Herbert Wiedermann
1956	GERMANY 3:49.6	U.S.S.R. 3:51.4	AUSTRIA 3:55.8
	Michael Scheuer Meinrad Miltenberger	Mikhail Kaaleste Antoliy Demitkov	Max Raub Herbert Wiedermann
1960	SWEDEN 3:34.7	HUNGARY 3:34.91	POLAND 3:37.34
	Gert Fredriksson Sven-Olov Sjödelius	András Szente György Mészáros	Stefan Kaplaniak Wladyslaw Zielinski
1964	SWEDEN 3:38.4	NETHERLANDS 3:39.30	GERMANY 3:40.69
	Sven-Olov Sjödelius Nils Utterberg	Antonius Geurts Paul Hoekstra	Heinz Buker Holger Zander
1968	U.S.S.R. 3:37.54	HUNGARY 3:38.44	AUSTRIA 3:40.71
	Aleksandr Shaparenko Vladimir Morozov	Csaba Giczi István Timár	Gerhard Seibold Gunther Pfaff
1972	U.S.S.R. 3:31.23	HUNGARY 3:32.00	POLAND 3:33.83
	Nikolai Gorbachev Viktor Kratassyuk	Jozsef Deme Janos Ratkai	Wladyslaw Szuszkiewicz Rafal Piszez
1976	U.S.S.R. 3:29.01	EAST GERMANY 3:29.33	HUNGARY 3:30.56
	Sergei Nagorny Vladimir Romanovski	Joachim Mattern Bernd Olbricht	Zoltan Bako Istvan Szabo
1980	U.S.S.R. 3:26.72	HUNGARY 3:28.49	SPAIN 3:28.66
	Vladimir Parfenovich Sergey Chukhrai	Istvan Szabo Istvan Joos	Luis Ramos-Misione Herminio Menendez

1984	CANADA 3:24.22	FRANCE 3:25.97	AUSTRALIA 3:26.80
	Hugh Fisher	Bernard Bregeon	Terry Kent
	Alwyn Morris	Patrick Lefoulon	Terry White

1,000 METERS KAYAK FOURS (K-4)

GOLD	SILVER	BRONZE
1896–1960 Event not held		
1964 U.S.S.R. 3:14.67	GERMANY 3:15.39	RUMANIA 3:15.51
Nikolay Chuzhikov	Günther Perleberg	Simion Cuciuc
Anatoly Grishin	Bernhard Schulze	Atanase Sciotnic
Vyatscheslav Ionov	Friedhelm Wentzke	Mihai Turcas
Vladimir Morozov	Holger Zander	Aurel Vernescu
1968 NORWAY 3:14.38	RUMANIA 3:14.81	HUNGARY 3:15.10
Steinar Amundsen	Anton Calenic	Csaba Giczi
Egil W. Söby	Dimitrie Ivanov	István Timár
Tore Berger	Haralambie Ivanov	Imre Szöllösi
Jan Johansen	Mihai Turcas	István Csizmadia
1972 U.S.S.R. 3:14.02	RUMANIA 3:15.07	NORWAY 3:15.27
Yuri Filatov	Aurel Vernescu	Egil W. Söby
Yuri Stezenko	Mihai Zafiu	Steinar Amundsen
Vladimir Morozov	Roman Vartolomeu	Tore Berger
Valeri Didenko	Atanase Sciotnic	Jan Johansen
1976 U.S.S.R. 3:08.69	SPAIN 3:08.95	EAST GERMANY 3:10.76
Sergei Chuhray	Jose Celorrio	Peter Bischof
Aleksandr Degtiarev	Jose Diaz-Flor	Bernd Duvigneau
Yuri Filatov	Herminio Menendez	Rudiger Helm
Vladimir Morozov	Luis Misone	Jurgen Lehnert
1980 EAST GERMANY 3:13.76	RUMANIA 3:15.35	BULGARIA 3:15.46
Bernd Olbricht	Mihai Zafiu	Boleslaw Borissov
Bernd Duvigneau	Vasile Diba	Boshidar Milenkov
Rudiger Helm	Ion Geanta	Lazar Christov
Harald Marg	Esanu Nicusor	Ivan Manev
1984 NEW ZEALAND 3:02.28	SWEDEN 3:02.81	FRANCE 3:03.94
Grant Bramwell	Per-Inge Bengtsson	Francois Barouh
Ian Ferguson	Tommy Karls	Philippe Boccara
Paul MacDonald	Lars-Erik Moberg	Pascal Boucherit
Alan Thompson	Thomas Ohlsson	Didier Vavasseur

500 METERS CANADIAN SINGLES (C-1)

1896–1972 Event not held		
1976 Aleksandr Rogov	John Wood	Matija Ljubek
(URS) 1:59.23	(CAN) 1:59.58	(YUG) 1:59.60
1980 Sergei Postrekhin	Lubomir Lubenov	Olaf Heukrodt
(URS) 1:53.37	(BUL) 1:53.49	(GDR) 1:54.38
1984 Larry Cain	Henning Jakobsen	Costica Olaru
(CAN) 1:57.01	(DEN) 1:58.45	(ROM) 1:59.86

1,000 METERS CANADIAN SINGLES (C-1)

1896–1932 Event not held		
1936 Francis Amyot	Bohuslav Karlik	Erich Koschik
(CAN) 5:32.1	(TCH) 5:36.9	(GER) 5:39.0
1948 Josef Holeček	Douglas Bennett	Robert Boutigny
(TCH) 5:42.0	(CAN) 5:53.3	(FRA) 5:55.9
1952 Josef Holeček	János Parti	Olavi Ojanperä
(TCH) 4:56.3	(HUN) 5:03.6	(FIN) 5:08.5
1956 Leon Rotman	István Hernek	Gennadiy Bukharin
(ROM) 5:05.3	(HUN) 5:06.2	(URS) 5:12.7

1960	János Parti (HUN) 4:33.93	Aleksandr Silayev (URS) 4:34.41	Leon Rotman (ROM) 4:35.87
1964	Jürgen Eschert (GER) 4:35.14	Andrei Igorov (ROM) 4:37.89	Yevgeny Penyayev (URS) 4:38.31
1968	Tibor Tatai (HUN) 4:36.14	Detlef Lewe (GER) 4:38.31	Vitaly Galkov (URS) 4:40.42
1972	Ivan Patzaichin (ROM) 4:08.94	Tamas Wichmann (HUN) 4:12.42	Detlef Lewe (GER) 4:13.63
1976	Matija Ljubek (YUG) 4:09.51	Vasiliy Urchenko (URS) 4:12.57	Tamas Wichmann (HUN) 4:14.11
1980	Lubomir Lubenov (BUL) 4:12.38	Sergei Postrekhin (URS) 4:13.53	Eckhard Leue (GDR) 4:15.02
1984	Ulrich Eicke (FRG) 4:06.32	Larry Cain (CAN) 4:08.67	Henning Jakobsen (DEN) 4:09.51

The Rumanian pair, Patzaichin and Covaliov, winning the 1968 Canadian Pairs event on the artificial lake, Canal de Quemanco, which was also used for rowing.

500 METERS CANADIAN PAIRS (C-2)

GOLD	SILVER	BRONZE
1896–1972 Event not held		
1976 **U.S.S.R. 1:45.81** Sergei Petrenko Aleksandr Vinogradov	**POLAND 1:47.77** Jerzy Opara Andrzej Gronowicz	**HUNGARY 1:48.35** Tamas Buday Oszkar Frey
1980 **HUNGARY 1:43.39** Laszlo Foltan Istvan Vaskuti	**RUMANIA 1:44.12** Ivan Patzaichin Istvan Capusta	**BULGARIA 1:44.83** Borislaw Ananiev Nikolai Ilkov
1984 **YUGOSLAVIA 1:43.67** Matija Ljubek Mirko Nisovic	**ROMANIA 1:45.68** Ivan Potzaichin Toma Simionov	**SPAIN 1:47.71** Enrique Miguez Narcisco Suarez

1,000 METERS CANADIAN PAIRS (C-2)

GOLD	SILVER	BRONZE
1896–1932 Event not held		
1936 CZECHOSLOVAKIA 4:50.1	AUSTRIA 4:53.8	CANADA 4:56.7
Vladimir Syrovátka	Rupert Weinstabl	Frank Saker
Jan-Felix Brzák	Karl Proisl	Harvey Charters
1948 CZECHOSLOVAKIA 5:07.1	U.S.A. 5:08.2	FRANCE 5:15.2
Jan-Felix Brzák	Stephen Lysak	Georges Dransart
Bohumil Kudrna	Stephan Macknowski	Georges Gandil
1952 DENMARK 4:38.3	CZECHOSLOVAKIA 4:42.9	GERMANY 4:48.3
Bent Peder Rasch	Jan-Felix Brzák	Egon Drews
Finn Haunstoft	Bohumil Kudrna	Wilfried Soltau
1956 RUMANIA 4:47.4	U.S.S.R. 4:48.6	HUNGARY 4:54.3
Alexe Dumitru	Pavel Kharin	Károly Wieland
Simion Ismailciuc	Gratsian Botev	Ferenc Mohácsi
1960 U.S.S.R. 4:17.94	ITALY 4:20.77	HUNGARY 4:20.89
Leonid Geyshtor	Aldo Dezi	Imre Farkas
Sergey Makarenko	Francesco La Macchia	András Törö
1964 U.S.S.R. 4:04.64	FRANCE 4:06.52	DENMARK 4:07.48
Andrey Khimich	Jean Boudehen	Peer N. Nielsen
Stepan Oschepkov	Michel Chapuis	John Sorenson
1968 RUMANIA 4:07.18	HUNGARY 4:08.77	U.S.S.R. 4:11.30
Ivan Patzaichin	Tamás Wichmann	Naum Prokupets
Serghei Covaliov	Gyula Petrikovics	Mikhail Zamotin
1972 U.S.S.R. 3:52.60	RUMANIA 3:52.63	BULGARIA 3:58.10
Vlados Chessyunas	Ivan Patzaichin	Fedia Damianov
Yuri Lobanov	Serghei Covaliov	Ivan Bourtchine
1976 U.S.S.R. 3:52.76	RUMANIA 3:54.28	HUNGARY 3:55.66
Sergei Petrenko	Gheorghe Danielov	Tamas Buday
Aleksandr Vinogradov	Gheorghe Simionov	Oszkar Frey
1980 RUMANIA 3:47.65	EAST GERMANY 3:49.93	U.S.S.R. 3:51.28
Ivan Patzaichin	Olaf Heukrodt	Vasiliy Yurchenko
Toma Simionov	Uwe Madeja	Yuriy Lobanov
1984 ROMANIA 3:40.60	YUGOSLAVIA 3:41.56	FRANCE 3:48.01
Ivan Potzaichin	Matija Ljubek	Didier Hoyer
Toma Simionov	Mirko Nisovic	Eric Renaud

Canoeing (Women)

500 METERS KAYAK SINGLES (K-1)

GOLD	SILVER	BRONZE
1896–1936 Event not held		
1948 Karen Hoff (DEN) 2:31.9	Alide Van de Anker-Doedans (HOL) 2:32.8	Fritzi Schwingl (AUT) 2:32.9
1952 Sylvi Saimo (FIN) 2:18.4	Gertrude Liebhart (AUT) 2:18.8	Nina Savina (URS) 2:21.6
1956 Elisaveta Dementyeva (URS) 2:18.9	Therese Zenz (GER) 2:19.6	Tove Söby (DEN) 2:22.3
1960 Antonina Seredina (URS) 2:08.08	Therese Zenz (GER) 2:08.22	Daniela Walkowiak (POL) 2:10.46

1964	Ludmila Khvedosyuk	Hilde Lauer	Marcia Jones
	(URS) 2:12.87	(ROM) 2:15.35	(USA) 2:15.68
1968	Ludmila Pinayeva-	Renate Breuer	Viorica Dumitru
	Khvedosyuk	(GER) 2:12.71	(ROM) 2:13.22
	(URS) 2:11.09		
1972	Yulia Ryabchlinskaya	Mieke Jaapies	Anna Pfeffer
	(URS) 2:03.17	(HOL) 2:04.03	(HUN) 2:05.50
1976	Carola Zirzow	Tatyana Korshunova	Klara Rajnai
	(GDR) 2:01.05	(URS) 2:03.07	(HUN) 2:05.01
1980	Birgit Fischer	Vania Checheva	Antonina Melnikova
	(GDR) 1:57.96	(BUL) 1:59.48	1:59.66
1984	Agneta Andersson	Barbara Schuttpelz	Annemiek Derckx
	(SWE) 1:58.72	(FRG) 1:59.93	(HOL) 2:00.11

500 METERS KAYAK PAIRS (K-2)

1896–1956 Event not held

1960	U.S.S.R. 1:54.76	GERMANY 1:56.66	HUNGARY 1:58.22
	Maria Zhubina	Therese Zenz	Vilma Egresi
	Antonina Seredina	Ingrid Hartmann	Klára Fried-Bánfalvi
1964	GERMANY 1:56.95	UNITED STATES	RUMANIA 2:00.25
		1:59.16	
	Roswitha Esser	Francine Fox	Hilde Lauer
	Annemarie Zimmermann	Gloriane Perrier	Cornelia Sideri
1968	GERMANY 1:56.44	HUNGARY 1:58.60	U.S.S.R. 1:58.61
	Annemarie Zimmermann	Anna Pfeffer	Ludmila Pinayeva
	Roswitha Esser	Katalin Rosznyói	Antonina Seredina
1972	U.S.S.R. 1:53.50	EAST GERMANY	RUMANIA 1:55.01
		1:54.30	
	Ludmila Pinayeva	Ilse Kaschube	Maria Nichiforov
	Ekaterina Kuryshko	Petra Grabowsky	Viorica Dumitru
1976	U.S.S.R. 1:51.15	HUNGARY 1:51.69	EAST GERMANY
			1:51.81
	Nina Gopova	Anna Pfeffer	Barbel Koster
	Galina Kreft	Klara Rajnai	Carola Zirzow
1980	EAST GERMANY	U.S.S.R. 1:46.91	HUNGARY 1:47.95
	1:43.88		
	Carsta Genauss	Galina Alexeyeva	Eva Rakusz
	Martina Bischof	Nina Trofimova	Maria Zakarias
1984	SWEDEN 1:45.25	CANADA 1:47.13	FEDERAL REPUBLIC
	Agneta Andersson	Alexandra Barre	OF GERMANY 1:47.32
	Anna Olsson	Sue Holloway	Josefa Idem
			Barbara Schuttpelz

500 METERS KAYAK FOURS

1984	ROMANIA 1:38.34	SWEDEN 1:38.87	CANADA 1:39.40
	Agafia Constantin	Agneta Andersson	Alexandra Barre
	Nastasia Ionescu	Anna Olsson	Lucie Guay
	Tecla Marinescu	Eva Karlsson	Sue Holloway
	Maria Stefan	Susanne Wiberg	Barb Olmsted

5. Cycling (Men)

1,000 METERS SPRINT

GOLD	SILVER	BRONZE

1896–1904 Event not held

1906	Francesco Verri	H. C. Bouffler	Eugène Debougnie
	(ITA) 1:42.2	(GBR)	(BEL)

1980[1]–1912 Event not held

---

[1] There was a 1,000 meters sprint event in the 1908 Games, but it was declared void because "the riders exceeded the time limit, in spite of repeated warnings."

1920	Maurice Peeters (HOL) 1:38.3	H. Thomas Johnson (GBR)	Harry Ryan (GBR)
1924[2]	Lucien Michard (FRA) 12.8	Jacob Meijer (HOL)	Jean Cugnot (FRA)
1928	René Beaufrand (FRA) 13.2	Antoine Mazairac (HOL)	Willy Falck-Hansen (DEN)
1932	Jacobus van Egmond (HOL) 12.6	Louis Chaillot (FRA)	Bruno Pellizzari (ITA)
1936	Toni Merkens (GER) 11.8	Arie Van Vliet (HOL)	Louis Chaillot (FRA)
1948	Mario Ghella (ITA) 12.0	Reginald Harris (GBR)	Axel Schandorff (DEN)
1952	Enzo Sacchi (ITA) 12.0	Lionel Cox (AUS)	Werner Potzernheim (GER)
1956	Michel Rousseau (FRA) 11.4	Guglielmo Pesenti (ITA)	Richard Ploog (AUS)
1960	Sante Gaiardoni (ITA) 11.1	Leo Sterckx (BEL)	Valentino Gasparella (ITA)
1964	Giovanni Pettenella (ITA) 13.69	Sergio Bianchetto (ITA)	Daniel Morelon (FRA)
1968	Daniel Morelon (FRA) 10.68	Giordano Turrini (ITA)	Pierre Trentin (FRA)
1972	Daniel Morelon (FRA) 11 .25	John M. Nicholson (AUS)	Omari Phakadze (URS)
1976	Anton Tkac (TCH) 10.78	Daniel Morelon (FRA)	Hans-Jurgen Geschke (GDR)
1980	Lutz Hesslich (GDR) 11.40	Yave Cahard (FRA)	Sergei Kopylov (URS)
1984	Mark Gorski (USA) 10.49	Nelson Vails (USA)	Tsutomu Sakamoto (JPN)

[2] Since 1924 only times over the last 200 meters of the event have been recorded.

1,000 METERS TIME-TRIAL

1896–1924 Event not held

1928	Willy Falck-Hansen (DEN) 1:14.4*	Gerard D. H. Bosch van Drakestein (HOL) 1:15.2	Edgar Gray (AUS) 1:15.6
1932	Edgar Gray (AUS) 1:13.0*	Jacobus van Egmond (HOL) 1:13.3	Charles Rampelberg (FRA) 1:13.4
1936	Arie van Vliet (HOL) 1:12.0*	Pierre Georget (FRA) 1:12.8	Rudolf Karsch (GER) 1:13.2
1948	Jacques Dupont (FRA) 1:13.5	Pierre Nihant (BEL) 1:14.5	Thomas Godwin (GBR) 1:15.0
1952	Russell Mockridge (AUS) 1:11.1*	Marino Morettini (ITA) 1:12.7	Raymond Robinson (SAF) 1:13.0
1956	Leandro Faggin (ITA) 1:09.8*	Ladislav Foucek (TCH) 1:11.4	J. Alfred Swift (SAF) 1:11.6
1960	Sante Gaiardoni (ITA) 1:07.27*	Dieter Gieseler (GER) 1:08.75	Rotislav Vargashkin (URS) 1:08.86
1964	Patrick Sercu (BEL) 1:09.59	Giovanni Pettenella (ITA) 1:10.09	Pierre Trentin (FRA) 1:10.42
1968	Pierre Trentin (FRA) 1:03.91*	Niels-Christian Fredborg (DEN) 1:04.61	Janusz Kierzkowski (POL) 1:04.63
1972	Niels-Christian Fredborg (DEN) 1:06.44	Daniel Clark (AUS) 1:06.87	Juergen Schuetze (GDR) 1:07.02
1976	Klaus-Jurgen Grunke (GDR) 1:05.93	Michel Vaarten (BEL) 1:07.52	Niels Fredborg (DEN) 1:07.62
1980	Lothar Thoms (GDR) 1:02.955	Aiexandr Panfilov (URS) 1:04.845	David Weller (JAM) 1:05.241
1984	Fredy Schmidtke (FRG) 1:06.10	Curtis Harnett (CAN) 1:06.44	Fabrice Colas (FRA) 1:06.65

4,000 METERS INDIVIDUAL PURSUIT

Note: Bronze medal times are set in a third place race, so can be faster than those set in the race for first and second place.

GOLD	SILVER	BRONZE
1896–1960 Event not held		
1964 Jiří Daler (TCH) 5:04.75	Giorgio Ursi (ITA) 5:05.96	Preben Isaksson (DEN) 5:01.90
1968 Daniel Rebillard (FRA) 4:41.71	Mogens Frey Jensen (DEN) 4:42.43	Xaver Kurmann (SUI) 4:39.42
1972 Knut Knudsen (NOR) 4:45.74	Xaver Kurmann (SUI) 4:51.96	Hans Lutz (GER) 4:50.80
1976 Gregor Braun (GDR) 4:47.61	Herman Ponsteen (HOL) 4:49.72	Thomas Huschke (GDR) 4:52.71
1980 Robert Dill-Bundi (SUI) 4:35.66	Alain Bondue (FRA) 4:42.96	Hans-Henrik Orsted (DEN) 4:36.54
1984 Steve Hegg (USA) 4:39.35	Rolf Golz (FRG) 4:43.82	Leonard Nitz (USA) 4:44.03

4,000 METERS TEAM PURSUIT

Note: Bronze medal times are set in a third place race, so can be faster than those set in the race for first and second place.

GOLD	SILVER	BRONZE
1896–1912 Event not held		
1920 ITALY 5:20.0	GREAT BRITAIN	SOUTH AFRICA
Franco Giorgetti	Albert White	James R. Walker
Ruggero Ferrario	H. Thomas Johnson	William R. Smith
Arnaldo Carli	William Stewart	Henry J. Kaltenbrun
Primo Magnani	C. Albert Alden	Harry W. Goosen
1924 ITALY 5:15.0	POLAND	BELGIUM
Alfredo Dinale	Jósef Lange	Léon Dahelinczky
Francesco Zucchetti	Franciszek Szymeczyk	Henry Hoevenaers
Angelo de Martino	Jan Lazarski	Fernand Saive
Aleardo Menegazzi	Tomas Sztankiewicz	Jean van den Bosch
1928 ITALY 5:01.8	NETHERLANDS 5:06.2	GREAT BRITAIN
Luigi Tasselli	Adriann Braspenninx	Frank Wyld
Giacomo Gaioni	Jan Maas	Leonard Wyld
Cesare Facciani	Johannes B. N. Pijnenburg	Percy Wyld
Mario Lusiani	Piet van der Horst	M. George Southall
1932 ITALY 4:53.0	FRANCE 4:55.7	GREAT BRITAIN 4:56.0
Marco Cimatti	Amédé Fournier	Ernest A. Johnson
Paolo Pedretti	René Legrèves	William Harvell
Alberto Ghilardi	Henri Mouillefarine	Frank W. Southall
Nino Borsari	Paul Chocque	Charles Holland
1936 FRANCE 4:45.0	ITALY 4:51.0	GREAT BRITAIN 4:52.6
Robert Charpentier	Bianco Bianchi	Harry H. Hill
Jean Goujon	Mario Gentili	Ernest A. Johnson
Guy Lapébie	Armando Latini	Charles T. King
Roger Le Nizerhy	Severino Rigoni	Ernest V. Mills
1948 FRANCE 4:57.8	ITALY 5:36.7	GREAT BRITAIN 4:55.8
Pierre Adam	Arnaldo Benefenati	Alan Geldard
Serge Blusson	Guido Bernardi	Thomas Godwin
Charles Coste	Anselmo Citterio	David Ricketts
Ferdinand Decanali	Rino Pucci	Wilfred Waters

GOLD	SILVER	BRONZE
1952 **ITALY 4:46.1**	**S. AFRICA 4:53.6**	**GREAT BRITAIN** 4:51.5
Marino Morettini	Thomas F. Shardelow	Ronald C. Stretton
Guido Messina	Alfred J. Swift	Alan Newton
Mino de Rossi	Robert G. Fowler	George A. Newberry
Loris Campana	George Estman	Donald C. Burgess
1956 **ITALY 4:37.4**	**FRANCE 4:39.4**	**GREAT BRITAIN** 4:42.2
Leandro Faggin	René Bianchi	Thomas Simpson
Valentino Gasparella	Jean Graczyk	Donald Burgess
Franco Gandini	Jean-Claude Lecante	John Geddes
Tonino Domenicali	Michel Vermeulin	Michael Gambrill
1960 **ITALY 4:30.90**	**GERMANY 4:35.78**	**U.S.S.R. 4:34.05**
Luigi Arienti	Peter Gröning	Stanislav Moskvin
Franco Testa	Manfred Klieme	Viktor Romanov
Mario Vallotto	Siegfried Köhler	Leonid Kolumbet
Marino Vigna	Bernd Barleben	Arnold Belgardt
1964 **GERMANY 4:35.67**	**ITALY 4:35.74**	**NETHERLANDS** 4:38.99
Lothar Claesges	Luigi Roncaglia	Gerard Koel
Karl-Heinz Henrichs	Vincenzo Mantovani	Hendrik Cornelisse
Karl Link	Carlo Rancati	Jacob Oudkerk
Ernest Streng	Franco Testa	Cornelis Schururing
1968 **DENMARK 4:22.44**	**GERMANY 4:18.94[1]**	**ITALY 4:18.35**
Gunnar Asmussen	Udo Hempel	Lorenzo Bossio
Per. P. Lyngemark	Karl Link	Cipirano Chemello
Reno B. Olsen	Karl-Heinz Henrichs	Luigi Roncaglia
Mogens Frey Jensen	Jürgen Kissner	Giorgio Morbiato
1972 **WEST GERMANY** 4:22.14	**EAST GERMANY** 4:25.25	**GREAT BRITAIN** 4:23.78
Jurgen Colombo	Thomas Huschke	Michael Bennett
Günter Haritz	Heinz Richter	Ian Hallam
Udo Hempel	Herbert Richter	Ronald Keeble
Günther Schumacher	Uwe Unterwalder	William Moore
1976 **WEST GERMANY** 4:21.06	**U.S.S.R. 4:27.15**	**GREAT BRITAIN** 4:22.41
Gregor Braun	Vladimir Osokin	Ian Banbury
Hans Lutz	Aleksandr Perov	Michael Bennett
Günther Schumacher	Vitaly Petrakov	Robin Croker
Peter Vonhof	Victor Sokolov	Ian Hallam
1980 **U.S.S.R. 4:15.70**	**EAST GERMANY** 4:19.67	**CZECHOSLOVAKIA[2]**
Viktor Manakov	Gerald Mortag	Teodor Cerny
Valeriy Movchan	Uwe Unterwalder	Martin Penc
Vladimir Osokin	Matthias Wiegand	Jiri Pokorny
Vitaliy Petrakov	Volker Winkler	Igor Slama
1984 **AUSTRALIA 4:25.99**	**USA 4:29.85**	**FEDERAL REPUBLIC OF GERMANY 4:25.60**
Michael Grenda	David Grylls	Reinhard Alber
Kevin Nichols	Steve Hegg	Rolf Golz
Michael Turtur	Patrick McDonough	Roland Gunther
Dean Woods	Leonard Nitz	Michael Marx

[1] Won final but disqualified.
[2] Italy disqualified in third place race.

POINTS RACE

1984 Roger Ilegems (BEL)	Uwe Messerschmidt (FRG)	Jose Manuel Youshimatz (MEX)

INDIVIDUAL ROAD RACE

GOLD	SILVER	BRONZE
1896	Aristides Konstantinidis (GRE) 3h 22:31.0	August Goedrich (GER) 3h 42:18.0	F. Battel (GBR) d.n.a.
1900–1904 Event not held			
1906	Fernand Vast (FRA) 2h 41:28.0	Maurice Bardonneau (FRA) 2h 41:28.4	Edmond Luguet (FRA) 2h 41:28.6
1908 Event not held			
1912	Rudolph Lewis (SAF) 10h 42:39.0	Frederick Grubb (GBR) 10h 51:24.2	Carl Schutte (USA) 10h 52:38.8
1920	Harry Stenqvist (SWE) 4h 40:01.8	Henry J. Kaltenbrun (SAF) 4h 41:26.6	Fernand Canteloube (FRA) 4h 42:54.4
1924	Armand Blanchonnet (FRA) 6h 20:48.0	Henry Hoevenaers (BEL) 6h 30:27.0	René Hamel (FRA) 6h 40:51.6
1928	Henry Hansen (DEN) 4h 47:18.0	Frank W. Southall (GBR) 4h 55:06.0	Gösta Carlsson (SWE) 5h 00:17.0
1932	Attilio Pavesi (ITA) 2h 28:05.6	Guglielmo Segato (ITA) 2h 29:21.4	Bernhard Britz (SWE) 2h 29:45.2
1936	Robert Charpentier (FRA) 2h 33:05.0	Guy Lapébie (FRA) 2h 33:05.2	Ernst Nievergelt (SUI) 2h 33:05.8
1948	José Beyaert (FRA) 5h 18:12.6	Gerardus P. Voorting (HOL) 5h 18:16.2	Lode Wouters (BEL) 5h 18:16.2
1952	André Noyelle (BEL) 5h 06:03.4	Robert Grondelaers (BEL) 5h 06:51.2	Edi Ziegler (GER) 5h 07:47.5
1956	Ercole Baldini (ITA) 5h 21:17.0	Arnaud Geyre (FRA) 5h 23:16.0	Alan Jackson (GBR) 5h 23:16.0
1960	Viktor Kapitonov (URS) 4h 20:37.0	Livio Trapè (ITA) 4h 20:37.0	Willy van den Berghen (BEL) 4h 20:57.0
1964	Mario Zanin (ITA) 4h 39:51.63	Kjell A. Rodian (DEN) 4h 39:51.65	Walter Godefroot (BEL) 4h 39:51.74
1968	Pierfranco Vianelli (ITA) 4h 41:25.24	Leif Mortensen (DEN) 4h 42:49.71	Gösta Pettersson (SWE) 4h 43:15.24
1972	Hennie Kuiper (HOL) 4h 14:37.0	Kevin C. Sefton (AUS) 4h 15:04.0	Jaime Huelamo (*disq*) (ESP) 4h 15:04.0
1976	Bernt Johansson (SWE) 4h 46:52.0	Giuseppe Martinelli (ITA) 4h 47:23.0	Mieczysl Nowicki (POL) 4h 47:23.0
1980	Sergei Sukhoruchenkov (URS) 4h 48:28.9	Czeslaw Lang (POL) 4h 51:26.9	Yuri Barinov (URS) 4h 51:26.9
1984	Alexi Grewal (USA) 4:59.57	Steve Bauer (CAN) close	Dag Otto Lauritzen (NOR) 5:00.18

This event has been held over the following distances:—1896—87 km; 1906—84 km; 1912—320 km; 1920—175 km; 1924—188 km; 1928—168 km; 1932 and 1936—100 km; 1948—194,63 km; 1952—190,4 km; 1956—187,73 km; 1960—175,38 km; 1964—194,83 km; 1968—196,2 km; 1972—200 km; 1976—176 km; 1980—189 km.

ROAD TEAM TIME-TRIAL

Held over 100 km except in 1964 (109,89 km) and 1968 (104 km)

1896–1956 Event not held			
1960	ITALY 2h 14:33.53	GERMANY 2h 16:56.31	U.S.S.R. 2h 18:41.67
	Antonio Bailetti	Gustav-Adolf Schur	Viktor Kapitonov
	Ottavio Cogliati	Egon Adler	Yevgeny Klevzov
	Giacomo Fornoni	Erich Hagen	Yuriy Melikhov
	Livio Trapè	Günter Lörke	Aleksey Petrov
1964	NETHERLANDS 2h 26:31.19	ITALY 2h 26:55.39	SWEDEN 2h 27:11.52
	Gerben Karstens	Severino Andreoli	Sven Hamrin
	Evert G. Dolman	Luciano dalla Bona	Erik Pettersson
	Johannes Pieterse	Pietro Guerra	Gösta Pettersson
	Hubertus Zoet	Ferrucio Manza	Sture Pettersson

1968	NETHERLANDS 2h 07:49.06	SWEDEN 2h 09:26.60	ITALY 2h 10:18.74
	Marinus Pijnen	Gösta Pettersson	Vittorio Marcelli
	Fedor den Hertog	Sture Pettersson	Mauro Simonetti
	Jan Krekels	Erik Pettersson	Pierfranco Vianelli
	Henk Zoetemelk	Tomas Pettersson	Giovanni Bramucci
1972	U.S.S.R. 2h 11:17.8	POLAND 2h 11:47.5	NETHERLANDS 2h 12:27.1
	Boris Chouhov	Lucjan Lis	Fedor den Hertog
	Valeri Iardy	Edward Barcik	Hennie Kuiper
	Gennady Komnatov	Stanislaw Szozda	Cees Priem
	Valery Likhachev	Ryszard Szurkowski	Aad van den Hoek
1976	U.S.S.R. 2h 08:53.0	POLAND 2h 09:13.0	DENMARK 2h 12:20.0
	Anatoli Chukanov	Tadeusz Mytnik	Verner Blaudzun
	Valeriy Chaplygin	Mieczysl Nowicki	Gert Frank
	Vladimir Kaminski	Stanisla Szozda	Jorgen Hansen
	Aavo Pikkuus	Ryszard Szurkowski	Jorn Lund
1980	U.S.S.R. 2h 01:21.7	EAST GERMANY 2h 02:53.2	CZECHOSLOVAKIA 2h 02:53.9
	Yuriy Kashirin	Falk Boden	Michal Klasa
	Oleg Logwin	Bernd Drogan	Vlastibor Konecny
	Sergey Shelpakov	Olaf Ludwig	Alipi Kostadinov
	Anatoliy Yarkin	Hans-Joachin Hartnick	Jiri Skoda
1984	ITALY 1:58.28	SWITZERLAND 2:02.38	USA 2:02.46
	Marcello Bartalini	Alfred Acherman	Ronald Kiefel
	Marco Giovannetti	Richard Trinkler	Roy Knickman
	Eros Poli	Laurent Vial	Davis Phinney
	Claudio Vandelli	Benno Wiss	Andrew Weaver

Cycling (Women)

INDIVIDUAL ROAD RACE

1984	Connie Carpenter-Phinney (USA) 2:11:14	Rebecca Twigg (USA) close	Sandra Schumacher (FRG) close

Held over a distance of 79.2km

6. Equestrian Sports

GRAND PRIX (JUMPING)

GOLD	SILVER	BRONZE
1896 Event not held		
1900 Aimé Haegeman	Georges van de Poele	de Champsavin
(BEL) *Benton II*	(BEL) *Windsor Squire*	(FRA) *Terpischore*
1904–1908 Event not held		
1912 Jean Cariou	Rabod W. von Kröcher	Emanuel de Blommaert de Soye
(FRA) 186 *Mignon*	(GER) 186 *Dohna*	(BEL) 185 *Clonmore*
Teams—SWEDEN 545 pts.	FRANCE 538	GERMANY 530
C. Gustav Lewenhaupt	Jean Cariou	Sigismund Freyer
Hans von Rosen	Michel d'Astafort	William Graf von Hohenau
Gustaf Kilman	Bernard Meyer	Ernst-Hubertus Deloch
1920 Tommaso Lequio	Alessandro Valerio	C. Gustaf Lewenhaupt
(ITA) 2 faults *Trebecco*	(ITA) 3 faults *Cento*	(SWE) 4 faults *Mon Coeur*
Teams—SWEDEN 14 faults	BELGIUM 16.25	ITALY 18.75
Hans von Rosen	Count Herman d'Oultremont	Ettore Caffaratti
Claes König	André Commans	Guilio Cacciandra
Daniel Norling	Baron Herman de Gaiffler d'Hestroy	Alessandro Alvisi
1924 Alphonse Gemuseus	Tommaso Lequio	Adam Królikiewicz
(SUI) 6 faults *Lucette*	(ITA) 8.75 *Trebecco*	(POL) 10 *Picador*
Teams—SWEDEN 42.25 pts.	SWITZERLAND 50	PORTUGAL 53
Ake Thelning	Alphonse Gemuseus	Antonio Borges d'Almeida
Axel Ståhle	Werner Stüber	Helder de Souza Martins
Age Lundström	Hans Bühler	José Mouzinho d'Albuquerque
1928 František Ventura	Pierre Bertrand de Balanda	Charles Kuhn
(TCH) no faults *Eliot*	(FRA) 2 *Papillon*	(SUI) 4 *Pepita*
Teams—SPAIN 4 faults	POLAND 8	SWEDEN 10
Marquis José Alvarez de los Trujillos	Kazimierz Gzowski	Karl Hansen
José Navarro Morenés	Kazimierz Szosland	Carl Björnstjerna
Julio Garcia Fernández	Michal Antoniewicz	Ernst Hallberg
1932[1] Takeichi Nishi	Harry Chamberlin	Clarence von Rosen jr.
(JPN) 8 pts. *Uranus*	(USA) 212 *Show Girl*	(SWE) 16 *Empire*
1936 Kurt Hasse	Henri Rang	József von Platthy
(GER) 4 faults *Tora*	(ROM) 4 *Delfis*	(HUN) 8 *Sellö*
Teams—GERMANY 44 faults	NETHERLANDS 51.5	PORTUGAL 56
Kurt Hasse	Jan A. de Bruine	Luis Mena e Silva
Marten von Barnekow	Johan J. Greter	Luis Marquéz do Funchal
Heinz Brandt	Henri L. M. van Schaik	José Beltrão
1948 Humberto Mariles Cortés	Rubén Uriza	Jean F. d'Orgeix
(MEX) 6.25 faults *Arete*	(MEX) 8 *Harvey*	(FRA) 8 *Sucre de Pomme*
Teams—MEXICO 34.25 faults	SPAIN 56.50	GREAT BRITAIN 67
Humberto Mariles Cortés	Jaime Garcia Cruz	Henry M. V. Nicoll
Rubén Uriza	Marcelino Gavilán y Ponce de Leon	Arthur Carr
Alberto Valdés	José Navarro Morenés	Harry M. Llewellyn
1952 Pierre Jonquières d'Oriola	Oscar Cristi	Fritz Thiedemann
(FRA) no faults *Ali Baba*	(CHI) 4 *Bambi*	(GER) 8 *Meteor*

---

[1] There was also a teams competition, but there was no nation of which all three riders completed the course.

Alwin Schockemöhle (GER) won the individual Grand Prix gold medal on "Warwick Rex" in 1976. He has also won 3 team medals, in 1960, 1968 and 1976.

	GOLD	SILVER	BRONZE
	Teams—**GREAT BRITAIN** 40.75 faults	**CHILE 45.75**	**UNITED STATES** 52.25
	Douglas Stewart	Oscar Cristi	Arthur J. McCashin
	Wilfred H. White	Ricardo Echeverria	John Russell
	Harry M. Llewellyn	Cesar Mendoza	William Steinkraus
1956	Hans Günter Winkler	Raimondo d'Inzeo	Piero d'Inzeo
	(GER) 4 faults *Halla*	(ITA) 8 *Merano*	(ITA) 11 *Uruguay*
	Teams—**GERMANY 40**	**ITALY 66**	**GREAT BRITAIN 69**
	Hans Günter Winkler	Raimondo d'Inzeo	Wilfred H. White
	Fritz Thiedemann	Piero d'Inzeo	Patricia Smythe
	Alfons Lütke-Westheus	Salvatore Oppes	Peter Robeson
1960	Raimondo d'Inzeo	Piero d'Inzeo	David Broome
	(ITA) 12 faults	(ITA) 16 *The Rock*	(GBR) 23 *Sunsalve*
	Posillippo		
	Teams—**GERMANY 46.50**	**UNITED STATES 66**	**ITALY 80.50**
	Alwin Schockemöhle	George Morris	Riamondo d'Inzeo
	Fritz Thiedemann	Frank Chapot	Piero d'Inzeo
	Hans Günter Winkler	William Steinkraus	Antonio Oppes
1964	Pierre Jonquières	Hermann Schridde	Peter Robeson
	d'Oriola	(GER) 13.75 faults	(GBR) 16 faults
	(FRA) 9 faults *Lutteur*	*Dozen*	*Firecrest*
	Teams—**GERMANY 68.50**	**FRANCE 77.75**	**ITALY 88.50**
	Hermann Schridde	Pierre Jonquières	Piero d'Inzeo
	Kurt Jarasinksi	d'Oriola	Raimondo d'Inzeo
	Hans Günter Winkler	Janou Lefebvre	Graziano Mancinelli
		Guy Lefrant	
1968	William Steinkraus	Marian Coakes	David Broome
	(USA) 4 faults	(GBR) 8 faults	(GBR) 12 faults
	Snowbound	*Stroller*	*Mister Softee*
	Teams—**CANADA 102.75**	**FRANCE 110.50**	**GERMANY 117.25**
	Thomas Gayford	Marcel Rozier	Hermann Schridde
	James Day	Janou Lefebvre	Alwin Schockemöhle
	James Elder	Pierre Jonquières	Hans Günter Winkler
		d'Oriola	

GOLD	SILVER	BRONZE
1972 Graziano Mancinelli (ITA) 8 faults *Ambassador*	Ann Moore (GBR) 9 faults *Psalm*	Neal Shapiro (USA) 8 faults *Sloopy*
Teams—WEST GERMANY 32	UNITED STATES 32.25	ITALY 48
Fritz Ligges	William Steinkraus	Vittorio Orlando
Gerhard Wiltfang	Neal Shapiro	Raimondo d'Inzeo
Hartwig Steenken	Kathryn Kusner	Graziano Mancinelli
Hans Günter Winkler	Frank Chapot	Piero d'Inzeo
1976 Alwin Schockemöhle (GER) No faults *Warwick Rex*	Michael Valliancourt (CAN) 12 faults *Branch County*	Francois Mathy (BEL) 12 faults *Gai Luron*
Teams—FRANCE 40	WEST GERMANY 44	BELGIUM 63
Hubert Parot	Hans Günter Winkler	Eric Wauters
Marcel Rozier	Paul Schockemöhle	Francois Mathy
Michel Roche	Alwin Shockemöhle	Edgar Guepper
Marc Roguet	Soenke Soenksen	Stanny Van Paeschen
1980 Jan Kowalczyk (POL) 8 faults *Artemor*	Nikolai Korolkov (URS) 9.5 faults *Espadron*	Joaquin Perez Heras[2] (MEX) 12 faults *Alymony*
Teams—U.S.S.R. 20.25	POLAND 56	MEXICO 59.75
Vyacheslav Chukanov	Marian Kozicki	Joaquin Perez Heras
Viktor Poganovsky	Jan Kowalczyk	Alberto Valdes Lacarra
Viktor Asmayev	Wieslaw Hartman	Gerardo Tazzer Valencia
Nikolai Korolkov	Janusz Bobik	Jesus Gomez Portugal
1984 Joe Fargis (USA) *Touch of Class*	Conrad Homfeld (USA) *Abdullah*	Heidi Robbiani (SUI) *Jessica V*
Teams—USA 12.00	GREAT BRITAIN 36.75	WEST GERMANY 39.25
Joe Fargis	Michael Whitaker	Paul Schockemohle
Conrad Homfeld	John Whitaker	Peter Luther
Leslie Burr	Steven Smith	Franke Sloothaak
Melanie Smith	Timothy Grubb	Fritz Ligges

---

[2] Won jump off.

GRAND PRIX (DRESSAGE)

GOLD	SILVER	BRONZE
1896–1908 Event not held		
1912 Carl Bonde (SWE) 15 pts. *Emperor*	Gustaf-Adolf Boltenstern Sr. (SWE) 21 *Neptun*	Hans von Blixen- Finecke (SWE) 32 *Maggie*
1920 Janne Lundblad (SWE) 27,937 pts. *Uno*	Bertil Sandström (SWE) 26,312 *Sabel*	Hans von Rosen (SWE) 25,125 *Running Sister*
1924 Ernst Linder (SWE) 276.4 pts. *Piccolomini*	Bertil Sandström (SWE) 275.8 *Sabel*	Xavier Lesage (FRA) 265.8 *Plumard*
1928 Carl F. F. von Langen (GER) 237.42 pts. *Draufgänger*	Charles Marion (FRA) 231.00 *Limon*	Ragnar Olsson (SWE) 229.78 *Günstling*
Teams—GERMANY 669.72 pts.	SWEDEN 650.86	NETHERLANDS 642.96
Carl von Langen	Ragnar Olsson	Jan van Reede
Hermann Linkenbach	Carl Bonde	Pierre Vesteegh
Eugen von Lotzbeck	Janne Lundblad	Gérard le Heux
1932 Xavier Lesage (FRA) 1,031.25 pts *Taine*	Charles Marion (FRA) 916.25 *Linon*	Hiram Tuttle (USA) 901.50 *Olympic*
Teams—FRANCE 2,818.75 pts.	SWEDEN 2,678.00	UNITED STATES 2,576.75
Xavier Lesage	Thomas Byström	Hiram Tuttle
Charles Marion	Gustaf-Adolf Boltenstern Jr.	Isaac Kitts
André Jousseaume	Bertil Sandström	Alvin Moore

GOLD	SILVER	BRONZE

1936 Heinz Pollay   Friedrich Gerhard   Alois Podhajsky
  (GER) 1,760 *Kronos* (GER)1,745.5 *Absinth* (AUT) 1,721.5 *Nero*
 Teams—GERMANY FRANCE 4,846   SWEDEN 4,660.5
   5,074 pts.
  Heinz Pollay   André Jousseaume Gregor von Aldercreutz
  Freidrich Gerhard Daniel Gillois   Folke Sandström
  Hermann von Oppeln Gérard de Ballorre Sven Colliander
   Bronikowski

1948 Hans Moser   André Jousseaume Gustaf-Adolf
  (SUI) 492.5 pts. (FRA) 480.0   Boltenstern Jr.
   Hummer   *Harpagon* (SWE) 477.5 *Trumpf*
 Teams—FRANCE 1,269 pts.[1] UNITED STATES 1,256 PORTUGAL 1,182
  André Jousseaume Robert Borg   Fernando da Silva Paes
  Jean Paillard   Earl Thomson   Francisco Valadas
  Maurice Buret   Frank Henry   Luis Mena e Silva

1952 Henri St. Cyr   Lis Hartel   André Jousseaume
  (SWE) 561 pts. (DEN) 541.5 *Jubilee* (FRA) 541.0 *Harpagon*
   Master Rufus
 Teams—SWEDEN SWITZERLAND GERMANY 1,501.0
   1,597.5 pts.   1,759.0
  Gustaf-Adolf   Gustav Fischer   Ida von Nagel
   Boltenstern Jr. Gottfried Trachsel Fritz Thiedemann
  Henri St. Cyr   Henri Chammartin Heinrich Pollay
  Gehnäll Persson

1956 Henri St. Cyr   Lis Hartel   Liselott Lisenhoff
  (SWE) 860 pts. *Juli* (DEN) 850 *Jubilee* (GER) 832 *Adular*
 Teams—SWEDEN,2,475pts. GERMANY 2,346 SWITZERLAND 2,346
  Henri St. Cyr   Liselott Lisenhoff Gustav Fischer
  Gehnäll Persson Hannelore Weygand Gottfried Trachsel
  Gustaf-Adolf   Anneliese Küppers Henri Chammartin
   Boltenstern Jr.

1960 Sergey Filatov   Gustav Fischer   Josef Neckermann
  (URS)2,144pts.*Absent* (SUI) 2,087 *Wald* (GER) 2,082 *Asbach*
         Team event not held

1964 Henri Chammartin Harry Boldt   Sergey Filatov
  (SUI) 1,504 pts. (GER) 1,503 *Remus* (URS) 1,486 *Absent*
   Woermann
 Teams—GERMANY SWITZERLAND   U.S.S.R. 2,311
   2,558 pts.   2,526
  Harry Boldt   Henri Chammartin Sergey Filatov
  Josef Neckermann Gustav Fischer   Ivan Kizimov
  Reiner Klimke   Marianne Gossweiler Ivan Kalita

1968 Ivan Kizimov   Josef Neckermann Reiner Klimke
  (URS) 1,572 pts.*Ikhor* (GER) 1,546 *Mariano* (GER) 1,537 *Dux*
 Teams—GERMANY U.S.S.R. 2,657 SWITZERLAND 2,547
   2,699 pts.
  Josef Neckermann Elena Petuchkova Henri Chammartin
  Liselott Linsenhoff Ivan Kizimov   Marianne Gossweiler
  Dr. Reiner Klimke Ivan Kalita   Gustav Fischer

1972 Liselott Linsenhoff Elena Petuchkova Josef Neckermann
  (GER) 1,229 pts. *Piaff* (URS) 1,185 *Pepel* (GER) 1,177 *Venetia*
 Teams—USSR 5,095 pts WEST GERMANY SWEDEN 4,849
         5,083
  Elena Petuchkova Liselott Linsenhoff Ulla Hakansson
  Ivan Kizimov   Josef Neckermann Ninna Swaab
  Ivan Kalita   Karin Schlüter   Maud van Rosen

	GOLD	SILVER	BRONZE
1976	Christine Stueckelberger (SUI) 1,486 pts.	Harry Boldt (GER) 1,432	Reiner Klimke (GER) 1,395
Teams—	WEST GERMANY 5,155 pts.	SWITZERLAND 4,684	USA 4,670
	Harry Boldt	Christine Stueckelberger	Hilda Gurney
	Reiner Klimke	Ulrich Lehmann	Dorothy Morkis
	Gabriela Grillo	Doris Ramseier	Edith Master
1980	Elizabeth Theurer (AUT) 1,370 pts. *Mon Cherie*	Yuri Kovshov (URS) 1,300 *Igrok*	Viktor Ugryumov (URS) 1,234 *Shkval*
Teams—	U.S.S.R. 4,383 pts.	BULGARIA 3,580	RUMANIA 3,346
	Yuriy Kovshov	Petar Mandajiev	Anghelache Donescu
	Viktor Ugryumov	Svetoslav Ivanov	Dumitru Veliku
	Vera Misevich	Gheorghi Gadjev	Petre Rosca
1984	Reiner Klimke (FRG) 1,504 pts. *Ahlerich*	Anne Grethe Jensen (DEN) 1,442 *Marzog*	Otto Hofer (SUI) 1,364 *Limandus*
Teams—	WEST GERMANY 4,955 pts.	SWITZERLAND 4,673	SWEDEN 4,630
	Reiner Klimke	Otto Hofer	Ulla Hakansson
	Uwe Sauer	Christine Stueckelberger	Ingamay Bylund
	Herbert Krug	Amy De Bary	Louise Nathhorst

---

[1] SWEDEN was originally declared the winner with 1,366 pts., but was disqualified subsequently—five years later.

THREE-DAY EVENT

	GOLD	SILVER	BRONZE
1896–1908	Event not held		
1912	Axel Nordlander (SWE) 46.59 pts. *Lady Artist*	Friedrich von Rochow (GER) 46.42 *Idealist*	Jean Cariou (FRA) 46.32 *Cocotte*
Teams—	SWEDEN 139.06 pts.	GERMANY 138.48	UNITED STATES 137.33
	Nils Adlercreutz	Friedrich von Rochow	Benjamin Lear
	Axel Nordlander	Eduard von Lütcken	John C. Montgomery
	Ernst G. Casparsson	Richard G. von Schaesberg-Thannheim	Guy Henry
1920	Helmer Mörner (SWE) 1,775 pts. *Germania*	Age Lundström (SWE) 1,738.75 *Yrsa*	Ettore Caffaratti (ITA) 1,733.75 *Traditore*
Teams—	SWEDEN 5.057.5 pts.	ITALY 4,735	BELGIUM 4,560
	Helmer Mörner	Ettore Caffaratti	Roger Moremans d'Emaus
	Age Lundström	Garibaldi Spighi	
	George von Braun	Guilio Cacciandra	Oswald Lints
			Jules Bonvalet
1924	Adolph D. C. van der Voort van Zijp (HOL) 1,976 pts. *Silver Piece*	Fröde Kirkebjerg (DEN) 1,853.5 *Meteor*	Sloan Doak (USA) 1,845.5 *Pathfinder*
Teams—	NETHERLANDS 5,297.5 pts.	SWEDEN 4,743.5	ITALY 4,512.5
	Adolph D. C. van der Voort van Zijp	Claes König	Alberto Lombardi
	Charles F. Pahud de Mortanges	Torsten Sylvan	Alessandro Alvisi
	Gerard P. C. de Kruyff	Gustaf Hagelin	Emanuele di Pralormo

The first winners of the Three-Day Event team competition were this Swedish trio at Stockholm in 1912.

	GOLD	SILVER	BRONZE
1928	Charles F. Pahud de Mortanges (HOL) 1,969.82 pts. *Marcoix*	Gerard P. C. de Kruyff (HOL) 1,967.26 *Va-t-en*	Bruno Neumann (GER) 1,944.42 *Ilja*
	Teams—NETHERLANDS 5.865.68 pts.	NORWAY 5,395.68	POLAND 5,067.92
	Charles F. Pahud de Mortanges Gerard P. C. de Kruyff Adolph D. C. van der Voort van Zijp	Arthur Quist Bjart Ording Eugen Johansen	Jósef Trenkwald Michal Antoniewicz Karol de Rómmel
1932	Charles F. Pahud de Mortanges (HOL) 1,813.83 pts. *Marcroix*	Earl Thomson (USA) 1,811 *Jenny Camp*	Clarence von Rosen Jr. (SWE) 1,809.42 *Sunnyside Maid*
	Teams—UNITED STATES 5,038.08 pts.	NETHERLANDS 4,689.08	—
	Earl Thomson Harry Chamberlin Edwin Argo	Charles F. Pahud de Mortanges Karel J. Schummelketel Aernout van Lennep	
1936	Ludwig Stubbendorff (GER) 37.7 faults *Nurmi*	Earl Thomson (USA) 99.9 *Jenny Camp*	Hans Mathiesen-Lunding (DEN) 102.2 *Jason*
	Teams—GERMANY 676.75 pts.	POLAND 991.70	GREAT BRITAIN 9,195.50
	Ludwig Stubbendorff Rudolf Lippert Konrad von Wangenheim	Severyn Kulesza Henryk Rojcewicz Zdislaw Kawecki	Edward Howard-Vyse Alec Scott Richard Fanshawe

1948   Bernard Chevallier   Frank Henry   J. Robert Selfelt

	GOLD	SILVER	BRONZE
1948	Bernard Chevallier (FRA) plus 4 pts. *Aiglonne*	Frank Henry (USA) minus 21 *Swing Low*	J. Robert Selfelt (SWE) minus 25 *Claque*
	Teams—UNITED STATES 161.50 faults	SWEDEN 165.00	MEXICO 305.25
	Frank Henry Charles Anderson Earl Thomson	J. Robert Selfelt Nils Olof Stahre Sigurd Svensson	Humberto Mariles Cortés Raúl Campero Joaquin Solano Chagoya
1952	Hans von Blixen-Finecke (SWE) 28.33 faults *Jubal*	Guy Lefrant (FRA) 54.50 *Verdun*	Wilhelm Büsing (GER) 55.50 *Hubertus*
	Teams—SWEDEN 221.49 pts.	GERMANY 235.49	UNITED STATES 587.16
	Hans von Blixen-Finecke Nils Olof Stahre Karl F. Frölén	Wilhelm Büsing Klaus Wagner Otto Rothe	Charles Hough Walter Staley Jr. John Wofford
1956	Petrus Kastenman (SWE) 66.53 faults *Iluster*	August Lütke-Westhues (GER) 84.87 *Trux von Kamax*	Francis Weldon (GBR) 85.48 *Kilbarry*
	Teams—GREAT BRITAIN 355.48 pts.	GERMANY 475.61	CANADA 572.72
	Albert E. Hill Francis Weldon A. Lawrence Rook	August Lütke-Westhues Klaus Wagner Otto Rothe	James Elder Brian Herbinson John Rumble
1960	Lawrence Morgan (AUS) plus 7.15 pts. *Salad Days*	Neale Lavis (AUS) minus 16.50 *Mirrabooka*	Anton Bühler (SUI) minus 51.21 *Gay Spark*
	Teams—AUSTRALIA 128.18 pts.	SWITZERLAND 386.02	FRANCE 515.71
	Lawrence Morgan Neale Lavis William Roycroft	Anton Bühler Hans Schwarzenbach Rudolf Günthardt	Jack L. Le Goff Jean R. Le Roy Guy Lefrant
1964	Mauro Checcoli (ITA) 64.40 pts. *Surbean*	Carlos Moratorio (ARG) 56.40 *Chalan*	Fritz Ligges (GER) 49.20 *Donkosak*
	Teams—ITALY 85.80 pts.	UNITED STATES 65.86	GERMANY 56.73
	Mauro Checcoli Paolo Angioni Giuseppe Ravano	Michael Page Kevin Freeman J. Michael Plumb	Fritz Ligges Horst Karsten Gerhard Schultz
1968	Jean-Jacques Guyon (FRA) 38.86 pts. *Pitou*	Derek Allhusen (GBR) 41.61 *Lochinvar*	Michael Page (USA) 52.31 *Faster*
	Teams—GREAT BRITAIN 175.93 pts.	UNITED STATES 245.87	AUSTRALIA 331.26
	Derek Allhusen Richard H. Meade Reuben Jones	Michael Page James Wofford J. Micheal Plumb	Wayne Roycroft Brian Cobcroft William Roycroft
1972	Richard H. Meade (GBR) 57.73 pts. *Laurieston*	Alessa Argenton (ITA) 43.33 *Woodland*	Jan Jonsson (SWE) 39.67 *Sarajevo*
	Teams—GREAT BRITAIN 95.53 pts.	UNITED STATES 10.81	WEST GERMANY minus 18.00
	Mary D. Gordon-Watson Bridget Parker Richard H. Meade Mark A. Phillips (non-scorer)	Kevin Freeman Bruce Davidson J. Michael Plumb	Harry Klugmann Karl Schultz Ludwig Goessing
1976	Edmund Coffin (US) 114.99 pts. *Bally—Cor*	Michael Plumb (USA) 125.85 *Better & Better*	Karl Schultz (GER) 129.45 *Madrigal*
	Teams—USA 441.00 pts.	WEST GERMANY 584.60	AUSTRALIA 599.54
	Edmund Coffin Michael Plumb Bruce Davidson Mary Tauskey	Karl Schultz Herbert Bloecker Helmut Rethemeier Otto Ammermann	Wayne Roycroft Mervyn Bennett William Roycroft Denis Pigott

1980	Frederico Euro Roman (ITA) 108.60 pts. *Rossinan*	Aleksandr Blinov (URS) 120.80 *Galzun*	Yuri Salnikov (URS) 151.60 *Pintset*

Teams—U.S.S.R. 457.00 pts.	ITALY 656.20	MEXICO 1,172.85
Aleksandr Blinov	Frederico Euro Roman	Manuel Mendivil Yocupicio
Yuri Salnikov	Anna Casagrande	David Barcena Rios
Valeriy Volkov	Mauro Roman	Jose Luis Perez Soto
Sergey Roghozhin	Marina Sciocchetti	Fabian Vazquez Lopez

1984	Mark Todd (NZL) 51.60 *Charisma*	Karen Stives (USA) 54.20 *Ben Arthur*	Virginia Holgate (GBR) 56.80 *Priceless*

Teams—USA 186.00	GREAT BRITAIN 189.20	WEST GERMANY 2340.00
Michael Plumb	Virginia Holgate	Dietmar Hogrefe
Karen Stives	Ian Stark	Bettina Overesch
Torrance Fleischmann	Diana Clapham	Burkhard Tesdorpf
Bruce Davidson	Lucinda Green	Claus Erhorn

---

7. Fencing (Men)

FOIL (INDIVIDUAL)

Wins are assessed on both wins (2 pts.) *and* draws (1 pt.) so, as in 1928, the winner does not necessarily have most wins.

	GOLD	SILVER	BRONZE
1896	Emile Gravelotte (FRA) 4 wins	Henri Callott (FRA) 3	Perikles Mavromichalis-Pierrakos (GRE) 2
1900	Emile Coste (FRA) 6 wins	Henri Masson (FRA) 5	Jacques Boulenger (FRA) 4
1904	Ramón Fonst (CUB) 3 wins	Albertson Van Zo Post (CUB) 2	Charles Tatham (CUB) 1
1906	Georges Dillon-Kavanagh (FRA) d.n.a.	Gustav Casmir (GER) d.n.a.	Pierre d'Hugues (FRA) d.n.a.
1908	Event not held		
1912	Nedo Nadi (ITA) 7 wins	Pietro Speciale (ITA) 5	Richard Verderber (AUT) 4
1920	Nedo Nadi (ITA) 10 wins	Phillippe Cattiau (FRA) 9	Roger Ducret (FRA) 9
1924	Roger Ducret (FRA) 6 wins	Philippe Cattiau (FRA) 5	Maurice van Damme (BEL) 4
1928	Lucien Gaudin (FRA) 9 wins	Erwin Casmir (GER) 9	Giulio Gaudini (ITA) 9
1932	Gustavo Marzi (ITA) 9 wins	Joseph Levis (USA) 6	Giulio Gaudini (ITA) 5
1936	Giulio Gaudini (ITA) 7 wins	Edouard Gardère (FRA) 6	Giorgio Bocchino (ITA) 4
1948	Jean Buhan (FRA) 7 wins	Christian d'Oriola (FRA) 5	Lajos Maszlay (HUN) 4
1952	Christian d'Oriola (FRA) 8 wins	Edoardo Mangiarotti (ITA) 6	Manlino di Rosa (ITA) 5

Jean Buhan of France (right), the winner of the individual foil event in 1948, is shown in an early bout with John Emrys Lloyd (GBR).

	GOLD	SILVER	BRONZE
1956	Christian d'Oriola (FRA) 6 wins	Giancarlo Bergamini (ITA) 5	Antonio Spallino (ITA) 5
1960	Viktor Zhdanovich (URS) 7 wins	Yuriy Sissikin (URS) 4	Albert Axelrod (USA) 3
1964	Egon Franke (POL) 3 wins	Jean-Claude Magnan (FRA) 2	Daniel Revenu (FRA) 1
1968	Ion Drimba (ROM) 4 wins	Jenö Kamuti (HUN) 3	Daniel Revenu (FRA) 3
1972	Witold Woyda (POL) 5 wins	Jenö Kamuti (HUN) 4	Christian Noël (FRA) 2
1976	Fabio Dal Zotto (ITA) 4 wins	Aleksandr Romankov (URS) 4	Bernard Talvard (FRA) 3
1980	Vladimir Smirnov (URS) 5 wins	Paskal Jolyot (FRA) 5	Aleksandr Romankov (URS) 5
1984	Mauro Numa (ITA)	Matthias Behr (FRG)	Stefano Cerioni (ITA)

FOIL (TEAM)

1896–1900 Event not held

1904 **CUBA**
Ramón Fonst
Albertson Van Zo Post
Manuel Diaz

INTERNATIONAL TEAM
Charles Tatham (CUB)
Charles Townsend (USA)
Arthur Fox (USA)

1906–1912 Event not held

1920 **ITALY**
Nedo Nadi
Aldo Nadi
Abelardo Olivier
Pietro Speciale
Rodolfo Terlizzi
Tomasso Costantino
Baldo Baldi
Oreste Puliti

FRANCE
Lionel Bony de
    Castellane
Gaston Amson
André Labatut
Georges Trombert
Marcel Perrot
Lucien Gaudin
Philippe Cattiau
Roger Ducret

UNITED STATES
Francis W. Honeycutt
Henry Breckinridge
Arthur Lyon
Robert V. Sears
Harold Rayner

Christian d'Oriola (FRA) (left) won 2 gold medals in the individual foil event and a gold and a silver medal in the team event, in 1952 and 1956.

	GOLD	SILVER	BRONZE
1924	**FRANCE**	**BELGIUM**	**HUNGARY**
	Lucien Gaudin	Désiré Beaurain	László Berti
	Roger Ducret	Charles Crahay	István Lichteneckert
	Philippe Cattiau	Fernand de Montigny	Sándor Posta
	Henri Jobier	Maurice van Damme	Zoltán Schenker
	Jacques Coutrot	Marcel Berré	Ödön Tersztyánszky
	Guy de Luget	Albert de Roocker	
	André Labatut		
	Joseph Peroteaux		
1928	**ITALY**	**FRANCE**	**ARGENTINA**
	Ugo Pignotti	Lucien Gaudin	Roberto Larraz
	Oreste Puliti	Philippe Cattiau	Raúl Anganuzzi
	Giulio Gaudini	Roger Ducret	Luis Lucchetti
	Giorgio Pessina	André Labatut	Hector Lucchetti
	Giorgio Chiavacci	Raymond Flacher	Carmelo Camet
	Gioacchino Guaragna	André Gaboriaud	
1932	**FRANCE**	**ITALY**	**UNITED STATES**
	Edouard Gardère	Gustavo Marzi	George C. Calnan
	René Lemoine	Ugo Pignotti	Frank Righeimer Jr.
	René Bougnol	Gioacchino Guaragna	Richard Steere
	Philippe Cattiau	Giulio Gaudini	Hugh Alessandroni
	René Bondoux	Giorgio Pessina	Dernell Every
	Jean Piot	Rodolfo Terlizzi	Joseph Levis
1936	**ITALY**	**FRANCE**	**GERMANY**
	Gustavo Marzi	André Gardère	Erwin Casmir
	Gioacchino Guaragna	René Bougnol	Julius Eisenecker
	Manlio di Rosa	René Lemoine	August Heim
	Ciro Verratti	Jacques Coutrot	Seigfrid Lerdon
	Giulio Gaudini	Edouard Gardère	Otto Adam
	Giorgio Bocchino	René Bondoux	Stefan Rosenbauer
1948	**FRANCE**	**ITALY**	**BELGIUM**
	André Bonin	Renzo Nostini	Georges de Bourguignon
	Christian d'Oriola	Manlio di Rosa	Henry Paternoster
	Jean Buhan	Edoardo Mangiarotti	Edoardo Yves
	René Bougnol	Giuliano Nostini	Raymond Bru
	Jacques Lataste	Giorgio Pellini	André van de W. de
	Adrien Rommel	Saverio Ragno	Vorsselaer
			Paul Valcke

GOLD	SILVER	BRONZE
1952 **FRANCE**	**ITALY**	**HUNGARY**
Jean Buhan	Giancarlo Bergamini	Endre Tilli
Christian d'Oriola	Antonio Spallino	Aladár Gerevich
Adrien Rommel	Manlio di Rosa	Endre Palócz
Claude Netter	Edoardo Mangiarotti	Lajos Maszlay
Jacques Nöel	Renzo Nostini	Tibor Berczelly
Jacques Lataste	Giorgio Pellini	József Sákovics
1956 **ITALY**	**FRANCE**	**HUNGARY**
Edoardo Mangiarotti	Christian d'Oriola	Lajos Somodi
Giancarlo Bergamini	Jacques Lataste	József Gyuricza
Antonio Spallino	René Coicaud	Endre Tilli
Vittorio Lucarelli	Claude Netter	József Marosi
Manlio di Rosa	Roger Closset	Mihály Fülöp
Luigi Carpaneda	Bernard Baudoux	József Sákovics
1960 **U.S.S.R.**	**ITALY**	**GERMANY**
Viktor Zhadanovich	Alberto Pellegrino	Jürgen Theuerkauff
Mark Midler	Luigi Carpaneda	Tim Gerresheim
Yuriy Sissikin	Mario Curletto	Eberhard Mehl
Gherman Sveshnikov	Aldo Aureggi	Jürgen Brecht
Yuriy Rudov	Edoardo Mangiarotti	
1964 **U.S.S.R.**	**POLAND**	**FRANCE**
Gherman Sveshnikov	Zbigniew Skrudik	Daniel Revenu
Yuriy Sissikin	Witold Woyda	Jacky Courtillat
Viktor Zhadanovich	Ryszard Parulski	Pierre Rodacanachi
Mark Midler	Egon Franke	Christian Noël
Yury Scharov	Janusz Rózycki	Jean-Claude Magnan
1968 **FRANCE**	**U.S.S.R.**	**POLAND**
Daniel Revenu	Gherman Sveshnikov	Witold Woyda
Gilles Berolatti	Yury Scharov	Zbigniew Skrudlik
Christian Noël	Vassily Stankovich	Ryszard Parulski
Jean-Claude Magnan	Viktor Putiatin	Egon Franke
Jacques Dimont	Yuriy Sissikin	Adam Lisewski
1972 **POLAND**	**U.S.S.R.**	**FRANCE**
Witold Woyda	Vassily Stankovich	Daniel Revenu
Lech Koziejowski	Anatoly Kotescev	Christian Noël
Jerzy Kaczmarek	Vladimir Demissov	Bernard Talvard
Marek Dabrowski	Leonid Romanov	Jean-Claude Magnan
Arkadiusz Godel	Viktor Putiatin	Gilles Berolatti
1976 **WEST GERMANY**	**ITALY**	**FRANCE**
Matthias Behr	Fabio Dal Zotto	Christian Noël
Thomas Bach	Carlo Montano	Bernard Talvard
Harald Hein	Stefano Simoncelli	Didier Flament
Klaus Reichert	Giovanni B. Coletti	Frederic Pietruska
1980 **FRANCE**	**U.S.S.R.**	**POLAND**
Didier Flament	Aleksandr Romankov	Adam Robak
Paskal Jolyot	Vladimir Smirnov	Boguslaw Zych
Bruno Boscherie	Sabiryan Rusiyev	Lech Koziejowski
Philippe Bonnin	Aschot Karagyan	Marian Sypniewski
1984 **ITALY**	**WEST GERMANY**	**FRANCE**
Mauro Numa	Matthias Behr	Philippe Omnes
Andrea Borella	Mathias Gey	Patrick Groc
Stefano Cerioni	Harald Hein	Frederick Pietruszka
Angelo Scuri	Frank Beck	Pascal Jolyot
Andrea Cipressa	Klaus Reichert	Marc Cerboni

EPEE (INDIVIDUAL)

	GOLD	SILVER	BRONZE
1896	Event not held		
1900	Ramón Fonst (CUB)	Louis Perrée (FRA)	Léon Sée (FRA)
1904	Ramón Fonst (CUB)	Charles Tatham (CUB)	Albertson Van Zo Post (CUB)
1906	Georges de la Falaise (FRA)	Georges Dillon-Kavanagh (FRA)	Alexander van Blijenburgh (HOL)
1908	Gaston Alibert (FRA) 5 wins	Alexandre Lippmann (FRA) 4	Eugène Olivier (FRA) 4
1912	Paul Anspach (BEL) 6 wins	Ivan Osiier (DEN) 5	Philippe Le Hardy de Beaulieu (BEL) 4
1920	Armand Massard (FRA) 9 wins	Alexandre Lippmann (FRA) 7	Gustave Buchard (FRA) 6
1924	Charles Delporte (BEL) 8 wins	Roger Ducret (FRA) 7	Nils Hellsten (SWE) 7
1928	Lucien Gaudin (FRA) 8 wins	Georges Buchard (FRA) 7	George Calnan (USA) 6
1932	Giancarlo Cornaggia-Medici (ITA) 8 wins	Georges Buchard (FRA) 7	Carlo Agostoni (ITA) 7
1936	Franco Riccardi (ITA) 5 wins	Saverio Ragno (ITA) 6	Giancarlo Cornaggia-Medici (ITA) 6
1948	Luigi Cantone (ITA) 7 wins	Oswald Zappelli (SUI) 5	Edoardo Mangiarotti (ITA) 5
1952	Edoardo Mangiarotti (ITA) 7 wins	Dario Mangiarotti (ITA) 6	Oswarld Zappelli (SUI) 6
1956	Carlo Pavesi (ITA) 5 wins	Giuseppe Delfino (ITA) 5	Edoardo Mangiarotti (ITA) 5
1960	Giuseppe Delfino (ITA) 5 wins	Allan L. N. Jay (GBR) 5	Bruno Khabarov (URS) 4
1964	Grigory Kriss (URS) 2 wins	H. William F. Hoskyns (GBR) 2	Guram Kostava (URS) 1
1968	Győző Kulcsár (HUN) 4 wins	Grigory Kriss (URS) 4	Gianluigi Saccaro (ITA) 4
1972	Csaba Fenyvesi (HUN) 4 wins	Jacques la Degaillerie (FRA) 3	Győző Kulcsár (HUN) 3
1976	Alexander Pusch (GER) 3 wins	Jurgen Hehn (GER) 3	Győző Kulcsár (HUN) 3
1980	Johan Harmenberg (SWE) 4 wins	Erno Kolczonay (HUN) 3	Philippe Riboud (FRA) 3
1984	Philippe Boisse (FRA)	Bjorne Vaggo (SWE)	Philippe Riboud (FRA)

EPEE (TEAM)

GOLD	SILVER	BRONZE
1896–1904 Event not held		
1906 FRANCE	**GREAT BRITAIN**	**BELGIUM**
Pierre d'Hugues	William H. Derborough	Constant Cloquet
George Dillon-Kavanagh	Cosmo E. Duff-Gordon	Fernard de Montigny
	Charles N. Robinson	Edmond Grahay
Mohr	Edgar Seligman	Philippe Le Hardy
Georges de la Falaise		de Beaulieu
1908 FRANCE	**GREAT BRITAIN**	**BELGIUM**
Gaston Alibert	C. Leaf Daniell	Paul Anspach
Bernard Gravier	Cecil Haig	Désiré Beaurain
Alexandre Lippmann	Martin Holt	Ferdinand Feyerick
Eugène Olivier	Robert Montgomerie	François Rom
Jean Stern	Edward Amphlett	Fernand de Montigny
Henri-Georges Berger	Edgar Seligman	Victor Willems
Charles Collignon	Sydney Martineau	Ferdnand Bosmans
1912 BELGIUM	**GREAT BRITAIN**	**NETHERLANDS**
Paul Anspach	Edgar Seligman	Adrianus E. W. de Jong
Henri Anspach	Edward Amphlett	W. P. Hubert van
Fernand de Montigny	Robert Montgomerie	Blijenburgh
Jacques Ochs	John Blake	Jetze Doorman
Gaston Salmon	Percival Davson	George van Rossem
Francois Rom	Arthur Everitt	Leo Nardus
Victor Willems	Sydney Martineau	
Robert Hennet	Martin Holt	
1920 ITALY	**BELGIUM**	**FRANCE**
Nedo Nadi	Paul Anspach	Armand Massard
Aldo Nadi	Léon Tom	Alexandre Lippmann
Abelardo Olivier	Ernest Gevers	Gustave Buchard
Giovanni Canova	Felix G. d'Alviella	Casanova
Dino Urbani	Victor Boin	Georges Trombert
Tullio Bozza	Joseph de Craecker	Gaston Amson
Andrea Marrazzi	Maurice de Wée	Moreau
Antonio Allocchio	Philippe Le Hardy	
Paolo Thaón di Revel	de Beaulieu	
1924 FRANCE	**BELGIUM**	**ITALY**
Lucien Gaudin	Fernand de Montigny	Vincenzo Cuccia
Roger Ducret	Joseph de Craecker	Giovanni Canova
Alexandre Lippmann	Paul Anspach	Giulio Basletta
Georges Buchard	Ernest Gevers	Marcello Bertinetti
André Labatut	Léon Tom	Virgilio Mantegazza
Georges Tainturier	Charles Delporte	Oreste Moricca
Lionel Lioteel		
1928 ITALY	**FRANCE**	**PORTUGAL**
Carlo Agostoni	Armand Massard	Paolo d'Eca Leal
Marcello Bartinetti	Georges Buchard	Mário de Noronha
Giancarlo Cornaggia-Medici	Gaston Amson	Jorge Paiva
	Emile Cornic	Frederico Paredes
Renzo Minoli	Bernard Schmetz	João Sassetti
Giulio Basletta	René Barbier	Henrique da Silveira
Franco Riccardi		
1932 FRANCE	**ITALY**	**UNITED STATES**
Bernard Schmetz	Carlo Agostoni	George Calnan
Philippe Cattiau	Franco Riccardi	Gustave Heiss
Georges Buchard	Saverio Ragno	Tracy Jaeckel
Jean Piot	Giancarlo Cornaggia-Medici	Frank Righeimer Jr.
Fernand Jourdant		Curtis Shears
Georges Tainturier	Renzo Minoli	Miguel de Capriles
1936 ITALY	**SWEDEN**	**FRANCE**
Giancarlo Cornaggia-Medici	Sven Thofelt	Georges Buchard
	Gustaf Dyrssen	Paul Wormser
Edoardo Mangiarotti	Gösta Almgren	Philippe Cattiau
Saverio Ragno	Hans Granfelt	Henri Dulieux
Alfredo Pezzano	Birger Cederin	Bernard Schmetz
Giancarlo Brusati	Hans van Drakenberg	Michel Pécheux
Franco Riccardi		

	GOLD	SILVER	BRONZE
1948	**FRANCE**	**ITALY**	**SWEDEN**
	Henri Guérin	Edoardo Mangiarotti	Carl Forssell
	Henri Lepage	Carlo Agostoni	Arne Tolbom
	Marcel Desprets	Fiorenzo Marini	Bengt H. Ljungquist
	Michel Pécheux	Antonio Mandruzzato	Sven Thofelt
	Maurice Huet	Luigi Cantone	Frank Cervell
	Edouard Artigas	Dario Mangiarotti	Per H. Carleson
1952	**ITALY**	**SWEDEN**	**SWITZERLAND**
	Edoardo Mangiarotti	Lennart Magnusson	Willy Fitting
	Dario Mangiarotti	Carl Forssell	Otto Rüfenacht
	Carlo Pavesi	Berndt-Otto Rehbinder	Oswald Zappelli
	Giuseppe Delfino	Per H. Carleson	Paul Barth
	Franco Bertinetti	Sven Fahlman	Marlo Valota
	Roberto Battaglia	Bengt H. Ljungquist	Paul Meister
1956	**ITALY**	**HUNGARY**	**FRANCE**
	Giuseppe Delfino	Béla Rerrich	Yves Dreyfus
	Franco Bertinetti	Ambrus Nagy	René Queyroux
	Alberto Pellegrino	Barnabás Berszenyi	Daniel Dagallier
	Giorgio Anglesio	József Marosi	Claude Nigon
	Carlo Pavesi	József Sákovics	Armand Mouyal
	Edoardo Mangiarotti	Lajos Balthazár	
1960	**ITALY**	**GREAT BRITAIN**	**U.S.S.R.**
	Alberto Pellegrino	Allan L. N. Jay	Valentin Chernikov
	Carlo Pavesi	Michael Howard	Arnold Chernusevich
	Giuseppe Delfino	John Pelling	Guram Kostava
	Edoardo Mangiarotti	H. William F. Hoskyns	Bruno Khabarov
	Gianluigi Saccaro	Michael Alexander	Aleksandr Pavlovsky
	Fiorenzo Marini	Raymond Harrison	
1964	**HUNGARY**	**ITALY**	**FRANCE**
	Gyözö Kulcsár	Gianluigi Saccaro	Jacques Brodin
	Zoltán Nemere	Giovanni Battista Breda	Yves Dreyfus
	Tamás Gabor	Gianfranco Paolucci	Claude Bourquard
	Istyán Kausz	Giuseppe Delfino	Jack Guittet
	Árpád Bárány	Alberto Pellegrino	Claude Brodin
1968	**HUNGARY**	**U.S.S.R.**	**POLAND**
	Csaba Fenyvesi	Grigory Kriss	Bogdan Andrzejewski
	Zoltán Nemere	Iosif Vitebsky	Michal Butkiewicz
	Pál Schmitt	Aleksey Nikanchikov	Bogdan Gonsior
	Gyözö Kulcsár	Yury Smolyakov	Henryk Nielaba
	Pál Nagy	Viktor Modzalevsky	Kazimierz Barburski
1972	**HUNGARY**	**SWITZERLAND**	**U.S.S.R.**
	Sandor Erdoes	Guy Evequoz	Viktor Modzalevsky
	Gyözö Kulcsár	Peter Lötscher	Sergei Paramonov
	Csaba Fenyvesi	Daniel Giger	Igor Valetov
	Pál Schmitt	Christian Kanter	Georgy Zajitsky
	Istvan Osztrics	François Suchanecki	Grigory Kriss
1976	**SWEDEN**	**WEST GERMNY**	**SWITZERLAND**
	Carl Von Essen	Alexander Pusch	Francois Suchanecki
	Hans Jacobson	Jurgen Hehn	Michel Poffet
	Leif Hogstrom	Reinhold Behr	Daniel Giger
	Rolf Edling	Volker Fischer	Christian Kauter
1980	**FRANCE**	**POLAND**	**U.S.S.R.**
	Philippe Riboud	Pyotr Jablowski	Aschot Karagyan
	Patrick Picot	Andrzej Lis	Boris Lukomski
	Hubert Gardas	Leszek Swornowski	Aleksandr Abushakhmetov
	Philippe Boisse	Ludomir Chronowski	Aleksandr Moshayev
1984	**WEST GERMANY**	**FRANCE**	**ITALY**
	Elmar Borrmann	Philippe Boisse	Stefano Bellone
	Volker Fischer	Jean Michel Henry	Sandro Cuomo
	Gerhard Heer	Olivier Lenglet	Cosimo Ferro
	Rafael Nickel	Philippe Riboud	Roberto Manzi
	Alexander Pusch	Michel Salesse	Angelo Mazzoni

SABRE (INDIVIDUAL)

	GOLD	SILVER	BRONZE
1896	Jean Georgiadis (GRE) 4 wins	Telemachos Karakalos (GRE) 3	Holger Nielsen (DEN) 2
1900	Georges de la Falaise (FRA) d.n.a.	Léon Thiébaut (FRA) d.n.a.	Siegfried Flesch (AUT) d.n.a.
1904	Manuel Diaz (CUB) d.n.a.	William Grebe (USA) d.n.a.	Albertson Van Zo Post (CUB) d.n.a.
1906	Jean Georgiadis (GR) d.n.a.	Gustav Casmir (GER) d.n.a.	Federico Cesarano (ITA) d.n.a.
1908	Jenö Fuchs (HUN) 6 wins	Béla Zulavsky (HUN) 6	Vilem Goppold von Lobsdorf (BOH) 4
1912	Jenö Fuchs (HUN) 6 wins	Béla Békéssy (HUN) 5	Ervin Mészáros (HUN) 5
1920	Nedo Nadi (ITA) 11 wins	Aldo Nadi (ITA) 9	Adrianus E. W. de Jong (HOL) 7
1924	Sándor Posta (HUN) 5 wins	Rogert Ducret (FRA) 5	János Garai (HUN) 5
1928	Ödön Tersztyánszky (HUN) 9 wins	Attila Petschauer (HUN) 9	Bino Bini (ITA) 8
1932	György Piller (HUN) 8 wins	Giulio Gaudini (ITA) 7	Endre Kabos (HUN) 5
1936	Endre Kabos (HUN) 7 wins	Gustavo Marzi (ITA) 6	Aladár Gerevich (HUN) 6
1948	Aladár Gerevich (HUN) 7 wins	Vincenzo Pinton (ITA) 5	Pál Kovács (HUN) 5
1952	Pál Kovács (HUN) 8 wins	Aladár Gerevich (HUN) 7	Tibor Berczelly (HUN) 5
1956	Rudolf Kárpáti (HUN) 6 wins	Jerzy Pawlowski (POL) 5	Lev Kuznyetsov (URS) 4
1960	Rudolf Kárpáti (HUN) 5 wins	Zoltán Horvath (HUN) 4	Wladimiro Calarese (ITA) 4
1964	Tibor Pézsa (HUN) 2 wins	Claude Arabo (FRA) 2	Umar Mavlikhanov (URS) 1
1968	Jerzy Powlowski (POL) 4 wins	Mark Rakita (URS) 4	Tibor Pézsa (HUN) 3
1972	Viktor Sidiak (URS) 4 wins	Peter Maroth (HUN) 3	Vladimir Nazlimov (URS) 3
1976	Viktor Krovopouskov (URS) 5 wins	Vladimir Nazlimov (URS) 4	Viktor Sidiak (URS) 3
1980	Viktor Krovopouskov (URS) 5 wins	Mikhail Burtsev (URS) 4	Imre Gedovari (HUN) 3
1984	Jean Francois Lamour (FRA)	Marco Marin (ITA)	Peter Westbrook (USA)

SABRE (TEAM)

1896–1904 Event not held

1906	**GERMANY**	**GREECE**	**NETHERLANDS**
	Gustav Casmir	Jean Georgiadis	James A. H. L. Melvill van Carnbée
	Jacob Erckrath de Bary	Menelaos Sakorraphos	
	August Petri	C. Zorbas	Johannes Franciscus Osten
	Emil Schön	Triantaphylos Kordogannis	George van Rossem
			Maurits Jacob van Löben Sels

Rudolf Karpati (HUN) (left) won the individual sabre competition in 1956 and 1960, one of 3 men who have won the gold medal twice.

Part of Hungary's successful sabre team poses in London in 1908. Since then, Hungarian teams have amassed 8 gold medals, a silver medal, and 3 bronze medals in this event.

	GOLD	SILVER	BRONZE

	GOLD	SILVER	BRONZE
1908	**HUNGARY**	**ITALY**	**BOHEMIA**
	Jenö Fuchs	Riccardo Nowak	Vilém Goppold von
	Oszkár Gerde	Alessandro Pirzio-Biroli	Lobsdorf
	Péter Tóth	Abelardo Olivier	Jaroslav Tucek
	Lajos Werkner	Marcello Bertinetti	Vlastimil Lada-
	Dezsö Földes	Sante Ceccherini	Sázavsky
			Otakar Lada
			Bedřich Schéjbal
1912	**HUNGARY**	**AUSTRIA**	**NETHERLANDS**
	László Berti	Richard Verderber	William P. Hubert
	Jenö Fuchs	Otto Herschmann	van Blijenburgh
	Ervin Mészáros	Rudolf Cvetko	Adrianus E. W. de Jong
	Zoltán Schenker	Friedrich Golling	Daik Scalongne
	Dezsö Földes	Andreas Suttner	Jetze Doorman
	Oszkár Gerde	Albert Bogen	George van Rossem
	Péter Tóth	Reinhold Trampler	Hendrik de Iongh
	Lajos Werkner		
1920	**ITALY**	**FRANCE**	**NETHERLANDS**
	Nedo Nadi	Marc Perrodon	Jan van der Wiele
	Aldo Nadi	Georges Trombert	Adrianus E. W. de Jong
	Oreste Puliti	J. Margraff	Jetze Doorman
	Dino Urbani	Henri de Saint Germain	William P. Hubert van
	Baldo Baldi	Jean Lacroix	Blijenburgh
	Francesco Gargano	Mondielli	Louis A. Delaunoy
	Giorgio Santelli		Salomon Zeldenrust
			Henri J. M. Wijnoldij-
			Daniels
1924	**ITALY**	**HUNGARY**	**NETHERLANDS**
	Oreste Puliti	László Berti	Adrianus E. W. De Jong
	Giulio Sarrocchi	János Garai	Jetzc Doorman
	Marcello Bertinetti	Sándor Posta	Hendrik D.
	Oreste Moricca	József Rády	Scherpenhuysen
	Renato Anselmi	Zoltán Schenker	Jan van der Wiele
	Guido Balzarini	Jeno Uhlyárik	Maarten H. van Dulm
	Bino Bini	László Széchy	
	Vincenzo Cuccia	Ödön Tersztyánszky	
1928	**HUNGARY**	**ITALY**	**POLAND**
	János Garai	Renato Anselmi	Kazimierz Laskowski
	Gyula Glykais	Bino Bini	Aleksander Malecki
	Sándor Gombos	Gustavo Marzi	Adam Papée
	József Rády	Oreste Puliti	Wladyslaw Segda
	Ödön Tersztyánszky	Emilio Salafia	Tadeusz Friedrich
	Attilla Petschauer	Giulio Sarrocchi	Jerzy Zabielski
1932	**HUNGARY**	**ITALY**	**POLAND**
	Endre Kabos	Renato Anselmi	Leszek Lubicz-Nycz
	Aladár Gerevich	Gustavo Marzi	Marian Suski
	György Piller	Arturo de Vecchi	Wladyslaw Dobrowolski
	Gyula Glykais	Giulio Gaudini	Adam Papée
	Attila Petschauer	Ugo Pignotti	Tadeusz Friedrich
	Ernö Nagy	Emilio Salafia	Wladyslaw Segda
1936	**HUNGARY**	**ITALY**	**GERMANY**
	Tibor Berczelly	Giulio Gaudini	Richard Wahl
	Aladár Gerevich	Gustavo Marzi	Erwin Casmir
	Endre Kabos	Aldo Masciotta	Julius Eisenecker
	László Rajcsányi	Aldo Montano	August Heim
	Imre Rajczy	Vincenzo Pinton	Hans Jörger
	Pál Kovács	Athos Tanzini	Hans Esser

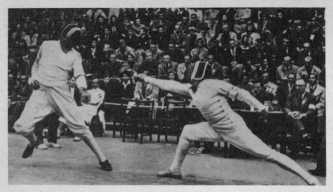

Aladár Gerevich (right), the Hungarian sabreur, won 7 gold, 1 silver, and 2 bronze medals from 1932 to 1960. This action took place in 1948.

1948 **HUNGARY**	**ITALY**	**UNITED STATES**
Aladár Gerevich	Gastone Darè	Norman Armitage
Rudolf Kárpáti	Carlo Turcato	George Worth
Pál Kovács	Vincenzo Pinton	Tibor Nyilas
Tibor Berczelly	Mauro Racca	Dean V. Cetrulo
László Rajcsányi	Renzo Nostini	Miguel de Capriles
Bertalan Papp	Aldo Montano	James Flynn
1952 **HUNGARY**	**ITALY**	**FRANCE**
Rudolf Kárpáti	Gastone Daré	Jean Laroyenne
Pál Kovács	Robert Ferrari	Jacques Lefèvre
Tibor Berczelly	Renzo Nostini	Jean Levavasseur
Aladár Gerevich	Giorgio Pellini	Bernard Morel
László Rajcsányi	Vincenzo Pinton	Maurice Piot
Bertalan Papp	Mauro Racca	Jean-François Tournon
1956 **HUNGARY**	**POLAND**	**U.S.S.R.**
Atilla Keresztes	Zygmunt Pawlas	Yakov Rylskiy
Aladár Gerevich	Jerzy Pawlowski	David Tychler
Rudolf Kárpáti	Wojciech Zablocki	Lev Kuznyetsov
Jenö Hámori	Andrzej Piatkowski	Evgeniy Cherepovskiy
Pál Kovács	Marek Kuszewski	Leonid Bogdanov
Dániel Magai	Ryszard Zub	
1960 **HUNGARY**	**POLAND**	**ITALY**
Zoltán Horváth	Jerzy Pawlowski	Pierluigi Chicca
Rudolf Kápráti	Wojciech Zablocki	Wladimiro Calarese
Tamás Mendelényi	Ryszard Zub	Mario Ravagnan
Pál Kovács	Emil Ochyra	Roberto Ferrari
Gabor Delneki	Andrzej Piatkowski	Gianpaolo Calanchini
Aladár Gerevich	Marek Kuszewski	
1964 **U.S.S.R.**	**ITALY**	**POLAND**
Nugzar Asatiani	Wladimiro Calarese	Emil Ochyra
Yakov Rylsky	Cesare Salvadori	Jerzy Pawlowski
Mark Rakita	Gianpaolo Calanchini	Ryszard Zub
Umar Mavlikhanov	Pierluigi Chicca	Andrzej Piatowski
Boris Melnikov	Mario Ravagnan	Wojciech Zablocki

GOLD	SILVER	BRONZE
1968 U.S.S.R.	ITALY	HUNGARY
Vladimir Nazlimov	Wladimiro Calarese	Tamás Kovács
Viktor Sidiak	Michele Maffei	János Kalamár
Eduard Vinokurov	Cesare Salvadori	Péter Bakonyi
Mark Rakita	Pierluigi Chicca	Miklós Meszéna
Umar Mavlikhanov	Rolando Rigoli	Tibor Pezsa
1972 ITALY	U.S.S.R.	HUNGARY
Michele Maffei	Vladimir Nazlimov	Pál Gerevich
Mario A. Montano	Eduard Vinokurov	Tamás Kovács
Rolando Rigoli	Viktor Sidiak	Peter Maroth
Mario T. Montano	Viktor Bajenov	Tibor Pezsa
Cesare Salvadori	Mark Rakita	Péter Bakonyi
1976 U.S.S.R.	ITALY	RUMANIA
Viktor Krovopouskov	Mario A. Montano	Dan Irimiciuc
Eduard Vinokurov	Michele Maffei	Ioan Pop
Viktor Sidiak	Angelo Arcidiacono	Marin Mustata
Vladimir Nazlimov	Tommaso Montano	Cornel Marin
1980 U.S.S.R.	ITALY	HUNGARY
Mikhail Burtsev	Michele Maffei	Imra Gedovari
Viktor Krovopuskov	Mario Montano	Rudolf Nebald
Viktor Sidyak	Marco Romano	Pal Gerevich
Vladimir Nazlymov	Ferdinando Meglio	Ferenc Hammang
1984 ITALY	FRANCE	ROMANIA
Marco Marin	Jean Francois Lamour	Marin Mustata
Gianfranco Dalla Barba	Pierre Guichot	Ioan Pop
Giovanni Scalzo	Herve Granger-Veyron	Alexandru Chiculita
Ferdinando Meglio	Philippe Delrieu	Corneliu Marin
Angelo Arcidiacono	Franck Ducheix	

Action during the sabre event in Rome, 1960, with Fimamizu of Japan (right), duelling with Van Celden of Israel.

Nedo Nadi (ITA), winner of an unprecedented 5 gold medals at the 1920 Games, poses here with Helène Mayer (GER), gold medallist in the women's fencing event at the 1928 Games.

Fencing (Women)

FOIL (INDIVIDUAL)

	GOLD	SILVER	BRONZE
1896–1920	Event not held		
1924	Ellen Osiier (DEN) 5 wins	Gladys M. Davis (GBR) 4	Grete Heckscher (DEN) 3
1928	Helène Mayer (GER) 7 wins	Muriel B. Freeman (GBR) 6	Olga Oelkers (GER) 4
1932	Ellen Preis (AUT) 9 wins	J. Heather Guinness (GBR) 8	Ena Bogen (HUN) 7
1936	Ilona Elek (HUN) 6 wins	Helène Mayer (GER) 5	Ellen Preis (AUT) 5
1948	Ilona Elek (HUN) 6 wins	Karen Lachmann (DEN) 5	Ellen Müller-Preis (AUT) 5
1952	Irene Camber (ITA) 5 wins	Ilona Elek (HUN) 5	Karen Lachmann (DEN) 4
1956	Gillian M. Sheen (GBR) 6 wins	Olga Orbán (ROM) 6	Renée Garilhe (FRA) 5
1960	Heidi Schmid (GER) 6 wins	Valentina Rastvorova (URS) 5	Maria Vicol (ROM) 4
1964	Ildikó Ujlaki-Rejtö (HUN) 2 wins	Helga Mees (GER) 2	Antonella Ragno (ITA) 2

1968	Elena Novikova (URS) 4 wins	Pilar Roldan (MEX) 3	Ildikó Ujlaki-Rejtö (HUN) 3
1972	Antonella Ragno-Lonzi (ITA) 4 wins	Ildikó Bóbis (HUN) 3	Galina Gorokhova (URS) 3
1976	Ildikó Schwarczenberger (HUN) 4 wins	Maria C. Collino (ITA) 4	Elene Novikova-Belova (URS) 3
1980	Pascale Trinquet (FRA) 4 wins	Magda Maros (HUN) 3	Barbara Wysoczanska (POL) 3
1984	Jujie Luan (CHN)	Cornelia Hanisch (FRG)	Dorina Vaccaroni (ITA)

FOIL (TEAM)

GOLD	SILVER	BRONZE
1896–1956 Event not held		
1960 U.S.S.R. Valentina Rastvorova Tatyana Petrenko Valentina Prudskova Lyudmila Shishova Galina Gorokhova Alexandra Zabelina	HUNGARY Katalin Juhász-Nagy Lidia Dömölky Ildikó Ujlaki-Rejtö Magda Kovács-Nyári Tiborné Szekély	ITALY Irene Camber Velleda Cesari Antonella Ragno Bruna Colombetti Claudia Pasini
1964 HUNGARY Ilkidó Ujlaki-Rejtö Katalin Juhász-Nagy Lidia Dömölky-Sakovics Judit Medelényi- Agoston Paula Földessy-Marosi	U.S.S.R. Galina Gorokhova Valentina Prudskova Tatyana Samusenko Lyudmila Shishova Valentina Rastvorova	GERMANY Heidi Schmid Helga Mees Rosemarie Scherberger Gudrun Theuerkauff
1968 U.S.S.R. Alexandra Zabelina Tatyana Samusenko Elena Novikova Galina Gorokhova Svetlana Chirkova	HUNGARY Lidia Dömölky- Sakovics Ildikó Bóbis Ildikó Ujlaki-Rejtö Mária Gulácsy Paula Földessy-Marosi	RUMANIA Clara Stahl-Iencic Ileana Drimba Maria Vicol Olga Szabo Ana Ene-Dersidan
1972 U.S.S.R. Elena Novikova-Belova Alexandra Zabelina Galina Gorokhova Tatyana Samusenko Svetlana Chirkova	HUNGARY Ildikó Sagine-Retjo Ildikó Schwarczenberger Maria Szolnoki Ildikó Bóbis Ildikó Matuscakene- Ronay	RUMANIA Olga Szabo Ileana Gyulai Ana Pascu Ecaterina Stahl
1976 U.S.S.R. Elena Novikova-Belova Olga Kniazeva Valentina Sidorova Nailia Guilazova	FRANCE Brigitte Latrille Brigitte Dumont Christi Muzio Veronique Trinquet	HUNGARY Ildikó Schwarczenberger Edit Kovacs Magda Maros Ildikó Sagi-Retjö
1980 FRANCE Brigitte Gaudin Pascale Trinquet Isabelle Boeri-Begard Veronique Brouquier	U.S.S.R. Valentina Sidorova Vailia Gilyasova Yelena Belova Irina Ushakova	HUNGARY Ildikó Schwarczenberger Magda Maros Gertrud Stefanek Zsusza Szocz
1984 WEST GERMANY Christiane Weber Cornelia Hanisch Sabine Bischoff Zita Funkenhauser Ute Wessel	ROMANIA Aurora Dan Koszto Veber Rozalia Oros Marcela Zsak Elisabeta Guzganu	FRANCE Laurence Modaine Pascale Trinquet-Hachin Brigitte Gaudin Veronique Brouquier Anne Meygret

Viktor Chukarin (URS), shown here on the pommelled horse, won a total of 7 gold medals in the gymnastics competitions of 1952 and 1956.

8. Gymnastics (Men)

In gymnastics there are eight events for men which are interlinked. First is the Team Competition which comprises one compulsory and one optional exercise for each of the six events: Floor Exercises, Side Horse, Rings, Horse Vault, Parallel Bars and Horizontal Bars. Each team competitor gets marks out of 10 for both his compulsory and optional exercise for each of the six events. The team of six with the greatest *total* of marks wins the gold medal.

Next, the best 36 competitors from the Team Competition qualify for the Individual All-Round Competition. They each complete a further optional exercise for each of the six events and gain new marks (out of 10) per event. These are then added to the *average* (not total) of their previous total marks in the compulsory and optional sections brought forward from the Team Competition previously decided.

Finally, the six best on each apparatus in the Team Competition qualify for the individual Final on that apparatus. This is decided by adding a new mark (out of 10) for a further optional exercise on that apparatus to the *average* (not total) of their previous marks in the compulsory and optional performances on that apparatus within the Team Competition previously decided.

In 1948 points for an event were marked out of 20 instead of 10 as in other recent years; otherwise scores since 1936 are of same comparative value.

TEAM COMPETITION

There was no team event in 1896 and 1900. From 1904 to 1932 this event often differed substantially from the current event as to program content, number of competitors and scoring values.

GOLD	SILVER	BRONZE
1936 **GERMANY** 657.430 pts.	**SWITZERLAND** 654.802	**FINLAND** 638.468
Franz Beckert	Walter Bach	Martti Uosikinen
Konrad Frey	Albert Bachmann	Heikki Savolainen
Alfred Schwarzmann	Eugen Mack	Mauri Noroma-Nyberg
Willi Stadel	Georges Miez	Aleksanteri Saarvala
Walter Steffens	Michael Reusch	Esa Seeste
Matthias Volz	Edi Seinemann	Veikkö Pakarinen
1948 **FINLAND** 1,358.3 pts.	**SWITZERLAND** 1,356.7	**HUNGARY** 1,330.35
A. Veikkö Huhtanen	Walter Lehmann	Lajos Tóth
Paavo Aaltonen	Josef Stalder	Lajos Sántha
Heikki Savolainen	Christian Kipfer	László Baranyai
Olavi Rove	Emil Studer	Ferenc Pataki
Einari Teräsvirta	Robert Lucy	János Mogyorósi-Klencs
Kalevi Laitinen	Michael Reusch	Ferenc Várköi
1952[1] **U.S.S.R.** 574.4 pts.	**SWITZERLAND** 567.5	**FINLAND** 564.2
Viktor Chukarin	Josef Stalder	Onni Lappalainen
Grant Shaginyan	Hans Eugster	Berndt Lindfors
Valentin Muratov	Jean Tschabold	Paavo Aaltonen
Yevgeniy Korolkov	Jack Günthard	Kaino Lempinen
Vladimir Belyakov	Melchior Thalmann	Heikki Savolainen
Yosif Berdiyev	Ernst Gebendinger	Kalevi Laitinen
Mikhail Perelman	Hans Schwarzentruber	Kalevi Viskari
Dimitriy Leonkin	Ernst Fivian	Olavi Rove
1956 **U.S.S.R.** 568.25 pts.	**JAPAN** 566.40	**FINLAND** 555.95
Viktor Chukarin	Takashi Ono	Raimo Heinonen
Valentin Muratov	Masao Takemoto	Onni Lappalainen
Boris Shakhlin	Akira Kono	Olavi Leimuvirta
Albert Azaryan	Nobuyuki Aihara	Berndt Lindfors
Yuriy Titov	Shinsaku Tsukawaki	Martti Mansikka
Pavel Stolbov	Masami Kubota	Kelevi Suoniemi
1960 **JAPAN** 575.20 pts.	**U.S.S.R.** 572.70	**ITALY** 559.05
Takashi Ono	Boris Shakhlin	Franco Menichelli
Shuji Tsurumi	Yuriy Titov	Giovanni Carminucci
Yukio Endo	Albert Azaryan	Gianfranco Marzolla
Masao Takemoto	Vladimir Portnoi	Angelo Vicardi
Nobuyuki Aihara	Valeriy Kerdemilidi	Orlando Polmonari
Takashi Mitsukuri	Nikolaya Miligulo	Pasquale Carminucci
1964 **JAPAN** 577.95 pts.	**U.S.S.R.** 575.45	**GERMANY** 565.10
Yukio Endo	Yury Tsapenko	Siegfried Fülle
Shuji Tsurumi	Boris Shakhlin	Klaus Köste
Haruhiro Yamashita	Victor Leontyev	Erwin Koppe
Takashi Mitsukuri	Victor Lisitsky	Peter Weber
Takuji Hayata	Sergey Diomidov	Philipp Fürst
Takashi Ono	Yuriy Titov	Günter Lyhs
1968 **JAPAN** 575.90 pts.	**U.S.S.R.** 571.10	**E. GERMANY** 557.15
Sawao Kato	Mikhail Voronin	Matthias Brehme
Akinori Nakayama	Sergey Diomidov	Klaus Köste
Eizo Kenmotsu	Vladimir Klimenko	Siegfried Fülle
Takeshi Kato	Valeriy Karassev	Peter Weber
Yukio Endo	Victor Lisitsky	Gerhard Dietrich
Mitsuo Tsukahara	Valeryi Iljinykh	Günter Beier

---

[1] In 1952 eight competitors counted instead of 6 as in other years.

GOLD	SILVER	BRONZE
1972 JAPAN 571.25 pts.	U.S.S.R. 564.05	E. GERMANY 559.70
Sawao Kato	Nikolai Andrianov	Klaus Köste
Eizo Kenmotsu	Mikhail Voronin	Matthias Brehme
Shigeru Kasamatsu	Viktor Klimenko	Wolfgang Thune
Akinori Nakayama	Edvard Mikhaelian	Wolfgang Klotz
Mitsuo Tsukahara	Aleksandre Maleev	Reinhard Rychly
Teriuihi Okamura	Vladimir Schukin	Jürgen Paeke
1976 JAPAN 576.85 pts.	U.S.S.R. 576.45	E. GERMANY 564.65
Hisato Igarashi	Vladimir Tikhonov	Bernd Jager
Shun Fujimoto	Gennadi Kryssin	Wolfgang Klotz
Sawao Kato	Alexandr Ditiatin	Rainer Hanschke
Hiroshi Kajiyama	Vladimir Marchenko	Michail Nikolay
Eizo Kenmotsu	Vladimir Markelov	Lutz Mack
Mitsuo Tsukahara	Nikolai Andrianov	Roland Bruckner
1980 U.S.S.R. 589.60 pts.	EAST GERMANY 581.15	HUNGARY 575.00
Nikolai Andrianov	Roland Bruckner	Ferenc Donath
Alexandr Ditiatin	Michael Nikolay	Zoltan Magyar
Eduard Asaryan	Lutz Hoffmann	Peter Kovacs
Alexandr Tkachyov	Ralf-Peter Hemmann	Gyorgy Guczoghy
Bogdan Makuts	Andreas Bronst	Istvan Vamos
Vladimir Markelov	Lutz Mack	Zoltan Kelemen
1984 USA 591.40	CHINA 590.80	JAPAN 586.70
Timothy Daggett	Yun Lou	Shinji Morisue
Scott Johnson	Li Yuejiu	Noritoshi Hirata
Mitchell Gaylord	Xu Zhiqiang	Koji Sotomura
James Hartung	Tong Fei	Nobuyuki Kajitani
Peter Vidmar	Li Ning	Kyoji Yamawaki
Bart Conner	Li Xiaoping	Koji Gushiken

Soviet gymnast Alexandr Ditiatin won a medal in each of the eight gymnastics categories in 1980, setting an all-Olympic record for the most medals won at one Games.

COMBINED EXERCISES (INDIVIDUAL)

This event was not held in 1896. From 1900 to 1932 this event often differed substantially from the current event as to program content and scoring values.

	GOLD	SILVER	BRONZE
1936	Alfred Schwarzmann (GER) 113.100	Eugen Mack (SUI) 112.334	Konrad Frey (GER) 111.532
1948	A. Veikkö Huhtanen (FIN) 229.7	Walter Lehmann (SUI) 229.0	Paavo Aaltonen (FIN) 228.8
1952	Viktor Chukarin (URS) 115.70	Grant Shaginyan (URS) 114.95	Josef Stalder (SUI) 114.75
1956	Viktor Chukarin (URS) 114.25	Takashi Ono (JPN) 114.20	Yuriy Titov (URS) 113.80
1960	Boris Shakhlin (URS) 115.95	Takashi Ono (JPN) 115.90	Yuriy Titov (URS) 115.60
1964	Yukio Endo (JPN) 115.95	Shuji Tsurumi (JPN) 115.40 Boris Shakhlin (URS) 115.40 Victor Lisitsky (URS) 115.40	
1968	Sawao Kato (JPN) 115.90	Mikhail Voronin (URS) 115.85	Akinori Nakayama (JPN) 115.65
1972	Sawao Kato (JPN) 114.650	Eizo Kenmotsu (JPN) 114.575	Akinori Nakayama (JPN) 114.325
1976	Nikolai Andrianov (URS) 116.650	Sawao Kato (JPN) 115.650	Mitsuo Tsukahara (JPN) 115.575
1980	Alexandr Ditiatin (URS) 118.650	Nikolai Andrianov (URS) 118.225	Stoyan Deltchev (BUL) 118.000
1984	Koji Gushiken (JPN) 118.700	Peter Vidmar (USA) 118.675	Li Ning (CHN) 118.575

FLOOR COMPETITION

1896–1928	Event not held		
1932	István Pelle (HUN) 9.60	Georges Miez (SUI) 9.47	Mario Lertora (ITA) 9.23
1936	Georges Miez (SUI) 18.666	Josef Walter (SUI) 18.5	Konrad Frey (GER) 18.466 Eugen Mack (SUI) 18.466
1948	Ferenc Pataki (HUN) 38.7	János Mogyorósi-Klencs (HUN) 38.4	Zdenek Ružička (TCH) 38.1
1952	William Thoresson (SWE) 19.25	Tadao Uesako (JPN) 19.15 Jerzy Jokiel (POL) 19.15	—
1956	Valentin Muratov (URS) 19.20	Nobuyuki Aihara (JPN) 19.10 William Thoresson (SWE) 19.10 Viktor Chukarin (URS) 19.10	—
1960	Nobuyuki Aihara (JPN) 19.450	Yuriy Titov (URS) 19.325	Franco Menichelli (ITA) 19.275
1964	Franco Menichelli (ITA) 19.45	Victor Lisitsky (URS) 19.35 Yukio Endo (JPN) 19.35	—
1968	Sawao Kato (JPN) 19.475	Akinori Nakayama (JPN) 19.400	Takeshi Kato (JPN) 19.275
1972	Nikolai Andrianov (URS) 19.175	Akinori Nakayama (JPN) 19.125	Shigeru Kasamatsu (JPN) 19.025
1976	Nikolai Andrianov (URS) 19.450	Vladimir Marchenko (URS) 19.425	Peter Kormann (USA) 19.300
1980	Roland Bruckner (GDR) 19.750	Nikolai Andrianov (URS) 19.725	Alexandr Ditiatin (URS) 19.700

| | 1984 | Li Ning (CHN) 19.925 | Yun Lou (CHN) 19.775 | Koji Sotomura (JPN) 19.700 Philippe Vatuone (FRA) 19.700 |

SIDE HORSE

		GOLD	SILVER	BRONZE
1896		Jules A. Zutter (SUI) d.n.a.	Hermann Weingärtner (GER)	
1900		Event not held		
1904		Anton Heida (USA) 42 pts	George Eyser (USA) 33	William A. Merz (USA)29
1906–1920		Event not held		
1924		Josef Wilhelm (SUI) 21.23	Jean Gutweniger (SUI) 21.13	Antoine Rebetez (SUI) 20.73
1928		Hermann Hänggi (SUI) 19.75	Georges Miez (SUI) 19.25	Heikki Savolainen (FIN) 18.83

RIGHT: Nikolai Andrianov (URS) has won more Olympic medals than any other male competitor, earning 15 in three Games from 1972 through 1980.

LEFT: Boris Shakhlin (URS) dominated the 1960 gymnastics competition with his 1 bronze, 2 silver, and 4 gold medals.

	GOLD	SILVER	BRONZE
1932	István Pelle (HUN) 19.07	Omero Bonoli (ITA) 18.87	Frank Haubold (USA) 18.57
1936	Konrad Frey (GER) 19.333	Eugen Mack (SUI) 19.167	Albert Bachmann (SUI) 19.067
1948	Paavo Aaltonen (FIN) 38.7 A. Veikkö Huhtanen (FIN) 38.7 Heikki Savolainen (FIN) 38.7	Luigi Zanetti (ITA) 38.3	Guido Figone (ITA) 38.2
1952	Viktor Chukarin (URS) 19.50	Yevgeniy Korolkov (URS) 19.40 Grant Shaginyan (URS) 19.40	—
1956	Boris Shakhlin (URS) 19.25	Takashi Ono (JPN) 19.20	Viktor Chukarin (URS) 19.10
1960	Eugen Ekman (FIN) 19.375 Boris Shakhlin (URS) 19.375		Shuji Tsurumi (JPN) 19.150
1964	Miroslav Cerar (YUG) 19.525	Shuji Tsurumi (JPN) 19.325	Yury Tsapenko (URS) 19.200
1968	Miroslav Cerar (YUG) 19.325	Olli E. Laiho (FIN) 19.225	Mikhail Voronin (URS) 19.200
1972	Viktor Klimenko (URS) 19.125	Sawao Kato (JPN) 19.000	Eizo Kenmotsu (JPN) 18.950
1976	Zoltan Magyar (HUN) 19.700	Eizo Kenmotsu (JPN) 19.575	Nikolai Andrianov (URS) 19.525
1980	Zoltan Magyar (HUN) 19.925	Alexandr Ditiatin (URS) 19.800	Michael Nikolay (GDR) 19.775
1984	Li Ning (CHN) 19.950 Peter Vidmar (USA) 19.950	—	Timothy Daggett (USA) 19.825

RINGS

	GOLD	SILVER	BRONZE
1896	Ioannis Mitropoulos (GRE) d.n.a.	Hermann Weingärtner (GER)	Petros Persakis (GRE)
1900	Event not held		
1904	Herman Glass (USA) 45	William A. Merz (USA) 35	Emil Voight (USA) 32
1906–1920	Event not held		
1924	Franco Martino (ITA) 21.553	Robert Pražák (TCH) 21.483	Ladislav Vácha (TCH) 21.430
1928	Leon Štukelj (YUG) 19.25	Ladislav Vácha (TCH) 19.17	Emanuel Löffler (TCH) 18.83
1932	George Gulack (USA) 18.97	William Denton (USA) 18.60	Giovanni Lattuada (ITA) 18.50
1936	Alois Hudec (TCH) 19.433	Leon Štukelj (YUG) 18.867	Matthias Volz (GER) 18.667
1948	Karl Frei (SUI) 39.60	Michael Reusch (SUI) 39.10	Zdenek Ružička (TCH) 38.50
1952	Grant Shaginyan (URS) 19.75	Viktor Chukarin (URS) 19.55	Hans Eugster (SUI) 19.40 Dimitriy Leonkin (URS) 19.40
1956	Albert Azaryan (URS) 19.35	Valentin Muratov (URS) 19.15	Masao Takemoto (JPN) 19.10 Masami Kubota (JPN) 19.10
1960	Albert Azaryan (URS) 19.725	Boris Shakhlin (URS) 19.500	Velik Kapsazov (BUL) 19.425 Takashi Ono (JPN) 19.425
1964	Takuji Hayata (JPN) 19.475	Franco Menichelli (ITA) 19.425	Boris Shakhlin (URS) 19.400

GOLD	SILVER	BRONZE
1968 Akinori Nakayama (JPN) 19.450	Mikhail Voronin (URS) 19.325	Sawao Kato (JPN) 19.225
1972 Akinori Nakayama (JPN) 19.350	Mikhail Voronin (URS) 19.275	Mitsuo Tsukahara (JPN) 19.225
1976 Nikolai Andrianov (URS) 19.650	Aleksandr Ditiatin (URS) 19.550	Danut Grecu (ROM) 19.500
1980 Alexandr Ditiatin (URS) 19.875	Alexandr Tkachyov (URS) 19.725	Jiri Tabak (TCH) 19.600
1984 Koji Gushiken (JPN) 19.850 Li Ning (CHN) 19.850	—	Mitchell Gaylord (USA) 19.825

HORSE VAULT

1896 Karl Schumann (GER) d.n.a.	Jules A. Zutter (SUI)	—
1900 Event not held		
1904 Anton Heida (USA) 36 George Eyser (USA) 36	—	William A. Merz (USA) 31
1906–1920 Event not held		
1924 Frank Kriz (USA) 9.98	Jan Koutny (TCH) 9.97	Bohumil Mořkovsky (TCH) 9.93
1928 Eugen Mack (SUI) 9.58	Emanuel Löffler (TCH) 9.50	Stane Derganc (YUG) 9.46
1932 Savino Guglielmetti (ITA) 18.03	Alfred Jochim (GER) 17.77	Edward Carmichael (USA) 17.53
1936 Alfred Schwarzmann (GER) 19.200	Eugen Mack (SUI) 18.967	Matthias Volz (GER) 18.467
1948 Paavo Aaltonen (FIN) 39.10	Olavi Rove (FIN) 39.00	János Mogyorósi-Klencs (HUN) 38.50 Ferenc Pataki (HUN) 38.50 Leos Sotornik (TCH) 38.50
1952 Viktor Chukarin (URS) 19.20	Masao Takemoto (JPN) 19.15	Tadao Uesako (JPN) 19.10 Takashi Ono (JPN) 19.10
1956 Helmuth Bantz (GER) 18.85 Valentin Muratov (URS) 18.85	—	Yuriy Titov (URS) 18.75
1960 Takashi Ono (JPN) 19.350 Boris Shakhlin (URS) 19.350	—	Vladimir Portnoi (URS) 19.225
1964 Haruhiro Yamashita (JPN) 19.600	Victor Lisitsky (URS) 19.325	Hannu Rantakari (FIN) 19.300
1968 Mikhail Voronin (URS) 19.000	Yukio Endo (JPN) 18.950	Sergey Diomidov (URS) 18.925
1972 Klaus Köste (GDR) 18.850	Viktor Klimenko (URS) 18.825	Nikolai Andrianov (URS) 18.800
1976 Nikolai Andrianov (URS) 19.450	Mitsuo Tsukahara (JPN) 19.375	Hiroshi Kajiyama (JPN) 19.275
1980 Nikolai Andrianov (URS) 19.825	Alexandr Ditiatin (URS) 19.800	Roland Bruckner (GDR) 19.775

ABOVE: Olympic champion of the rings in both 1956 and 1960 was Albert Azaryan of Russia.

RIGHT: Akinori Nakayama (JPN) repeated his 1968 triumph on the rings in 1972 at Munich.

| 1984 | Yun Lou
(CHN) 19.950 | Li Ning
(CHN) 19.825
Koji Gushiken
(JPN) 19.825
Mitchell Gaylord
(USA) 19.825
Shinji Morisue
(JPN) 19.825 | — |

PARALLEL BARS

	GOLD	SILVER	BRONZE
1896	Alfred Flatow (GER) d.n.a.	Jules A. Zutter (SUI)	Hermann Weingärtner (GER)
1900	Event not held		
1904	George Eyser (USA) 44	Anton Heida (USA) 43	John Duha (USA) 40
1906–1920	Event not held		
1924	August Güttinger (SUI) 21.63	Robert Pražák (TCH) 21.61	Giorgio Zampori (ITA) 21.45
1928	Ladislav Vácha (TCH) 18.83	Josip Primožič (YUG) 18.50	Hermann Hänggi (SUI) 18.08
1932	Romeo Neri (ITA) 18.97	István Pelle (HUN) 18.60	Heikki Savolainen (FIN) 18.27
1936	Konrad Frey (GER) 19.067	Michael Reusch (SUI) 19.034	Alfred Schwarzmann (GER) 18.967
1948	Michael Reusch (SUI) 39.5	Veikkö Huhtanen (FIN) 39.3	Christian Kipfer (SUI) 39.1 Josef Stalder (SUI) 39.1
1952	Hans Eugster (SUI) 19.65	Viktor Chukarin (URS) 19.60	Josef Stalder (SUI) 19.50
1956	Viktor Chukarin (URS) 19.20	Masami Kubota (JPN) 19.15	Takashi Ono (JPN) 19.10 Masao Takemoto (JPN) 19.10
1960	Boris Shakhlin (URS) 19.400	Giovanni Carminucci (ITA) 19.375	Takashi Ono (JPN) 19.350
1964	Yukio Endo (JPN) 19.675	Shuji Tsurumi (JPN) 19.450	Franco Menichelli (ITA) 19.350
1968	Akinori Nakayama (JPN) 19.475	Mikhail Voronin (URS) 19.425	Vladimir Klimenko (URS) 19.225
1972	Sawao Kato (JPN) 19.475	Shigeru Kasamatsu (JPN) 19.375	Eizo Kenmotsu (JPN) 19.250
1976	Sawao Kato (JPN) 19.675	Nikolai Andrianov (URS) 19.500	Mitsuo Tsukahara (JPN) 19.475
1980	Alexandr Tkachyov (URS) 19.775	Alexandr Ditiatin (URS) 19.750	Roland Bruckner (GDR) 19.650
1984	Bart Conner (USA) 19.950	Nobuyuki Kajitani (JPN) 19.925	Mitchell Gaylord (USA) 19.850

HORIZONTAL BAR

1896	Hermann Weingärtner (GER) d.n.a.	Alfred Flatow (GER)	
1900	Event not held		
1904	Anton Heida (USA) 40 Edward Hennig (USA) 40	—	George Eyser (USA) 39
1906–1920	Event not held		
1924	Leon Štukelj (YUG) 19.730	Jean Gutweniger (SUI) 19.236	André Higelin (FRA) 19.163
1928	Georges Miez (SUI) 19.17	Romeo Neri (ITA) 19.00	Eugen Mack (SUI) 18.92

1932	Dallas Bixler (USA) 18.33	Heikki Savolainen (FIN) 18.07	Einari Teräsvirta (FIN) 18.07[1]
1936	Aleksanteri Saarvala (FIN) 19.367	Konrad Frey (GER) 19.267	Alfred Schwarzmann (GER) 19.233
1948	Josef Stalder (SUI) 39.7	Walter Lehmann (SUI) 39.4	Veikkö Huhtanen (FIN) 39.2
1952	Jack Günthard (SUI) 19.55	Josef Stalder (SUI) 19.50 Alfred Schwarzmann (GER) 19.50	—

---

[1]Teräsvirta conceded second place to Savolainen.

	GOLD	SILVER	BRONZE
1956	Takashi Ono (JPN) 19.60	Yuriy Titov (URS) 19.40	Masao Takemoto (JPN) 19.30
1960	Takashi Ono (JPN) 19.60	Masao Takemoto (JPN) 19.525	Boris Shakhlin (URS) 19.475
1964	Boris Shakhlin (URS) 19.625	Yuriy Titov (URS) 19.55	Miroslav Cerar (YUG) 19.50
1968	Mikhail Voronin (URS) 19.550 Akinori Nakayama (JPN) 19.550	—	Eizo Kenmotsu (JPN) 19.375
1972	Mitsuo Tsukahara (JPN) 19.725	Sawao Kato (JPN) 19.525	Shigeru Kasamatsu (JPN) 19.450
1976	Mitsuo Tsukahara (JPN) 19.675	Eizo Kenmotsu (JPN) 19.500	Eberhard Gienger (GER) 19.475
1980	Stoyan Deltchev (BUL) 19.825	Alexandr Ditiatin (URS) 19.750	Nikolai Andrianov (URS) 19.675
1984	Shinji Morisue (JPN) 20.00	Tong Fei (CHN) 19.975	Koji Gushiken (JPN) 19.950

Gymnastics (Women)

In women's gymnastics there are six events which are interlinked. First is the Team Competition which comprises one compulsory and one optional exercise for each of the four events: Horse Vault, Uneven Bars, Balance Beam and Floor Exercises. Each team competitor gets marks out of 10 for both her compulsory and optional exercise for each of the four events. The team of six with the greatest *total* of marks wins the gold medal.

Next the best 36 competitors from the Team Competition qualify for the Individual All-Round Competition. They each complete a further optional exercise for each of the four events and gain new marks (out of 10) per event. These are then added to the *average* (not total) of their previous total marks in the compulsory and optional sections brought forward from the Team Competition previously decided.

Finally, the six best on each apparatus in the Team Competition qualify for the individual Final on that apparatus. This is decided by adding a new mark (out of 10) for a further optional exercise on that apparatus and the *average* (not total) of their previous marks in the compulsory and optional performances on that apparatus within the Team Competition previously decided.

COMBINED EXERCISES (TEAM)

There was no team event from 1896 to 1924 nor in 1932. A team event was introduced in 1928 and was also held in 1936 to 1956 but the fundamental conditions make the results not comparable with the current event and conditions which started in 1960.

GOLD	SILVER	BRONZE
1960 U.S.S.R. 382.320	CZECHOSLOVAKIA 373.323	RUMANIA 372.053
Larissa Latynina	Vera Čáslavská	Sonia Iovan
Sofia Muratova	Eva Bosáková	Elena Leustean
Polina Astakhova	Ludmila Švedová	Antanasia Ionescu
Margarita Nikolayeva	Adolfina Tkačiková	Uta Poreceanu
Lydia Ivanova	Mathydla Matoušková-Šinová	Emilia Lita
Tamara Lyukhina	Hana Ružičková	Elena Niculescu
1964 U.S.S.R. 380.890	CZECHOSLOVAKIA 379.989	JAPAN 377.889
Larissa Latynina	Vera Čáslavská	Keiko Ikeda-Tanaka
Elena Volchetskaya	Hana Ružičková	Toshiko Aihara-Shirasu
Polina Astakhova	Jaroslava Sedlačková	
Tamara Lyukhina	Adolfina Tkačiková	Kiyoko Ono
Tamara Manina	Mária Krajčirová	Taniko Nakamura
Ludmila Gromova	Jana Posnerová	Hiroko Tsuji
		Ginko Chiba-Abukawa
1968 U.S.S.R. 382.85	CZECHOSLOVAKIA 382.20	E. GERMANY 379.10
Zinaida Voronina	Vera Čáslavská	Erika Zuchold
Natalya Kuchinskaya	Bohumila Rimnácova	Karin Janz
Larissa Petrik	Miroslava Skleničková	Maritta Bauerschmidt
Olga Karasseva	Maria Krajčirová	Ute Starke
Lyudmila Tourischeva	Hana Lišková	Marianne Noack
Ljubov Burda	Jana Kubičková	Magdalena Schmidt
1972 U.S.S.R. 380.50	E. GERMANY 376.55	HUNGARY 368.25
Lyudmila Tourischeva	Karin Janz	Ilona Bekesi
Olga Korbut	Erika Zuchold	Monika Csaszar
Tamara Lazakovitch	Angelika Hellmann	Krisztina Medveczky
Ljubov Burda	Irene Abel	Aniko Kery
Elvira Saadi	Christine Schmitt	Marta Kelemen
Antonina Koshel	Richarda Schmeisser	Zsuzsa Nagy
1976 U.S.S.R. 390.35	RUMANIA 387.15	E. GERMANY 385.10
Svetlana Grozdova	Gabriela Trusca	Angelika Hellmann
Elvira Saadi	Georgeta Gabor	Marion Kische
Maria Filatova	Anca Grigoras	Kerstin Gerschau
Olga Corbut	Mariana Constantin	Gitta Escher
Lyudmila Tourischeva	Teodora Ungureanu	Steffi Kraker
Nelli Kim	Nadia Comaneci	Carola Dombeck
1980 U.S.S.R. 394.90	RUMANIA 393.50	EAST GERMANY 392.55
Natalya Shaposhnikova	Emilia Eberle	Maxi Gnauck
Yelena Davydova	Nadia Comaneci	Katharina Rensch
Nelli Kim	Rodica Dunka	Steffi Kraker
Maria Filatova	Melita Ruhn	Birgit Suss
Stella Zacharova	Cristina Grigoras	Silvia Hindorff
Yelena Naimushina	Dumitrita Turner	Karola Sube
1984 ROMANIA 392.20	USA 391.20	CHINA 388.60
Simona Pauca	Pamela Bileck	Qun Huang
Cristina Grigoras	Michelle Dusserre	Qiurui Zhou
Mihaela Stanulet	Kathy Johnson	Jiani Wu
Laura Cutina	Tracee Talavera	Yanhong Ma
Lavinia Agache	Julianne McNamara	Ping Zhou
Ecaterina Szabo	Mary Lou Retton	Yongyan Chen

COMBINED EXERCISES (INDIVIDUAL)

GOLD	SILVER	BRONZE
1896–1948	Event not held	
1952 Maria Gorokhovskaya (URS) 76.78	Nina Bocharova (URS) 75.94	Margit Korondi (HUN) 75.82
1956 Larissa Latynina (URS) 74.933	Agnes Keleti (HUN) 74.633	Sofia Muratova (URS) 74.466

At the 1976 Games in Montreal, 14-year-old Nadia Comaneci of Romania became the first gymnast to be awarded a perfect score in Olympic competition.

Mary Lou Retton (US) was voted best all-around Olympic gymnast in the 1984 games. She won a gold medal in that category, a silver in the vault and a bronze in the uneven parallel bars.

1960 Larissa Latynina (URS) 77.031	Sofia Muratova (URS) 76.696	Polina Astakhova (URS) 76.164
1964 Vera Caslavská (TCH) 77.564	Larissa Latynina (URS) 76.998	Polina Astakhova (URS) 76.965
1968 Vera Cáslavská (TCH) 78.25	Zinaida Voronina (URS) 76.85	Natalya Kuchinskaya (URS) 76.75
1972 Lyudmila Tourischeva (URS) 77.025	Karin Janz (GDR) 76.875	Tamara Lazakovitch (URS) 76.850
1976 Nadia Comaneci (ROM) 79.275	Nelli Kim (URS) 78.675	Lyudmila Tourischeva (URS) 78.625
1980 Yelena Davydova (URS) 79.150	Maxi Gnauck (GDR) 79.075 Nadia Comaneci (ROM) 79.075	—
1984 Mary Lou Retton (USA) 79.175	Ecaterina Szabo (ROM) 79.125	Simona Pauca (ROM) 78.675

HORSE VAULT

GOLD	SILVER	BRONZE
1896–1948 Event not held		
1952 Yekaterina Kalinchuk (URS) 19.20	Maria Gorokhovskaya (URS) 19.19	Galina Minaitscheva (URS) 19.16
1956 Larissa Latynina (URS) 18.833	Tamara Manina (URS) 18.800	Ann-Sofi Colling (SWE) 18.733 Olga Tass (HUN) 18.733
1960 Margarita Nikolayeva (URS) 19.316	Sofia Muratova (URS) 19.049	Larissa Latynina (URS) 19.016
1964 Vera Čáslavská (TCH) 19.483	Larissa Latynina (URS) 19.283 Birgit Radochla (GER) 19.283	—
1968 Vera Čáslavská (TCH) 19.775	Erika Zuchold (GDR) 19.625	Zinaida Voronina (URS) 19.500
1972 Karin Janz (GDR) 19.525	Erika Zuchold (GDR) 19.275	Lyudmila Tourischeva (URS) 19.250
1976 Nelli Kim (URS) 19.800	Lyudmila Tourischeva (URS) 19.650 Carola Dombeck (GDR) 19.650	—
1980 Natalia Shaposhnikova (URS) 19.725	Steffi Kraker (GDR) 19.675	Melita Ruhn (ROM) 19.650
1984 Ecaterina Szabo (ROM) 19.875	Mary Lou Retton (USA) 19.850	Lavinia Agache (ROM) 19.750

ASYMMETRICAL BARS

GOLD	SILVER	BRONZE
1896–1948 Event not held		
1952 Margit Korondi (HUN) 19.40	Maria Gorokhovskaya (URS) 19.26	Agnes Keleti (HUN) 19.16
1956 Agnes Keleti (HUN) 18.966	Larissa Latynina (URS) 18.833	Sofia Muratova (URS) 18.800
1960 Polina Astakhova (URS) 19.616	Larissa Latynina (URS) 19.416	Tamara Lyukhina (URS) 19.399
1964 Polina Astakhova (URS) 19.332	Katalin Makray (HUN) 19.216	Larissa Latynina (URS) 19.199
1968 Vera Čáslavská (TCH) 19.650	Karin Janz (GDR) 19.500	Zinaida Voronina (URS) 19.425
1972 Karin Janz (GDR) 19.675	Olga Korbut (URS) 19.450 Erika Zuchold (GDR) 19.450	—
1976 Nadia Comaneci (ROM) 20.000	Teodora Ungureanu (ROM) 19.800	Marta Egervari (HUN) 19.775
1980 Maxi Gnauck (GDR) 19.875	Emilia Eberle (ROM) 19.850	Steffi Kraker (GDR) 19.775 Melita Ruhn (ROM) 19.775 Maria Filatova (URS) 19.775
1984 Yanhong Ma (CHN) 19.950 Julianne McNamara (USA) 19.950	—	Mary Lou Retton (USA) 19.800

RIGHT: The Soviet gymnast Larissa Semyonovna Latynina has won more medals than any other Olympic competitor—9 gold, 5 silver, and 4 bronze. She now coaches the U.S.S.R. team.

BELOW: Lyudmila Tourischeva (URS), winner of 4 gold medals in 3 Games, married Soviet track and field gold medallist Valery Borzov after the 1976 Olympics.

BALANCE BEAM

1896–1948   Event not held

	GOLD	SILVER	BRONZE
1952	Nina Bocharova (URS) 19.22	Maria Gorokhovskaya (URS) 19.13	Margit Korondi (HUN) 19.02
1956	Agnes Keleti (HUN) 18.80	Eva Bosáková (TCH) 18.63 / Tamara Manina (URS) 18.63	—
1960	Eva Bosáková (TCH) 19.283	Larissa Latynina (URS) 19.233	Sofia Muratova (URS) 19.232
1964	Vera Čáslavská (TCH) 19.449	Tamara Manina (URS) 19.399	Larissa Latynina (URS) 19.382
1968	Natalya Kuchinskaya (URS) 19.650	Vera Čáslavská (TCH) 19.575	Larissa Petrik (URS) 19.250
1972	Olga Korbut (URS) 19.575	Tamara Lazakovitch (URS) 19.375	Karin Janz (GDR) 18.975
1976	Nadia Comaneci (ROM) 19.950	Olga Korbut (URS) 19.725	Teodora Ungureanu (ROM) 19.700
1980	Nadia Comaneci (ROM) 19.800	Yelena Davydova (URS) 19.750	Natalia Shaposhnikova (URS) 19.725
1984	Simona Pauca (ROM) 19.800 / Ecaterina Szabo (ROM) 19.800	—	Kathy Johnson (USA) 19.650

FLOOR EXERCISES

	GOLD	SILVER	BRONZE
1896–1948	Event not held		
1952	Agnes Keleti (HUN) 19.36	Maria Gorokhovskaya (URS) 19.20	Margit Korondi (HUN) 19.00
1956	Larissa Latynina (URS) 18.733 / Agnes Keleti (HUN) 18.733	—	Elena Leustean (ROM) 18.70
1960	Larissa Latynina (URS) 19.583	Polina Astakhova (URS) 19.532	Tamara Lyukhina (URS) 19.449
1964	Larissa Latynina (URS) 19.599	Polina Astakhova (URS) 19.500	Anikó Jánosi (HUN) 19.300
1968	Larissa Petrik (URS) 19.675 / Vera Čáslavská (TCH) 19.675	—	Natalya Kuchinskaya (URS) 19.650
1972	Olga Korbut (URS) 19.575	Lyudmila Tourischeva (URS) 19.550	Tamara Lazakovitch (URS) 19.450
1976	Nelli Kim (URS) 19.850	Lyudmila Tourischeva (URS) 19.825	Nadia Comaneci (ROM) 19.750
1980	Nelli Kim (URS) 19.875 / Nadia Comaneci (ROM) 19.875	—	Natalia Shaposhnikova (URS) 19.825 / Maxi Gnauck (GDR) 19.825
1984	Ecaterina Szabo (ROM) 19.975	Julianne McNamara (USA) 19.950	Mary Lou Retton (USA) 19.775

RHYTHMIC GYMNASTICS

	GOLD	SILVER	BRONZE
1984	Lori Fung (CAN) 57.950	Doina Staiculescu (ROM) 57.900	Regina Weber (FRG) 57.700

9. Handball, Men (Indoor)

It should be noted that in 1936 there was a Field Handball (i.e. outdoor) competition. The medals went to Germany (gold), Austria (silver) and Switzerland (bronze).

	GOLD	SILVER	BRONZE
1972	**YUGOSLAVIA** Zoran Zivkovic Abaz Arslanagic Miroslav Pribanic Petar Fajfric Milorad Karaiic Djoko Lavrnic Slobodan Miskovic Hrvoje Horvat Branislav Pokrajac Zdravko Miljak Milan Lazarevic Nebojsa Popovic	**CZECHOSLOVAKIA** František Krabik Peter Pospisil Ivan Satrapa Vladimir Jary Jiri Kavan Andrej Lukosik Vladimir Haber Jindrich Krepinal Ladislav Benes Vincent Lavko Jaroslav Konecny Pavel Mikes	**RUMANIA** Cornel Penu Alexandru Dinca Gavril Kicsid Ghita Licu Cristian Gatu Roland Gunnesch Radu Voina Simion Schobel Gheorghe Gruia Werner Stockl Dan Marin Adrian Cosma
1976	**U.S.S.R.** Mikhail Istchenko Anatoli Fedjukin Vladimir Maximov Sergei Kushnirjuk Vladimir Kravsov Yuri Klimov Aleksandr Anpilogov Evgeniy Tchernyshov Valeriy Gassiy Anatoli Tomin Yuri Kidjayev Aleksandr Rezanov	**RUMANIA** Cornel Penu Gavril Kicsid Cristian Gatu Ghita Licu Radu Voina Roland Gunnesch Stefan Birtalan Adrian Cosma Constantin Tudosie Nicolae Munteanu Werner Stockl Mircea Grabovschi	**POLAND** Andrzej Szymczak Piotr Ciesla Zdzislaw Antczak Zygfryd Kuchta Jerzy Klempel Janusz Brzozowski Ryszard Przybysz Jerzy Melcer Andrzej Sokolowski Jan Gmyrek Henryk Rozmiarek Alfred Kaluzinski
1980	**EAST GERMANY** Siegfried Voigt Gunter Dreibrodt Peter Rost Klaus Gruner Hans-Georg Beyer Dietmar Schmidt Hartmut Kruger Lothar Doering Ernst Gerlach Frank Wahl Ingolf Wiegert Wieland Schmidt Rainer Hoft Georg Jaunich	**U.S.S.R.** Mikhail Istchenko Viktor Machorin Sergei Kushnirjuk Aleksandr Karshakevich Vladimir Belov Anatoli Fedjukin Aleksandr Anpilogov Yevgeniy Cheryshov Aleksey Zhuk Nikolai Tomin Yuri Kidjayev Valdemar Novitsky Vladimir Kravsov Vladimir Repiyev	**RUMANIA** Nicolae Munteanu Marian Dumitru Iosif Boros Maricel Voinea Vasile Stinga Radu Voina Cornel Durau Stefan Birtalan Alexandru Folker Neculai Vasilca Adrian Cosma Claudiu Eugen Ionescu Cezar Draganita Lucian Vasilache
1984	**YUGOSLAVIA** Zlatan Amautovic Veselin Vukovic Milan Kalina Jovan Elezovic Zdravko Zovko Branko Strbac Davo Jurina Veselin Vujovic Slobodan Kuzmanovski Mirko Basic Zdravko Radjenovic Mile Isakovic Momir Rnic	**WEST GERMANY** Andreas Thiel Arnulf Meffle Rudiger Neitzel Martin Schwalb Dirk Rauin Michael Paul Michael Roth Thomas Happe Erhard Wunderlich Thomas Springel Klaus Woller Jochen Fraatz Ulrich Roth	**ROMANIA** Nicolae Munteanu Marian Dumitru Iosif Boros Maricel Voinea Vasile Stinga George Dogarescu Gheorghe Covaciu Cornel Durau Alexandru Folker Alexandru Buligan Vasile Oprea Mircea Bedivan Adrian Simion

Handball, Women (Indoor)

GOLD	SILVER	BRONZE

1896–1972   Event not held

1976	**U.S.S.R.**	**EAST GERMANY**	**HUNGARY**
	Natalia Sherstjuk	Hannelore Zober	Agota Bujdoso
	Rafiga Shabanova	Gabriele Badorek	Marta Megyeri
	Lubov Berezhnaya	Evelyn Matz	Borbala Toth-Harsanyi
	Zinaida Turchina	Roswitha Krause	Katalin Laki
	Tatyana Makarets	Christina Rost	Amalia Sterbinszky
	Maria Litoshenko	Petra Uhlig	Marianna Nagy
	Ludmila Bobrus	Christina Voss	Klaru Csik
	Tatyana Glustchenko	Liane Michaelis	Rozalia Lelkes
	Ludmila Shubina	Silvia Siebert	Maria Vadasz
	Galina Zakharova	Marion Tietz	Erzsebet Nemeth
	Aldona Chesaitite	Kristina Richter	Eva Angyal
	Nina Lobova	Eva Paskuy	Maria Berzsenyi
	Ludmila Pantchuk	Waltraud Kretzschmar	Ilona Nagy
	Larisa Karlova	Hannelore Burosch	Zsuzsa Kezi

1980	**U.S.S.R.**	**YUGOSLAVIA**	**EAST GERMANY**
	Natalia Timoshkina	Ana Titlic	Hannelore Zober
	Larisa Karlova	Slavica Jeremic	Katrin Kruger
	Irina Palchikova	Zorica Vojinovic	Evelyn Matz
	Tatiana Kochergina	Radmila Drljaca	Roswitha Krause
	Ludmila Poradnik	Katica Iles	Christina Rost
	Larisa Savkina	Mirjana Ognjenovic	Petra Uhlig
	Aldona Nenenene	Svetlana Anastasovski	Claudia Wunderlich
	Yulia Safina	Svetlana Kitic	Savine Rother
	Olga Zubareva	Mirjana Djurica	Kornelia Kunisch
	Valentina Lutaeva	Biserka Visnjic	Marion Tietz
	Lubov Odinokova	Jasna Merdan	Kristina Richter
	Sigita Strechen	Vesna Radovic	Waltraud Kretzschmar
	Natalia Lukianenko	Vesna Milosevic	Birgit Heinicke
	Zinaida Turchina	Rada Savic	Renate Rudolph

1984	**YUGOSLAVIA**	**KOREA**	**CHINA**
	Jasna Ptujec	Mi-Na Son	Xingjiang Wu
	Mirjana Ognjenovic	Kyung-Soon Kim	Jianping He
	Ljubinka Jankovic	Soon-Ei Lee	Juefeng Zhu
	Svetlana Anastasovski	Hyoi-Soon Jeong	Weihong Zhang
	Svetlana Dasic-Kitic	Mi-Sook Kim	Xiumin Gao
	Alenka Cuderman	Hwa-Soo Han	Linwei Wang
	Svetlana Mugosa	Ok-Hwa Kim	Liping Liu
	Mirjana Djurica	Choon-Yei Kim	Xiulan Sun
	Biserka Visnjic	Soon-Bok Jeung	Yumei Liu
	Slavica Djukic	Byung-Soon Yoon	Lan Li
	Jasna Kolar-Merdan	Young-Ja Lee	Mingxing Wang
	Ljiljana Mugosa	Kyung-Hwa Sung	Zhen Chen
	Zorica Pavicevic	Soo-Kyung Youn	Peijun Zhang
	Emilija Ercic		

Grahannandan Singh (left) scores one of India's four winning goals in the 1948 finals.

10. Hockey (Field)

GOLD	SILVER	BRONZE
1896–1906 Event not held		
1908 ENGLAND	IRELAND	SCOTLAND & WALES
H. I. Wood	E. P. C. Holmes	(tied for third place)
L. C. Baillon	Henry J. Brown	d.n.a.
Harold Scott-Freeman	Walter E. Peterson	
Alan H. Noble	Henry L. Murphy	
Edgar W. Page	Walter J. H. Campbell	
John Y. Robinson	William E. Graham	
Eric Green	Robert L. Kennedy	
Reginald G. Pridmore	Frank L. Robinson	
Stanley H. Shoveller	Eric P. Allman-Smith	
Gerald Logan	G. S. Gregg	
Percy M. Rees	C. F. Power	
	W. G. McCormick	
1912 Event not held		
1920 ENGLAND	DENMARK	BELGIUM
Harry E. Haslam	Andreas Rasmussen	Charles Delelienne
John H. Bennett	Hans-Christian Herlak	Maurice van den
Charles S. Atkin	Frans Faber	Bemden
Harold D. R. Cooke	Erik Husted	Raoul Daufresne de la
Eric B. Crockford	Henning Holst	Chevalerie
Cyril T. A. Wilkinson	Hans-Jörgen Hansen	René Strauwen
William F. Smith	Hans-Adolf Bjerrum	Fernand de Montigny
George F. McGrath	Thorvald Eigenbrod	Adolphe Goemaere
John McBryan	Sven Blach	Pierre Chibert
Stanley H. Shoveller	Steen Due	André Becquet
Rex W. Crummack	Ejvind Blach	Raymond Keppens
Arthur F. Leighton		Pierre Valcke
Colin H. Campbell		Jean van Nerom
Charles Marcon		Robert Gevers
Harold K. Cassels		Louis Diercxens
1924 Event not held		

GOLD	SILVER	BRONZE

1928 INDIA

GOLD	SILVER	BRONZE
INDIA	**NETHERLANDS**	**GERMANY**
Richard J. Allen	Adriaan J. L. Katte	George Brunner
Michael E. Rocque	Albert W. Tresling	Werner Proft
Leslie C. Hammond	Reindert B. J. de Waal	Heinz Wöltje
Rex A. Norris	Johannes W. Brand	Werner Freyberg
Broome E. Pinniger	Emile P. J. Duson	Theo Haag
Sayed M. Yusuf	Jan G. Ankerman	Erich Zander
E. John Goodsir-Cullen	Hendrik P. Visser t'Hooft	Friedrich Horn
Maurice A. Gateley	Robert van der Veen	Herbert Müller
George E. Marthins	Paulus van de Rovaert	Bruno Boche
Dhyan Chand	Gerrit J. A. Jannink	Herbert Hobein
Frederick S. Seaman	August J. Kop	Herbert Kemmer
Khair Singh		Erwin Franzkowiak
Jaipal Singh		Hans Haussmann
Shaukat Ali		Karl Heinz Immer
Feroze Khan		Aribert Heymann
		Kurt Haverbeck
		Rolf Wollner
		Gerd Strantzen
		Heinz Förstendorf

1932

GOLD	SILVER	BRONZE
INDIA	**JAPAN**	**UNITED STATES**
Sayed Mohammed Jaffar	Junzo Inohara	David McMullin
	Toshio Usami	William Boddington
Roop Singh	Kenichi Konishi	James Gentle
Dhyan Chand	Hiroshi Nagata	Charles Shaeffer
Gurmit Singh	Haruhiko Kon	Lawrence Knapp
Richard J. Carr	Eiichi Nakamura	Horace Disston
Lal Shah Bokhari	Yoshio Sakai	Samuel Ewing
Broome E. Pinniger	Katsumi Shibata	Henry Greer
M. A. K. Minhas	Sadayoshi Kobayashi	Leonard O'Brien
Leslie C. Hammond	Akio Sohda	Frederick Wolters
Carlyle C. Tapsell	Shumkichi Hamada	Harold Brewster
Arthur C. Hind		Amos Deacon
Richard Allen		
Masud Minhas		

1936

GOLD	SILVER	BRONZE
INDIA	**GERMANY**	**NETHERLANDS**
Richard J. Allen	Karl Dröse	Jan de Looper
Carlyle C. Tapsell	Erich Zander	Reindert B. J. de Waal
Mohammed Hussain	Herbert Kemmer	Max Westerkamp
Baboo N. Nimal	Heinz Schmalix	Hendrik C. de Looper
E. John Goodsir-Cullen	Erwin Keller	Rudolf J. van der Haar
Joseph Galibardy	Alfred Gerdes	Anton R. van Lierop
Shabban Shahab ud Din	Fritz Messner	Pieter A. Gunning
Dara ali Iqtidar Shah	Hans Scherbart	Henri C. W. Schnitger
Dhyan Chand	Kurt Weiss	Ernst W. van den Berg
Roop Singh	Werner Hamel	Agathon de Roos
Sayed Mohammed Jaffar	Harald Huffmann	René Sparenberg
	Werner Kubitzki	Carl E. Heybroek
Ahmed Sher Khan	Tito Warnholtz	
Garewal Gurcharan Singh	Detlef Okrent	
	Hermann Auf der Heide	
Ahsan Mohomed Khan	Heinrich Peter	
Lionel C. Emmett	Carl Menke	
Mirza Nasir ud Din Masood	Heinz Raack	
	Paul Mehlitz	
Cyril J. Michie	Ludwig Beisiegel	
Fernandes Paul Peter	Karl Ruck	
Joseph Phillip	Erich Cuntz	

	GOLD	SILVER	BRONZE
1948	**INDIA**	**GREAT BRITAIN**	**NETHERLANDS**
	Leo H. K. Pinto	David L. S. Brodie	Antonius M. Richter
	Trilochan Singh	George B. Sime	Henri J. J. Derckx
	Randhir Singh Gentle	William L. C. Lindsay	Johan F. Drijver
	Keshav C. Datt	Michael M. Walford	Jenne Langhout
	Amir C. Kumar	Frank O. Reynolds	Hermanus P. Loggere
	Maxie Vaz	F. Robin Lindsay	Edvard H. Tiel
	Kishan Lal	John M. Peak	Willem van Heel
	Kunwa Digvijai Singh	W. Neil White	Andries C. Boerstra
	Grahanandan Singh	Robert E. Adlard	Pieter M. J. Bromberg
	Patrick A. Jansen	Norman F. Borrett	Jan H. Kruize
	Lawrie Fernandes	William S. Griffiths	Rius T. Esser
	Ranganadhan Francis	Ronald Davies	Henricus N. Bouwman
	Akhtar Hussain	G. Hudson	
	Leslie W. Claudius	R. T. Lake	
	Jaswant S. Rajput	Peter Whitbread	
	Reginald Rodrigues		
	Latifur Rehman		
	Balbir Singh		
	Walter J. L. D'Souza		
	Gerry R. Glacken		
1952	**INDIA**	**NETHERLANDS**	**GREAT BRITAIN**
	Ranganadhan Francis	Laurens S. Mulder	Graham B. Dadds
	Dharam Singh	Henri J. J. Derckx	Roger K. Midgley
	Randhir S. Gentle	Johan F. Drijver	Denys J. Carnill
	Leslie W. Claudius	Julius T. Ancion	John A. Cockett
	Keshav C. Datt	Hermanus P. Loggere	Dennis M. R. Eagan
	Govind Perumal	Edvard H. Tiel	Anthony J. B. Robinson
	Raghbir Lal	Willem van Heel	Anthony S. Nunn
	Kunwar D. Singh	Rius T. Esser	Robin A. Fletcher
	Balbir Singh	Jan H. Kruize	Richard O. A. Norris
	Udham Singh	Andries C. Boerstra	John V. Conroy
	Muniswamy Rajagopal	Leonard H. Wery	John P. Taylor
	Meldric St. C. Daluz		Derek M. Day
	Grahanandan Singh		S. T. Theobald
	Chinadorai Deshmutu		
1956	**INDIA**	**PAKISTAN**	**GERMANY**
	Shankar Laxman	Zakir Hussain	Alfred Lücker
	Bakshish Singh	Ghulam Rasul	Helmut Nonn
	Randhir S. Gentle	Anwar Ahmad Khan	Günther Ullerich
	Leslie W. Claudius	Hussain Mussarat	Günther Brennecke
	Amir Kumar	Noor Alam	Werner Delmes
	Govind Perumal	Abdul Hamid	Eberhard Ferstl
	Charles Stephen	Habibur Rehman	Hugo Dollheiser
	Gurdev Singh	Mutih Ullah	Heinz Radzikowski
	Balbir Singh	Hussain Akhtar	Wolfgang Nonn
	Udham Singh	Nasir Ahmad	Hugo Budinger
	Raghbir S. Bhola	Manzur H. Atif	Werner Rozenbaum
	Ranganadhan Francis	Habib Alikiddi	
	Balkishan Singh	Munir Ahmad Dar	
	Amit Singh Bakshi	Latifur Rehman	
	Kaushi Haripal		
	Hardyal Singh		
	Raghbir Lal		

1960 PAKISTAN

GOLD	SILVER	BRONZE
PAKISTAN	**INDIA**	**SPAIN**
Abdul Rashid	Shankar Laxman	Carlos Del Coso Iglesias
Bashir Ahmad	Prithipal Singh	José Colomer Rivas
Manzur H. Atif	Jamanlal Sharma	Rafael Egusquiza
Ghulam Rasul	Leslie W. Claudius	Basterva
Anwar Ahmad Khan	Joseph Antic	Juan Angel Calzado
Ali Habib Kidi	Mohinder Lal	de Castro
Noor Alam	Joginder Singh	José Antonio Dinares
Abdul Hamid	John V. Peter	Massaqué
Abdul Waheed	Jaswant Singh	Edouardo Dualde
Nasir Ahmad	Udham Singh	Santos de Lamadrid
Mutih Ullah	Raghbir S. Bhola	Joachim Dualde
Khurshid Aslam	Charanjit Singh	Santos de Lamadrid
Mushtaq Ahmad	Govind Savant	Pedro Amat Fontanais
Munir Ahmad Dar		Francisco Caballer
		Soteras
		Ignacio Macaya
		Santos de Lamadrid
		Pedro Murúa
		Leguizamón
		Pedro Roig Junyent
		Luis Maria Usoz
		Quintana
		Narciso Ventalló
		Surralles

1964 INDIA	**PAKISTAN**	**AUSTRALIA**
Shankar Laxman	Abdul Hamid	Paul Dearing
Prithipal Singh	Munir Ahmad Dar	Donald McWatters
Dhara M. Singh	Manzur H. Atif	Brian Glencross
Mohinder Lal	Saeed Anwar	John McBride
Charanjit Singh	Anwar Ahmad Khan	Julian Pearce
Gurbux Singh	Muhammad Rashid	Graham Wood
Joginder Singh	Khalid Mahmood Hussain	Robin Hodder
John V. Peter	Zaka-ud-Din	Raymond Evans
Harbinder Singh	Muhammad Afzal	Eric Pearce
Kashik Haripal	Manna	Patrick Nilan
Darshan Singh	Mohammad Asad Malik	Donald Smart
Jagjit Singh	Mutih Ullah	Antony Waters
Bandu Patil	Tariq Niazi	Mervyn Crossman
Udham Singh	Zafar Hayat	Desmond Piper
Ali Sayeed	Khizar Nawaz	
	Kurshid Aslam	

1968 PAKISTAN	**AUSTRALIA**	**INDIA**
Zakir Hussain	Paul Dearing	Rajendra A. Christy
Tanvir A. Dar	James Mason	Gurbux Singh
Tariq Aziz	Brian Glencross	Prithipal Singh
Saeed Anwar	Gordon Pearce	Balbir Singh II
Riaz Ahmed	Julian Pearce	Ajitpal Singh
Bulrez Akhtar	Robert Haigh	Krishna Murtay
Khalid Mahmood	Donald Martin	Perumal
Hussain	Eric Pearce	Balbir Singh III
Mohammad Ashfaq	Raymond Evans	Balbir Singh I
Abdul Rashid	Frederick Quinn	Harbinder Singh
Mohammad Asad Malik	Ronald Riley	Inamur Rehman
Jahangir Ahmad Butt	Patrick Nilan	Inder Singh
Riaz Ud Din	Donald Smart	Munir Sait
Tariq Niazi	Desmond Piper	Harmik Singh
		John V. Peter
		Tarsem Singh

1972 WEST GERMANY	**PAKISTAN**	**INDIA**
Peter Kraus	Saleem Sherwan	Cornelius Charles
Michael Peter	Akhtarul Islam	Mukhbain Singh
Dieter Freise	Munawaruz Zaman	Michael Kindo
Michael Krause	Saeed Anwar	Krishna Murtay
Eduard Thelen	Riaz Ahmed	Perumal

1976

1980

1984

Hockey (Field) Women

1896–1976 Event not held

1980	ZIMBABWE	CZECHOSLOVAKIA	U.S.S.R.
	Sarah English	Berta Hruba	Nelli Gorbatkova
	Anne Mary Grant	Jirina Kadlecova	Valentina Zazdravnykh
	Brenda Joan Phillips	Jirina Cermakova	Nadyezda Ovechkina
	Patricia Jean McKillop	Marta Urbanova	Natella Krasnikova
	Sonia Robertson	Kveta Petrickova	Natalya Bykova
	Patricia Joan Davies	Marie Sykorova	Lidiya Glubokova
	Maureen Jean George	Ida Hubackova	Galina Vyuzhanina
	Linda Margaret Watson	Milada Blazkova	Natalya Bozunova
	Susan Huggett	Jana Lahodova	Lyailya Akhmerova
	Gillian Margaret Cowley	Alena Kyselicova	Nadyezda Filipova
	Elizabeth Murial Chase	Jirina Hajkova	Tatyana Yembakhtova
	Sandra Chick	Viera Podhanyiova	Tatyana Shviganova
	Helen Volk	Jarmila Kralickova	Ludmila Frolova
	Christine Prinsloo	Iveta Srankova	Galina Inzhuvatova
	Arlene Nadine Boxhall	Lenka Vymazalova	Yelena Gureva
	Anthea Doreen Stewart	Jirina Krizova	Alina Kham

1984	NETHERLANDS	WEST GERMANY	USA
	Bernadette De Beus	Ursula Thielemann	Gwen Cheeseman
	Alette Pos	Beate Deininger	Beth Anders
	Margriet Zegers	Christina Moser	Kathleen McGahey
	Laurien Wllemse	Hella Roth	Anita Miller
	Marjolein Eysvogel	Dagmar Breiken	Regina Buggy
	Josephine Boekhorst	Birgit Hagen	Christine Larson-Mason
	Carina Benninga	Birgit Hahn	Beth Beglin
	Alexandra LePoole	Gabriele Appel	Marcella Place
	Francisca Hillen	Andrea Weiermann-Lietz	Julie Staver
	Marieke Van Doorn	Corinna Lingnau	Diane Moyer
	Sophie Von Weiler	Martina Koch	Sheryl Johnson
	Aletta Van Manen	Gabriele Schley	Charlene Morett
	Irene Hendriks	Patricia Ott	Karen Shelton
	Elisabeth Sevens	Susanne Schmid	Brenda Stauffer
	Martine Ohr	Sigrid Landgraf	Leslie Milne
	Anneloes Nieuwenhuizen	Elke Drull	Judy Strong

---

11. Judo

Sport introduced in 1964.

OPEN CATEGORY, NO WEIGHT LIMIT

	GOLD	SILVER	BRONZE
1964	Antonius Geesink (HOL)	Akio Kaminaga (JPN)	Theodore Boronovskis (AUS) Klaus Glahn (GER)
1968	Event not held		
1972	Wilhelm Ruska (HOL)	Vitali Kusnezov (URS)	Jean-Claude Brondani (FRA) Angelo Parisi (GBR)
1976	Haruki Uemura (JPN)	Keith Remfry (GBR)	Shota Chochoshvili (URS) Jeaki Cho (KOR)
1980	Dietmar Lorenz (GDR)	Angelo Parisi (FRA)	Arthur Mapp (GBR) Andras Ozsvar (HUN)

| 1984 | Yasuhiro Yamashita (JPN) | Mohamed Rashwan (EGY) | Mihai Cioc (ROM) Arthur Schnabel (FRG) |

New weight categories were introduced in 1980

OVER 95 kg (209¼ lb)

	GOLD	SILVER	BRONZE
1980	Angelo Parisi (FRA)	Dimitar Zaprianov (BUL)	Vladimir Kocman (TCH) Radomir Kovacevic (YUG)
1984	Hitoshi Saito (JPN)	Angelo Parusi (FRA)	Yong-Chul Cho (KOR) Mark Berger (CAN)

UP TO 95 kg (209¼ lb)

| 1980 | Robert Van De Walle (BEL) | Tengiz Khubuluri (URS) | Dietmar Lorenz (GDR) Henk Numan (HOL) |
| 1984 | Hyoung-Zoo Ha (KOR) | Douglas Vieira (BRA) | Bjarni Fridriksson (ISL) Gunter Neureuther (FRG) |

UP TO 86 kg (189½ lb)

| 1980 | Juerg Roethlisberger (SUI) | Issac Azcuy (CUB) | Alexandr Iatskevich (URS) Detlef Ultsch (GDR) |
| 1984 | Peter Seisenbacher (AUT) | Robert Berland (USA) | Seiki Nose (JPN) Walter Carmona (BRA) |

UP TO 78 kg (171¾ lb)

| 1980 | 'Shota Khabareli (URS) | Juan Ferrer (CUB) | Bernard Tchoullouyan (FRA) Harald Heinke (GDR) |
| 1984 | Frank Wieneke (FRG) | Neil Adams (GBR) | Michel Nowak (FRA) Mircea Fratica (ROM) |

UP TO 71kg (156½ lb)

| 1980 | Ezio Gamba (ITA) | Neil Adams (GBR) | Karl-Heinz Lehmann (GDR) Ravdan Davaadalai (MGL) |
| 1984 | Byeoung-Keun Ahn (KOR) | Ezio Gamba | Luis Onmura (ITA) Kerrith Brown (GBR) |

UP TO 65 kg (143¼ lb)

| 1980 | Nikolay Solodukhin (URS) | Tsendying Damdin (MGL) | Ilian Nedkov (BUL) Janusz Pawlowski (POL) |
| 1984 | Yoshiyuki Matsuoka (JPN) | Jung-Oh Hwang | Josef Reiter (KOR) Marc Alexandre (FRA) |

UP TO 60 kg (132¼ lb)

| 1980 | Thierry Rey (FRA) | Jose Rodriguez (CUB) | Aramby Emizh (URS) Tibor Kinces (HUN) |
| 1984 | Shinji Hosokawa (JPN) | Jae-Yup Kim | Edward Liddie (KOR) Neil Eckersley (GBR) |

PREVIOUS WINNERS

OVER 93 kg (205 lb)

	GOLD	SILVER	BRONZE
1964	Isao Inokuma (JPN)	A. H. Douglas Rogers (CAN)	Parnaoz Chikviladze (URS) Anzor Kiknadze (URS)
1968	Event not held		
1972	Wilhelm Ruska (HOL)	Klaus Glahn (GER)	Givi Onashvili (URS) Motoki Nishimura (JPN)
1976	Sergei Novikov (URS)	Gunther Neureuther (GER)	Sumio Endo (JPN) Allen Coage (USA)

80 to 93 kg (176¼ to 205 lb)

1964–1968	Event not held		
1972	Shota Chochoshvili (URS)	David C. Starbrook (GBR)	Chiaki Ishii (BRA) Paul Barth (GER)
1976	Kazuhiro Ninomiya (JPN)	Ramaz Harshiladze (URS)	David C. Starbrook (GBR) Juerg Roethlisberger (SUI)

Shinobu Sekine of Japan (left) defeated Brian Jacks of Great Britain (right) in this semi-final match and went on to win the gold medal in the middleweight category in 1972.

70 to 80 kg (154¼ to 176¼ lb)

	GOLD	SILVER	BRONZE
1964	Isao Okano (JPN)	Wolfgang Hofmann (GER)	James Bregman (USA) Eui Tae Kim (KOR)
1968	Event not held		
1972	Shinobu Sekine (JPN)	Seung-Lip Oh (KOR)	Brian Jacks (GBR) Jean-Paul Coche (FRA)
1976	Isamu Sonoda (JPN)	Valeriy Dvoinikov (URS)	Slavko Obadov (YUG) Youngchul Park (KOR)

63 to 70 kg (138¾ to 154¼ lb)

1964–1968	Event not held		
1972	Toyokazu Nomura (JPN)	Anton Zajkowski (POL)	Dietmar Hoetger (GDR) Anatoli Novikov (URS)
1976	Vladimir Nevzorov (URS)	Koji Kuramoto (JPN)	Patrick Vial (FRA) Marian Talaj (POL)

Up to 63 kg (138¾ lb)

GOLD	SILVER	BRONZE
1964 Takehide Nakatani (JPN)	Eric Haenni (SUI)	Oleg Stepanov (URS) Aron Bogulubov (URS)
1968 Event not held		
1972 Takao Kawaguchi (JPN)		Yong Ik Kim (PRK) Jean-Jacques Mounier (FRA)
1976 Hector Rodriguez (CUD)	Eunkyung Chang (KOR)	Felice Mariani (ITA) Jozsef Tuncsik (HUN)

---

[1]Bakhaavaa Buidaa (MGL) disqualified after positive drug test.

---

12. Modern Pentathlon

The five events [currently in the order Riding (800 m course), Fencing (epée), Shooting (pistol 25 m), Swimming (300 m free-style), and Cross-country running (4,000 m)] have remained constant although there have inevitably been changes of rules, time allowed and order over the years.

Competitors were placed by lowest number of placing points (e.g. 1 for 1st in an event and 10 for a 10th place in another) until an international graduated points scoring table was introduced in 1956.

1896–1908 Event not held		
1912 Gustaf Lilliehöök (SWE) 27	Gösta Åsbrink (SWE) 28	Georg de Laval (SWE) 30
1920 Gustaf Dryssen (SWE) 18	Erik de Laval (SWE) 23	Gösta Rüno (SWE) 27
1924 Bo Lindman (SWE) 18	Gustaf Dryssen (SWE) 39.5	Bertil Uggla (SWE) 45
1928 Sven Thofelt (SWE) 47	Bo Lindman (SWE) 50	Helmuth Kahl (GER) 52
1932 Johan Gabriel Oxenstierna (SWE) 32	Bo Lindman (SWE) 35.5	Richard Mayo (USA) 38.5
1936 Gotthard Handrick (GER) 31.5	Charles Leonard (USA) 39.5	Silvano Abba (ITA) 45.5
1948 William Grut (SWE) 16	George Moore (USA) 47	Gösta Gärdin (SWE) 49
1952 Lars Hall (SWE) 32	Gábor Benedek (HUN) 39	István Szondi (HUN) 41
Teams—HUNGARY 166 Gábor Benedek István Szondi Aladár Kovácsi	SWEDEN 182 Lars Hall Torsten Lindqvist Cläes Egnell	FINLAND 213 Olavi Mannonen Lauri Vikko Olavi Rokka
1956 Lars Hall (SWE) 4,843	Olavi Mannonen (FIN) 4,774.5	Väinö Korhonen (FIN) 4,750
Teams—U.S.S.R. 13,690.5 Igor Novikov Aleksandr Tarassov Ivan Deryugin	UNITED STATES 13,482 George H. Lambert William Andre Jack T. Daniels	FINLAND 13,185.5 Olavi Mannonen Väinö Korhonen Berndt Katter

Andras Balczo (HUN) was the most successful of all modern pentathletes with 3 gold and 2 silver medals.

GOLD	SILVER	BRONZE
1960 Ferenc Németh (HUN) 5,024	Imre Nagy (HUN) 4,988	Robert L. Beck (USA) 4,981
Teams—HUNGARY 14,863	U.S.S.R. 14,309	UNITED STATES 14,192
Ferenc Németh	Igor Novikov	Robert L. Beck
Imre Nagy	Nikolai Tatarinov	George H. Lambert
András Balczó	Hanno Selg	Jack T. Daniels
1964 Ferenc Török (HUN) 5,116	Igor Novikov (URS) 5,067	Albert Mokeyev (URS) 5,039
Teams—U.S.S.R. 14,961	UNITED STATES 14,189	HUNGARY 14,173
Igor Novikov	James Moore	Ferenc Török
Albert Mokeyev	David Kirkwood	Imre Nagy
Victor Mineyev	Paul Pesthy	Otto Török
1968 Björn Ferm (SWE) 4,964	András Balczó (HUN) 4,953	Pavel Lednev (URS) 4,795
Teams—HUNGARY 14,325	U.S.S.R. 14,248	FRANCE 13,289
András Balczó	Boris Onischenko	Raoul Gueguen
István Móna	Pavel Lednev	Lucien Guiguet
Ferenc Török	Stasis Shaparnis	Jean-Pierre Giudicelli
1972 András Balczó (HUN) 5,412	Boris Onischenko (URS) 5,335	Pavel Lednev (URS) 5,328
Teams—U.S.S.R. 15,968	HUNGARY 15,348	FINLAND 14,812
Boris Onischenko	András Balczó	Risto Hurme
Pavel Lednev	Zsigmond Villanyi	Veikko Salminen
Vladimir Shmelev	Pal Bako	Martti Ketelae
1976 Janusz Pyciak-Peciak (POL) 5,520	Pavel Lednev (URS) 5,485	Jan Bartu (TCH) 5,466
Teams—GREAT BRITAIN 15,559	CZECHOSLOVAKIA 15,451	HUNGARY 15,395
Adrian Parker	Jan Bartu	Tamas Kancsal
Robert Nightingale	Bohumil Starnovsky	Tibor Maracsko
Jeremy Fox	Jiri Adam	Szvetiszlav Sasics
1980 Anatoly Starostin (URS) 5,568	Tamas Szmobathelyi (HUN) 5,502	Pavel Lednev (URS) 5,382
Teams—U.S.S.R. 16,126	HUNGARY 15,912	SWEDEN 15,845
Anatoliy Starostin	Tamas Szombathelyi	Svante Rasmuson
Pavel Lednev	Tibor Maracsko	Lennart Pettersson
Yevgeniy Lipeyev	Laszlo Horvath	George Horvath

1984	Daniele Masala	Svante Rasmuson	Carlo Massullo
	(ITA) 5,469	(SWE) 5,456	(ITA) 5,406
Teams—ITALY 16,060	Carlo Massullo	USA 15,568	FRANCE 15,565
	Carlo Massullo	Deam Glenesk	Paul Four
	Daniele Masala	Robert Losey	Didier Boube
	Pierpaolo Cristofori	Michael Storm	Joel Bouzou

---

13. Rowing (Men)

The standard Olympic course is now 1 mile 427 yards *2 000 m* in length.

In 1904, however, the course was 2 miles *3 218,7 m;* in 1908 1½ miles *2 414 m*; and in 1948 1 mile 350 yards *1 929 m*.

Times: The water conditions can vary sufficiently from one Games to another, even over a course of the same length, so as to make comparison between Games of little value.

There can thus be no Olympic *records* as such, but as a matter of interest the following are the *fastest times* achieved in any Olympic regatta over 2,000 meters:

Single Sculls	6:52.46	S. Drea (IRL)	1976
Double Sculls	6:12.48	Norway	1976
Quadruple Sculls	5:47.83	U.S.S.R.	1976
Coxless Pairs	6:33.02	East Germany	1976
Coxed Pairs	7:01.10	Bulgaria	1976
Coxless Fours	5:53.65	East Germany	1976
Coxed Fours	6:09.28	U.S.S.R.	1976
Eights	5:32.17	East Germany	1976

The times given of the Bronze medal winners in 1928 are those achieved in a losing semi-final or race between beaten semi-finalists.

SINGLE SCULLS

	GOLD	SILVER	BRONZE
1896	Event not held		
1900	Henri Barrelet	André Gaudin	St. George Ashe
	(FRA) 7:35.6	(FRA) 7:41.6	(GBR) 8:15.6
1904	Frank Greer	James Juvenal	Constance Titus
	(USA) 10:08.5	(USA) 2 lengths	(USA) 1 length
1906	Gaston Delaplane	Joseph Larran	
	(FRA) 5:53.4	(FRA) 6:07.2	
1908	Harry Blackstaffe	Alexander McCulloch	Bernhard von Gaza
	(GBR) 9:26.0	(GBR) 1 length	(GER) d.n.a.
			Károly Levitzky
			(HUN) d.n.a.
1912	William D. Kinnear	Polydore Veirman	Everard B. Butler
	(GBR) 7:47.6	(BEL) 1 length	(CAN) d.n.a.
			Mikhail Kusik
			(URS) d.n.a.

One of only five oarsmen to take three gold medals, Jack Beresford of Great Britain won rowing events in 1924, 1932, and 1936.

	GOLD	SILVER	BRONZE
1920	John Kelly (USA) 7:35.0	Jack Beresford (GBR) 7:36.0	Clarence Hadfield d'Arcy (NZL) 7:48.0
1924	Jack Beresford (GBR) 7:49.2	William E. Garrett-Gilmore (USA) 7:54.0	Josef Schneider (SUI) 8:01.1
1928	Henry Pearce (AUS) 7:11.10	Kenneth Myers (USA) 7:20.8	T. David Collet (GBR) 7:19.8
1932	Henry Pearce (AUS) 7:44.4	William Miller (USA) 7:45.2	Guillermo Douglas (URU) 8:13.6
1936	Gustav Schäfer (GER) 8:21.5	Josef Hasenöhrl (AUT) 8:25.8	Daniel Barrow (USA) 8:28.0
1948	Mervyn Wood (AUS) 7:24.4	Eduardo Risso (URU) 7:38.2	Romolo Catasta (ITA) 7:51.4
1952	Yuri Tyukalov (URS) 8:12.8	Mervyn Wood (AUS) 8:14.5	Teodor Kocerka (POL) 8:19.4
1956	Vyacheslav Ivanov (URS) 8:02.5	Stuart Mackenzie (AUS) 8:07.7	John B. Kelly (USA) 8:11.8
1960	Vyacheslav Ivanov (URS) 7:13.96	Achim Hill (GER) 7:20.21	Teodor Kocerka (POL) 7:21.26
1964	Vyacheslav Ivanov (URS) 8:22.51	Achim Hill (GER) 8:26.34	Gottfried Kottmann (SUI) 8:29.68
1968	Henri Jan Wienese (HOL) 7:47.80	Jochen Meissner (GER) 7:52.00	Alberto Demiddi (ARG) 7:57.19
1972	Yuri Malishev (URS) 7:10.12	Alberto Demiddi (ARG) 7:11.53	Wolfgang Gueldenpfennig (GDR) 7:14.45
1976	Pertti Karppinen (FIN) 7:29.03	Peter Kolbe (GER) 7:31.67	Joachim Dreifke (GDR) 7:38.03
1980	Pertti Karppinen (FIN) 7:09.61	Vasily Yakusha (URS) 7:11.66	Peter Kersten (GDR) 7:14.88
1984	Pertti Karppinen (FIN) 7:00.24	Peter-Michael Kolbe (FRG) 7:02.19	Robert Mills (CAN) 7:10.38

DOUBLE SCULLS

	GOLD	SILVER	BRONZE
1896–1900	Event not held		
1904	**UNITED STATES** 10:03.2	UNITED STATES d.n.a.	UNITED STATES d.n.a.
	John Mulcahy William Varley	John Hoben James McLoughlin	John Wells Joseph Ravanack
1906–1912	Event not held		
1920	**UNITED STATES** 7:09.0	ITALY 7:19.0	FRANCE 7:21.0
	John Kelly Paul Costello	Erminio Dones Pietro Annoni	Alfred Plé Gaston Giran
1924	**UNITED STATES** 7:45.0	FRANCE 7:54.8	SWITZERLAND d.n.a.
	John Kelly Paul Costello	Jean-Pierre Stock Marc Detton	Rudolf Bosshard Heini Thoma
1928	**UNITED STATES** 6:41.4	CANADA 6:51.0	AUSTRIA 6:48.8
	Charles J. McIlvaine Paul Costello	Jack Guest Joseph Wright	Viktor Flessl Leo Losert
1932	**UNITED STATES** 7:17.4	GERMANY 7:22.8	CANADA 7:27.6
	William E. Garrett-Gilmore Kenneth Myers	Gerhard Boetzelen Herbert Buhtz	Nöel de Mille Charles Pratt
1936	**GREAT BRITAIN** 7:20.8	GERMANY 7:26.2	POLAND 7:36.2
	Leslie F. Southwood Jack Beresford	Joachim Pirsch Willy Kaidel	Jerzy Ustupski Roger Verey
1948	**GREAT BRITAIN** 6:51.3	DENMARK 6:55.3	URUGUAY 7:12.4
	B. Herbert T. Bushnell Richard D. Burnell	Aage E. Larsen Ebbe Parsner	Juan Rodriguez William Jones
1952	**ARGENTINA** 7:32.2	U.S.S.R. 7:38.3	URUGUAY 7:43.7
	Tranquilo Capozzo Eduardo Guerrero	Georgiy Zhilin Igor Emchuk	Miguel Seijas Juan Rodriguez
1956	**U.S.S.R.** 7:24.0	UNITED STATES 7:32.3	AUSTRALIA 7:37.4
	Aleksandr Berkutov Yuri Tyukalov	Bernard Costello James Gardiner	Murray Riley Mervyn Wood
1960	**CZECHOSLOVAKIA** 6:47.50	U.S.S.R. 6:50.49	SWITZERLAND 6:50.59
	Václav Kozák Pavel Schmidt	Aleksandr Berkutov Yuri Tyukalov	Ernst Huerlimann Rolf Larcher
1964	**U.S.S.R.** 7:10.66	UNITED STATES 7:13.16	CZECHOSLOVAKIA 7:14.23
	Oleg Tyurin Boris Dubrovsky	Seymour Cromwell James Storm	Vladimir Andrs Pavel Hofman
1968	**U.S.S.R.** 6:51.82	NETHERLANDS 6:52.80	UNITED STATES 6:54.21
	Anatoly Sass Aleksandr Timoshinin	Henricus A. Droog Leendert F. van Dis	John Nunn William Maher
1972	**U.S.S.R.** 7:01.77	NORWAY 7:02.58	EAST GERMANY 7:05.55
	Aleksandr Timoshinin Gennadi Korshikov	Frank Hansen Svein Thogersen	Joachim Boehmer Hans-Ulrich Schmied
1976	**NORWAY** 7:13.20	GREAT BRITAIN 7:15.26	EAST GERMANY 7:17.45
	Frank Hansen Alf Hansen	Chris Baillieu Michael Hart	Hans-Ulrich Schmied Jurgen Bertow
1980	**EAST GERMANY** 6:24.33	YUGOSLAVIA 6:26.34	CZECHOSLOVAKIA 6:29.07
	Joachim Dreifke Klaus Kroppelien	Zoran Pancic Milorad Stanulov	Zdenek Pecka Vaclav Vochoska

1984	USA 6:36.87	BELGIUM 6:38.19	YUGOSLAVIA 6:39.59
	Bradley Lewis	Pierre-Marie Deloof	Zoran Pancic
	Paul Enquist	Dirk Crois	Milorad Stanulov

COXLESS QUADRUPLE SCULLS

GOLD	SILVER	BRONZE

1896–1972 Event not held

1976	EAST GERMANY	U.S.S.R. 6:19.89	CZECHOSLOVAKIA
	6:18.65		6:21.77
	Wolfgang	Yevgeni Duleyev	Jaroslav Helebrand
	Guldenpfennig	Yuri Yakimov	Vaclav Vochoska
	Rudiger Reiche	Aivar Lazdenieks	Zdenek Pecka
	Karl-Heinz Bussert	Vitautas Butkus	Vladek Lacina
	Michael Wolfgramm		
1980	EAST GERMANY	U.S.S.R.	BULGARIA
	5:49.81	5:51.47	5:52.38
	Frank Dundr	Yuriy Shapochka	Mintscho Nikolov
	Karsten Bunk	Yevgeniy Barbakov	Lubomir Petrov
	Uwe Heppner	Valeriy Kleshnev	Ivo Russev
	Martin Winter	Nikolai Dovgan	Bogdan Dobrev
1984	WEST GERMANY	AUSTRALIA	CANADA
	5:57.55	5:57.98	5:59.07
	Albert Hedderich	Paul Reedy	Doug Hamilton
	Raimund Hormann	Gary Gullock	Mike Hughes
	Dieter Wiedenmann	Timothy McLaren	Phil Monckton
	Michael Dursch	Anthony Lovrich	Bruce Ford

COXLESS PAIRS

1896–1906 Event not held

1908	GREAT BRITAIN	GREAT BRITAIN ——	
	9:41.0	2½ lengths	
	(Leander I)	(Leander II)	
	J. R. K. Fenning	George E. Fairbairn	
	Gordon L. Thomson	Philip E. Verdon	

1912–1920 Event not held

1924	NETHERLANDS	FRANCE 8:21.6 ——	
	8:19.4		
	Wilhelm H. Rösingh	Maurice Bouton	
	Antonie C. Beijnen	George Piot	
1928	GERMANY 7:06.4	GREAT BRITAIN	UNITED STATES
		7:08.8	7:20.4
	Bruno Müller	R. Archibald Nisbet	John Schmitt
	Kurt Moeschter	Terence O'Brien	Paul McDowell
1932	GREAT BRITAIN	NEW ZEALAND 8:02.4	POLAND 8:08.2
	8:00.0		
	H. R. Arthur Edwards	Frederick Thompson	Janusz Mikolajczyk
	Lewis Clive	Cyril Stiles	Henryk Budzynski
1936	GERMANY 8:16.1	DENMARK 8:19.2	ARGENTINA 8:23.0
	Hugo Strauss	Harry J. Larsen	Julio Curatella
	Willi Eichhorn	Richard Olsen	Horacio Podestá
1948	GREAT BRITAIN	SWITZERLAND 7:23.9	ITALY 7:31.5
	7:21.1		
	John H. T. Wilson	Josef Kalt	Bruno Boni
	William G. R. M. Laurie	Hans Kalt	Felice Fanetti
1952	UNITED STATES	BELGIUM 8:23.5	SWITZERLAND
	8:20.7		8:32.7
	Charles Logg	Michel Knuysen	Kurt Schmid
	Thomas Price	Robert Baetens	Hans Kalt
1956	UNITED STATES	U.S.S.R. 8:03.9	AUSTRIA 8:11.8
	7:55.4		
	James Fifer	Igor Buldakov	Josef Kloimstein
	Duvall Hecht	Viktor Ivanov	Alfred Sageder

1960 **U.S.S.R.** 7:02.01	**AUSTRIA** 7:03.69	**FINLAND** 7:03.80
Valentin Boreyko	Josef Kloimstein	Veli Lehtelä
Olyeg Golovanov	Alfred Sageder	Toimi Pitkänen
1964 **CANADA** 7:32.94	**NETHERLANDS** 7:33.40	**GERMANY** 7:38.63
George Hungerford	Steven Blaisse	Michael Schwan
Roger C. Jackson	Ernst W. Veenemans	Wolfgang Hottenrott
1968 **EAST GERMANY** 7:26.56	**UNITED STATES** 7:26.71	**DENMARK** 7:31.84
Jörg Lucke	Lawrence Hough	Peter F. Christiansen
Hans-Jürgen Bothe	Philip Johnson	Ib Ivan Larsen

GOLD	SILVER	BRONZE
1972 **EAST GERMANY** 6:53.16	**SWITZERLAND** 6:57.06	**NETHERLANDS** 6:58.70
Siegfried Brietzke	Heinrich Fischer	Roelof Luyernburg
Wolfgang Mager	Alfred Bachmann	Rund Stokvis
1976 **EAST GERMANY** 7:23.31	**UNITED STATES** 7:26.73	**GERMANY** 7:30.03
Jorg Landvoigt	Calvin Coffey	Peter Vanroye
Bernd Landvoigt	Michael Staines	Thomas Strauss
1980 **EAST GERMANY** 6:48.01	**U.S.S.R.** 6:50.50	**GREAT BRITAIN** 6:51.47
Jorg Landvoigt	Yuriy Pimenov	Charles Wiggin
Bernd Landvoigt	Nikolai Pimenov	Malcolm Carmichael
1984 **ROMANIA** 6:45.39	**SPAIN** 6:48.47	**NORWAY** 6:51.81
Petru Iosub	Fernando Climent	Hans Magnus Grepperud
Valer Toma	Luis Lasurtegui	Sverre Loken

COXED PAIRS

1896 Event not held		
1900 **NETHERLANDS** 7:34.2	**FRANCE I** 7:34.4	**FRANCE II** 7:57.2
(Minerva, Amsterdam)	(Soc. Nautique de la Marne)	(Rowing Club Castillonais)
1904–1912 Event not held		
1920 **ITALY** 7:56.0	**FRANCE** 7:57.0	**SWITZERLAND** d.n.a.
Ercole Olgeni	Gabriel Poix	Edouard Candeveau
Giovanni Scatturin	Maurice Bouton	Alfred Felber
Guido de Filip (cox)	Ernest Barberolle (cox)	Paul Piaget (cox)
1924 **SWITZERLAND** 8:39.0	**ITALY** 8:39.1	**UNITED STATES** d.n.a.
Edouard Candeveau	Ercole Olgeni	Leon Butler
Alfred Felber	Giovanni Scatturin	Harold Wilson
Emil Lachapelle (cox)	Gino Sopracordevole (cox)	Edward Jennings (cox)
1928 **SWITZERLAND** 7:42.6	**FRANCE** 7:48.4	**BELGIUM** 7:59.4
Hans Schöchlin	Armand Marcelle	Léon Flament
Karl Schöchlin	Edouard Marcelle	François de Coninck
Hans Bourquin (cox)	Henri Préaux (cox)	Georges Anthony (cox)
1932 **UNITED STATES** 8:25.8	**POLAND** 8:31.2	**FRANCE** 8:41.2
Charles Kieffer	Janusz Slazak	André Giriat
Joseph Schauers	Jerzy Braun	Anselme Brusa
Edward Jennings (cox)	Jerzy Skolimowski (cox)	Pierre Brunet (cox)
1936 **GERMANY** 8:36.9	**ITALY** 8:49.7	**FRANCE** 8:54.0
Herbert Adamski	Guido Santin	Georges Tapie
Gerhard Gustmann	Almiro Bergamo	Marceau Fourcade
Dieter Arend (cox)	Luciano Negrini (cox)	Nöel Vandernotte (cox)
1948 **DENMARK** 8:00.5	**ITALY** 8:12.2	**HUNGARY** 8:25.2
Tage Henriksen	Aldo Tarlao	Béla Zsitnik
Finn Pedersen	Giovanni Steffe	Antal Szendey
Carl Ebbe Andersen (cox)	Alberto Radi (cox)	Róbert Zimonyi (cox)

GOLD	SILVER	BRONZE
1952 **FRANCE** 8:28.6 Raymond Salles Gaston Mercier Bernard Malivoire (cox)	**GERMANY** 8:32.1 Heinz Manchen Helmut Heinhold Helmut Noll (cox)	**DENMARK** 8:34.9 Svend Petersen Paul Svendsen Jörgen Frandsen (cox)
1956 **UNITED STATES** 8:26.1 Arthur Ayrault F. Conn Findlay Kurt Seiffert (cox)	**GERMANY** 8:29.2 Karl-Heinrich von Groddeck Horst Arndt Rainer Borkowsky (cox)	**U.S.S.R.** 8:31.0 Igor Yemtschuk Georgiy Zhilin Vladimir Petrov (cox)
1960 **GERMANY** 7:29.14 Bernhard Knubel Heinz Renneberg Klaus Zerta (cox)	**U.S.S.R.** 7:30.17 Antanas Bogdanavichus Zigmas Yukna Igor Rudakov (cox)	**UNITED STATES** 7:34.58 F. Conn Findlay Richard Draeger H. Kent Mitchell (cox)

GOLD	SILVER	BRONZE
1964 **UNITED STATES** 8:21.23 Edward Ferry F. Conn Findlay H. Kent Mitchell (cox)	**FRANCE** 8:23.15 Georges Morel Jacques Morel Jean-Claude Darouy (cox)	**NETHERLANDS** 8:23.42 Jan J. Bos Herman J. Rouwé Frederik Hartsuiker (cox)
1968 **ITALY** 8:04.81 Primo Baran Renzo Sambo Bruno Cipolla (cox)	**NETHERLANDS** 8:06.80 Herman J. Suselbeek Hadriaan van Nes Roderick Rijnders (cox)	**DENMARK** 8:08.07 Jörn Krab Harry Jörgensen Preben Krab (cox)
1972 **EAST GERMANY** 7:17.25 Wolfgang Gunkel Joerg Lucke Klaus-Dieter Neubert (cox)	**CZECHOSLOVAKIA** 7:19.57 Oldrich Svojanovsky Pavel Svojanovsky Vladimir Petricek (cox)	**RUMANIA** 7:21.36 Stefan Tudor Petre Ceapura Ladislau Lowrenschi (cox)
1976 **EAST GERMANY** 7:58.99 Harald Jahrling Friedrich Ulrich George Spohr (cox)	**U.S.S.R.** 8:01.82 Dmitri Bekhterev Yuri Shurkalov Yuri Lorentson (cox)	**CZECHOSLOVAKIA** 8:03.28 Oldrich Svojanovsky Pavel Svojanovsky Ludvik Vebr (cox)
1980 **EAST GERMANY** 7:02.54 Harald Jahrling Friedrich-Wilhelm Ulrich Georg Spohr (cox)	**U.S.S.R.** 7:03.35 Viktor Prevertsev Gennadiy Kryuchkin Aleksandr Lukyanov (cox)	**YUGOSLAVIA** 7:04.92 Dusko Mrduljas Zlatko Celent Josip Reic (cox)
1984 **ITALY** 7:05.99 Carmine Abbagnale Giuseppe Abbagnale Giuseppe Di Capua	**ROMANIA** 7:11.21 Dimitrie Popescu Vasile Tomoiaga Dumitru Raducanu	**USA** 7:12.81 Kevin Still Robert Espeseth Douglas Herland

COXLESS FOURS

1896–1900 Event not held

1904 **UNITED STATES** 9:53.8 (Century B.C., St. Louis) Arthur M. Stockhoff August C. Erker George Dietz Albert Nasse	**UNITED STATES** d.n.a. (Mound City R.C., St. Louis) Frederick Suerig Martin Fromanack Charles Aman Michael Begley	——

1906 Event not held

1908	**GREAT BRITAIN**	**GREAT BRITAIN**	
	8:34.0	1½ lengths	
	(Magdalen B.C., Oxford)	(Leander)	
	C. Robert Cudmore	Philip R. Filleul	
	James A. Gillan	Harold R. Barker	
	Duncan McKinnon	J. R. K. Fenning	
	John R. Somers-Smith	Gordon L. Thomson	
1912–1920	Event not held		
1924	**GREAT BRITAIN**	**CANADA** 7:18.0	**SWITZERLAND**
	7:08.6		d.n.a.
	Charles R. M. Eley	Archibald C. Black	Emile Albrecht
	James A. McNabb	Colin H. B. Finlayson	Alfred Probst
	Robert E. Morrison	George F. McKay	Eugen Sigg
	T. Robert B. Sanders	William Wood	Hans Walter
1928	**GREAT BRITAIN**	**UNITED STATES**	**ITALY** 6:31.6
	6:36.0	6:37.0	
	Edward V. Bevan	Charles Karle	Cesare Rossi
	Richard Beesly	William Miller	Pietro Freschi
	Michael H. Warriner	George Heales	Umberto Bonadè
	John G. H. Lander	Ernest Bayer	Paolo Gennari
1932	**GREAT BRITAIN**	**GERMANY** 7:03.0	**ITALY** 7:04.0
	6:58.2		
	Rowland D. George	Hans Maier	Antonio Provenzani
	Jack Beresford	Walter Flinsch	Giliante d'Este
	Hugh R. A. Edwards	Ernst Gaber	Francesco Cossu
	John C. Badcock	Karl Aletter	Antonio Ghiardello

East Germany, the eventual gold medalist, leads Great Britian in a preliminary heat of coxless fours at the 1972 Games in Munich.

	GOLD	SILVER	BRONZE
1936	**GERMANY** 7:01.8	**GREAT BRITAIN**	**SWITZERLAND**
		7:06.5	7:10.6
	Wilhelm Menne	Thomas Bristow	Karl Schmid
	Martin Karl	Alan Barrett	Alex Homberger
	Anton Rom	Peter Jackson	Hans Homberger
	Rudolf Eckstein	John D. Sturrock	Hermann Betschart
1948	**ITALY** 6:39.0	**DENMARK** 6:43.5	**UNITED STATES**
			6:47.7
	Franco Faggi	Ib Storm Larsen	Robert Perew
	Giovanni Invernizzi	Helge Schroeder	Gregory Gates
	Elio Morille	A. Bonde Hansen	Stuart Griffing
	Giuseppe Moioli	Helge Halkjaer	F. John Kingsbury

	GOLD	SILVER	BRONZE
1952	**YUGOSLAVIA** 7:16.0	**FRANCE** 7:18.9	**FINLAND** 7:23.3
	Duje Bonačič	Pierre Blondiaux	Veikko Lommi
	Vleimir Valenta	Jacques Guissart	Kauko Wahlsten
	Mate Trojanovič	Marc Bouissou	Oiva Lommi
	Peter Šegvič	Roger Gautier	Lauri Nevalainen
1956	**CANADA** 7:08.8	**UNITED STATES**	**FRANCE** 7:20.9
		7:18.4	
	Archibald McKinnon	John Welchli	Guy Guillabert
	Lorne Loomer	John McKinlay	Gaston Mercier
	I. Walter d'Hondt	Arthur McKinlay	Yves Delacour
	Donald Arnold	James McIntosh	René Guissart
1960	**UNITES STATES**	**ITALY** 6:28.78	**U.S.S.R.** 6:29.62
	6:26.26		
	Arthur Ayrault	Tullio Baraglia	Igor Akhremchik
	Theodore Nash	Renato Bosatta	Yuriy Batschurov
	John Sayre	Giancarlo Crosta	Valentin Morkovkin
	Richard Wailes	Giuseppe Galante	Anatoliy Tarabrin
1964	**DENMARK** 6:59.30	**GREAT GRITAIN**	**UNITED STATES**
		7:00.47	7:01.37
	John Orsted Hansen	John M. Russell	Geoffrey Picard
	Björn Haslöv	Hugh A.	Richard Lyon
	Erik Petersen	Wardell-Yerburgh	Theodore Mittet
	Kurt Helmudt	William Barry	Theodore Nash
		John James	
1968	**EAST GERMANY**	**HUNGARY** 6:41.64	**ITALY** 6:44.01
	6:39.18		
	Frank Forberger	Zoltán Melis	Renato Bosatta
	Dieter Grahn	György Sarlós	Tullio Baraglia
	Frank Rühle	József Csermely	Pier Angelo Conti
	Dieter Schubert	Antal Melis	Abramo Albini Manzini
1972	**EAST GERMANY**	**NEW ZEALAND**	**WEST GERMANY**
	6:24.27	6:25.64	6:28.41
	Frank Forberger	Dick Tonks	Joachim Ehrig
	Frank Rühle	Dudley Storey	Peter Funnekoetter
	Dieter Grahn	Ross Collinge	Franz Weld
	Dieter Schubert	Noel Mills	Wolfgang Plottke
1976	**EAST GERMANY**	**NORWAY** 6:41.22	**U.S.S.R.** 6:42.52
	6:37.42		
	Siegfried Brietzke	Ole Nafstad	Raul Arnemann
	Andreas Decker	Arne Bergodd	Nikolai Kuznetsov
	Stefan Semmler	Finn Tveter	Valeri Dolinin
	Wolfgang Mager	Rolf Andreassen	Anushavan Gasan-Dzhalalov
1980	**EAST GERMANY** 6:08.17	**U.S.S.R.** 6:11.81	**GREAT BRITAIN** 6:16.58
	Jurgen Thiele	Aleksey Kamkin	John Beattie
	Andreas Decker	Valeri Dolinin	Ian McNuff
	Stefan Semmler	Aleksandr Kulagin	David Townsend
	Siegfried Brietzke	Vitaliy Yeliseyev	Martin Cross
1984	**NEW ZEALAND** 6:03.48	**USA** 6:06.10	**DENMARK** 6:07.72
	Leslie O'Connell	David Clark	Michael Jessen
	Shane O'Brien	Jonathan Smith	Lars Nielsen
	Conrad Robertson	Philip Stekl	Per Rasmussen
	Keith Trask	Alan Forney	Erik Christiansen

COXED FOURS

	GOLD	SILVER	BRONZE
1896	Event not held		
1900	**GERMANY** 5:59.0	**NETHERLANDS**	**GERMANY** 6:35.0
	(Germania, Hamburg)	6:33.0	(Ruderverein,
	Oskar Gossler	(Minerva, Amsterdam)	Ludwigshafen)
	Katzenstein		
	Tietgens		
	G. Gossler		
	G. Gossler (cox)		

GOLD	SILVER	BRONZE
1904 Event not held		
1906 **ITALY** 8:13.0	**FRANCE** d.n.a.	**FRANCE** d.n.a.
(Bucintoro)	(Soc. Nautique de la Basse Siene)	(Soc. Nautique de Bayonne)
Enrico Bruna	Gaston Delaplane	Adolphe Bernard
Emilio Fontanella	Charles Delaporte	Joseph Halcet
Riccardo Jandinoni	León Deliguières	Jean-Baptiste Laporte
Giorgio Cesana	Paul Echard	Jean-Baptiste Mathieu
Giuseppe Poli (cox)	Marcel Frébourg (cox)	Pierre Sourbé (cox)
1908 Event not held		
1912 **GERMANY** 6:59.4	**GREAT BRITAIN** 2 lengths	**NORWAY** d.n.a.
(Ludwigshafener R.C.)	(Thames R.C.)	(Christiania R.C.)
Albert Arnheiter	Julius Beresford	Henry Larsen
Otto Fickeisen	Charles Rought	Matias Torstensen
Rudolf Fickeisen	Bruce Logan	Theodor Klem
Herman Wilker	Charles G. Vernon	Haakon Tonsager
Otto Maier (cox)	Geoffrey Carr (cox)	Ejnar Tonsager (cox)
		DENMARK
		(Polyteknic R.C.)
		Erik Bisgaard
		Rasmus P. Frandsen
		Magnus Simonsen
		Poul Thymann
		Eigil Clemmensen (cox)
1920 **SWITZERLAND** 6:54.0	**UNITED STATES** 6:58.0	**NORWAY** 7:02.0
Hans Walter	Kenneth Myers	Henry Larsen
Max Rudolf	Carl O. Klose	Per Gulbrandsen
Willy Brüderlin	Franz Federschmidt	Theodor Klem
Paul Rudolf	Erich Federschmidt	Birger Var
Paul Staub (cox)	Sherman Clark (cox)	Thoralf Hagen (cox)
1924 **SWITZERLAND** 7:18.4	**FRANCE** 7:21.6	**UNITED STATES** 1 length
Hans Walter	Louis Gressier	Robert Gerhardt
Alfred Probst	Georges Lecointe	Sidney Jelinek
Emile Albrecht	Raymond Thalleux	Edward Mitchell
Eugen Sigg	Eugène Constant	Henry Welsford
Walter Loosli (cox)	Marcel Lepan (cox)	John Kennedy (cox)
1928 **ITALY** 6:47.8	**SWITZERLAND** 7:03.4	**POLAND** 7:12.8
Valerio Perentin	Ernst Haas	František Bronikowski
Giliante d'Este	Joseph Meyer	Edmund Jankowski
Nicolo Vittori	Otto Bucher	Leszek Birkholz
Giovanni Delise	Karl Schwegler	Bernard Ormanowski
Renato Petronio (cox)	Fritz Boesch (cox)	Bronislaw Drewek (cox)
1932 **GERMANY** 7:19.0	**ITALY** 7:19.2	**POLAND** 7:26.8
Joachim Spemberg	Bruno Parovel	Edward Kobylinski
Walter Meyer	Riccardo Divora	Stanislaw Urban
Horst Hoeck	Giovanni Plazzer	Janusz Ślazak
Hans Eller	Bruno Vattovaz	Jerzy Braun
Karlheinz Neumann (cox)	Giovanni Scherl (cox)	Jerzy Skolimowski (cox)
1936 **GERMAY** 7:16.2	**SWITZERLAND** 7:24.3	**FRANCE** 7:33.3
Paul Söllner	Karl Schmid	Fernand Vandernotte
Ernst Gaber	Hans Homberger	Marcel Vandernotte
Walter Volle	Alex Homberger	Marcel Cosmat
Hans Maier	Hermann Betschart	Marcel Chauvigné
Fritz Bauer (cox)	Rolf Spring (cox)	Noel Vandernotte (cox)
1948 **UNITED STATES** 6:50.3	**SWITZERLAND** 6:53.3	**DENMARK** 6:58.6
Gordon Giovanelli	Pierre Stebler	Harry M. Knudsen
Robert W. Eill	Erich Schriever	Henry C. Larsen
Robert Martin	Emile Knecht	Börge R. Nielsen
Warren Westlund	Rudolf Reichling	Erik C. Larsen
Allen Morgan (cox)	André Moccand (cox)	Jörgen Ib Olsen (cox)

GOLD	SILVER	BRONZE
1952 CZECHOSLOVAKIA 7:33.4	SWITZERLAND 7:36.5	UNITED STATES 7:37.0
Karel Mejta	Enrico Bianchi	Carl Lovested
Jiři Havlis	Karl Weidmann	Alvin Ulbrickson
Jan Jindra	Heinrich Scheller	Richard Wahlström
Stanislav Lusk	Emile Ess	Matthew Leanderson
Miroslav Koranda (cox)	Walter Leiser (cox)	Albert Rossi (cox)
1956 ITALY 7:19.4	SWEDEN 7:22.4	FINLAND 7:30.9
Alberto Winkler	Olof Larsson	Kauko Hänninen
Romano Sgheiz	Gösta Eriksson	Reino Poutanen
Angelo Vanzin	Ivar Aronsson	Veli Lehtelä
Franco Trincavelli	Sven E. Gunnarsson	Toimi Pitkänen
Ivo Stefanoni (cox)	Bertil Göransson (cox)	Matti Niemi (cox)
1960 GERMANY 6:39.12	FRANCE 6:41.62	ITALY 6:43.72
Gerd Cintl	Robert Dumantois	Fulvio Balatti
Horst Effertz	Claude Martin	Romano Sgheiz
Jürgen Litz	Jacques Morel	Franco Trincavelli
Klaus Riekemann	Guy Nosbaum	Giovanni Zucchi
Michael Obst (cox)	Jean Klein (cox)	Ivo Stefanoni (cox)
1964 GERMANY 7:00.44	ITALY 7:02.84	NETHERLANDS 7:06.46
Peter Neusel	Renato Bosatta	Alex Mullink
Bernhard Britting	Emilio Trivini	Jan van de Graaf
Joachim Werner	Giuseppe Galante	Frederick R. van de Graaf
Egbert Hirschfelder	Franco de Pedrina	Robert van de Graaf
Jürgen Oelke (cox)	Giovanni Spinola (cox)	Marius Klumperbeek (cox)
1968 N. ZEALAND 6:45.62	E. GERMANY 6:48.20	SWITZERLAND 6:49.04
Richard J. Joyce	Peter Kremtz	Denis Oswald
Dudley L. Storey	Roland Göhler	Hugo Waser
Warren J. Cole	Klaus Jacob	Jakob Grob
Ross H. Collinge	Manfred Gelpke	Peter Bolliger
Simon C. Dickie (cox)	Dieter Semetzky (cox)	Gottlieb Fröhlich (cox)
1972 W. GERMANY 6:31.85	E. GERMANY 6:33.30	CZECHOSLOVAKIA 6:35.64
Peter Berger	Dietrich Zander	Otakar Marecek
Hans-Johann Faerber	Reinhard Gust	Karel Neffe
Gerhard Auer	Eckhard Martens	Vladimir Janos
Alois Bierl	Rolf Jobst	František Provaznik
Uwe Benter (cox)	Klaus-Dieter Ludwig (cox)	Vladimir Petricek (cox)
1976 U.S.S.R. 6:40.22	E. GERMANY 6:42.70	W. GERMANY 6:46.96
Vladimir Eshinov	Andreas Schulz	Johann Faerber
Nikolai Ivanov	Rudiger Kunze	Ralph Kubail
Mikhail Kuznetsov	Walter Diessner	Siegfried Frickle
Alexandr Klepikov	Ullrich Diessner	Peter Niehusen
Alexandr Lukianov (cox)	Johannes Thomas (cox)	Hartmut Wenzel (cox)
1980 EAST GERMANY 6:14.51	U.S.S.R. 6:19.05	POLAND 6:22.52
Dieter Wendisch	Artur Garonskis	Grzegorz Stellak
Ullrich Diessner	Dimant Krisianis	Adam Tomasiak
Walter Diessner	Dzintars Krisianis	Grzegorz Nowak
Gottfried Dohn	George Tikmers	Ryszard Stadniuk
Andreas Gregor (cox)	Juris Berzynsh (cox)	Ryszard Kubiak (cox)
1984 GREAT BRITAIN 6:18.64	USA 6:20.28	NEW ZEALAND 6:23.68
Martin Cross	Thomas Kiefer	Kevin Lawton
Richard Budgett	Gregory Springer	Donald Symon
Andrew Holmes	Michael Bach	Barrie Mabbott
Steven Redgrave	Edward Ives	Ross Tong
Adrian Ellison	John Stillings	Brett Hollister

The United States wins by a nose over Italy, Canada, and Great Britain in the final eights race at Los Angeles in 1932.

EIGHTS

GOLD	SILVER	BRONZE
1896	Event not held		
1900	**UNITED STATES** 6:09.8 (Vesper B.C., Philadelphia)	**BELGIUM** 6:13.8 (Royal Club Nautique de Ghent)	**NETHERLANDS** 6:23.0 (Minerva, Amsterdam)
	Roscoe Lockwood	Marcel van Crombrugghe	Walker M. Timmerman Thijssen
	Edward Marsh		
	Edward Hedley	Maurice Hemelsoet	Ruurd G. Leegstra
	William Carr	Oscar de Cock	Johannes W. van Djik
	John E. Geiger	Maurice Verdonck	Henricus Tromp
	James Juvenal	Prospère Bruggeman	Hendrick K. Offerhaus
	Harry Debaecke	Oscar de Somville	Roelof Klein
	John N. Exley	Frank Odberg	François A. Brandt
	Louis G. Abell	Jules de Bisschop	Walter Middelberg
		Alfred Vanlandeghem	Hermanus G. Brockmann
1904	**UNITED STATES** 7:50.0 (Vesper B.C., Philadelphia)	**CANADA** d.n.a. (Argonaut, R.C. Toronto)	—
	Fred Cresser	Joseph Wright	
	M. D. Gleason	Donald Mackenzie	
	Frank Schell	William Wadsworth	
	J. S. Flanigan	Geroge Strange	
	C. E. Armstrong	Phil Boyd	
	H. H. Lott	C. R. 'Pat' Reiffensteim	
	J. F. Dempsey	W. Rice	
	John N. Exley	R. Bailey	
	Louis G. Abell	Thomas Loudon	
1906	Even not held		

GOLD	SILVER	BRONZE
1908 **GREAT BRITAIN I** 7:52.0	**BELGIUM** 2 lenghts (Royal C.N. Gand)	**GREAT BRITAIN II** (Cambridge University B.C.)
(Leander Club)	Oscar Taelman	Frederick Jerwood
Albert C. Gladstone	Marcel Morimont	Eric W. Powell
Frederick S. Kelly	Rémy Orban	Guy A. Carver
Banner C. Johnstone	Georges Mijs	Edward G. Williams
Guy Nickalls	François Vergucht	Henry M. Goldsmith
Charles D. Burnell	Polydore Veirman	Harold E. Kitching
Ronald H. Sanderson	Oscar de Somville	John S. Burn
Raymond B. Etherington-Smith	Rodolphe Poma	Douglas C. R. Stuart
Henry C. Bucknall	Alfred Vanlandeghem	Richard F. Boyle (cox)
Gilchrist S. Maclagen (cox)	(cox)	**CANADA** (Argonaut R. C. (Toronto)
		Irvine R. Robertson
		George F. Wright
		Julius A. Thomson
		Walter A. Lewis
		Gordon B. Balfour
		Becher R. Gale
		Charles Riddy
		Geoffrey Taylor
		Douglas E. Kertland (cox)
1912 **GREAT BRITAIN I** 6:15.0	**GREAT BRITAIN II** 1 length	**GERMANY** d.n.a. (Berliner R.V. 1876)
(Leander Club)	(New College, Oxford)	
Sidney E. Swann	Sir William Parker	Otto Leibing
Leslie G. Wormald	William Fison	Max Broeske
Ewart D. Horsfall	Thomas Gillespie	Max Vetter
James A. Gillan	Beaufort Burdekin	Wilhelm Bartholomae
Arthur S. Garton	Frederick Pitman	Fritz Bartholomae
Alister G. Kirby	Arthur Wiggins	Werner Dehn
Philip Fleming	Charles Littlejohn	Rudolf Reichelt
Edgar R. Burgess	Robert Bourne	Hans Mathiae
Henry B. Wells (cox)	John Walker (cox)	Kurt Runge (cox)
1920 **UNITED STATES** 6:02.6	**GREAT BRITAIN** (Leander Club) 6:05.0	**NORWAY** 6:36.0
(Navy)	Rev. Sidney Swann	Theodor Nag
Virgil Jacomini	Ralph Shove	Conrad Olsen
Edwin Graves	Sebastian Earl	Adolf Nilsen
Willian Jordan	John Campbell	Haakon Ellingsen
Edward Moore	Walter James	Thore Michelsen
Allen Sanborn	Richard Lucas	Arne Mortensen
Donald Johnston	Guy O. Nickalls	Karl Nag
Vincent Gallagher	Ewart Horsfall	Tollef Tollefsen
Clyde King	Robin Johnston (cox)	Thoralf Hagen (cox)
Sherman Clark (cox)		
1924 **UNITED STATES** (Yale B.C.) 6:33.4	**CANADA** 6:49.0 (Toronto B.C.)	**ITALY** d.n.a. (Zara R.C.)
Leonard G. Carpentier	Arthur Bell	Antonio Cattalinich
Howard T. Kingsbury	Robert Hunter	Francesco Cattalinich
Alfred M. Wilson	William Langford	Simeone Cattalinich
J. David Lindley	Harold Little	Guiseppe Crivelli
John L. Miller	John Smith	Latino Galasso
James S. Rockefeller	Warren Snyder	Pietro Ivanov
Frederick Sheffield	Norman Taylor	Bruno Sorich
Benjamin M. Spock	William Wallace	Carlo Toniatti
Laurence R. Stoddard (cox)	Ivor Campbell (cox)	Vittorio Gliubich (cox)

GOLD	SILVER	BRONZE
1928 **UNITED STATES** (Univ. of Calif.) 6:03.2	**GREAT BRITAIN** (Thames R.C.) 6:05.6	**CANADA** 6:03.8
Marvin Stalder	Harold West	Frederick Hedges
John Brinck	Jack Beresford	Frank Fiddes
Francis Frederick	Gordon Killick	John Hand
Walter Thompson	Harold Lane	Herbert Richardson
William Dally	Donald Gollan	Jack Murdock
James Workman	John Badcock	Athol Meech
Hubert Caldwell	Guy O. Nickalls	Edgar Norris
Peter Donlon	James Hamilton	William Ross
Donald Blessing (cox)	Arthur Sulley (cox)	Jack Donelly (cox)
1932 **UNITED STATES** (Univ. of Calif.) 6:37.6	**ITALY** 6:37.8	**CANADA** 6:40.4
Winslow Hall	Renato Barbieri	Albert Taylor
Harold Tower	Enrico Garzelli	Donald Boal
Charles Chandler	Guglielmo del Bimbo	William Thoburn
Burton Jastram	Roberto Vestrini	Cedric Liddell
David Dunlap	Dino Barsotti	Harry Fry
Duncan Gregg	Renato Bracci	Stanley Stanyar
James Blair	Mario Balleri	Joseph Harris
Edwin Salisbury	Vittorio Cioni	Earl Eastwood
Norris Graham (cox)	Cesare Milani (cox)	George MacDonald (cox)
1936 **UNITED STATES** 6:25.4 (Univ. Washington)	**ITALY** 6:26.0	**GERMANY** 6:26.4
Donald Hume	Guglielmo del Bimbo	Herbert Schmidt
Joseph Rantz	Dino Barsotti	Hans-Joachim
George Hunt	Oreste Grossi	Hannemann
James McMillin	Enzo Bartolini	Werner Loeckle
John White	Mario Checcacci	Gerd Völs
Gordon Adam	Dante Secchi	Hein Kaufmann
Charles·Day	Ottorino Quaglierini	Hans Kuschke
Herbert Morris	Enrico Garzelli	Helmut Radach
Robert Moch (cox)	Cesare Milani (cox)	Alfred Rieck
		Wilhelm Mahlow (cox)
1948 **UNITED STATES** (Univ. of Calif.) 5:56.7	**GREAT BRITAIN** 6:06.9	**NORWAY** 6:10.3
John Stack	Andrew Mellows	Carl H. Monssen
Justus Smith	David Meyrick	Thor Pedersen
David Brown	C. Brian Lloyd	Leif Naess
Lloyd Butler	Paul Massey	Harald Kråkenes
George Ahlgren	E. A. Paul Bircher	Halfdan Gran-Olsen
James Hardy	Guy Richardson	Hans E. Hansen
David Turner	Maurice Lapage	Torstein Kråkenes
Ian Turner	Christopher Barton	Kristoffer Lepsöe
Ralph Purchase (cox)	Jack Dearlove(cox)	Sigurd Monssen (cox)
1952 **UNITED STATES** (Navy) 6:25.9	**U.S.S.R.** 6:31.2	**AUSTRALIA** 6:33.1
Frank Shakespeare	Yevgeniy Brago	Robert Tinning
William Fields	Vladimir Rodimushkin	Ernest Chapman
James Dunbar	Aleksey Komarov	Nimrod Greenwood
Richard Murphy	Igor Borisov	Mervyn Finlay
Robert Detweiler	Slava Amiragov	Edward Pain
Henry Proctor	Leonid Gissen	Philip Cayzer
Wayne Frye	Yevgeniy Samsonov	Thomas Chessel
Edward Stevens	Vladimir Krukov	David Anderson
Charles Manring (cox)	Igor Polyakov (cox)	Geoffrey Williamson (cox)

	GOLD	SILVER	BRONZE

	GOLD	SILVER	BRONZE
1956	**UNITED STATES** (Yale Univ.) 6:35.2	**CANADA** 6:37.1	**AUSTRALIA** 6:39.2
	Thomas Charlton	Philip Kueber	Michael Aikman
	David Wight	Richard McClure	David Boykett
	John Cooke	Robert Wilson	Angus Benfield
	Donald Beer	David Helliwell	James Howden
	Caldwell Esselstyn	Donald Pretty	Garth Manton
	Charles Grimes	William McKerlich	Walter Howell
	Richard Wailes	Douglas McDonald	Adrian Monger
	Robert Morey	Lawrence West	Bryan Doyle
	William Becklean (cox)	Carlton Ogawa (cox)	Harold Hewitt (cox)
1960	**GERMANY** 5:57.18	**CANADA** 6:01.52	**CZECHOSLOVAKIA** 6:04.84
	Klaus Bittner	Donald Arnold	Josef Ventus
	Karl-Heinz Hopp	I. Walter d'Hondt	Bohumil Janoušek
	Hans Lenk	Nelson Kuhn	Jan Jindra
	Manfred Rulffs	John Lecky	Jiri Lundák
	Frank Schepke	Lorne Loomer	Stanislav Lusk
	Kraft Schepke	Archibald McKinnon	Václav Pavkovič
	Walter Schröeder	William McKerlich	Ludek Pojezny
	Karl-Heinz von Groddeck	Glen Mervyn	Jan Švéda
	Willi Padge (cox)	Sohen Biln (cox)	Miroslav Koniček (cox)
1964	**UNITED STATES** 6:18.23	**GERMANY** 6:23.29	**CZECHOSLOVAKIA** 6:25.11
	Joseph Amlong	Klaus Aeffke	Petr Čermák
	Thomas Amlong	Klaus Bittner	Jiri Lundák
	Harold Budd	Karl-Heinz von Groddeck	Jan Mrvik
	Emory Clark		Julnis Toček
	Stanley Cwiklinski	Hans-Jürgen Wallbrecht	Josef Ventus
	Hugh Foley	Klaus Behrens	Ludek Pojezny
	William Knecht	Jürgen Schroeder	Bohumil Janoušek
	William Stowe	Jürgen Plagemann	Richard Novy
	Robert Zimonyi (cox)	Horst Meyer	Miroslav Koniček (cox)
		Thomas Ahrens (cox)	
1968	**W. GERMANY** 6:07.00	**AUSTRALIA** 6:07.98	**U.S.S.R.** 6:09.11
	Horst Meyer	Alfred Duval	Zigmas Yukna
	Dirk Schreyer	Michael Morgan	Antanas Bagdonavichus
	Ruediger Henning	Joseph Fazio	Vladimir Sterlik
	Lutz Ulbricht	Peter Dickson	Yozanas Yagelavichus
	Wolfgang Hottenrott	David Douglas	Alexander Matryshkin
	Egbert Hirschfelder	John Ranch	Vitautas Briedis
	Joerg Siebert	Gary Pearce	Valentin Kravtschuk
	Nico Ott	Robert Shirlaw	Victor Suslin
	Gunther Thiersch (cox)	Alan Grover (cox)	Yury Lorentsson (cox)
1972	**NEW ZEALAND** 6:08.94	**UNITED STATES** 6:11.61	**EAST GERMANY** 6:11.67
	Tony Hurt	Lawrence Terry	Hans-Joachim Borzym
	Wybo Veldman	Fritz Hobbs	Joerg Landvoigt
	Dick Joyce	Peter Raymond	Harold Dincke
	John Hunter	Timothy Mickelson	Manfred Schneider
	Lindsay Wilson	Eugene Clapp	Hartmut Schreiber
	Arhol Earl	William Hobbs	Manfred Schmorde
	Trevor Coker	Cleve Livingstone	Bernd Landvoigt
	Gary Robertson	Michael Livingstone	Heinrich Mederow
	Simon C. Dickie (cox)	Paul Hoffman (cox)	Dietmar Schwartz (cox)

1976	EAST GERMANY 5:58.29	GREAT BRITAIN 6:00.82	NEW ZEALAND 6:03.51
	Bernd Baumgart	Richard Lester	Ivan Sutherland
	Gottfried Döhn	John Yallop	Trevor Coker
	Werner Klatt	Timothy Crooks	Peter Dignan
	Hans-Joachim Lück	Hugh Matheson	Lindsay Wilson
	Dieter Wendisch	David Maxwell	Athol Earl
	Roland Kostulski	James Clark	Dave Rodger
	Ulrich Karnatz	Fred Smallbone	Alex McLean
	Karl-Heinz Prudohl	Leonard Robertson	Tony Hurt
	Karl-Heinz Danielowski (cox)	Patrick Sweeney (cox)	Simon Dickie (cox)
1980	EAST GERMANY 5:49.05	GREAT BRITAIN 5:51.92	U.S.S.R. 5:52.66
	Bernd Krauss	Duncan McDougall	Viktor Kokoshkin
	Hans-Peter Koppe	Allan Whitwell	Andrej Tishchenko
	Ulrich Kons	Henry Clay	Aleksandr Tkachenko
	Jorg Friedrich	Chris Mahoney	Ionas Pintskus
	Jens Doberschutz	Andrew Justice	Ionas Normantas
	Ulrich Karnatz	John Pritchard	Andrej Lugin
	Uwe Duhring	Malcolm McGowan	Aleksandr Manzevich
	Bernd Hoing	Richard Stanhope	Igor Maistrenko
	Klaus-Dieter Ludwig (cox)	Colin Moynihan (cox)	Grigori Dmitrenko (cox)
1984	CANADA 5:41.32	USA 5:41.74	AUSTRALIA 5:43.40
	Pat Turner	Walter Lubsen Jr	Craig Muller
	Kevin Neufield	Andrew Sudduth	Clyde Hefer
	Mark Evans	John Terwilliger	Sam Patten
	Grant Main	Christopher Penny	Timothy Willoughby
	Paul Steele	Thomas Darling	Ian Edmunds
	Mike Evans	Earl Borchelt	James Battersby
	Dean Crawford	Charles Clapp	Ion Popa
	Blair Horm	Bruce Ibbetson	Steve Evans
	Brian McMahon	Robert Jaugstetter	Gavin Thredgold

Rowing (Women)

Women's rowing was introduced in 1976 over a course of 1,000 meters. In 1988 the course for women will also be over 2000m, as for the men.

SINGLE SCULLS

1976	Christine Scheiblich (GDR) 4:05.56	Joan Lind (USA) 4:06.21	Elena Antonova (URS) 4:10.24
1980	Sanda Toma (ROM) 3:40.69	Antonina Makhina (URS) 3:41.65	Martina Schroter (GDR) 3:43.54
1984	Valeria Racila (ROM) 3:40.68	Charlotte Geer (USA) 3:43.89	Ann Haesebrouck (BEL) 3:45.72

DOUBLE SCULLS

	GOLD	SILVER	BRONZE
1976	BULGARIA 3:44.36	EAST GERMANY 3:47.86	U.S.S.R. 3:49.93
	Svetla Otzetova	Sabine Jahn	Leonora Kaminskaite
	Zdravka Yordanova	Petra Boesler	Genovate Ramoshkene
1980	U.S.S.R. 3:16.27	EAST GERMANY 3:17.63	RUMANIA 3:18.91
	Elena Khloptseva	Cornelia Linse	Olga Homeghi
	Larisa Popova	Heidi Westphal	Valeria Rosca-Racila
1984	ROMANIA 3:26.75	NETHERLANDS 3:29.13	CANADA 3:29.82
	Marioara Popescu	Greet Hellemans	Daniele Laumann
	Elisabeta Oleniuc	Nicolette Hellemans	Silken Laumann

COXLESS PAIRS

1976	BULGARIA 4:01.22	EAST GERMANY 4:01.64	WEST GERMANY 4:02.35
	Siika Kelbetcheva	Angelika Noack	Edith Eckbauer
	Stoyanka Grouitcheva	Sabine Dahne	Thea Einoeder
1980	EAST GERMANY 3:30.49	POLAND 3:30.95	BULGARIA 3:32.39
	Ute Steindorf	Malgorzata Dluzewska	Siika Barboulova
	Cornelia Klier	Czeslawa Koscianska	Stoyanka Kubatova
1984	ROMANIA 3:32.60	CANADA 3:36.06	WEST GERMANY 3:40.50
	Rodica Arba	Betty Craig	Ellen Becker
	Elena Horvat	Tricia Smith	Iris Volkner

COXED QUADRUPLE SCULLS

1976	EAST GERMANY 3:29.99	U.S.S.R. 3:32.49	RUMANIA 3:32.76
	Anke Borchmann	Anna Kondrachina	Ioana Tudoran
	Jutta Lau	Mira Bryunina	Maria Micsa
	Viola Poley	Larisa Alexandrova	Felicia Afrasiloaia
	Roswitha Zobelt	Galina Ermolaeva	Elisabeta Lazar
	Liane Weigelt (cox)	Nadyezda Chernysheva (cox)	Elena Giurca (cox)
1980	EAST GERMANY 3:15.32	U.S.S.R 3:15.73	BULGARIA 3:16.10
	Sybille Reinhardt	Antonina Pustovit	Mariana Serbezova
	Jutta Ploch	Yelena Matyevskaya	Rumeliana Boneva
	Jutta Lau	Olga Vasilchenko	Dolores Nakova
	Roswitha Zobelt	Nadyezda Lubimova	Ani Bakova
	Liane Buhr (cox)	Nina Cheremisina (cox)	Anka Georgieva (cox)
1984	ROMANIA 3:14.11	USA 3:15.57	DENMARK 3:16.02
	Titie Taran	Anne Marden	Hanne Eriksen
	Anisoara Sorohan	Lisa Rohde	Birgitte Hanel
	Ioana Badea	Joan Lind	Charlotte Koefoed
	Sofia Corban	Virginia Gilder	Bodil Rasmussen
	Ecaterina Oancia	Kelly Rickon	Jette Soeresen

COXED FOURS

1976	EAST GERMANY 3:45.08	BULGARIA 3:48.24	U.S.S.R. 3:49.38
	Karin Metze	Ginka Gurova	Nadyezda Sevostyanova
	Bianka Schwede	Liliana Vasseva	Ludmila Krokhina
	Gabriele Lohs	Reni Yordanova	Galina Mishenina
	Andrea Kurth	Mariika Modeva	Anna Pasokha
	Sabine Hess (cox)	Kapka Gueorguieva (cox)	Lidia Krylova (cox)
1980	EAST GERMANY 3:19.27	BULGARIA 3:20.75	U.S.S.R. 3:20.92
	Ramona Kapheim	Ginka Gurova	Mariya Fadeyeva
	Silvia Frohlich	Mariika Modeva	Galina Sovetnikova
	Angelika Noack	Rita Todorova	Marina Studneva
	Romy Saalfeld	Iskra Velinova	Svetlana Semyonova
	Kristen Wenzel (cox)	Nadelda Filipova (cox)	Nina Cheremisina (cox)
1984	ROMANIA 3:19.30	CANADA 3:21.55	AUSTRALIA 3:23.39
	Florica Lavric	Marilyn Brain	Robyn Grey-Gardner
	Maria Fricioiu	Angie Schneider	Karen Brancourt
	Chira Apostol	Barbara Armbrust	Susan Chapman
	Olga Bularda	Jane Tregunno	Margot Foster
	Viorica Ioja	Lesley Thompson	Susan Lee

GOLD	SILVER	BRONZE
1976 **EAST GERMANY** 3:33.32	**U.S.S.R.** 3:36.17	**UNITED STATES** 3:38.68
Viola Goretzki	Lubov Tatalayeva	Jacqueline Zoch
Christiane Knetsch	Nadyezda Roshchina	Anita DeFrantz
Ilona Richter	Klavdiya Kozenkova	Carie Graves
Brigitte Ahrenholz	Elena Zubko	Marion Greig
Monika Kallies	Olga Kolkova	Anne Warner
Henrietta Ebert	Nelli Tarakanova	Peggy Ann McCarthy
Helma Lehmann	Nadyezda Rozgon	Carol Brown
Irina Muller	Olga Guzenko	Gail Ricketson
Marina Wilke (cox)	Olga Pugovskaya (cox)	Lynn Silliman (cox)
1980 **EAST GERMANY** 3:03.32	**U.S.S.R.** 3:04.39	**RUMANIA** 3:05.63
Martina Boesler	Olga Pivovarova	Angelica Aposteanu
Kersten Neisser	Nina Umanets	Marlena Zagoni
Christiane Kopke	Nadyezda Prischepa	Rodica Frintu
Birgit Schutz	Valentina Zhulina	Florica Bucur
Gabriele Kuhn	Tatyana Stetzenko	Rodica Puscatu
Ilona Richter	Yelena Tereshina	Ana Iliuta
Marita Sandig	Nina Preobrazhenskaya	Maria Constantinescu
Karin Metze	Maria Pazyun	Elena Bondar
Marina Wilke (cox)	Nina Frolova (cox)	Elena Dobritoiu (cox)
1984 **USA** 5:59.80	**ROMANIA** 3:00.87	**NETHERLANDS** 3:02.92
Shyril O'Steen	Doina Balan	Nicolette Hellemans
Harriet Metcalf	Marioara Trasca	Lynda Cornet
Caroll Brewer	Aurora Plesca	Harriet Van Ettekoven
Carie Graves	Aneta Mihaly	Greet Hellemans
Jeanne Flanagan	Adriana Chelariu	Marieke Van
Kristine Norellus	Minaela Armasescu	Drogenbroek
Kristen Thorsness	Camelia Diaconescu	Anne Marie Quist
Kathryn Keeler	Lucia Sauca	Catharina Neelissen
Betsy Beard	Viorica Ioja	Willemien Vaandrager
		Martha Laurijsen

14. Shooting

FREE PISTOL (50 meters)

1896	Summer Paine (USA) 442	Viggo Jensen (DEN) 285	Holger Nielsen (DEN) d.n.a.
1900	Karl Röderer (SUI) 503	Achille Paroche (FRA) 466	Konrad Stäheli (SUI) 453
1904	Event not held		
1906	Georgios Orphanidis (GRE) 221	Jean Fouconnier (FRA) 219	Aristides Rangavis (GRE) 218
1908	Event not held		
1912	Alfred Lane (USA) 499	Peter J. Dolfen (USA) 474	Charles E. Stewart (GBR) 470
1920	Karl T. Frederick (USA) 496	Afranio da Costa (BRA) 489	Alfred P. Lane (USA) 481
1924–1932	Event not held		
1936	Torsten Ullmann (SWE) 559	Erich Krempel (GER) 544	Charles des Jammonières
1948	Edwin Vazquez Cam (PER) 545	Rudolf Schnyder (SUI) 539	Torsten Ullmann (SWE) 539

1952	Huelet Benner (USA) 553	Angel Léon de Gozalo (ESP) 550	Ambrus Balogh (HUN) 549
1956	Pentti Linnosvuo (FIN) 556	Makhmud Oumarov (URS) 556	Offutt Pinion (USA) 551
1960	Aleksey Gushchin (URS) 560	Makhmud Oumarov (URS) 552	Yoshihisa Yoshikawa (JPN) 552
1964	Väinö Markkanen (FIN) 560	Franklin Green (USA) 557	Yoshihisa Yoshikawa (JPN) 554
1968	Grigory Kossykh (URS) 562	Heinz Mertel (GER) 562	Harald Vollmar (GDR) 560

	GOLD	SILVER	BRONZE
1972	Ragnar Skanakar (SWE) 567*	Dan Iuga (ROM) 562	Rudolf Dollinger (AUT) 560
1976	Uwe Potteck (GDR) 573*	Harald Vollmar (GDR) 567	Rudolf Dollinger (AUT) 562
1980	Aleksandr Melentev (URS) 581*	Harald Vollmar (GDR) 568	Lubtcho Diakov (BUL) 565
1984	Haifeng Xu (CHN) 566	Ragnar Skanaker (SWE) 565	Yifu Wang (CHN) 564

SMALL-BORE RIFLE—PRONE POSITION

	GOLD	SILVER	BRONZE
1896–1920	Event not held		
1924	Pierre Coquelin de Lisle (FRA) 398	Marcus W. Dinwiddie (USA) 396	Josias Hartmann (SUI) 394
1928	Event not held		
1932	Bertil Rönnmark (SWE) 294	Gustavo Huet (MEX) 294	Zoltán Hradetsky-Soós (HUN) 293
1936	Willy Rögeberg (NOR) 300	Ralph Berzsenyi (HUN) 296	Wladyslaw Karás (POL) 296
1948	Arthur Cook (USA) 599	Walter Tomsen (USA) 599	Jonas Jonsson (SWE) 597
1952	Iosif Sarbu (ROM) 400	Boris Andreyev (URS) 400	Arthur Jackson (USA) 399
1956	Gerald Rouellette (CAN) 600[1]	Vasiliy Borissov (URS) 599	Gilmour S. Boa (CAN) 598
1960	Peter Kohnke (GER) 590	James Hill (USA) 589	Enrico Forcella Pelliccione (VEN) 587
1964	László Hammerl (HUN) 597	Lones Wigger (USA) 597	Tommy Pool (USA) 596
1968	Jan Kurka (TCH) 598	László Hammerl (HUN) 598	Ian Ballinger (NZL) 597
1972	Ho Jun Li (PRK) 599*	Victor Auer (USA) 598	Nicolae Rotaru (ROM) 598
1976	Karlheinz Smieszek (GER) 599*	Ulrich Lind (GER) 597	Gennadi Lushchikov (URS) 595
1980	Karoly Varga (HUN) 599*	Hellfried Heilfort (GDR) 599*	Petar Zaprianov (BUL) 598
1984	Edward Etzel (USA) 599*	Michel Bury (FRA) 596	Michael Sullivan (GBR) 596

---

[1]Range found to be slightly short—record not allowed.

Lones Wigger (USA) receiving the silver medal for small-bore rifle shooting from the prone position at Tokyo in 1964. He earned a gold medal for small-bore rifle shooting in the three-position event at the same Games.

SMALL-BORE RIFLE—THREE POSITIONS
(prone, kneeling, standing)

GOLD	SILVER	BRONZE
1896–1948 Event not held		
1952 Erling Kongshaug (NOR) 1,164	Vilho Ylönen (FIN) 1,164	Boris Andreyev (URS) 1,163
1956 Anatoliy Bogdanov (URS) 1,172	Otakar Hořínek (TCH) 1,172	Nils J. Sundberg (SWE) 1,167
1960 Viktor Shamburkin (URS) 1,149	Marat Niyasov (URS) 1,145	Klaus Zähringer (GER) 1,139
1964 Lones Wigger (USA) 1,164	Velitchko Khristov (BUL) 1,152	László Hammerl (HUN) 1,151
1968 Bernd Klingner (GER) 1,157	John Writer (USA) 1,156	Vitaly Parkhimovich (URS) 1,154
1972 John Writer (USA) 1,166*	Lanny Bassham (USA) 1,157	Werner Lippoldt (GDR) 1,153
1976 Lanny Bassham (USA), 1,162	Margaret Murdock (USA) 1,162	Werner Seibold (GER) 1,160
1980 Viktor Vlasov (URS) 1,173*	Bernd Hartstein (GDR) 1,166	Sven Johansson (SWE) 1,165
1984 Malcolm Cooper (GBR) 1173*	Daniel Nipkow (SUI) 1163	Alister Allan (GBR) 1162

RAPID-FIRE PISTOL

1896	Jean Phrangoudis (GRE) 344	Georgios Orphanidis (GRE) 249	Holger Nielsen (DEN) d.n.a.
1900	Maurice Larony (FRA) 58	Léon Moreaux (FRA) 57	Eugène Balne (FRA) 57
1904	Event not held		
1906	Maurice Lecoq (FRA) 250	Léon Moreaux (FRA) 249	Aristides Rangavis (GRE) 245
1908	Paul van Asbroeck (BEL) 490	Réginald Storms (BEL) 487	James E. Gorman (USA) 485
1912	Alfred Lane (USA) 287	Paul Palén (SWE) 286	Johan H. von Holst (SWE) 283
1920	Guilherne Paraense (BRA) 274	Raymond C. Bracken (USA) 272	Fritz Zulauf (SUI) 269
1924	H. M. Bailey (USA) 18	Vilhelm Carlberg (SWE) 18	Lennart Hannelius (FIN) 18
1928	Event hot held		
1932	Renzo Morigi (ITA) 36	Heinz Hax (GER) 36	Domenico Matteucci (ITA) 36
1936	Cornelius van Oyen (GER) 36	Heinz Hax (GER) 35	Torsten Ullmann (SWE) 34
1948	Károly Takács (HUN) 580	Carlos E. Diaz Sáenz Valiente (ARG) 571	Sven Lundqvist (SWE) 569
1952	Károly Takács (HUN) 579	Szilárd Kun (HUN) 578	Gheorghe Lichiardopol (ROM) 578
1956	Stefan Petrescu (ROM) 587	Evgeniy Shcherkasov (URS) 585	Gheorghe Lichiardopol (ROM) 581
1960	William McMillan (USA) 587	Pentti Linnosvuo (FIN) 587	Aleksandr Zabelin (URS) 587
1964	Pentti Linnosvuo (FIN) 592	Ion Tripsa (ROM) 591	Lubomi T. Nacovsky (TCH) 590
1968	Jozef Zapedzki (POL) 593	Marcel Rosca (ROM) 591	Renart Suleimanov (URS) 591
1972	Josef Zapedzki (POL) 595*	Ladislav Faita (TCH) 594	Victor Torshin (URS) 593
1976	Norbert Klaar (GDR) 597*	Jurgen Wiefel (GDR) 596	Roberto Ferraris (ITA) 595
1980	Corneliu Ion (ROM) 596	Jurgen Wiefel (GDR) 596	Gerhard Petritsch (AUT) 596
1984	Takeo Kamachi (JPN) 595	Corneliu Ion (ROM) 593	Rauno Bies (FIN) 591

OLYMPIC TRAP SHOOTING

	GOLD	SILVER	BRONZE
1896	Event not held		
1900	Roger de Barbarin (FRA) 17	René Guyot (FRA) 17	Justinien de Clary (FRA) 17
1904	Event not held		
1906	Two events were held under different conditions.		
1908	Walter H. Ewing (CAN) 72	George Beattie (CAN) 60	Alexander Maunder (GBR) 57 Anastassios Metaxas (GRE) 57
1912	James Graham (USA) 96	Alfred Goeldel (GER) 94	Harry Blau (URS) 91
1920	Mark Arie (USA) 95	Frank Troeh (USA) 93	Frank Wright (USA) 87
1924	Gyula Halasy (HUN) 98	Konrad Huber (FIN) 98	Frank Hughes (USA) 97
1928–1948	Event not held		
1952	George P. Généreux (CAN) 192	Knut Holmqvist (SWE) 191	Hans Liljedahl (SWE) 190
1956	Galliano Rossini (ITA) 195	Adam Smelczynski (POL) 190	Alessandro Ciceri (ITA) 188

1960	Ion Dumitrescu (ROM) 192	Galliano Rossini (ITA) 191	Sergey Kalinin (URS) 190
1964	Ennio Mattarelli (ITA) 198	Pavel Senichev (URS) 194	William Morris (USA) 194
1968	J. Robert Braithwaite (GBR) 198	Thomas Garrigus (USA) 196	Kurt Czekalla (GDR) 196
1972	Angelo Scalzone (ITA) 199*	Michel Carrega (FRA) 198	Silvano Basagni (ITA) 195
1976	Donald Haldeman (USA) 190	Armando Silva Marques (POR) 189	Ubaldesc Baldi (ITA) 189
1980	Luciano Giovannetti (ITA) 198	Rustan Yambulatov (URS) 196	Jorg Damme (GDR) 196
1984	Luciano Giovannetti (ITA) 192	Francisco Boza (PER) 192	Daniel Carlisle (USA) 192

SKEET SHOOTING

1896–1964	Event not held		
1968	Evgeny Petrov (URS) 198*	Romano Garagnani (ITA) 198*	Konrad Wirnhier (GER) 198*
1972	Konrad Wirnhier (GER) 195	Evgeny Petrov (URS) 195	Michael Buchheim (GDR) 195
1976	Josef Panacek (TCH) 198	Eric Swinkels (HOL) 198	Wieslaw Gawlikowski (POL) 196
1980	Hans Kjeld Rasmussen (DEN) 196	Lars-Goran Carlsson (SWE) 196	Roberto Castrillo (CUB) 196
1984	Matthew Dryke (USA) 198*	Ole Rasmussen (DEN) 196	Luca Scribani Rossi (ITA) 196

RUNNING GAME TARGET

1896	Event not held		
1900	Louis Debray (FRA) 20	P. Nivet (FRA) 20	de Lambert (FRA) 19
1904–1968	Event not held		
1972	Lakov Zhelezniak (URS) 569*	Hanspeter Bellingrodt (COL) 565	John Kynoch (GBR) 562
1976	Alexander Gazov (URS) 579*	Alexander Kedyarov (URS) 576	Jerzy Greszkiewicz (POL) 571
1980	Igor Sokolov (URS) 589*	Thomas Pfeffer (GDR) 589*	Alexandr Gazov (URS) 587
1984	Yuwei Li (CHN) 587	Helmut Bellingrodt (COL) 584	Shiping Huang (CHN) 581

AIR RIFLE

1984	Philippe Heberle (FRA) 589*	Andreas Kronthaler (AUT) 587	Barry Dagger (GBR) 587

Shooting (Women)

SPORT PISTOL

1984	Linda Thom (CAN) 585*	Ruby Fox (USA) 585*	Patricia Dench (AUS) 583

STANDARD RIFLE

1984	Xiaoxuan Wu (CHN) 581*	Ulrike Holmer (FRG) 578	Wanda Jewell (USA) 578

AIR RIFLE

1984	Pat Spurgin (USA) 393*	Edith Gufler (ITA) 391	Xiaoxuan Wu (CHN) 389

15. Soccer

There was no Soccer event in 1896. In the 1900, 1904 and 1906 Games most of the medal winning teams were merely clubs rather than strictly international teams.

	GOLD	SILVER	BRONZE
1896	Event not held		

	GOLD	SILVER	BRONZE
1908	**GREAT BRITAIN**	**DENMARK**	**NETHERLANDS**
	Harold P. Bailey	Ludwig Drescher	Reinier B. Beeuwkes
	Walter S. Corbett	Charles Buchwald	Karel Heijting
	Herbert Smith	Harald Hansen	Lou Otten
	Kenneth R. G. Hunt	Harald Bohr	Johan W. E. Sol
	Frederick W. Chapman	Christian Middelboe	Johannes M. de Korver
	Robert M. Hawkes	Nils Middelboe	Emil G. Mundt
	Arthur Berry	Oscar Nielsen-Nörland	Jan H. Welcker
	Vivian J. Woodward	August Lindgreen	Edu Snethlage
	Harold S. Stapley	Sophus Nielsen	Gerard S. Reeman
	Claude H. Parnell	Vilhelm Wolffhagen	Jan Thomée
	Harold P. Hardman	Björn Rasmussen	Georges F. de
		Marius Andersen	Bruyn Kops
		Johannes Gandil	Johan A. F. Kok

	GOLD	SILVER	BRONZE
1912	**GREAT BRITAIN**	**DENMARK**	**NETHERLANDS**
	Ronald G. Brebner	Sophus Hansen	Marius J. Göbel
	Thomas C. Burn	Nils Middelboe	David Wijnfeldt
	Arthur E. Knight	Harald Hansen	Piet Bouman
	Douglas McWhirter	Charles Buchwald	Gerardus Fortgens
	Horace C. Littlewort	Emil Jörgensen	Constant W. Feith
	James Dines	Paul Berth	Nicolaas de Wolff
	Arthur Berry	Oscar Nielsen-Nörland	Dick N. Lotsy
	Vivian J. Woodward	Axel Thufason	Johannes W. Boutmy
	Harold A. Walden	Anton Olsen	Jan G. van Bredakolff
	Gordon R. Hoare	Sophus Nielsen	Huug F. de Groot
	Ivan G. A. Sharpe	Vilhelm Wolffhagen	Caesar H. ten Cate
	Edward Hanney	Askel M. Petersen	Jan van der Sluis
	Harold Stamper	Hjalmar Christoffersen	Jan Vos
	E. Gordon D. Wright	Poul Nielsen	Nico J. Bouvy
		Ivar L. Seidelin-Neilsen	Johannes M. de Korver

	GOLD	SILVER	BRONZE
1916	Event not held		

	GOLD	SILVER	BRONZE
1920	**BELGIUM**	**SPAIN**	**NETHERLANDS**
	Jan de Bie	Ricardo Zamora	Robert McNeill
	Armand Swartenbroeks	Pedro Vallana	Henri L. B. Denis
	Oscar Verbeek	Mariano Arrate	Leonard F. G. Bosschart
	Joseph Musch	Juan Artola	Frederick C. Kuipers
	Emile Hanse	Agustin Sancho	Hermanus H. Steeman
	André Fierens	Ramón Eguiazábal	Johannes D. de Natris
	Louis van Hege	Francisco	Jacob E. Bulder
	Robert Coppée	Pagazaurtundúa	Bernardus Groosjohan
	Mathiew Bragard	Felix Sesúmaga	Jan L. van Dort
	Henri Larnoe	Patricio Arbolaza	Oscar E. van Rappard
	Désiré Bastin	Rafael Moreno	Herman C. G. van
	Fernand Nisot	Domingo Acedo	Heijden
	Georges Hebden	José Samitier	Bernard W. J. Verweij
	Félix Balyu	José M. Belausteguigoitia	Evert J. Bulder
		Louis Otero	Adrianus G. Bieshaar
		Joaquin Vázquez	
		Ramón Moncho Gil	
		Sabino Bilbao	
		Silverio Izaguirre	

GOLD	SILVER	BRONZE
1924		
URUGUAY	**SWITZERLAND**	**SWEDEN**
Andrés Mazali	Hans Pulver	Sigfrid Lindberg
José Nasazzi	Adolphe Reymond	Axel Alfredsson
Pedro Arispe	Rudolf Ramseyer	Fritjof Hillén
José L. Andrade	August Oberhauser	Sven Friberg
José Vidal	Paul Schmiedlin	Gustaf Carlson
Alfredo Ghierra	Aron Pollitz	Harry Sundberg
Santos Urdinarán	Karl Ehrenbolger	Charles Brommesson
Hector Scarone	Robert Pache	Sven Rydell
Pedro Petrone	Walter Dietrich	Per Kaufeldt
Pedro Céa	Max Abbeglen	Albin Dahl
Alfredo Romano	Paul Fässler	Rudolf Kock
Umberto Tomasina	Paul Sturzenegger	Gunnar Holmberg
Juan Naya	Edmond Kramer	Evert Lundqvist
Alfredo Zibechi	Félix Bédouret	Tore Keller
Antonio Urdinarán	Adolphe Mengotti	Thorsten Svensson
		Konrad Hirsch
		Sven Linqvist
		Sten Mellgren
1928		
URUGUAY	**ARGENTINA**	**ITALY**
Andrés Mazali	Angel Bossio	Giampiero Combi
José Nasazzi	Fernando Paternoster	Delfo Bellini
Pedro Arispe	Ludovico Bidoglio	Umberto Caligaris
José L. Andrade	Juan Evaristo	Alfredo Pitto
Lorenzo Fernández	Luis F. Monto	Fulvio Bernardini
Alvaro Gestido	Segundo Medici	Pietro Genovesi
Santos Urdináran	Raimundo Orsi	Adolfo Baloncieri
Hector Castro	Enrique Gainzarain	Elvio Banchero
Pedro Petrone	Manuel Ferreira	Angelo Schiavio
Pedro Céa	Domingo Tarasconi	Mario Magnozzi
Hector Scarone	Adolfo Carricaberri	Virgilio F. Levratto
Antonio Campolo	Feliciano A. Perducca	Giovanni Deprà
Juan Arremón	Saúl Calandra	Antonio Janni
René Borjas	Roberto Cherro	Silvio Pietroboni
Juan Piriz	Rodolfo Orlandini	Enrico Rivolta
Adhemar Canavesi	Octavio Diaz	Virginio Rosetta
Roberto Figueroa		Gino Rossetti
1932 Event not held		
1936		
ITALY	**AUSTRIA**	**NORWAY**
Bruno Venturini	Eduard Kainberger	Henry Johansen
Alfredo Foni	Ernst Künz	Nils Eriksen
Pietro Rava	Martin Kargl	Öivind Holmsen
Giuseppe Baldo	Anton Krenn	Frithjof Ulleberg
Achille Piccini	Karl Wahlmüller	Jörgen Juve
Ugo Locatelli	Max Hofmeister	Rolf Holmberg
Annibale Frossi	Walter Werginz	Magdalon Monsen
Libero Marchini	Adolf Laudon	Reidar Kvammen
Sergio Bertoni	Klement Steinmetz	Alf Martinsen
Carlo Biagi	Karl Kainberger	Odd Frantzen
Francesco Gabriotti	Franz Fuchsberger	Arne Brustad
Luigi Scarabello	Josef Kitzmüller	Frederik Horn
Giulio Cappelli	Franz Mandl	Sverre Hansen
Alfonso Negro		Magnar Isaksen

	GOLD	SILVER	BRONZE
1948	**SWEDEN**	**YUGOSLAVIA**	**DENMARK**
	Torsten Lindberg	Ljubomir Lovrič	Ejgil Nielsen
	Knut Nordahl	Miroslav Brozovič	Viggo Jensen
	Erik Nilsson	Branislav Stankovič	Knud B. Overgaard
	Birger Rosengren	Zlatko Cajkoviski	Axel Pilmark
	Bertil Nordahl	Miodrag Jovanovič	Dion Örnvold
	Sune Andersson	Aleksandar Atanakovič	Ivan Jensen
	Kjell Rosén	Zvonko Cimermančič	Johannes Plöger
	Gunnar Grén	Rajko Mitič	Knud Lundberg
	Gunnar Nordahl	Stejpan Bobek	Carl A. Praest
	Henry Carlsson	Željko Čajkovski	John Hansen
	Nils Liedholm	Bernard Vukas	Jörgen Sörensen
	Börje Leander	Franjo Šoštarič	Holger Seebach
		Prvoslav Mihajlovič	Karl Aage Hansen
		Franjo Völfl	
		Kosta Tomasevič	

This hard-fought match resulted in a bronze medal for Denmark (dark shirts) in the 1948 Games.

	GOLD	SILVER	BRONZE
1952	**HUNGARY**	**YUGOSLAVIA**	**SWEDEN**
	Gyula Grosics	Vladimir Beara	Karl Svensson
	Jenö Buzánszky	Branko Stankovič	Lennart Samuelsson
	Gyula Lóránt	Tomislav Crnkovič	Erik Nilsson
	Mihály Lantos	Zlatko Cajkovski	Olle Åhlund
	József Bozsik	Ivan Horvat	Bengt Gustavsson
	Nándor Hidegkuti	Vujadin Boškov	Gösta Lindh
	Sándor Kocsis	Tihomir Ognjanov	Sylve Bengtsson
	Pétér Palotás	Rajko Mitič	Gösta Löfgren
	Ferenc Puskás	Bernard Vukas	Ingvar Rydell
	Zoltán Csibor	Stjepan Bobek	Yngve Brodd
	József Zakariás	Branko Zebec	Gösta Sandberg
	Jenö Dalnoki		Holger Hansson
	Imre Kovács		
	László Budai		
	Lajos Csordás		

GOLD	SILVER	BRONZE
1956 **U.S.S.R.**	**YUGOSLAVIA**	**BULGARIA**
Lev Yashin	Petar Radenkovič	Georgi Naydenov
Boris Kuznyetsov	Mladen Koščak	Kiril Rakarov
Mikhail Ogognikov	Nikola Radovič	Yosif Yosifor
Aleksey Paramanov	Ivan Santek	Stefan Stefanov
Anatoliy Bashashkin	Ljubiša Spajič	Manol Manolov
Igor Netto	Dobrošlav Krstič	Nikola Kovatchev
Boris Tatushin	Dragoslav Sekularac	Gavril Stojanov
Anatoliy Issayev	Zlatko Papec	Miltcho Goranov
Edouard Streltsov	Sava Antič	Panayot Panayotov
Sergey Salnikov	Todor Vaselinovič	Ivan Kolev
Anatoliy Ilin	Muhamed Mujič	Kroum Yanev
Anatoliy Maslenkin	Blagoje Vidinič	Todor Diyev
Nikita Simonian	Ibrahim Biogradlič	Dimiter Milanov
Nikolay Tyshenko	Luka Liposinovič	Georgy Dimitrov
Vladimir Ryjkin		
Iosif Betsa		
Valentin Ivanov		
Boris Rasinsky		
1960 **YUGOSLAVIA**	**DENMARK**	**HUNGARY**
Blagoje Vidinič	Poul Andersen	Gábor Török
Vladimir Djurkovic	Poul Jensen	Zoltán Dudás
Fahrudin Jusufi	Bent Hansen	Jenö Dalnoki
Ante Zanetic	Hans C. Nielsen	Ernö Sölymösi
Novak Roganovič	Flemming Nielsen	Pál Várhidi
Želijko Perušič	Poul Pedersen	Ferenc Kovács
Andreja Ankovič	Tommy Troelsen	Imre Sátori
Zelijko Matuš	Harald Nielsen	János Göröcs
Milan Galič	Henning Enoksen	Flórián Albert
Tomislav Knez	Jörn Sörensen	Pál Orosz
Borivoje Kostič	Henry Fröm	János Dunai
Velimir Sombolac	John Danielsen	Dezsö Novák
Alexsandar Kozlina		Oszkár Vilezsál
Dušan Maravič		Gyula Rákosi
Silvester Takač		Lajos Faragó
Milutin Soskič		László Pál
		Tibor Pál
1964 **HUNGARY**	**CZECHOSLOVAKIA**	**GERMANY**
Antal Szentmihàlyi	František Schmucker	Hans J. Heinsch
Dezsö Novák	Anton Urban	Peter Rock
Kálmán Ihász	Karel Z. Pičman	Manfred Geisler
Árpád Orban	Josef Vojta	Herbert Pankau
Ferenc Nógrádi	Vladimir Weiss	Manfred Walter
János Farkas	Jan Geleta	Gerhard Koerner
Tibor Csernai	Jan Bramovsky	Hermann Stoeker
Ferenc Bene	Ivan Mráz	Otto Fraessdorf
Imre Komora	Karel Lichtnégl	Henning Frenzel
Gustáv Szepesi	Vojtech Masny	Jürgen Noeldner
Sándor Katona	František Valošek	Eberhard Vogel
József Gelei	Anton Svajlen	Horst Weigang
Károly Palotai	Karel Knesl	Klaus Urbánczyk
Zoltán Varga	Stefan Matlák	Klaus-Dieter Seehaus
	Karel Nepomucky	Werner Unger
	Ludevit Cvet	Dieter Engelhardt
	František Knebort	Wolfgang Bartels
		Bernd Bauchspiess
		Klaus Lisiewicz

TIMETABLE OF THE XVth
WINTER OLYMPIC GAMES—CALGARY, CANADA
(FEBRUARY 13–28 1988)

Event	Venue	Date
OPENING CEREMONY	McMahon Stadium	February 13

Ice Hockey

Preliminary matches	Saddledome	February 13
Preliminary matches	Saddledome	February 14
Preliminary matches	Saddledome	February 15
Preliminary matches	Saddledome	February 16
Preliminary matches	Saddledome	February 17
Preliminary matches	Saddledome	February 18
Preliminary matches	Saddledome	February 19
Preliminary matches	Saddledome	February 20
Preliminary matches	Saddledome	February 21
Preliminary matches	Saddledome	February 22
Preliminary matches	Stampede Corral	February 13
Preliminary matches	Stampede Corral	February 15
Preliminary matches	Stampede Corral	February 16
Preliminary matches	Stampede Corral	February 17
Preliminary matches	Stampede Corral	February 18
Preliminary matches	Stampede Corral	February 19
Preliminary matches	Stampede Corral	February 20
Preliminary matches	Stampede Corral	February 21
Medal Round	Saddledome	February 24
Medal Round	Saddledome	February 25
Medal Round	Saddledome	February 26
Medal Round	Saddledome	February 27
Bronze Medal Game	Saddledome	February 28
Final Game	Saddledome	February 28

Figure Skating

Pairs, Short programme	Stampede Corral	February 14
Pairs, Free programme	Saddledome	February 16
Men's, Short programme	Stampede Corral	February 18
Men's, Free programme	Saddledome	February 20
Dance, Compulsory programme	Stampede Corral	February 21
Dance, Original Set Pattern	Saddledome	February 22
Dance, Free programme	Saddledome	February 23
Ladies', Short programme	Saddledome	February 25
Ladies', Free programme	Saddledome	February 27
Exhibition	Stampede Corral	February 28

Speed Skating

Men's 500m	Olympic Oval	February 14
Men's 5000m	Olympic Oval	February 17
Men's 1000m	Olympic Oval	February 18
Men's 1500m	Olympic Oval	February 20
Men's 10000m	Olympic Oval	February 21
Ladies' 500m	Olympic Oval	February 22
Ladies' 3000m	Olympic Oval	February 23
Ladies' 1000m	Olympic Oval	February 26
Ladies' 1500m	Olympic Oval	February 27
Ladies' 5000m	Olympic Oval	February 28

Bobsleigh

2-man	Canada Olympic Park	February 20
2-man	Canada Olympic Park	February 21
4-man	Canada Olympic Park	February 27
4-man	Canada Olympic Park	February 28

Luge

Men's, 1st & 2nd runs	Canada Olympic Park	February 14
Men's, 3rd & 4th runs	Canada Olympic Park	February 15
Ladies' 1st & 2nd runs	Canada Olympic Park	February 16
Ladies' 3rd & 4th runs	Canada Olympic Park	February 17
Doubles 1st & 2nd runs	Canada Olympic Park	February 19

Ski Jumping

70m hill	Canada Olympic Park	February 14
90m hill, team	Canada Olympic Park	February 17
90m hill	Canada Olympic Park	February 20

Nordic Skiing

Ladies' 10km	Canmore Nordic Centre	February 14
Men's 30km	Canmore Nordic Centre	February 15
Ladies' 5km	Canmore Nordic Centre	February 17
Men's 15km	Canmore Nordic Centre	February 19
Ladies' 4 × 5km relay	Canmore Nordic Centre	February 21
Men's 4 × 10km relay	Canmore Nordic Centre	February 22
Ladies' 20km	Canmore Nordic Centre	February 25
Men's 50km	Canmore Nordic Centre	February 27

Nordic Combined

70m hill, team	Canada Olympic Park	February 23
3 × 10km relay, team	Canada Olympic Park	February 24
70m hill, individual	Canada Olympic Park	February 27
15km individual	Canada Olympic Park	February 28

Biathlon

20km individual	Canmore Nordic Centre	February 20
10km individual	Canmore Nordic Centre	February 23
4 × 7.5km relay	Canmore Nordic Centre	February 26

Alpine Skiing

Men's Downhill	Nakiska, Mt Allan	February 14
Men's Combined Downhill	Nakiska, Mt Allan	February 15
Men's Combined Slalom	Nakiska, Mt Allan	February 16
Ladies' Downhill	Nakiska, Mt Allan	February 18
Ladies' Combined Downhill	Nakiska, Mt Allan	February 19
Ladies' Combined Slalom	Nakiska, Mt Allan	February 20
Men's Super Giant Slalom	Nakiska, Mt Allan	February 21
Ladies' Super Giant Slalom	Nakiska, Mt Allan	February 22
Ladies' Giant Slalom	Nakiska, Mt Allan	February 24
Men's Giant Slalom	Nakiska, Mt Allan	February 25
Ladies' Slalom	Nakiska, Mt Allan	February 26
Men's Slalom	Nakiska, Mt Allan	February 27

Freestyle Skiing (Demonstration Sport)

Aerials	Canada Olympic Park	February 21
Moguls	Canada Olympic Park	February 22
Ballet	Canada Olympic Park	February 25

Curling (Demonstration Sport)

Preliminary rounds	Max Bell Arena	February 15
Preliminary rounds	Max Bell Arena	February 16
Preliminary rounds	Max Bell Arena	February 17
Preliminary rounds	Max Bell Arena	February 18
Semi-finals	Max Bell Arena	February 20
Final	Max Bell Arena	February 21

Short Track Speed Skating (Demonstration Sport)

Men's 1500m] Ladies' 500m]	Father David Bauer Arena	February 22
Men's 500m] Ladies' 1500m]	Father David Bauer Arena	February 23
Men's 1000m] Ladies' 3000m] Relay heats]	Father David Bauer Arena	February 24
Men's 3000m] Ladies' 1000m] Relay Final]	Father David Bauer Arena	February 25

Disabled Skiing (Exhibition)

Giant Slalom	Canada Olympic Park	February 16
5km Cross-country	Canada Olympic Park	February 17
CLOSING CEREMONY	McMahon Stadium	February 28

TIMETABLE OF THE XXIVth OLYMPIC GAMES—SEOUL, KOREA (SEPTEMBER 17–OCTOBER 2 1988)

Some of the data is still provisional due to negotiations with the People's Republic of Korea which have not yet been resolved.

Archery (at Hwarang Archery Field)

Women 70m, Men 90m	September 27
Women 60m, Men 70m	September 27
Women 50m, Men 50m	September 28
Women 30m, Men 30m	September 28
Women 70m, 60m, 50m, 30m	September 29
Men 90m, 70m, 50m, 30m	September 29
Women and Men, Semi-finals	September 30
Women and Men, Finals	September 30
Women and Men, Team Contests	October 1
Women and Men, Team Finals	October 1

Basketball (at Changchoong Gymnasium)

Preliminary games, Men	September 17
Preliminary games, Men	September 18
Preliminary games, Women	September 19
Preliminary games, Men	September 20
Preliminary games, Men	September 21
Preliminary games, Women	September 22
Preliminary games, Men	September 23
Preliminary games, Men	September 24
Preliminary games, Women	September 25
Preliminary games, Men	September 26
Preliminary games, Women	September 27
Preliminary games, Men	September 28
Placings match (7-8 places), Women Bronze medal match, Women	September 28
Placings match (5-6 places), Women Final, Women	September 29
Placings match (11-12 places), Men Placings match (9-10 places), Men Placings match (7-8 places), Men Bronze medal match, Men	September 29
Placings match (5-6 places), Men Final, Men	September 30

Boxing (at Chamshil Gymnasium)

Preliminary bouts	September 17
Preliminary bouts	September 18
Preliminary bouts	September 19
Preliminary bouts	September 20

Preliminary bouts	September 21
Preliminary bouts	September 22
Preliminary bouts	September 23
Preliminary bouts	September 24
Preliminary bouts	September 25
Preliminary bouts	September 26
Quarter-finals	September 27
Quarter-finals	September 28
Semi-finals	September 29
Finals (6)	October 1
Finals (6)	October 2

Canoeing (at Han River Regatta Course)

500m heats, Men & Women (K1,C1,K2,C2)	September 26
500m repechages, Men & Women (K1,C1,K2,C2)	September 26
1000m heats, Men (K1,C1,K2,C2,K4)	September 27
500m heats & repechages, Women (K4)	September 27
1000m repechages, Men	September 27
500m semi-finals, Men & Women (K1,C1,K2,C2)	September 28
1000m semi-finals, Men (K1,C1,K2,C2,K4)	September 29
500m semi-finals, Women (K4)	September 29
500m Finals, Men & Women (K1,C1,K2,C2)	September 30
500m Finals, Women (K4)	October 1
1000m Finals, Men (K1,C1,K2,C2,K4)	October 1

Cycling (at Sports Complex Velodrome)

100km Team Time Trial, Final	September 18
Individual Pursuit—qualification	September 20
1000m Time Trial, Final	September 20
Sprint—qualification, Men & Women	September 21
Individual Pursuit—⅛ final	September 21
Individual Points Race, Men—qualification	September 21
Individual Pursuit—Quarter-finals	September 21
Sprint—⅛ finals, Men & Women	September 22
Individual Pursuit—Semi-finals	September 22
Individual Points Race—qualification	September 22
Sprint—quarter-finals, Men & Women	September 22
Individual Pursuit—Final	September 22
Team Pursuit—qualification	September 23
Sprint—semi-finals, Men & Women	September 23
Team Pursuit—quarter-finals	September 23
Team Pursuit—semi-finals	September 24
Sprint—Finals, Men & Women	September 24

Team Pursuit—Final	September 24
Individual Points Race—Final	September 24
Individual Road Race, Women—Final	September 25
Individual Road Race, Men—Final	September 26

Equestrianism (at Nam Seoul Equestrian Arena)

Three-day event, Dressage	September 19
Three-day event, Dressage	September 20
Three-day event, Endurance	September 21
Three-day event, Jumping	September 22
Training Jumping competition	September 23
Qualifying for Individual Jumping	September 24
Team Dressage	September 25
Team Dressage	September 26
Team Jumping	September 27
Individual Dressage	September 28
Qualifying for Individual Jumping	September 30
Individual Jumping	October 2

Fencing (at Sports Complex Gymnasium)

Foil, Individual, Men—Preliminaries	September 20
Foil, Individual, Women—Preliminaries	September 21
Foil, Individual, Men—Direct Elimination	September 21
Foil, Individual, Men—Final	September 21
Sabre, Individual, Men—Preliminaries	September 22
Foil, Individual, Women—Direct Elimination	September 22
Foil, Individual, Women—Final	September 22
Epee, Individual, Men—Preliminaries	September 23
Sabre, Individual, Men—Direct Elimination	September 23
Sabre, Individual, Men—Final	September 23
Epee, Individual, Men—Direct Elimination	September 24
Epee, Individual, Men—Final	September 24
Foil Team, Men—Preliminaries	September 26
Foil Team, Women—Preliminaries	September 27
Foil Team, Men—Direct Elimination	September 27
Foil Team, Men—Final	September 27
Sabre Team, Men—Preliminaries	September 28
Foil Team, Women—Direct Elimination	September 28
Foil Team, Women—Final	September 28
Epee Team, Men—Preliminaries	September 29
Sabre Team, Men—Direct Elimination	September 29
Sabre Team, Men—Final	September 29
Epee Team, Men—Direct Elimination	September 30
Epee Team, Men—Final	September 30

Football (Soccer) (at Seoul Municipal Stadium)

| Preliminary matches (4) | September 17 |
| Preliminary matches (4) | September 18 |

Preliminary matches (4)	September 19
Preliminary matches (4)	September 20
Preliminary matches (4)	September 21
Preliminary matches (4)	September 22
Quarter-finals (2)	September 24
Quarter-finals (2)	September 25
Semi-finals (2)	September 27
3rd and 4th place match	September 30
Final	October 1

Gymnastics (at Sports Complex Gymnasium)

Compulsory Exercises, Team, Men	September 18
Compulsory Exercises, Team, Women	September 19
Optional Exercises, Team, Men	September 20
Optional Exercises, Team, Women	September 21
All-around Finals, Men	September 22
All-around Finals, Women	September 23
Apparatus Finals, Men	September 24
Apparatus Finals, Women	September 25
Rhythmic preliminaries, Women	September 28
Rhythmic preliminaries, Women	September 29
Rhythmic Finals, Women	September 30

Handball (at Suwon Centre)

Preliminary matches, Men	September 20
Preliminary matches, Women	September 21
Preliminary matches, Men	September 22
Preliminary matches, Women	September 23
Preliminary matches, Men	September 24
Preliminary matches, Women	September 25
Preliminary matches, Men	September 26
Final Round, Women	September 27
Preliminary matches, Men	September 28
Final Round, Women	September 29
Final, Women	September 29
11th & 12th place match, Men	September 30
9th & 10th place match, Men	September 30
7th & 8th place match, Men	September 30
5th & 6th place match, Men	September 30
3rd & 4th place match, Men	October 1
Final, Men	October 1

Hockey (Field) (at Songnam Stadium)

Preliminary matches, Men	September 18
Preliminary matches, Men	September 20
Preliminary matches, Women	September 21
Preliminary matches, Men	September 22

Preliminary matches, Women	September 23
Preliminary matches, Men	September 24
Preliminary matches, Women	September 25
Preliminary matches, Men	September 26
Match 4A—3B, Women	September 27
Match 3A—4B, Women	September 27
Semi-final 1A—2B, Women	September 27
Semi-final 1B—2A, Women	September 27
Match 5A—6B, Men	September 28
Match 5B—6A, Men	September 28
Match 3A—4B, Men	September 28
Match 3B—4A, Men	September 28
Semi-final 1B—2A, Men	September 28
Semi-final 1A—2B, Men	September 28
5th & 6th place match, Women	September 29
7th & 8th place match, Women	September 29
9th & 10th place match, Men	September 29
11th & 12th place match, Men	September 29
5th & 6th place match, Men	September 30
7th & 8th place match, Men	September 30
3rd & 4th place match, Women	September 30
Final, Women	September 30
3rd & 4th place match, Men	October 1
Final, Men	October 1

Judo (At Yongin Judo School)

Extra Lightweight (60kg)	September 25
Half Lightweight (65kg)	September 26
Lightweight (71kg)	September 27
Half Middleweight (78kg)	September 28
Middleweight (86kg)	September 29
Half Heavyweight (95kg)	September 30
Heavyweight (95kg+)	October 1

Modern Pentathlon (at various sites)

Riding at Seoul Equestrian Park	September 18
Fencing at Olympic Park	September 19
Swimming at Olympic Park	September 20
Shooting at Taenung Shooting Range	September 21
Cross-country at Taenung Country Club	September 22

Rowing (at Han River Regatta Course)

Elimination heats, Men & Women	September 19
Elimination heats, Men & Women	September 20
Repechages, Men & Women	September 21
Semi-finals, Men & Women (if necessary)	September 22
7th-12th place Finals, Men & Women	September 23
Coxed Fours, Women—Final	September 24
Double Sculls, Women—Final	September 24

Coxless Pairs, Women—Final	September 24
Coxed Fours, Men—Final	September 24
Double Sculls, Men—Final	September 24
Coxless Pairs, Men—Final	September 24
Single Sculls, Men—Final	September 24
Single Sculls, Women—Final	September 25
Quadruple Sculls, Women—Final	September 25
Eights, Women—Final	September 25
Coxed Pairs, Men—Final	September 25
Coxless Fours, Men—Final	September 25
Quadruple Sculls, Men—Final	September 25
Eights, Men—Final	September 25

Shooting (at Taerung International Shooting Range)

Air Rifle, Women	September 18
Free Pistol, Men	September 18
Trap (75 targets)	September 18
Small-bore Rifle, English match, Men	September 19
Sport Pistol, Women	September 19
Trap (75 targets)	September 19
Air Rifle, Men	September 20
Trap (50 targets)	September 20
Air Pistol, Women	September 21
Standard Rifle, Women	September 21
Rapid Fire Pistol, Men (30 shots)	September 22
Skeet (75 targets)	September 22
Small-bore Rifle, 3 pos, Men	September 22
Running Game Target, Men (30 shots)	September 22
Rapid Fire Pistol, Men (30 shots)	September 23
Running Game Target, Men (30 shots)	September 23
Skeet (75 targets)	September 23
Air Pistol, Men	September 24
Skeet (50 targets)	September 24

Swimming (at Sports Complex Pool)

Heats—100m freestyle, Women	September 18
Heats—100m breaststroke, Men	September 18
Heats—400m I medley, Women	September 18
Heats—200m freestyle, Men	September 18
Final—100m freestyle, Women	September 19
Final—100m breaststroke, Men	September 19
Final—400m I medley, Women	September 19
Final—200m freestyle, Men	September 19
Heats—100m butterfly, Men	September 20
Heats—200m freestyle, Women	September 20
Heats—400m I medley, Men	September 20
Heats—200m breaststroke, Women	September 20
Heats—40 × 200m freestyle, Men	September 20
Final—100m butterfly, Men	September 21
Final—200m freestyle, Women	September 21
Final—400m I medley, Men	September 21
Final—200m breaststroke, Women	September 21

Final—4 × 200m freestyle, Men	September 21
Heats—400m freestyle, Women	September 22
Heats—100m freestyle, Men	September 22
Heats—100m backstroke, Women	September 22
Heats—200m backstroke, Men	September 22
Heats—4 × 100m freestyle, Women	September 22
Final—400m freestyle, Women	September 22
Final—100m freestyle, Men	September 22
Final—100m backstroke, Women	September 22
Final—200m backstroke, Men	September 22
Final—4 × 100m freestyle, Women	September 22
Heats—400m freestyle, Men	September 23
Heats—100m butterfly, Women	September 23
Heats—200m breaststroke, Men	September 23
Heats—100m breaststroke, Women	September 23
Heats—4 × 100m freestyle, Men	September 23
Heats—800m freestyle, Women	September 23
Final—400m freestyle, Men	September 23
Final—100m butterfly, Women	September 23
Final—200m breaststroke, Men	September 23
Final—100m breaststroke, Women	September 23
Final—4 × 100m freestyle, Men	September 23
Heats—200m I medley, Women	September 24
Heats—200m butterfly, Men	September 24
Heats—100m backstroke, Men	September 24
Heats—4 × 100m medley, Women	September 24
Heats—50m freestyle, Men	September 24
Heats—1500m freestyle, Men	September 24
Final—200m I medley, Women	September 24
Final—200m butterfly, Men	September 24
Final—50m freestyle, Men	September 24
Final—800m freestyle, Women	September 24
Final—100m backstroke, Men	September 24
Final—4 ×10m medley, Women	September 24
Heats—200m I medley, Men	September 25
Heats—200m butterfly, Women	September 25
Heats—200m backstroke, Women	September 25
Heats—4 × 100m medley, Men	September 25
Heats—50m freestyle, Women	September 25
Final—200m I medley, Men	September 25
Final—200m butterfly, Women	September 25
Final—50m freestyle, Women	September 25
Final—1500m freestyle, Men	September 25
Final—200m backstroke, Women	September 25
Final—4 × 100m medley, Men	September 25

Diving

Platform—preliminaries, Women	September 17
Platform—Final, Women	September 18
Springboard—preliminaries, Men	September 19
Springboard—Final, Men	September 20
Springboard—preliminaries, Women	September 26
Springboard—Final, Women	September 27
Platform—preliminaries, Men	September 28
Platform—Final, Men	September 29

Synchronized Swimming

Solo—preliminaries	September 26
Duet—preliminaries	September 27
Figures	September 28
Solo—Final	September 30
Duet—Final	October 1

Water Polo

Preliminary rounds	September 21
Preliminary rounds	September 22
Preliminary rounds	September 23
Final round (3 games)	September 26
Final round (3 games)	September 27
Final round (3 games)	September 30
Final round (3 games)	October 1

Table Tennis (at Seoul University Gymnasium)

Singles, Men—preliminary matches	September 23
Singles, Women—preliminary matches	September 23
Doubles, Men—preliminary matches	September 23
Doubles, Women—preliminary matches	September 23
Doubles, Men—preliminary matches	September 24
Singles, Women—preliminary matches	September 24
Singles, Men—preliminary matches	September 24
Doubles, Men—preliminary matches	September 24
Doubles, Women—preliminary matches	September 24
Singles, Men—preliminary matches	September 25
Singles, Women—preliminary matches	September 25
Doubles, Men—preliminary matches	September 25
Doubles, Women—preliminary matches	September 25
Doubles, Men—preliminary matches	September 26
Singles, Women—preliminary matches	September 26
Singles, Men—preliminary matches	September 26
Doubles, Women—preliminary matches	September 26
Singles, Men—preliminary matches	September 27
Singles, Women—preliminary matches	September 27
Doubles, Men—preliminary matches	September 27
Doubles, Women—preliminary matches	September 27
Singles, Men—preliminary matches	September 28
Singles, Women—preliminary matches	September 28
Doubles, Men—preliminary matches	September 28
Doubles, Women—preliminary matches	September 28
Doubles, Women—quarter-finals	September 29
Doubles, Men—quarter-finals	September 29
Singles, Women—quarter-finals	September 29
Singles, Men—quarter-finals	September 29
Singles, Women—losers of quarter-finals	September 30
Singles, Men—losers of quarter-finals	September 30
Doubles, Women—semi-finals	September 30
Doubles, Men—semi-finals	September 30

Singles, Women—semi-finals	September 30
Singles, Men—semi-finals	September 30
Doubles, Women—5th to 8th places	October 1
Doubles, Men—5th to 8th places	October 1
Singles, Women—5th to 8th places	October 1
Singles, Men—5th to 8th places	October 1
Doubles, Women—3rd & 4th place	October 1
Doubles, Men—3rd & 4th place	October 1
Singles, Women—3rd & 4th place	October 1
Singles, Men—3rd & 4th place	October 1
Doubles, Women—Final	October 1
Doubles, Men—Final	October 1
Singles, Women—Final	October 1
Singles, Men—Final	October 1

Tennis (at Suwon Campus of Kyunghee University)

Singles, Men—1st round (16 matches)	September 20
Singles, Men—1st round (16 matches)	September 21
Singles, Men—2nd round (16 matches)	September 22
Doubles, Men—1st round (16 matches)	September 23
Singles, Women—1st round (8 matches)	September 23
Singles, Men—3rd round (8 matches)	September 24
Singles, Women—1st round (8 matches)	September 24
Doubles, Women—1st round (8 matches)	September 24
Doubles, Men—2nd round (8 matches)	September 25
Singles, Women—2nd round (8 matches)	September 25
Singles, Men—quarter-finals	September 26
Doubles, Women—quarter-finals	September 26
Doubles, Men—quarter-finals	September 27
Singles, Women—quarter-finals	September 27
Singles, Men—semi-finals	September 28
Doubles, Women—semi-finals	September 28
Singles, Women—semi-finals	September 29
Doubles, Men—semi-finals	September 29
Singles, Men—Final	September 30
Doubles, Women—Final	September 30
Doubles, Men—Final	October 1
Singles, Women—Final	October 1

Track & Field (at Olympic Stadium)

September 23	Heptathlon 100m hurdles, shot(m) qualifying, MARATHON(W), 100m(m) heats, heptathlon high jump, triple jump qualifying, 400m hurdles(m) heats, 400m(w) heats, 100m(m) 2nd round, heptathlon shot, 20KM WALK(M), 800m(m) heats, 3000m(w) heats, heptathlon 200m, SHOT PUT(M), 10000m(m) heats
September 24	400m(m) heats, javelin(m) qualifying, heptathlon long jump, 400m(w) 2nd round, 100m(w) heats, 100m(m) semi-finals, high jump(m) qualifying, TRIPLE JUMP, 100M FINAL(M), 100m(w) 2nd round, heptathlon javelin, 800m(w) heats, 400m hurdles(m) semi-finals, HEPTATHLON 800M

September 25	Hammer qualifying, 400m hurdles(w) heats, 110m hurdles(m) heats, JAVELIN(M), 100m(w) semi-finals, HIGH JUMP(M), 400m(m) 2nd round, 400m(w) semi-finals, long jump(m) qualifying, 110m hurdles(m) 2nd round, 400M HURDLES(M), 100M FINAL(W), javelin(w) qualifying, 800m(w) semi-finals, 800m(m) semi-finals, 3000M FINAL(W), 5000m(m) heats
September 26	Pole vault qualifying, 10000m(w) heats, 200m(m) heats, 400m hurdles(w) semi-finals, HAMMER, 110m hurdles(m) semi-finals, 800M FINAL(W), 800M FINAL(M), 200m(m) 2nd round, LONG JUMP(M), 3000m steeplechase heats, JAVELIN(W), 110M HURDLES(M), 400m(m) semi-finals, 400M FINAL(W), 10000M FINAL(M)
September 28	Decathlon 100m, discus(w) qualifying, decathlon long jump, 200m(w) heats, decathlon shot put, POLE VAULT, 400M HURDLES(W), 400M FINAL(M), decathlon high jump, 200m(w) 2nd round, 200m(m) semi-finals, 1500m(w) heats, long jump(w) qualifying, 1500m(m) heats, 200M FINAL(M), 3000m steeplechase semi-finals, decathlon 400m
September 29	Decathlon 110m hurdles, high jump(w) qualifying, decathlon discus, 100m hurdles(w) heats, decathlon pole vault, DISCUS(W), 200m(w) semi-finals, 1500m(m) semi-finals, decathlon javelin, 100m hurdles(w) 2nd round, LONG JUMP(W), 1500m(w) semi-finals, 200M FINAL(W), 5000m(m) semi-finals, DECATHLON 1500M
September 30	50KM WALK, discus(m) qualifying, 4 × 400m relay(w) heats, 4 × 400m relay(m) heats, 100m hurdles(w) semi-finals, shot put (w) qualifying, HIGH JUMP(W), 100M HURDLES FINAL(W), 4 × 100m relay(m) heats, 4 × 100m relay(w) heats, 3000M STEEPLE-CHASE, 4 × 400m(m) semi-finals, 4 × 400m relay(w) semi-finals, 10000M FINAL(W)
October 1	4 × 100m relay(w) semi-finals, SHOT PUT(W), 4 × 100m relay(m) semi-finals, DISCUS(M), 1500 M FINAL(W), 1500M FINAL(M), 5000M FINAL(M), 4 × 100M RELAY(W), 4 × 100 M RELAY(M), 4 × 400M RELAY(W), 4 × 400M RELAY(M)
October 2	MARATHON(M)

(Finals shown in capitals)

Volleyball (at Hanyang University Gym)

Preliminary matches, Men	September 17
Preliminary matches, Men	September 18
Preliminary matches, Men	September 19
Preliminary matches, Women	September 20
Preliminary matches, Men	September 22
Preliminary matches, Women	September 23
Preliminary matches, Men	September 24
Preliminary matches, Women	September 25
Preliminary matches, Men	September 26
Semi-finals, Women	September 27
Semi-finals, Men	September 28
7th & 8th place match, Women	September 29
5th & 6th place match, Women	September 29
3rd & 4th place match, Women	September 29
Final, Women	September 29

Semi-final, Men	September 30
11th & 12 place match, Men	September 30
9th & 10th place match, Men	September 30
Semi-final, Men	September 30
7th & 8th place match, Men	October 1
5th & 6th place match, Men	October 1
3rd & 4th place match, Men	October 2
Final, Men	October 2

Weightlifting (at Sports Complex Gymnasium)

52kg, Group C	September 18
52kg, Group B	September 18
52kg, Group A	September 18
56kg, Group C	September 19
56kg, Group B	September 19
56kg, Group A	September 19
60kg, Group C	September 20
60kg, Group B	September 20
60kg, Group A	September 20
67.5kg, Group C	September 21
67.5kg, Group B	September 21
67.5kg, Group A	September 21
75kg, Group C	September 22
75kg, Group B	September 22
75kg, Group A	September 22
82.5kg, Group C	September 24
82.5kg, Group B	September 24
82.5kg, Group A	September 24
90kg, Group C	September 25
90kg, Group B	September 25
90kg, Group A	September 25
100kg, Group C	September 26
100kg, Group B	September 26
100kg, Group A	September 26
110kg, Group C	September 27
110kg, Group B	September 27
110kg, Group A	September 27
110kg +, Group B	September 28
110kg, Group A	September 29

Wrestling (at Sangnru Gymnasium)

Greco-Roman Style
Preliminaries—48kg, 52kg, 90kg	September 18
Preliminaries—48kg, 52kg, 62kg, 74kg, 90kg, 100kg	September 19
Preliminaries—52kg, 57kg, 68kg, 74kg, 82kg, 100kg, 100kg +	September 20
Group finals—48kg, 62kg, 90kg	September 20
Finals—48kg, 62kg, 90kg	September 20
Preliminaries—57kg, 68kg, 82kg, 100kg +	September 21
Group finals—52kg, 74kg, 100kg	September 21
Finals—52kg, 74kg, 100kg	September 21
Group finals—57kg, 68kg, 82kg, 100kg +	September 22
Finals—57kg, 68kg, 82kg, 100kg +	September 22

Freestyle

Preliminaries—48kg, 62kg, 90kg	September 27
Preliminaries—48kg, 52kg, 62kg, 74kg, 90kg, 100kg	September 28
Preliminaries—52kg, 57kg, 68kg, 74kg, 82kg, 100kg, 100kg +	September 29
Group finals—48kg, 62kg, 90kg	September 29
Finals—48kg, 62kg, 90kg	September 29
Preliminaries—57kg, 68kg, 82kg, 100kg +	September 30
Group finals—52kg, 74kg, 100kg	September 30
Finals—52kg, 74kg, 100kg	September 30
Group finals—57kg, 68kg, 82kg, 100kg +	October 1
Finals—57kg, 68kg, 82kg, 100kg +	October 1

Yachting (at Pusan)

First race, all classes	September 20
Second race, all classes	September 21
Third race, all classes	September 22
Fourth race, all classes	September 23
Fifth race, all classes	September 26
Sixth race, all classes	September 27
Seventh race, all classes	September 28

Opening & Closing Ceremonies

Opening Ceremony	Olympic Stadium	September 17
Closing Ceremony	Olympic Stadium	October 2

Demonstration Sports

Baseball

Preliminary games	September 19
Preliminary games	September 20
Preliminary games	September 21
Preliminary games	September 22
Preliminary games	September 23
Preliminary games	September 24
Semi-finals	September 26
3rd & 4th place match	September 28
Final	September 28

Judo, Women

Extra Lightweight	September 25
Half Lightweight	September 26
Lightweight	September 27
Half Middleweight	September 28
Middleweight	September 29
Half Heavyweight	September 30
Heavyweight	October 1

Taekwondo

Finweight, Men	September 17
Flyweight, Men	September 17
Finweight, Women	September 17

Flyweight, Women		September 17
Bantamweight, Men		September 18
Featherweight, Men		September 18
Bantamweight, Women		September 18
Featherweight, Women		September 18
Lightweight, Men		September 19
Welterweight, Men		September 19
Lightweight, Women		September 19
Welterweight, Women		September 19
Middleweight, men		September 20
Heavyweight, Men		September 20
Middleweight, Women		September 20
Heavyweight, Women		September 20

Exhibition Events

Bowling		
Men's Masters		September 18
Women's Masters		September 18
Badminton		
Singles, Men	Seoul University Gymnasium	September 19
Doubles, Men	Seoul University Gymnasium	September 19
Singles, Women	Seoul University Gymnasium	September 19
Doubles, Women	Seoul University Gymnasium	September 19
Doubles, Mixed	Seoul University Gymnasium	September 19
Wheelchair Races for the Disabled		
800m, Women	Olympic Stadium	September 30
1500m, Men	Olympic Stadium	September 30

GOLD	SILVER	BRONZE
1968 HUNGARY	**BULGARIA**	**JAPAN**
Károly Fatér	Stoyan Yordanov	Kenzo Yokayama
Dezsö Novák	Atanas Gerov	Hirosci Katayama
Lajos Dunai	Gueorgui Christakiev	Yoshitada Yamaguchi
Miklós Pancsics	Milko Gaidarski	Mitsuo Kamata
Iván Menczel	Kiril Ivkov	Takaji Mori
Lajos Szücs	Ivailo Georgiev	Aritatsu Ogi
László Fazekas	Tzvetan Dimitrov	Teruki Miyamoto
Antal Dunai	Evgueni Yantchovski	Masashi Watanabe
László Nagy	Petar Jekov	Kunishige Kamamoto
Ernö Noskó	Atanas Christov	Ikuo Matsumoto
István Juhász	Asparukh Donev	Ryuichi Sugiyama
Lajos Kocsis	Georgi Vassilev	Masakatsu Miyamoto
László Keglovich	Kiril Christov	Shigeo Yaegashi
István Sárközi	Mikhail Giionin	Yasuyuki Kuwahara
István Basti	Yantcho Dimitrov	
	Georgi Ivanov	
	Ivan Zafirov	
	Todor Nikolov	
1972 POLAND	**HUNGARY**	**EAST GERMANY**[1]
Hubert Kostka	Istvan Geczi	Jürgen Croy
Zbigniew Gut	Peter Vepi	Manfred Zapf
Jerzy Gorgon	Miklós Pancsics	Konrad Weise
Zygmunt Anczok	Peter Juhasz	Bernd Bransch
Lesław Cmikiewicz	Lajos Szucs	Jürgen Pommerenke
Jerzy Kraska	Mihaly Kozma	Jürgen Sparwasser
Kazimierz Deyna	Antal Dunai	Hans-Jürgen Kreische
Zygfryd Szoltysik	Lajos Ku	Achim Streich
Włodzimierz Łubanski	Bela Varadi	Wolfgang Seguin
Robert Gadocha	Ede Dunai	Peter Ducke
Ryszard Szymczak	Laszlo Balint	Frank Ganzera
Antoni Szymanowski	Lajos Kocsis	Lothar Kurbjuweit
Marian Ostafinski	Kalman Toth	Eberhard Vogel
Kazimierz Kmiecik	Jozsef Kovacs	Ralf Schulenberg
Zygmunt Maszczyk	Laszlo Branikovics	Reinhard Häfner
Joachim Marx	Csaba Vidacs	Harald Irmscher
Grzegorz Lato	Adam Rothermel	Siegmar Wätzlich

	BRONZE	BRONZE
	U.S.S.R.[1]	
	Oleg Blohin	Gennadi Yevrushikhin
	Murtaz Hurcilava	Oganes Zanazanian
	Yuri Istomin	Andrei Yakubik
	Vladimir Kaplichnyi	Arkadiy Andriasian
	Viktor Kolotov	Revaz Dsodzuashvili
	Evgeniy Lovchev	Iojef Sabo
	Sergei Olshanskiy	Vladimir Onischenko
	Evgeniy Rudakov	Anatoliy Kuksov
	Viacheslav Semenov	Yuri Eliseev
		Vladimir Pilguy

---

[1]Third place declared a tie after extra time played.

This British soccer team took home the gold medal in 1912 with a final victory of 18 to 1 over Denmark.

The Italian goalkeeper protects his team's 2-to-1 edge from Austrian attack in the 1936 soccer final.

1976	EAST GERMANY	POLAND	U.S.S.R.
	Jurgen Croy	Jan Tomaszewski	Vladimir Astapovski
	Hans Jurgen Dorner	Piotr Mowlik	Viktor Matvienko
	Konrad Weise	Antoni Szymanowski	Mikhail Fomenko
	Lothar Kurbjuweit	Wladyslaw Zmuda	Stefan Reshko
	Reinhard Lauck	Zygmunt Maszczyk	Vladimir Troshkin
	Reinhard Häfner	Grzegorz Lato	Vladimir Onischenko
	Hans Jurgen Riediger	Henryk Kasperczak	Leonid Nazarenko
	Bernd Bransch	Kazimierz Deyna	Viktor Kolotov
	Martin Hoffmann	Andrzej Szarmach	Oleg Blokhin
	Gerd Kische	Kazimierz Kmiecik	Leonid Buriak
	Wolfram Lowe	Henryk Wawrowski	Aleksandr Minayev
	Wilfried Grobner	Henryk Wieczorek	Viktor Zviagintsev
	Hartmut Schade		

1980	CZECHOSLOVAKIA	EAST GERMANY	U.S.S.R.
	Stanislav Seman	Bodo Rudwaleit	Rinat Dasayev
	Ludek Macela	Artur Ullrich	Tengiz Sulakvelidze
	Josef Mazura	Lothar Hause	Aleksandr Chivadze
	Libor Radimec	Frank Baum	Vagiz Khidiyatullin
	Zdenek Rygel	Rudiger Schnuphase	Oleg Romantsev
	Petr Nemec	Frank Terletzki	Sergey Shavlo
	Ladislav Vizek	Wolfgang Steinbach	Sergey Andreyev
	Jan Berger	Werner Peter	Vladimir Bessonov
	Jindrich Svoboda	Dieter Kuhn	Yuriy Gavrilov
	Lubos Pokluda	Norbert Trieloff	Feodor Chernenkov
	Werner Licka	Matthias Muller	Valeriy Gazzayev
	Rostislav Vaclavicek	Matthias Liebers	Sergey Baltacha
	Jaroslav Netolicka	Wolf-Rudiger Netz	Khoren Oganesyan
	Oldrich Rott	Frank Uhlig	Vladimir Pilgu
	Frantisek Stambacher	Jurgen Bahringer	Sergey Nikulin
	Frantisek Kunzo	Bernd Jakubowski	Aleksandr Prokopenko

1984	FRANCE	BRAZIL	YUGOSLAVIA
	Albert Rust	Gilmar Rinaldi	Ivan Pudar
	William Ayache	Ronaldo Silva	Vlado Capljic
	Michel Bibard	Jorge Luiz Brum	Mirsad Baljic
	Dominique Bjotat	Mauro Galvao	Srecko Katanec
	Francois Brisson	Ademir Kaeser	Marko Elsner
	Patrick Cubaynes	Andre Luiz Ferreira	Ljubomir Radanovic
	Patrice Garande	Paulo Santos	Admir Smajic
	Philippe Jeannol	Carlos Verri	Nenad Gracan
	Guy Lacombe	Joao Leiehardt Neto	Milko Djurovski
	Jean-Claude Lemoult	Augilmar Oliveira	Mehmed Bazdarevic
	Jean-Philippe Rohr	Silvio Paiva	Borislav Cvetkovic
	Didier Senac	Luiz Dias	Tomislav Ivkovic
	Jean-Christoph Thouvenel	Luiz Carlos Winck	Jovica Nikolic
		Davi Cortez Silva	Stjepan Deveric
	Jose Toure	Antonio Jose Gil	Branko Miljus
	Daniel Xoureb	Francisco Vidal	Dragan Stojkovic
	Jean-Louis Zanon	Milton Cruz	Mitar Mrkela
	Michel Bensoussan		

16. Swimming and Diving (Men)

100 METERS FREE-STYLE (109 yd. 1 ft.)

GOLD	SILVER	BRONZE
1896 Alfréd Hajós (HUN) 1:22.2*	Efstathios Choraphas (GRE) 1:23.0	Otto Herschmann (AUT) d.n.a.
1900–1904 Event not held		
1906 Charles M. Daniels (USA) 1:13.4*	Zóltán von Halmay (HUN) 1:14.2	Cecil Healy (AUS) d.n.a.
1908 Charles M. Daniels (USA) 1:05.6*	Zóltán von Halmay (HUN) 1:06.2	Harald Julin (SWE) 1:08.0
1912 Duke P. Kahanamoku (USA) 1:03.4	Cecil Healy (AUS/NZL) 1:04.6	Kenneth Huszagh (USA) 1:05.6
1920 Duke P. Kahanamoku (USA) 1:01.4	Pua K. Kealoha (USA) 1:02.2	William W. Harris (USA) 1:03.0
1924 Johnny Weissmuller (USA) 59.0*	Duke P. Kahanamoku (USA) 1:01.4	Samuel Kahanamoku (USA) 1:01.8
1928 Johnny Weissmuller (USA) 58.6*	István Bárány (HUN) 59.8	Katsuo Takaishi (JPN) 1:00.0
1932 Yasuji Miyazaki (JPN) 58.2	Tatsugo Kawaishi (JPN) 58.6	Albert Schwartz (USA) 58.8
1936 Ferenc Csik (HUN) 57.6	Masanori Yusa (JPN) 57.9	Shigeo Arai (JPN) 58.0
1948 Walter Ris (USA) 57.3*	Alan Ford (USA) 57.8	Géza Kádas (HUN) 58.1
1952 C. Clarke Scholes (USA) 57.4	Hiroshi Suzuki (JPN) 57.4	Göran Larsson (SWE) 58.2
1956 Jon Henricks (AUS) 55.4*	John Devitt (AUS) 55.8	Gary Chapman (AUS) 56.7
1960 John Devitt (AUS) 55.2*	Lance M. Larson (USA) 55.2*	Manuel dos Santos (BRA) 55.4
1964 Donald Schollander (USA) 53.4*	Robert McGregor (GBR) 53.5	Hans-Joachim Klein (GER) 54.0
1968 Michael V. Wenden (AUS) 52.2*	Kenneth Walsh (USA) 52.8	Mark A. Spitz (USA) 53.0
1972 Mark A. Spitz (USA) 51.22*	Jerry Heidenreich (USA) 51.65	Vladimir Bure (URS) 51.77
1976 Jim Montgomery (USA) 49.99*	Jack Babashoff (USA) 50.81	Peter Nocke (GER) 51.31
1980 Jorg Woithe (GDR) 50.40	Per Holmertz (SWE) 50.91	Per Johansson (SWE) 51.29
1984 Ambrose Gaines (USA) 49.80*	Mark Stockwell (AUS) 50.24	Per Johansson (SWE) 50.31

The following Olympic records were set in addition to those medal-winning performances marked with an asterisk*.

1:08.2	von Halmay	1908	1:00.4	Kahanamoku	1920	57.5	Ris	1948
1:05.8	Daniels	1908		(in a final prior		57.1	Scholes	1952
1:04.8	Perry McGillivray (USA)	1912		to a re-swim)		56.8	L. Reid Patterson (USA)	1956
			58.6	Weissmuller	1928			
			58.0	Miyazaki	1932			
1:02.6	Kahanamoku	1912	57.7	Peter Fick (USA)	1936	55.7	Henricks	1956
						54.0	Gary Ilman (USA)	1964
1:02.4	Kahanamoku	1912	57.7	Arai	1936	53.9	Ilman	1964
			57.5	Masaharu Taguchi (JPN)	1936	53.4	Zachary Zorn (USA)	1968
1:01.8	Kahanamoku	1920				52.9	Wenden	1968
1:01.4	Kahanamoku	1920	57.5	Yusa	1936	50.39	Montgomery	1976

Michael Gross of West Germany set two world records in the 1984 Olympics at Los Angeles in the 200 meters freestyle and the 100 meters butterfly.

LEFT: Mark Spitz (USA) won 7 gold medals at the Munich Games in 1972, an Olympic record for a single year in any sport.

ABOVE: The dominant free-style swimmers at 400 meters and 1,500 meters in 1956 and 1960 were (left to right) George Breen (USA), I. Murray Rose (AUS) and Tsuyoshi Yamanaka (JPN).

200 METERS FREE-STYLE (218 yd. 2 ft.)

	GOLD	SILVER	BRONZE
1896	Event not held		
1900	Frederick C. V. Lane (AUS) 2:25.2	Zóltán von Halmay (HUN) 2:31.4	Karl Ruberl (AUT) 2:32.0
1904–1964	Event not held		
1968[1]	Michael V. Wenden (AUS) 1:55.2*	Donald A. Schollander (USA) 1:55.8	John M. Nelson (USA) 1:58.1
1972	Mark A. Spitz (USA) 1:52.78*	Steven Genter (USA) 1:53.73	Werner Lampe (GER) 1:53.99
1976	Bruce Furniss (USA) 1:50.29*	John Naber (USA) 1:50.50	Jim Montgomery (USA) 1:50.58
1980	Sergei Kopliakov (URS) 1:49.81*	Andrei Krylov (URS) 1:50.76	Graeme Brewer (AUS) 1:51.60
1984	Michael Gross (FRG) 1:47.44*	Michael Heath (USA) 1:49.10	Thomas Fahrner (FRG) 1:49.69

The following Olympic records were set in addition to those medal-winning performances already marked with an asterisk*

1:59.5	Nelson	1968	1:51.41	Klaus		1:50.93	Furniss	1976
1:59.3	Wenden	1968		Steinbach		1:48.03	Michael	
1:52.71	Bogdanov (URS)	1976		(GER)	1976		Gross (FRG)	1984

400 METERS FREE-STYLE (437 yd. 1 ft.)

	GOLD	SILVER	BRONZE
1896–1904	Event not held		
1906	Otto Scheff (AUT) 6:23.8*	Henry Taylor (GBR) 6:24.4	John A. Jarvis (GBR) 6:27.2
1908	Henry Taylor (GBR) 5:36.8*	Frank E. Beaurepaire (AUS/NZL) 5:44.2	Otto Scheff (AUT) 5:46.0
1912	George R. Hodgson (CAN) 5:24.4	John G. Hatfield (GBR) 5:25.8	Harold H. Hardwick (AUS/NZL) 5:31.2
1920	Norman Ross (USA) 5:26.8	Ludy Langer (USA) 5:29.2	George Vernot (CAN) 5:29.8
1924	Johnny Weissmuller (USA) 5:04.2*	Arne Borg (SWE) 5:05.6	Andrew M. Charlton (AUS) 5:06.6
1928	V. Alberto Zorilla (ARG) 5:01.6*	Andrew M. Charlton (AUS) 5:03.6	Arne Borg (SWE) 5:04.6
1932	Clarence L. Crabbe (USA) 4:48.4*	Jean Taris (FRA) 4:48.5	Tautomu Oyokota (JPN) 4:52.3
1936	Jack Medica (USA) 4:44.5*	Shumpei Uto (JPN) 4:45.6	Shozo Makino (JPN) 4:48.1
1948	William Smith (USA) 4:41.0*	James McLane (USA) 4:34.4	John B. Marshall (AUS) 4:47.7
1952	Jean Boiteaux (FRA) 4:30.7*	Ford Konno (USA) 4:31.3	Per-Olof Ostrand (SWE) 4:35.2
1956	I. Murray Rose (AUS) 4:27.3*	Tsuyoshi Yamanaka (JPN) 4:30.4	George T. Breen (USA) 4:32.5
1960	I. Murray Rose (AUS) 4:18.3*	Tsuyoshi Yamanaka (JPN) 4:21.4	John Konrads (AUS) 4:21.8
1964	Donald A. Schollander (USA) 4:12.2*	Frank Wiegand (GER) 4:14.9	Allan Wood (AUS) 4:15.1
1968	Michael J. Burton (USA) 4:09.0*	Ralph W. Hutton (CAN) 4:11.7	Alain Mosconi (FRA) 4:13.3
1972[1]	Bradford P. Cooper (AUS) 4:00.27*	Steven Genter (USA) 4:01.94	Tom McBreen (USA) 4:02.64
1976	Brian Goodell (USA) 3:51.93*	Tim Shaw (USA) 3:52.54	Vladimir Raskatov (URS) 3:55.76
1980	Vladimir Salnikov (URS) 3:51.31*	Andrei Krylov (URS) 3:53.24	Ivar Stukolkin (URS) 3:53.95
1984	George Dicarlo (USA) 3:51.23*	John Mykkanen (USA) 3:51.49	Justin Lemberg (AUS) 3:51.79

[1]Rick DeMont (USA) finished first but was subsequently disqualified.

The following Olympic records were set in addition to those medal-winning performances already marked with an asterisk *

5:48.8 T. Sydney Battersby (GBR) 1908	5:13.6 Weissmuller 1924	4:17.2 Wiegand 1964
5:42.2 Taylor 1908	4:53.2 Takashi Yokoyama (JPN) 1932	4:15.8 Schollander 1964
5:40.6 Scheff 1908	4:51.4 Yokoyama 1932	4:06.59 Bengt Gingsjoe (SWE) 1972
5:36.0 Hardwick 1912	4:45.5 Uto 1936	4:05.89 Genter 1972
5:34.0 Cecil Healy (AUS/NZL) 1912	4:42.2 McLane 1948	4:04.59 Cooper 1972
5:25.4 Hodgson 1912	4:38.6 Ostrand 1952	3:59.62 Djan Madruga (BRA) 1976
5:22.4 Breyer (USA) 1924	5:33.1 Boiteaux 1952	3:57.56 Raskatov 1976
5:22.2 Weissmuller 1924	4:21.0 Yamanaka 1960	3:56.40 Shaw 1976
	4:19.2 Alan Somers (USA) 1960	3:55.24 Goodell 1976
		3:50.91 Thomas Fahrner (FRG) 1984

1,500 METERS FREE-STYLE (1,640 yd. 1 ft.)

GOLD	SILVER	BRONZE
1896–1906 Event not held		
1908 Henry Taylor (GBR) 22:48.4*	T. Sydney Battersby (GBR) 22:51.2	Frank E. Beaurepaire (AUS/NZL) 22:56.2
1912 George R. Hodgson (CAN) 22:00.0*	John G. Hatfield (GBR) 22:39.0	Harold Hardwick (AUS/NZL) 23:15.4
1920 Norman Ross (USA) 22:23.2	George Vernot (CAN) 22:36.4	Frank E. Beaurepaire (AUS) 23:04.0
1924 Andrew M. Charlton (AUS) 20:06.6*	Arne Borg (SWE) 20:41.4	Frank E. Beaurepaire (AUS) 21:48.4
1928 Arne Borg (SWE) 19:51.8*	Andrew M. Charlton (AUS) 20:02.6	Clarence L. Crabbe (USA) 20:28.8
1932 Kusuo Kitamura (JPN) 19:12.4*	Shozo Makino (JPN) 19:14.1	James C. Christy (USA) 19:39.5
1936 Noboru Terada (JPN) 19:13.7	Jack Medica (USA) 19:34.0	Shumpei Uto (JPN) 19:34.5
1948 James McLane (USA) 19:18.5	John B. Marshall (AUS) 19:31.3	György Mitró (HUN) 19:43.2
1952 Ford Konno (USA) 18:30.0*	Shiro Hashizume (JPN) 18:41.4	Tetsuo Okamoto (BRA) 18:51.3
1956 I. Murray Rose (AUS) 17:58.9	Tsuyoshi Yamanaka (JPN) 18:00.3	George T. Breen (USA) 18:08.2
1960 John Konrads (AUS) 17:19.6*	I. Murray Rose (AUS) 17:21.7	George T. Breen (USA) 17:30.6
1964 Robert Windle (AUS) 17:01.7*	John Nelson (USA) 17:03.0	Allan Wood (AUS) 17:07.7
1968 Michael J. Burton (USA) 16:38.9*	John Kinsella (USA) 16:57.3	Gregory Brough (AUS) 17:04.7
1972 Michael J. Burton (USA) 15:52.58*	Graham Windeatt (AUS) 15:58.48	Douglas Northway (USA) 16:09.25
1976 Brian Goodell (USA) 15:02.40*	Bobby Hackett (USA) 15:03.91	Stephen Holland (AUS) 15:04.66
1980 Vladimir Salnikov (URS) 14:58.27*	Alexandr Chaev (URS) 15:14.30	Max Metzker (AUS) 15:14.49
1984 Michael O'Brien (USA) 15:05.20	George Dicarlo (USA) 15:10.59	Stefan Pfeiffer (FRG) 15:12.11

The following Olympic records were set in addition to those medal-winning perform-ances already marked with an asterisk * .

25:02.6	Paul Radmilovic (GBR) 1908	21:11.4	Borg 1924	17:15.9	Windle 1964
23:45.8	Beaurepaire 1908	19:51.6	Kitamura 1932	16:34.63	Hans-Joachim Fassnacht
		19:38.7	Makino 1932		(GER) 1972
23:42.8	Battersby 1908	18:34.0	Hashizume 1952	15:59.63	Windeatt 1972
23:24.4	Taylor 1908	18:04.1	Rose 1956	15:37.61	Zoltan Wladar
22:54.0	Taylor 1908	17:52.9	Breen 1956		(HUN) 1976
22:23.0	Hodgson 1912	17:46.5	Yamanaka 1960	15:20.74	Paul Hartloff
21:20.4	Charlton 1924	17:32.8	Rose 1960		(USA) 1976

Michael Burton of the United States doubled in 1968 in the 400 meters and 1,500 meters free-style, and won a third gold medal in 1972, again in the 1,500 meters free-style.

100 METERS BACK STROKE (109 yd. 1 ft.)

GOLD	SILVER	BRONZE
1896–1906 Event not held		
1908 Arno Bieberstein (GER) 1:24.6*	Ludvig Dam (DEN) 1:26.6	Herbert Haresnape (GBR) 1:27.0
1912 Harry J. Hebner (USA) 1:21.2	Otto Fahr (GER) 1:22.4	Paul Kellner (GER) 1:24.0
1920 Warren P. Kealoha (USA) 1:15.2	Ray Kegeris (USA) 1:16.2	Gérard Blitz (BEL) 1:19.0
1924 Warren P. Kealoha (USA) 1:13.2*	Paul Wyatt (USA) 1:15.4	Károly Bartha (HUN) 1:17.8
1928 George H. Kojac (USA) 1:08.2*	Walter Laufer (USA) 1:10.0	Paul Wyatt (USA) 1:12.0
1932 Masaji Kiyokawa (JPN) 1:08.6	Toshio Irie (JPN) 1:09.8	Kentaro Kawatsu (JPN) 1:10.0
1936 Adolf Kiefer (USA) 1:05.9*	Albert Van de Weghe (USA) 1:07.7	Masaji Kiyokawa (JPN) 1:08.4
1948 Allen Stack (USA) 1:06.4	Robert Cowell (USA) 1:06.5	Georges Vallerey (FRA) 1:07.8
1952 Yoshinobu Oyakawa (USA) 1:05.4*	Gilbert Bozon (FRA) 1:06.2	Jack Taylor (USA) 1:06.4
1956 David Thiele (AUS) 1:02.2*	John Monckton (AUS) 1:03.2	Frank E. McKinney (USA) 1:04.5

1960	David Thiele (AUS) 1:01.9*	Frank E. McKinney (USA) 1:02.1	Robert E. Bennett (USA) 1:02.3
1964	Event not held		
1968	Roland Matthes (GDR) 58.7*	Charles Hickcox (USA) 1:00.2	Ronnie P. Mills (USA) 1:00.5
1972	Roland Matthes (GDR) 56.58*	Mike Stamm (USA) 57.70	John Murphy (USA) 58.35
1976	John Naber (USA) 55.49*	Peter Rocca (USA) 56.34	Roland Matthes (GDR) 57.22
1980	Bengt Baron (SWE) 56.53	Viktor Kuznetsov (URS) 56.99	Vladimir Dolgov (URS) 57.63
1984	Rick Carey (USA) 55.79	David Wilson (USA) 56.35	Mike West (CAN) 56.49

The following Olympic records were set in addition to those medal-winning performances already marked with an asterisk *.

1:25.6 (twice)	Bieberstein	1908	1:06.9	Kiefer	1936	1:01.9	Larry Barbiere (USA)	1968
1:21.1	Hebner	1912	1:06.8	Kiefer	1936	1:01.0	Matthes	1968
1:20.8	Hebner	1912	1:05.7	Oyakawa	1952	58.63	Stamm	1972
1:17.8	Ray Kegeris (USA)	1920	1:04.2	Robert Christophe (FRA)	1956	58.15	Mitchell Ivey (USA)	1972
1:14.8	Kealoha	1920	1:03.4	Monckton	1956	57.99	Ivey	1972
1:13.4	Kealoha	1924	1:02.0	Bennett	1960	56.30†	Matthes	1972
1:09.2	Kojac	1928				56.19	Naber	1976

†In medley relay.

200 METERS BACK STROKE (218 yd. 2 ft.)

	GOLD	SILVER	BRONZE
1896	Event not held		
1900	Ernst Hoppenberg (GER) 2:47.0*	Karl Ruberl (AUT) 2:56.0	Johannes Drost (HOL) 3:01.0
1904–1960	Event not held		
1964	Jed Graef (USA) 2:10.3*	Gary Dilley (USA) 2:10.5	Robert E. Bennett (USA) 2:13.1
1968	Roland Matthes (GDR) 2:09.6*	Mitchell Ivey (USA) 2:10.6	Jack Horsley (USA) 2:10.9
1972	Roland Matthes (GDR) 2:02.82*	Mike Stamm (USA) 2:04.09	Mitchell Ivey (USA) 2:04.33
1976	John Naber (USA) 1:59.19*	Peter Rocca (USA) 2:00.55	Don Harrigan (USA) 2:01.35
1980	Sandor Wladar (HUN) 2:01.93	Zoltan Verraszto (HUN) 2:02.40	Mark Kerry (AUS) 2:03.14
1984	Rick Carey (USA) 2:00.23	Frederic Delcourt (FRA) 2:01.75	Cameron Henning (CAN) 2:02.37

The following Olympic records were set in addition to those medal-winning performances already marked with an asterisk *.

2:16.1	Bennett	1964	2:14.5	Graef	1964	2:07.51	Stamm	1972
2:14.7	Shigeo Fukushima (JPN)	1964	2:14.2	Dilley	1964	2:06.62	Matthes	1972
			2:13.8	Dilley	1964	2:02.25	Harrigan	1976
			2:13.7	Graef	1964	2:02.01	Naber	1976
						1:58.99	Carey	1984

100 METERS BREAST STROKE (109 yd. 1 ft.)

1896–1964 Event not held

1968 Donald McKenzie (USA) 1:07.7*	Vladimir Kossinsky (URS) 1:08.0	Nickolay Pankin (URS) 1:08.0
1972 Nobutaka Taguchi (JPN) 1:04.94*	Tom Bruce (USA) 1:05.43	John Hencken (USA) 1:05.61
1976 John Hencken (USA) 1:03.11*	David Wilkie (GBR) 1:03.43	Arvidas Iuozaytis (URS) 1:04.23
1980 Duncan Goodhew (GBR) 1:03.34	Arsen Miskarov (URS) 1:03.82	Peter Evans (AUS) 1:03.96
1984 Steve Lundquist (USA) 1:01.65*	Victor Davis (CAN) 1:01.99	Peter Evans (AUS) 1:02.97

The following Olympic records were set in addition to those medal-winning performances already marked with an asterisk *

1:08.9 Pankin 1968	1:05.68 Hencken 1972	1:03.88 Hencken 1976
1:08.1 McKenzie 1968	1:05.13 Taguchi 1972	1:03.62 Hencken 1976
1:08.1 Pankin 1968	1:04.92 Duncan	1:02.87 Evans 1984
1:07.9 Kossinsky 1968	Goodhew	1:02.16 Lundquist1984
1:05.89 Mark Chatfield	(GBR) 1976	
(USA) 1972	1:04.78 Iuozaytis 1976	

200 METERS BREAST STROKE (218 yd. 2 ft.)

1896–1906 Event not held

1908 Frederick Holman (GBR) 3:09.2*	William W. Robinson (GBR) 3:12.8	Pontus Hansson (SWE) 3:14.6
1912 Walter Bathe (GER) 3:01.8*	Wilhelm Lützow (GER) 3:05.0	Kurt Malisch (GER) 3:08.0
1920 Häken Malmroth (SWE) 3:04.4	Thor Henning (SWE) 3:09.2	Arvo Aaltonen (FIN) 3:12.2
1924 Robert D. Skelton (USA) 2:56.5	Joseph de Combe (BEL) 2:59.2	William Kirschbaum (USA) 3:01.0
1928 Yoshiyuki Tsuruta (JPN) 2:48.8*	Erich Rademacher (GER) 2:50.6	Teofilo Yldefonzo (PHI) 2:56.4
1932 Yoshiyuki Tsuruta (JPN) 2:45.4	Reizo Koike (JPN) 2:46.4	Teofilo Yldefonzo (PHI) 2:47.1
1936 Tetsuo Hamuro (JPN) 2:42.5*	Erwin Sietas (GER) 2:42.9	Reizo Koike (JPN) 2:44.2
1948 Joseph Verdeur (USA) 2:39.3*	Keith Carter (USA) 2:40.2	Robert Sohl (USA) 2:43.9
1952 John Davies (AUS) 2:34.4*	Bowen Stassforth (USA) 2:34.7	Herbert Klein (GER) 2:35.9
1956 Masura Furukawa (JPN) 2:34.7*	Masahiro Yoshimura (JPN) 2:36.7	Charis Yunitschev (URS) 2:36.8
1960 William D. Mulliken (USA) 2:37.4	Yoshihiko Osaki (JPN) 2:38.0	Wieger E. Mensonides (HOL) 2:39.7
1964 Ian O'Brien (AUS) 2:27.8*	Georgy Prokopenko (URS) 2:28.2	Chester Jastremski (USA) 2:29.6
1968 Felipe Muñoz (MEX) 2:28.7	Vladimir Kossinsky (URS) 2:29.2	Brian Job (USA) 2:29.9
1972 John Hencken (USA) 2:21.55*	David A. Wilkie (GBR) 2:23.67	Nobutaka Taguchi (JPN) 2:23.88
1976 David Wilkie (GBR) 2:15.11*	John Hencken (USA) 2:17.26	Rick Colella (USA) 2:19.20
1980 Robertas Zulpa (URS) 2:15.85	Alban Vermes (HUN) 2:16.93	Arsen Miskarov (URS) 2:17.28
1984 Victor Davis (CAN) 2:13.34*	Glenn Beringen (AUS) 2:15.79	Etienne Dagon (SUI) 2:17.41

Two of the greatest back stroke experts ever seen in Olympic competition are Roland Matthes (GDR) at left and John Naber (USA) at right. Matthes won the gold medal at 100 meters and 200 meters in both 1968 and 1972. Naber set Olympic and world records at both distances at the 1976 Games.

In the 100 meters breast stroke event in 1976, John Hencken (USA) in lane 3 beat David Wilkie (GBR) in lane 5 by just over half a second. At 200 meters Wilkie beat the defending champion Hencken.

The following Olympic records were set in addition to those medal-winning performances already marked with an asterisk *.

3:10.0	Holman	1908	2:46.2	Koike	1932	2:38.0	Mulliken	1960
3:10.6	Holman	1908	2:44.9	Koike	1932	2:37.2	Mulliken	1960
3:07.4	Lützow	1912	2:42.5	Hamuro	1936	2:31.4	O'Brien	1964
3:03.4	Bathe	1912	2:40.0†	Verdeur	1948	2:30.1	Egon	
3:02.2	Bathe	1912	2:38.9†	L. Komadel			Henninger	
2:56.0	Skelton	1924		(TCH)	1952		(GER)	1964
2:52.0	Rademacher		2:36.8†	G. Holan		2:28.7	O'Brien	1964
		1928		(USA)	1952	2:26.32	Klaus Katzur	
2:50.0	Tsuruta	1928	2:36.8†	Davies	1952		(GDR)	1972
2:49.2	Tsuruta	1928	2:36.1†	Furukawa		2:23.45	Taguchi	1972
2:46.2	Tsuruta	1932			1956	2:21.08	Colella	1976
						2:18.29	Wilkie	1976

† In the 1948 and 1952 Games the records for this event were achieved by the then
permissible butterfly stroke. Furukawa's 1956 record was achieved by the now also
disallowed underwater technique.

100 METERS BUTTERFLY (109 yd. 1 ft.)

1896–1964 Event not held
1968	Douglas A. Russell (USA) 55.9*[1]	Mark A. Spitz (USA) 56.4	Ross Wales (USA) 57.2
1972	Mark A. Spitz (USA) 54.27*	Bruce Robertson (CAN) 55.56	Jerry Heidenreich (USA) 55.74
1976	Matt Vogel (USA) 54.35	Joseph Bottom (USA) 54.50	Gary Hall (USA) 54.65
1980	Par Arvidsson (SWE) 54.92	Roger Pyttel (GDR) 54.94	David Lopez (ESP) 55.13
1984	Michael Gross (FRG) 53.08*	Pedro Morales (USA) 53.23	Glenn Buchanan (AUS) 53.85

[1] In 1968 Russell set an inaugural record of 57.3 which he improved to 55.9 in the
semi-finals.
Olympic record performances: 54.02 by Michael Gross 1984, and 53.78 by Pedro
Morales 1984

200 METERS BUTTERFLY (218 yd. 2 ft.)

1896–1952 Event not held
1956	William Yorzyk (USA) 2:19.3	Takashi Ishimoto (JPN) 2:23.8	György Tumpek (HUN) 2:23.9
1960	Michael F. Troy (USA) 2:12.8*	Neville Hayes (AUS) 2:14.6	J. David Gillanders (USA) 2:15.3
1964	Kevin J. Berry (AUS) 2:06.6*	Carl Robie (USA) 2:07.5	Fred Schmidt (USA) 2:09.3
1968	Carl Robie (USA) 2:08.7	Martyn Woodroffe (GBR) 2:09.0	John Ferris (USA) 2:09.3
1972	Mark A. Spitz (USA) 2:00.70*	Gary Hall (USA) 2:02.86	Robin Backhaus (USA) 2:03.23

GOLD	SILVER	BRONZE
1976 Michael Bruner (USA) 1:59.23*	Steven Gregg (USA) 1:59.54	William Forrester (USA) 1:59.96
1980 Sergei Fesenko (URS) 1:59.76	Philip Hubble (GBR) 2:01.20	Roger Pyttel (GDR) 2:01.39
1984 Jon Sieben (AUS) 1:57.04*	Michael Gross (FRG) 1:57.40	Rafael Vidal Castro (VEN) 1:57.51

There were six record butterfly performances (then permissible) in the 1948 and 1952 breast stroke events culminating in John Davies' (AUS) 2:34.4 in 1952. Thereafter the non-medal-winning records were:

2:18.6	Yorzyk	1956	2:09.3	Robie	1964	2:00.24	Gregg	1976
2:15.5	Troy	1960	2:03.70	Hall	1972	1:59.19	Pedro Morales	
2:10.0	Robie	1964	2:03.11	Backhaus	1972		(USA)	1984
			2:02.11	Spitz	1972	1:58.72	Gross	1984

200 METERS INDIVIDUAL MEDLEY

GOLD	SILVER	BRONZE
1896–1964 Event not held		
1968 Charles Hickcox (USA) 2:12.0	Greg Buckingham (USA) 2:13.0	John Ferris (USA) 2:13.3
1972 Gunnar Larsson (SWE) 2:07.17*	Tim McKee (USA) 2:08.37	Steve Furniss (USA) 2:08.45
1976–1980 Event not held		
1984 Alex Baumann (CAN) 2:01.42*	Pedro Morales (USA) 2:03.05	Neil Cochran (GBR) 2:04.38

400 METERS INDIVIDUAL MEDLEY (437 yd. 1 ft.)

GOLD	SILVER	BRONZE
1896–1960 Event not held		
1964 Richard Roth (USA) 4:45.4*	Roy Saari (USA) 4:47.1	Gerhard Hetz (GER) 4:51.0
1968 Charles Hickcox (USA) 4:48.4	Gary Hall (USA) 4:48.7	Michael Holthaus (GER) 4:51.4
1972 Gunnar Larsson (SWE) 4:31.98*	Tim McKee (USA) 4:31.98*	Andras Hargitay (HUN) 4:32.70
1976 Rod Strachan (USA) 4:23.68*	Tim McKee (USA) 4:24.62	Andrei Smirnov (URS) 4:26.90
1980 Aleksandr Sidorenko (URS) 4:22.89*	Sergei Fesenko (URS) 4:23.43	Zoltan Verraszto (HUN) 4:24.24
1984 Alex Baumann (CAN) 4:17.41*	Ricardo Prado (BRA) 4:18.45	Robert Woodhouse (AUS) 4:20.50

The following non-medal-winning performances were also Olympic Records:

4:52.0	Robie	1964	4:34.99	Larsson	1972	4:27.15	Strachan	1976
4:37.51	Hargitay	1972	4:27.76	Steve Furniss (USA)	1976			

4 × 100 METERS MEDLEY RELAY (4 × 109 yd. 1 ft.)
(Order of strokes: back stroke, breast stroke, butterfly, free-style.)

GOLD	SILVER	BRONZE
1896–1956 Event not held		
1960 UNITED STATES 4:05.4*	AUSTRALIA 4:12.0	JAPAN 4:12.2
Frank E. McKinney	David Theile	Kazuo Tomita
Paul W. Hait	Terry Gathercole	Koichi Hirakida
Lance M. Larson	Neville Hayes	Yoshihiko Osaki
F. Jeffrey Farrell	Gary Shipton	Keigo Shimizu
1964 UNITED STATES 3:58.4*	GERMANY 4:01.6	AUSTRALIA 4:02.3
Harold T. Mann	Ernst-Joachim Küppers	Peter Reynolds
William Craig	Egon Henninger	Ian O'Brien
Fred Schmidt	Horst-Günther Gregor	Kevin J. Berry
Stephen Clark	Hans-Joachim Klein	David Dickson
1968 UNITED STATES 3:54.9*	EAST GERMANY 3:57.5	U.S.S.R. 4:00.7
Charles Hickcox	Roland Matthes	Yuri Gromak
Donald McKenzie	Egon Henninger	Vladimir Kossinsky
Douglas A. Russell	Horst-Günther Gregor	Vladimir Nemshilov
Kenneth Walsh	Frank Wiegand	Leonid Ilyichev
1972 UNITED STATES 3:48.16*	EAST GERMANY 3:52.12	CANADA 3:52.26
Mike Stamm	Roland Matthes	Eric Fish
Tom Bruce	Klaus Katzur	William Mahony
Mark A. Spitz	Hartmut Floekner	Bruce Robertson
Jerry Heidenerich	Lutz Unger	Robert A. Kasting
1976 UNITED STATES 3:42.22*	CANADA 3:45.94	WEST GERMANY 3:47.29
John Naber	Stephen Pickell	Klaus Steinbach
John Hencken	Graham Smith	Walter Kusch
Matt Vogel	Clay Evans	Michael Kraus
Jim Montgomery	Gary MacDonald	Peter Nocke
1980 AUSTRALIA 3:45.70	U.S.S.R. 3:45.92	GREAT BRITAIN 3:47.71
Mark Kerry	Viktor Kuznetsov	Gary Abraham
Peter Evans	Arsen Miskarov	Duncan Goodhew
Mark Tonelli	Yevgeniy Seredin	David Lowe
Neil Brooks	Sergei Kopliakov	Martin Smith
1984 USA 3:39.30*	CANADA 3:43.23	AUSTRALIA 3:43.25
Rick Carey	Mike West	Mark Kerry
Steve Lundquist	Victor Davis	Peter Evans
Pedro Morales	Tom Ponting	Glenn Buchanan
Ambrose Gaines	Sandy Goss	Mark Stockwell

The following Olympic records were set in addition to those medal-winning performances already marked with an asterisk*.

4:14.8 Australia 1960	4:05.1 United States 1964	3:51.98 United States 1972
4:08.2 United States 1960		3:47.28 United States 1976

4 × 100 METERS FREE-STYLE RELAY (4 × 109 yd. 1 ft.)

1896–1960 Event not held

1964 USA 3:33.2	GERMANY 3:37.2	AUSTRALIA 3:39.1
Steve Clark	Horst Loffler	David Dickson
Mike Austin	Frank Wiegand	Peter Doak
Gary Ilman	Uwe Jacobsen	John Ryan
Don Schollander	Hans-Joachim Klein	Robert Windle
1968 USA 3:31.7*	USSR 3:34.2	AUSTRALIA 3:34.7
Zachary Zorn	Semyon Belits-Geiman	Greg Rogers
Steve Rerych	Viktor Mazanov	Robert Windle
Mark Spitz	Georgy Kulikov	Robert Cusack
Ken Walsh	Leonid Ilichev	Mike Wenden
1972 USA 3:26.42*	USSR 3:29.72	GDR 3:32.42
David Edgar	Vladimir Bure	Roland Matthes
John Murphy	Viktor Mazanov	Wilfried Hartung
Jerry Heidenreich	Viktor Aboimov	Peter Bruch
Mark Spitz	Igor Grivennikov	Lutz Unger

1976–1980 Event not held

1984 USA 3:19.03*	AUSTRALIA 3:19.68	SWEDEN 3:22.69
Chris Cavanaugh	Greg Fasala	Thomas Leidstrom
Michael Heath	Neil Brooks	Bengt Baron
Matthew Bond	Michael Delany	Mikael Orn
Ambrose Gaines	Mark Stockwell	Per Johansson

4 × 200 METERS FREE-STYLE RELAY (4 × 218 yd. 2 ft.)

1896–1906 Event not held

1908 GREAT BRITAIN 10:45.6	HUNGARY 10:59.0	UNITED STATES 11:02.8
John H. Derbyshire	József Munk	Harry Hebner
Paul Radmilovic	Imre Zachár	Leo Goodwin
William Foster	Béla von Las Torres	Charles M. Daniels
Henry Taylor	Zóltán von Halmay	Leslie G. Rich
1912 AUSTRALASIA 10:11.6*	UNITED STATES 10:20.2	GREAT BRITAIN 10:28.2
Cecil Healy	Kenneth Huszagh	William Foster
Malcolm Champion[1]	Harry J. Hebner	T. Sydney Battersby
Leslie Boardman	Perry McGillivray	John Hatfield
Harold Hardwick	Duke P. Kahanamoku	Henry Taylor
1920 UNITED STATES 10:04.4*	AUSTRALIA 10:25.4	GREAT BRITAIN 10:37.2
Perry McGillivray	Henry Hay	Leslie Savage
Pua K. Kealoha	William Herald	E. Percy Peter
Norman Ross	Ivan Stedman	Henry Taylor
Duke P. Kahanamoku	Frank E. Beaurepaire	Harold E. Annison
1924 UNITED STATES 9:53.4*	AUSTRALIA 10:02.2	SWEDEN 10:06.8
Wallace O'Connor	Maurice Christie	George Werner
Harry Glancy	Ernest Henry	Orvar Trolle
Ralph Breyer	Frank E. Beaurepaire	Åke Borg
Johnny Weissmuller	Andrew M. Charlton	Arne Borg
1928 UNITED STATES 9:36.2*	JAPAN 9:41.4	CANADA 9:47.8
Austin Clapp	Hiroshi Yoneyama	F. Munro Bourne
Walter Laufer	Nobuo Arai	James Thompson
George Kojac	Tokuhei Sada	Garnet Ault
Johnny Weissmuller	Katsuo Takaishi	Walter Spence
1932 JAPAN 8:58.4*	UNITED STATES 9:10.5	HUNGARY 9:31.4
Yasuji Miyazaki	Frank Booth	András Wannié
Masanori Yusa	George Fissier	László Szabados
Takashi Yokoyama	Marola Kalili	András Székely
Hisakichi Toyoda	Manuella Kalili	István Bárány

---

[1] A New Zealander; the other three members of the team were Australians. The two countries entered a composite team in the Olympic Games until 1920.

	GOLD	SILVER	BRONZE
1936	**JAPAN** 8:51.5*	**UNITED STATES** 9:03.0	**HUNGARY** 9:12.3
	Masanori Yusa	Ralph Flanagan	Arpád Lengyel
	Shigeo Sugiura	John Macionis	Oszkár Abay-Nemes
	Masaharu Taguchi	Paul Wolf	Ödön Gróf
	Shigeo Arai	Jack Medica	Ferenc Csik
1948	**UNITED STATES** 8:46.0*	**HUNGARY** 8:48.4	**FRANCE** 9:08.0
	Walter Ris	Elemér Szathmári	Joseph Bernardo
	James McLane	György Mitró	Henri Padou
	Wallace Wolf	Imre Nyéki	René Cornu
	William Smith	Géza Kádas	Alexandre Jany
1952	**UNITED STATES** 8:31.1*	**JAPAN** 8:33.5	**FRANCE** 8:45.9
	Wayne Moore	Hiroshi Suzuki	Joseph Bernardo
	William Woolsey	Yoshihiro Hamaguchi	Aldo Eminente
	Ford Konno	Toru Goto	Alexandre Jany
	James McLane	Teijiro Tanikawa	Jean Boiteaux
1956	**AUSTRALIA** 8:23.6*	**UNITED STATES** 8:31.5	**U.S.S.R.** 8:34.7
	Kevin O'Halloran	Richard Hanley	Vitaliy Sorokin
	John Devitt	George T. Breen	Vladimir Struschanov
	I. Murray Rose	William Woolsey	Gennadiy Nikolayev
	Jon Henricks	Ford Konno	Boris Nikitin
1960	**UNITED STATES** 8:10.2*	**JAPAN** 8:13.2	**AUSTRALIA** 8:13.8
	George P. Harrison	Makoto Fukui	David G. Dickson
	Richard A. Blick	Hiroshi Ishii	John Devitt
	Michael F. Troy	Tsuyoshi Yamanaka	I. Murray Rose
	F. Jeffrey Farrell	Tatsuo Fujimoto	John Konrads
1964	**UNITED STATES** 7:52.1*	**GERMANY** 7:59.3	**JAPAN** 8:03.8
	Stephen Clark	Horst-Günther Gregor	Makoto Fukui
	Roy Saari	Gerhard Hetz	Kunihiro Iwasaki
	Gary Ilman	Frank Wiegand	Toshio Shoji
	Donald A. Schollander	Hans-Joachim Klein	Yukiaki Okabe
1968	**UNITED STATES** 7:52.3	**AUSTRALIA** 7:53.7	**U.S.S.R.** 8:01.6
	John M. Nelson	Gregory Rogers	Vladimir Bure
	Stephen Rerych	Graham White	Semyon Belitz-Geiman
	Mark A. Spitz	Robert Windle	Georgy Kulikov
	Donald A. Schollander	Michael V. Wenden	Leonid Ilyichev
1972	**UNITED STATES** 7:35.78*	**WEST GERMANY** 7:41.69	**U.S.S.R.** 7:45.76
	John Kinsella	Klaus Steinbach	Igor Grivennilkov
	Frederick Tyler	Werner Lampe	Viktor Mazanov
	Steven Genter	Hans-Günter Vosseler	Georgy Kulikov
	Mark Spitz	Hans-Joachim Fassnacht	Vladimir Bure
1976	**UNITED STATES** 7:23.22*	**U.S.S.R.** 7:27.97	**GREAT BRITAIN** 7:32.11
	Michael Bruner	Vladimir Raskatov	Alan McClatchey
	Bruce Furniss	Andrei Bogdanov	David Dunne
	John Naber	Sergei Kopliakov	Gordon Downie
	Jim Montgomery	Andrei Krylov	Brian Brinkley
1980	**U.S.S.R.** 7:23.50	**EAST GERMANY** 7:28.60	**BRAZIL** 7:29.30
	Sergei Kopliakov	Frank Pfutze	Jorge Fernades
	Vladimir Salnikov	Jorg Woithe	Marcus Mattioli Laborne
	Ivar Stukolkin	Detlef Grabs	Cyro Delgado Marques
	Andrei Krylov	Rainer Strohbach	Djan Madruga Garrido

1984	USA 7:15.69*	WEST GERMANY 7:15.73	GREAT BRITAIN 7:24.78
	Michael Heath	Thomas Fahrner	Neil Cochran
	David Larson	Dirk Korthals	Paul Easter
	Jeff Float	Alexander Schowtka	Paul Howe
	Lawrence Hayes	Michael Gross	Andrew Astbury

The following Olympic records were set in addition to those medal-winning performances already marked with an asterisk*.

11:35.0	Australia 1908	9:59.4	United States 1924	8:09.0	United States 1964
10.53.4	Great Britain 1908	9:38.8	United States 1928	7:49.03	Australia 1972
10:26.4	United States 1912	8:56.1	Japan 1936	7:46.42	United States 1972
10:14.0	Australia 1912	8:42.1	Japan 1952	7:33.21	U.S.S.R. 1976
		8:17.1	Japan 1960	7:30.33	U.S.A 1976
		8:09.7	Germany 1964	7:18.87	U.S.A. 1984

SPRINGBOARD DIVING

1896–1906 Event not held

1908	Albert Zurner (GER) 85.5	Kurt Behrens (GER) 85.3	George Gaidzik (USA) 80.8 Gottlob Walz (GER) 80.8
1912	Paul Günther (GER) 79.23	Hans Luber (GER) 76.78	Kurt Behrens (GER) 73.73
1920	Louis E. Kuehn (USA) 675.4	Clarence Pinkston (USA) 655.3	Louis J. Balbach (USA) 649.5
1924	Albert C. White (USA) 696.4	Peter Desjardins (USA) 693.2	Clarence Pinkston (USA) 653
1928	Peter Desjardins (USA) 185.04	Michael Galitzen (USA) 174.06	Farid Simaika (EGY) 172.46
1932	Michael Galitzen (USA) 161.38	Harold Smith (USA) 158.54	Richard Degener (USA) 151.82
1936	Richard Degener (USA) 163.57	Marshall Wayne (USA) 159.56	Al Greene (USA) 146.29
1948	Bruce Harlan (USA) 163.64	Miller Anderson (USA) 157.29	Samuel Lee (USA) 145.52
1952	David Browning (USA) 205.29	Miller Anderson (USA) 199.84	Robert Clotworthy (USA) 184.92
1956	Robert Clotworthy (USA) 159.56	Donald Harper (USA) 156.23	Joaquin Capilla Pérez (MEX) 150.69
1960	Gary M. Tobian (USA) 170.00	Samuel N. Hall (USA) 167.08	Juan Botella (MEX) 162.30

	GOLD	SILVER	BRONZE
1964	Kenneth Sitzberger (USA) 159.90	Francis Gorman (USA) 157.63	Larry Andreasen (USA) 143.77
1968	Bernard Wrightson (USA) 170.15	Klaus Dibiasi (ITA) 159.74	James Henry (USA) 158.09
1972	Vladimir Vasin (URS) 594.09	Franco Cagnotto (ITA) 591.63	Craig Lincoln (USA) 577.29
1976	Philip Boggs (USA) 619.05	Franco Cagnotto (ITA) 570.48	Aleksandr Kosenkov (URS) 567.24
1980	Aleksandr Portnov (URS) 905.025	Carlos Giron (MEX) 892.140	Franco Cagnotto (ITA) 871.500
1984	Greg Louganis (USA) 754.41	Liangde Tan (CHN) 662.31	Ronald Merriott (USA) 661.32

PLATFORM DIVING

1896-1904 Event not held

1906	Gottlob Walz (GER) 156.00	Georg Hoffman (GER) 150.20	Otto Satzinger (AUT) 147.40
1908	Hjalmar Johansson (SWE) 83.75	Karl Malström (SWE) 78.73	Arvid Spångberg (SWE) 74.00
1912	Erik Adlerz (SWE) 73.94	Albert Zürner (GER) 72.60	Gustaf Blomgren (SWE) 69.56
1920	Clarence Pinkston (USA) 100.67	Erik Adlerz (SWE) 99.08	Haig Prieste (USA) 93.73
1924	Albert C. White (USA) 97.46	David Fall (USA) 97.30	Clarence Pinkston (USA) 94.60
1928	Peter Desjardins (USA) 98.74	Farid Simaika (EGY) 99.58	Michael Galitzen (USA) 92.34
1932	Harold Smith (USA) 124.80	Michael Galitzen (USA) 124.28	Frank Kurtz (USA) 121.98
1936	Marshall Wayne (USA) 113.58	Elbert Root (USA) 110.60	Hermann Stork (GER) 110.31
1948	Samuel Lee (USA) 130.05	Bruce Harlan (USA) 122.30	Joaquin Capilla Pérez (MEX) 113.52
1952	Samuel Lee (USA) 156.28	Joaquin Capilla Pérez (MEX) 145.21	Günther Haase (GER) 141.31
1956	Joaquin Capilla Pérez (MEX) 152.44	Gary M. Tobian (USA) 152.41	Richard Connor (USA) 149.79
1960	Robert D. Webster (USA) 165.56	Gary M. Tobian (USA) 165.25	Brian E. Phelps (GBR) 157.13
1964	Robert D. Webster (USA) 148.58	Klaus Dibiasi (ITA) 147.54	Thomas Gompf (USA) 146.57
1968	Klaus Dibiasi (ITA) 164.18	Alvaro Gaxiola (MEX) 154.49	Edwin Young (USA) 153.93
1972	Klaus Dibiasi (ITA) 504.12	Richard Rydze (USA) 480.75	Franco Cagnotto (ITA) 475.83
1976	Klaus Dibiasi (ITA) 600.51	Gregory Louganis (USA) 576.99	Vladimir Aleynik (URS) 548.61
1980	Falk Hoffmann (GDR) 835.65	Vladimir Alcinik (URS) 819.705	David Ambartsumyan (URS) 817.44
1984	Greg Louganis (USA) 710.91	Bruce Kimball (USA) 643.40	Kungzheng Li (CHN) 638.28

Greg Louganis (US), considered the world's best diver today, earned perfect 10's in competition several times in world championship meets. In the 1984 Olympics he won 2 gold medals and set new world records for springboard and platform diving.

Swimming and Diving (Women)

100 METERS FREE-STYLE (109 yd. 1 ft.)

1896–1908 Event not held

1912	Fanny Durack (AUSTRALASIA) 1:22.2	Wilhelmina Wylie (AUSTRALASIA) 1:25.4	Jennie Fletcher (GBR) 1:27.0
1920	Ethelda M. Bleibtrey (USA) 1:13.6*	Irene M. Guest (USA) 1:17.0	Frances C. Schroth (USA) 1:17.2
1924	Ethel Lackie (USA) 1:12.4	Mariechen Wehselau (USA) 1:12.8	Gertrude C. Ederle (USA) 1:14.2

	GOLD	SILVER	BRONZE
1928	Albina Osipowich (USA) 1:11.0*	Eleanor A. Gerratti (USA) 1:11.4	M. Joyce Cooper (GBR) 1:13.6
1932	Helene Madison (USA) 1:06.8*	Willemijntje den Ouden (HOL) 1:07.8	Eleanor A. Saville (USA) 1:08.2
1936	Hendrika W. Mastenbroek (HOL) 1:05.9*	Jeanette Campbell (ARG) 1:06.4	Gisela Arendt (GER) 1:06.6
1948	Greta M. Andersen (DEN) 1:06.3	Ann E. Curtis (USA) 1:06.5	Marie-Louise J. Vaessen (HOL) 1:07.6
1952	Katalin Szöke (HUN) 1:06.8	Johanna Termeulen (HOL) 1:07.0	Judit Temes (HUN) 1:07.1
1956	Dawn Fraser (AUS) 1:02.0*	Lorraine J. Crapp (AUS) 1:02.3	Faith Leech (AUS) 1:05.1
1960	Dawn Fraser (AUS) 1:01.2*	S. Christine von Saltza (USA) 1:02.8	Natalie Steward (GBR) 1:03.1
1964	Dawn Fraser (AUS) 59.5*	Sharon Stouder (USA) 59.9	Kathleen Ellis (USA) 1:00.8
1968	Jan M. Henne (USA) 1:00.0	Susan Pedersen (USA) 1:00.3	Linda Gustavson (USA) 1:00.3
1972	Sandra Neilson (USA) 58.59*	Shirley Babashoff (USA) 59.02	Shane E. Gould (AUS) 59.06
1976	Kornelia Ender (GDR) 55.65*	Petra Priemer (GDR) 56.49	Enith Brigitha (HOL) 56.65
1980	Barbara Krause (GDR) 54.78*	Caren Metschuck (GDR) 55.16	Ines Diers (GDR) 55.65
1984	Carrie Steinseifer (USA) 55.92 Nancy Hogshead (USA) 55.92	—	Annemarie Verstappen (HOL) 56.08

The following Olympic records were set in addition to those medal-winning performances already marked with an asterisk*.

1:29.8	Bella Moore (GBR)	1912	1:08.5	Saville	1932	59.9 Fraser	1964
1:23.6	Daisy Curwen (GBR)	1912	1:07.6	den Ouden	1932	59.5 (.47) Magdolna Patoh (HUN)	1972
1:19.8	Durack	1912	1:06.4	(twice) Mastenbroek	1936	59.5 (.51) Neilson	1972
1:18.0	Schroth	1920	1:05.9	Andersen	1948	59.5 (.51) Babashoff	1972
1:14.4	Bleibtrey	1920	1:05.5	Temes	1952	59.44 Gould	1972
1:12.2	Wehselau	1924	1:03.4	Crapp	1956	59.05 Babashoff	1972
1:12.2	Osipowich	1928	1:02.4	Fraser	1956	56.95 Priemer	1976
1:11.4	Gerratti	1928	1:01.9	von Saltza	1960	56.61 Brigitha	1976
1:09.0	Cooper	1932	1:01.4	Fraser	1960	55.81 Ender	1976
1:08.9	Madison	1932	1:00.6	Fraser	1964	54.98 Krause	1980

200 METERS FREE-STYLE (218 yd. 2 ft.)

1896–1964 Event not held

	GOLD	SILVER	BRONZE
1968	Debbie Meyer (USA) 2:10.5*	Jan M. Henne (USA) 2:11.0	Jane Barkman (USA) 2:11.2
1972	Shane E. Gould (AUS) 2:03.56*	Shirley Babashoff (USA) 2:04.33	Keena Rothhammer (USA) 2:04.92
1976	Kornelia Ender (GDR) 1:59.26*	Shirley Babashoff (USA) 2:01.22	Enith Brigitha (HOL) 2:01.40
1980	Barbara Krause (GDR) 1:58.33*	Ines Diers (GDR) 1:59.64	Carmela Schmidt (GDR) 2:01.44
1984	Mary Wayte (USA) 1:59.23	Cynthia Woodhead (USA) 1:59.50	Annemarie Verstappen (HOL) 1:59.69

The following Olympic records were set in addition to those medal-winning performances already marked with an asterisk*.

2:13.1	Meyer	1968	2:07.48	Rothhammer 1972	2:07.05	Andrea Eife
2:08.12	Ann Marshall (USA)	1972			2:01.54	(GDR) 1972 Brigitha 1976

The first time women's swimming made the Olympic schedule was in 1912 at Stockholm. This is the final of the 100 meters free-style event.

400 METERS FREE-STYLE (437 yd. 1 ft.)

	GOLD	SILVER	BRONZE
1896–1920	Event not held		
1924	Martha Norelius (USA) 6:02.2*	Helen Wainwright (USA) 6:03.8	Gertrude C. Ederle (USA) 6:04.8
1928	Martha Norelius (USA) 5:42.8*	Marie J. Braun (HOL) 5:57.8	Josephine McKim (USA) 6:00.2
1932	Helene Madison (USA) 5:28.5*	Lenore Kight (USA) 5:28.6	Jennie Maakal (SAF) 5:47.3
1936	Hendrika W. Maestenbrock (HOL) 5:26.4*	Ragnhild Hveger (DEN) 5:27.5	Lenore Wingard (USA) 5:29.0
1948	Ann E. Curtis (USA) 5:17.8*	Karen-Margrete Harup (DEN) 5:21.2	Catherine Gibson (GBR) 5:22.5
1952	Valéria Gyenge (HUN) 5:12.1*	Éva Novák (HUN) 5:13.7	Evelyn T. Kawamoto (USA) 5:14.6

At the 1976 Montreal Games, Kornelia Ender (GDR) became one of only 3 women to win 4 Olympic gold medals in swimming.

	GOLD	SILVER	BRONZE
1956	Lorraine J. Crapp (AUS) 4:54.6*	Dawn Fraser (AUS) 5:02.5	Sylvia Ruuska (USA) 5:07.1
1960	S. Christine von Saltza (USA) 4:50.6*	Jane Cederqvist (SWE) 4:53.9	Catharina Lagerberg (HOL) 4:56.9
1964	Virginia Duenkel (USA) 4:43.3*	Marilyn Ramenofsky (USA) 4:44.6	Terri L. Stickles (USA) 4:47.2
1968	Debbie Meyer (USA) 4:31.8*	Linda Gustavson (USA) 4:35.5	Karen L. Moras (AUS) 4:37.0
1972	Shane E. Gould (AUS) 4:19.04*	Novella Calligaris (ITA) 4:22.44	Gudrun Wegner (GDR) 4:23.11
1976	Petra Thuemer (GDR) 4:09.89*	Shirley Babashoff (USA) 4:10.46	Shannon Smith (CAN) 4:14.60
1980	Ines Diers (GDR) 4:08.76*	Petra Schneider (GDR) 4:09.16	Carmela Schmidt (GDR) 4:10.86
1984	Tiffany Cohen (USA) 4:07.10*	Sarah Hardcastle (GBR) 4:10.27	June Croft (GBR) 4:11.49

The following Olympic records were set in addition to those medal-winning performances already marked with an asterisk*.

6:12.2	Ederle	1924	5:02.5	Fraser	1956	4:27.53	Jenny Wylie (USA)	1972
5:45.4	Norelius	1928	5:00.2	Crapp	1956			
5:40.9	Kight	1932	4:53.6	von Saltza	1960	4:24.14	Calligaris	1972
5:28.0	Hveger	1936	4:48.6	Duenkel	1964	4:15.71	Rebecca	
5:25.7	Harup	1948	4:47.7	Ramenofsky	1964		Perrott	
5:16.6	Kawamoto	1952	4:35.0	Meyer	1968		(NZL)	1976
5:07.6	Marley L. Shriver (USA)	1956						

800 METERS FREE-STYLE (874 yd. 2 ft.)

1896–1964 Event not held

1968 Debbie Meyer (USA) 9:24.0*	Pamela Kruse (USA) 9:35.7	Maria T. Ramirez (MEX) 9:38.5
1972 Keena Rothhammer (USA) 8:53.68*	Shane E. Gould (AUS) 8:56.39	Norvella Calligaris (ITA) 8:57.46
1976 Petra Thuemer (GDR) 8:37.14*	Shirley Babashoff (USA) 8:37.59	Wendy Weinberg (USA) 8:42.60
1980 Michelle Ford (AUS) 8:28.90*	Ines Diers (GDR) 8:32.55	Heike Dahne (GDR) 8:33.48
1984 Tiffany Cohen (USA) 8:24.95*	Michele Richardson (USA) 8:30.73	Sarah Hardcastle (GBR) 8:32.60

The following Olympic records were set in addition to those medal-winning performances already marked with an asterisk*.

9:42.8	Meyer	1968	9:02.96	Calligaris 1972	8:46.81 Nicole Kramer
9:38.3	Karen L. Moras		8:59.69	Rothhammer	(USA) 1976
	(AUS)	1968		1972	8:46.58 Thuemer 1976

100 METERS BACK STROKE (109 yd. 1 ft.)

1896–1920 Event not held

1924 Sybil Bauer (USA) 1:23.2*	Phyllis Harding (GBR) 1:27.4	Aileen Riggin (USA) 1:28.2
1928 Marie J. Braun (HOL) 1:22.0	Ellen King (GBR) 1:22.2	M. Joyce Cooper (GBR) 1:22.8
1932 Eleanor Holm (USA) 1:19.4	Philomena Mealing (AUS) 1:21.3	Elizabeth V. Davies (GBR) 1:22.5
1936 Dina W. J. Senff (HOL) 1:18.9	Hendrika W. Maestenbroek (HOL) 1:19.2	Alice Bridges (USA) 1:19.4

Shane Gould (AUS) dominated women's swimming in 1972 with a bronze, a silver and 3 gold medals in the six events she entered.

GOLD	SILVER	BRONZE
1948 Karen M. Harup (DEN) 1:14.4*	Suzanne W. Zimmermann (USA) 1:16.0	Judy-Joy Davies (AUS) 1:16.7
1952 Joan C. Harrison (SAF) 1:14.3	Geertje Wielema (HOL) 1:14.5	Jean Stewart (NZL) 1:15.8
1956 Judith B. Grinham (GBR) 1:12.9*	Carin Cone (USA) 1:12.9*	Margaret Edwards (GBR) 1:13.1
1960 Lynn E. Burke (USA) 1:09.3	Natalie Steward (GBR) 1:10.8	Satoko Tanaka (JPN) 1:11.4
1964 Cathy Ferguson (USA) 1:07.7*	Christine Caron (FRA) 1:07.9	Virginia Duenkel (USA) 1:08.0
1968 Kaye Hall (USA) 1:06.2*	Elaine B. Tanner (CAN) 1:06.7	Jane Swaggerty (USA) 1:08.1
1972 Melissa Belote (USA) 1:05.78*	Andrea Gyarmati (HUN) 1:06.26	Susie Atwood (USA) 1:06.34
1976 Ulrike Richter (GDR) 1:01.83*	Birgit Treiber (GDR) 1:03.41	Nancy Garapick (CAN) 1:03.71
1980 Rica Reinisch (GDR) 1:00.86*	Ina Kleber (GDR) 1:02.07	Petra Reidel (GDR) 1:02.64
1984 Theresa Andrews (USA) 1:02.55	Betsy Mitchell (USA) 1:02.63	Jolanda De Rover (HOL) 1:02.91

The following Olympic records were set in addition to those medal-winning performances already marked with an asterisk*

1:24.0	Bauer	1924	1:13.0	Edwards	1956	1:07.6	Tanner	1968	
1:22.0	King	1928	1:12.0	Laura Ranwell		1:07.4	Tanner	1968	
1:21.6	Braun	1928		(SAF)	1960	1:06.08	Belote	1972	
1:18.3	Holm	1932	1:09.4	Burke	1960	1:05.00	Tauna		
1:16.6	Senff	1936	1:09.0	Burke			Vandeweghe		
1:15.6	Harup	1948		(relay leg)	1960		(USA)	1976	
1:15.5	Harup	1948	1:08.9	Duenkel	1964	1:03.28	Garapick	1976	
1:13.8	Wielema	1952	1:08.8	Ferguson	1964	1:02.39	Richter	1976	
1:13.1	Grinham	1956	1:08.5	Caron	1964	1:01.50	Reinisch	1980	

200 METERS BACK STROKE (218 yd. 2 ft.)

1896–1964 Event not held

1968	Lillian D. Watson (USA) 2:24.8*	Elaine B. Tanner (CAN) 2:27.4	Kaye Hall (USA) 2:28.9
1972	Melissa Belote (USA) 2:19.19*	Susie Atwood (USA) 2:20.38	Donna Marie Gurr (CAN) 2:23.22
1976	Ulrike Richter (GDR) 2:13.43*	Birgit Treiber (GDR) 2:14.97	Nancy Garapick (CAN) 2:15.60
1980	Rica Reinisch (GDR) 2:11.77*	Cornelia Polit (GDR) 2:13.75	Birgit Treiber (GDR) 2:14.14
1984	Jolanda De Rover (HOL) 2:12.38	Amy White (USA) 2:13.04	Aneta Patrascoiu (ROM) 2:13.29

The following Olympic records were set in addition to those medal-winning performances already marked with an asterisk*.

2:31.1	Hall	1968	2:29.2	Watson	1968	2:20.58	Belote	1972
2:30.9	Tanner	1968	2:22.13	Atwood	1972	2:16.49	Garapick	1976

100 METERS BREAST STROKE (109 yd. 1 ft.)

GOLD	SILVER	BRONZE
1896–1964 Event not held		
1968 Djurdjica Bjedov (YUG) 1:15.8*	Galina Prozumenshchikova (URS) 1:15.9	Sharon Wichman (USA) 1:16.1
1972 Catherine Carr (USA) 1:13.58*	Galina Stepanova (URS) 1:14.99	Beverley J. Whitfield (AUS) 1:15.73
1976 Hannelore Anke (GDR) 1:11.16	Lyubov Rusanova (URS) 1:13.04	Marina Koshevaia (URS) 1:13.30
1980 Ute Geweniger (GDR) 1:10.22	Elvira Vasilkova (URS) 1:10.41	Susanne Nielsson (DEN) 1:11.16
1984 Petra Van Staveren (HOL) 1:09.88*	Anne Ottenbrite (CAN) 1:10.69	Catherine Poirot (FRA) 1:10.70

The following Olympic records were set in addition to those medal-winning performances already marked with an asterisk*.

1:18.8	Catie Ball (USA)	1968	1:17.4	Ana Maria Norbis (URU)	1968	1:16.7 Norbis	1968
1:17.7	Bjedov	1968				1:15.00 Carr	1972
			1:16.8	Wichman	1968	1:11.11 Anke	1976
						1:10.86 Anke	1976
						1:10.11 Geweniger	1980

200 METERS BREAST STROKE (218 yd. 2 ft.)

GOLD	SILVER	BRONZE
1896–1920 Event not held		
1924 Lucy Morton (GBR) 3:33.2	Agnes Geraghty (USA) 3:34.0	Gladys H. Carson (GBR) 3:35.4
1928 Hilde Schrader (GER) 3:12.6	Mietje Baron (HOL) 3:15.2	Lotte Mühe (GER) 3:17.6
1932 Claire Dennis (AUS) 3:06.3*	Hideko Maehata (JPN) 3:06.4	Else Jacobson (DEN) 3:07.1
1936 Hideko Maehata (JPN) 3:03.6	Martha Genenger (GER) 3:04.2	Inge Sörensen (DEN) 3:07.8
1948 Petronella van Vliet (HOL) 2:57.2	Beatrice Lyons (AUS) 2:57.7	Éva Novák (HUN) 2:00.2
1952 Éva Székely (HUN) 2:51.7*†	Eva Novák (HUN) 2:54.4	Helen O. Gordon (GBR) 2:57.6
1956 Ursula Happe (GER) 2:53.1*‡	Éva Székely (HUN) 2:54.8	Éva-Maria ten Elsen (GER) 2:55.1
1960 Anita Lonsbrough (GBR) 2:49.5*	Wiltrud Urselmann (GER) 2:50.0	Barbara Göbel (GER) 2:53.6
1964 Galina Prozumenshchikova (URS) 2:46.4*	Claudia A. Kolb (USA) 2:47.6	Svetlana Babanina (URS) 2:48.6
1968 Sharon Wichman (USA) 2:44.4*	Djurdjica Bjedov (YUG) 2:46.4	Galina Prozumenshchikova (URS) 2:47.0
1972 Beverley J. Whitfield (AUS) 2:41.71*	Dana Schoenfield (USA) 2:42.05	Galina Stepanova (URS) 2:42.36
1976 Marina Koshevaia (URS) 2:33.35*	Marina Iurchenia (URS) 2:36.08	Lyubov Rusanova (URS) 2:36.22
1980 Lina Kachushite (URS) 2:29.54*	Svetlana Varganova (URS) 2:29.61	Yulia Bogdanova (URS) 2:32.39

1984 Anne Ottenbrite   Susan Rapp   Ingrid Lempereur
      (CAN) 2:30.38   (USA) 2:31.15   (BEL) 2:31.40

The following Olympic records were set in addition to those medal-winning
performances already marked with an asterisk*.

3:27.6	Geraghty	1924	2:57.4	van Vliet	1948	2:48.3 Babanina 1964
3:11.6	Schrader	1928	2:57.0	van Vliet	1948	2:43.13 Agnes Kissne-
3:11.2	Schrader	1928	2:54.0	Novák	1952	Kaczander
3:08.2	Dennis	1932	2:54.0†	Székely	1952	(HUN) 1972
3:03.0	Genenger	1936	2:52.0	Urselmann	1960	2:35.14 Koshevaia 1976
3:01.9	Maehata	1936	2:48.6	Bärbel Grimmer		2:29.77 Varganova 1980
3:01.2†	Székely	1948		(GER)	1964	

---

†Butterfly stroke (then permitted) used.
‡Underwater technique (then permitted) used.

100 METERS BUTTERFLY (109 yd. 1 ft.)

1896–1952 Event not held
1956	Shelley Mann	Nancy J. Ramey	Mary J. Sears
	(USA) 1:11.0	(USA) 1:11.9	(USA) 1:14.4
1960	Carolyn J. Schuler	Marianne Heemskerk	Janice Andrew
	(USA) 1:09.5*	(HOL) 1:10.4	(AUS) 1:12.2
1964	Sharon Stouder	Aagje Kok	Kathleen Ellis
	(USA) 1:04.7*	(HOL) 1:05.6	(USA) 1:06.0
1968	Lynette McClements	Ellie Daniel	Susan Shields
	(AUS) 1:05.5	(USA) 1:05.8	(USA) 1:06.2
1972	Mayumi Aoki	Roswitha Beier	Andrea Gyarmati
	(JPN) 1:03.34*	(GDR) 1:03.61	(HUN) 1:03.73
1976	Kornelia Ender	Andrea Pollack	Wendy Boglioli
	(GDR) 1:00.13*	(GDR) 1:00.98	(USA) 1:01.17
1980	Caren Metschuck	Andrea Pollack	Christiane Knacke
	(GDR) 1:00.42	(GDR) 1:00.90	(GDR) 1:01.44
1984	Mary Meagher	Jenna Johnson	Karin Seick
	(USA) 59.26	(USA) 1:00.19	(FRG) 1:01.36

**Aagje Kok (HOL) won the 200 meters butterfly when it was introduced in the
Olympic program in 1968.**

The following Olympic records were set in addition to those medal-winning performances already marked with an asterisk*.

1:11.2	Mann	1956	1:07.0	Stouder	1964	1:01.84	Boglioli	1976
1:09.8	Schuler	1960	1:05.6	Stouder	1964	1:01.43	Pollack	1976
1:07.8	Ellis	1964	1:04.00	Aoki	1972	1:01.03	Ender	1976
1:07.5	Donna De Varona (USA)	1964	1:03.80	Gyarmati	1972	0:59.05	Meagher	1984

200 METERS BUTTERFLY (218 yd. 2 ft.)

GOLD	SILVER	BRONZE
1896–1964	Event not held	
1968	Aagje Kok (HOL) 2:24.7*	Helga Lindner (GDR) 2:24.8	Ellie Daniel (USA) 2:25.9
1972	Karen Moe (USA) 2:15.57*	Lynn Colella (USA) 2:16.34	Ellie Daniel (USA) 2:16.74
1976	Andrea Pollack (GDR) 2:11.41*	Ulrike Tauber (GDR) 2:12.50	Rosemarie Gabriel (GDR) 2:12.86
1980	Ines Geissler (GDR) 2:10.44*	Sybille Schonrock (GDR) 2:10.45	Michelle Ford (AUS) 2:11.66
1984	Mary Meagher (USA) 2:06.90*	Karen Phillips (AUS) 2:10.56	Ina Beyermann (FRG) 2:11.91

The following Olympic records were set in addition to those medal-winning performances already marked with an asterisk *. The butterfly stroke was permissible in the 1948 and 1952 breast stroke competition. The fastest time then recorded was 2:54.0 by Éva Székely in 1952.

2:33.0	Diane Giebel (USA)	1968	2:26.3	Kok	1968	2:14.53	Karen Thornton (USA)	1976
2:29.4	Daniel	1968	2:18.32	Rosemarie Kother (GDR)	1972	2:14.39	Tamara Shelofastova (URS)	1976
2:29.1	Toni Hewitt (USA)	1968	2:17.18	Daniel	1972	2:11.56	Pollack	1976

200 METERS INDIVIDUAL MEDLEY

1896–1964	Event not held		
1968	Claudia Kolb (USA) 2:24.7	Susan Pedersen (USA) 2:28.8	Jan Henne (USA) 2:31.4
1972	Shane Gould (AUS) 2:23.07*	Kornelia Ender (GDR) 2:23.59	Lynn Vidali (USA) 2:24.06
1976–1980	Event not held		
1984	Tracy Caulkins (USA) 2:12.64*	Nancy Hogshead (USA) 2:15.17	Michele Pearson (AUS) 2:15.92

400 METERS INDIVIDUAL MEDLEY

1896–1960	Event not held		
1964	Donna De Varona (USA) 5:18.7*	Sharon Finneran (USA) 5:24.1	Martha Randall (USA) 5:24.2
1968	Claudia A. Kolb (USA) 5:08.5*	Lynn Vidali (USA) 5:22.2	Sabine Steinbach (GDR) 5:25.3
1972	Gail Neall (AUS) 5:02.97*	Leslie Cliff (CAN) 5:03.57	Novella Calligaris (ITA) 5:03.99
1976	Ulrike Tauber (GDR) 4:42.77*	Cheryl Gibson (CAN) 4:48.10	Becky Smith (CAN) 4:50.48
1980	Petra Schneider (GDR) 4:36.29*	Sharron Davies (GBR) 4:46.83	Agnieszka Czopek (POL) 4:48.17

1984 Tracy Caulkins   Suzanne Landells   Petra Zindler
     (USA) 4:39.24   (AUS) 4:48.30   (FRG) 4:48.57

The following Olympic records were set in addition to those medal-winning
performances already marked with an asterisk *.

5:30.6	Anita	5:26.8	Veronika	5:17.2	Kolb	1968
	Lonsbrough		Holletz	5:06.96	Evelin Stolze
	(GBR) 1964		(GDR) 1964		(GDR) 1972
5:27.8	Randall 1964	5:24.2	De Varona 1964	4:52.90	Smith 1976
				4:51.24	Tauber 1976

4 × 100 METERS FREE-STYLE RELAY

GOLD	SILVER	BRONZE
1896–1908 Event not held		
1912 **GREAT BRITAIN**	**GERMANY** 6:04.6	**AUSTRIA** 6:17.0
5:52.8*		
Bella Moore	Wally Dressel	Margarete Adler
Jennie Fletcher	Louise Otto	Klara Milch
Annie Spiers	Hermine Stindt	Josephine Sticker
Irene Steer	Grete Rosenberg	Berta Zahourek
1920 **UNITED STATES**	**GREAT BRITAIN**	**SWEDEN** 5:43.6
5:11.6*	5:40.8	
Margaret D. Woodbridge	Hilda James	Aina Berg
Frances C. Schroth	Constance M. Jeans	Emy Machnow
Irene M. Guest	Charlotte Radcliffe	Karin Nilsson
Ethelda M. Bleibtrey	Grace McKenzie	Jane Gylling
1924 **UNITED STATES**	**GREAT BRITAIN**	**SWEDEN** 5:35.6
4:58.8*	5:17.0	
Gertrude C. Ederle	Florence Barker	Aina Berg
Euphrasia Donnelly	Grace McKenzie	Vivan Petersson
Ethel Lackie	Iris V. Tanner	Gulli Everlund
Mariechen Wehselau	Constance M. Jeans	Hjördis Töppel
1928 **UNITED STATES**	**GREAT BRITAIN**	**SOUTH AFRICA**
4:47.6*	5:02.8	5:13.4
Adelaide Lambert	M. Joyce Cooper	Katharine Russell
Eleonora Gerratti	Sarah Stewart	Rhoda Rennie
Albina Osipowich	Iris V. Tanner	Marie Bedford
Martha Norelius	Ellen E. King	Frederica J. van der
		Goes
1932 **UNITED STATES**	**NETHERLANDS**	**GREAT BRITAIN**
4:38.0*	4:47.5	4:52.4
Josephine McKim	Maria Vierdag	Elizabeth V. Davies
Helen Johns	Maria Oversloot	Helen Varcoe
Eleonora Saville	Cornelia Ladde	M. Joyce Cooper
Helene Madison	Willemijntje den Ouden	Edna Hughes
1936 **NETHERLANDS**	**GERMANY** 4:36.8	**UNITED STATES**
4:36.0*		4:40.2
Johanna K. Selbach	Ruth Halbsguth	Katherine L. Rawls
Catherina W. Wagner	Leni M. Lohmar	Bernice R. Lapp
Willemijntje den Ouden	Ingeborg Schmitz	Mavis Freeman
Hendrika W.	Gisela Arendt	Olive M. McKean
Mastenbroek		
1948 **UNITED STATES**	**DENMARK** 4:29.6	**NETHERLANDS**
4:29.2*		4:31.6
Marie L. Corridon	Eva J. Riise	Irma Schuhmacher
Thelma M. Kalama	Karen M. Harup	Margot Marsman
Brenda M. Helser	Greta M. Andersen	Marie-Louise J. Vaessen
Ann E. Curtis	Fritze W. Carstensen	Johanna M. Termeulen
1952 **HUNGARY** 4:24.4*	**NETHERLANDS**	**UNITED STATES**
	4:29.0	4:30.1
Ilona Novák	Marie-Louise Linssen	Jacqueline La Vine
Judit Temes	Koosje van Voorn	Marilee Stepan
Éva Novák	Johanna M. Termeulen	Joan Alderson
Katalin Szöke	Irma Heijting	Evelyn Kawamoto

Tracy Caulkins (US), here wearing 5 World Championship gold medals and one silver from 1978, added 2 Olympic golds in 1984 in the 200 and 400 meters individual medleys.

Shirley Babashoff (USA) holds a total of 8 Olympic medals, including 2 golds in the 4 × 100 meters free-style relay events in 1972 and 1976 and 6 silvers in team and individual competition.

GOLD	SILVER	BRONZE
1956 AUSTRALIA 4:17.1*	UNITED STATES 4:19.2	SOUTH AFRICA 4:25.7
Dawn Fraser	Sylvia Ruuska	Jeanette Myburgh
Faith Leech	Shelley Mann	Susan Roberts
Sandra Morgan	Nancy Simons	Natalie Myburgh
Lorraine J. Crapp	Joan Rosazza	Moira Abernethy
1960 UNITED STATES 4:08.9*	AUSTRALIA 4:11.3	GERMANY 4:19.7
Joan A. Spillane	Dawn Fraser	Christel Steffin
Shirley A. Stobs	Ilsa Konrads	Heidi Pechstein
Carolyn V. Wood	Lorraine J. Crapp	Gisela Weiss
S. Christine von Saltza	Alva Colquhoun	Ursula Brunner
1964 UNITED STATES 4:03.8*	AUSTRALIA 4:06.9	NETHERLANDS 4:12.0
Sharon Stouder	Robyn Thorn	Paulina van der Wildt
Donna De Varona	Janice Murphy	Catharina Beumer
Lillian Watson	Lynette Bell	Winnie Van Weerdenburg
Kathleen Ellis	Dawn Fraser	Erica Terpstra
1968 UNITED STATES 4:02.5*	EAST GERMANY 4:05.7	CANADA 4:07.2
Jane Barkman	Gabriele Wetzko	Angela Coughlan
Linda Gustavson	Roswitha Krause	Marilyn Corson
Susan Pedersen	Uta Schmuck	Elaine B. Tanner
Jan M. Henne	Martina Grunert	Marion Lay
1972 UNITED STATES 3:55.19*	EAST GERMANY 3:55.55	WEST GERMANY 3:57.93
Sandra Neilson	Gabriele Wetzko	Jutta Weber
Jennifer Kemp	Andrea Eife	Heidemarie Reineck
Jane Barkman	Elke Sehmisch	Gudrun Beckmann
Shirley Babashoff	Kornelia Ender	Angela Steinbach
1976 UNITED STATES 3:44.82*	EAST GERMANY 3:45.50	CANADA 3:48.81
Kim Peyton	Kornelia Ender	Gail Amundrud
Wendy Boglioli	Petra Priemer	Barbara Clark
Jill Sterkel	Andrea Pollack	Becky Smith
Shirley Babashoff	Claudia Hempel	Anne Jardin
1980 EAST GERMANY 3:42.71*	SWEDEN 3:48.93	NETHERLANDS 3:49.51
Barbara Krause	Carina Ljungdahl	Conny van Bentum
Caren Metschuck	Tina Gustafsson	Wilma van Velsen
Ines Diers	Agneta Martensson	Reggie de Jong
Sarina Hulsenbeck	Agneta Eriksson	Annelies Maas
1984 USA 3:43.43	NETHERLANDS 3:44.40	WEST GERMANY 3:45.56
Jenna Johnson	Annemarie Verstappen	Iris Zscherpe
Carrie Steinseifer	Elles Voskes	Susanne Schuster
Dara Torres	Desi Reijers	Christiane Pielke
Nancy Hogshead	Conny Van Bentum	Karin Seick

The following Olympic records were set in addition to those medal-winning performances already marked with an asterisk *.

4:55.6	United States 1928	4:28.1	United States 1952	3:50.27	United States 1976
4:33.5	Denmark 1948	3:58.11	East Germany 1972	3:48.95	East Germany 1976
4:31.3	Netherlands 1948				

4 × 100 METERS MEDLEY RELAY

(Order of strokes: back stroke, breast stroke, butterfly, free-style.)

GOLD	SILVER	BRONZE
1896–1956 Event not held		
1960 **UNITED STATES** 4:41.1*	**AUSTRALIA** 4:45.9	**GERMANY** 4:47.6
Lynn E. Burke	Marilyn Wilson	Ingrid Schmidt
Patty Kempner	Rosemarie Lassig	Ursula Küper
Carolyn J. Schuler	Janice Andrew	Bärbel Fuhrmann
S. Christine von Saltza	Dawn Fraser	Ursula Brunner
1964 **UNITED STATES** 4:33.9*	**NETHERLANDS** 4:37.0	**U.S.S.R.** 4:39.2
Cathy Ferguson	Kornelia Winkel	Tatyana Savelieva
Cynthia Goyette	Klena Bimolt	Svetlana Babanina
Sharon Stouder	Aagje Kok	Tatyana Deviatova
Kathleen Ellis	Erica Terpstra	Natalya Ustinova
1968 **UNITED STATES** 4:28.3*	**AUSTRALIA** 4:30.0	**WEST GERMANY** 4:36.4
Kaye Hall	Lynette P. Watson	Angelika Kraus
Catie Ball	Lynette McClements	Uta Frommater
Ellie Daniel	Judy Playfair	Heike Hustede
Susan Pedersen	Janet Steinbeck	Heidi Reineck
1972 **UNITED STATES** 4:20.75*	**EAST GERMANY** 4:24.91	**WEST GERMANY** 4:26.46
Melissa Belote	Christine Herbst	Silke Pielen
Catherine Carr	Renate Vogel	Verena Eberle
Deena Deardurff	Roswitta Beier	Gudrun Beckmann
Sandra Neilsen	Kornelia Ender	Heidi Reineck
1976 **EAST GERMANY** 4:07.95*	**UNITED STATES** 4:14.55	**CANADA** 4:15.22
Ulrike Richter	Linda Jeszek	Wendy Hogg
Hannelore Anke	Lauri Siering	Robin Corsiglia
Andrea Pollack	Camille Wright	Susan Sloan
Kornelia Ender	Shirley Babashoff	Anne Jardin
1980 **EAST GERMANY** 4:06.67*	**GREAT BRITAIN** 4:12.24	**U.S.S.R.** 4:13.61
Rica Reinisch	Helen Jameson	Yelena Kruglova
Ute Geweniger	Margaret Kelly	Elvira Vasilkova
Andrea Pollack	Ann Osgerby	Alla Grishchenkova
Caren Metschuck	June Croft	Natalya Strunnikova
1984 **USA** 4:08.34	**WEST GERMANY** 4:11.97	**CANADA** 4:12.98
Theresa Andrews	Svenja Schlicht	Reema Abdo
Tracy Caulkins	Ute Hasse	Anne Ottenbrite
Mary Meagher	Ina Beyermann	Michelle MacPherson
Nancy Hogshead	Karin Seick	Pamela Rai

The following Olympic records were set in addition to those medal-winning performances already marked with an asterisk *

4:49.0	Gt. Britain 1960	4:27.58	East Germany 1972	4:20.10	Canada 1976
4:47.7	Holland 1960			4:13.98	East Germany 1976
4:39.1	U.S.S.R. 1964	4:27.57	United States 1972		

SYNCHRONIZED SWIMMING—SOLO

1896–1980 Event not held		
1984 Tracie Ruiz (USA) 198.467	Carolyn Waldo (CAN) 195.300	Miwako Motoyoshi (JPN) 187.050

1896–1980 Event not held
1984   **USA** 195.584   **CANADA** 194.234   **JAPAN** 187.992
     Candy Costie   Sharon Hambrock   Saeko Kimura
     Tarcie Ruiz   Kelly Kryczka   Miwako Motoyoshi

SPRINGBOARD DIVING

	GOLD	SILVER	BRONZE
1896–1912	Event not held		
1920	Aileen M. Riggin (USA) 539.9	Helen E. Wainwright (USA) 534.8	Thelma R. Payne (USA) 534.1
1924	Elizabeth Becker (USA) 474.5	Aileen M. Riggin (USA) 460.4	Caroline Fletcher (USA) 434.4
1928	Helen Meany (USA) 78.62	Dorothy Poynton (USA) 75.62	Georgia Coleman (USA) 73.38
1932	Georgia Coleman (USA) 87.52	Katherine Rawls (USA) 82.56	Jane Fauntz (USA) 82.12
1936	Marjorie Gestring (USA) 89.27	Katherine Rawls (USA) 88.35	Dorothy Hill (USA) 82.36
1948	Victoria Draves (USA) 108.74	Zoe Ann Olsen (USA) 108.23	Patricia Elsener (USA) 101.30
1952	Patricia McCormick (USA) 147.30	Madeleine Moreau (FRA) 139.34	Zoe Ann Jensen (USA) 127.57
1956	Patricia McCormick (USA) 142.36	Jeanne Stunyo (USA) 125.89	Irene Macdonald (CAN) 121.40
1960	Ingrid Krämer (GER) 155.81	Paula J. Pope (USA) 141.24	Elizabeth Ferris (GBR) 139.09
1964	Ingrid Engel (GER) 145.00	Jeanne Collier (USA) 138.36	Mary Willard (USA) 138.18
1968	Sue Gossick (USA) 150.77	Tamara Pogozheva (URS) 145.30	Keala O'Sullivan (USA) 145.23
1972	Micki J. King (USA) 450.03	Ulrika Knape (SWE) 434.19	Marina Janicke (GDR) 430.92
1976	Jennifer Chandler (USA) 506.19	Christa Kohler (GDR) 469.41	Cynthia McIngvale (USA) 466.83
1980	Irina Kalinina (URS) 725.910	Martina Proeber (GDR) 698.895	Karin Guthke (GDR) 685.245
1984	Sylvie Bernier (CAN) 530.70	Kelly McCormick (USA) 527.46	Christina Seufert (USA) 422.07

PLATFORM DIVING

1896–1908	Event not held		
1912	Greta Johansson (SWE) 39.9	Lisa Regnell (SWE) 36.0	Isabelle White (GBR) 34.0
1920	Stefani Fryland-Clausen (DEN) 34.6	Eileen Armstrong (GBR) 33.3	Eva Ollivier (SWE) 33.3
1924	Caroline Smith (USA) 10.5	Elizabeth Becker (USA) 11.0	Hjördis Töpel (SWE) 15.5
1928	Elizabeth Pinkston (USA) 31.6	Georgia Coleman (USA) 30.6	Lala Sjöqvist (SWE) 29.2
1932	Dorothy Poynton (USA) 40.26	Georgia Coleman (USA) 35.56	Marion Roper (USA) 35.22
1936	Dorothy Hill (USA) 33.93	Velma Dunn (USA) 33.63	Käthe Köhler (GER) 33.43
1948	Victoria Draves (USA) 68.87	Patricia Elsener (USA) 66.28	Birte Christoffersen (DEN) 66.04
1952	Patricia McCormick (USA) 79.37	Paula J. Myers (USA) 71.63	Juno Irwin (USA) 70.49

1956	Patricia McCormick (USA) 84.85	Juno Irwin (USA) 81.64	Paula J. Myers (USA) 81.58
1960	Ingrid Krämer (GER) 91.28	Paula J. Pope (USA) 88.94	Ninel Krutova (URS) 86.99
1964	Lesley Bush (USA) 99.80	Ingrid Engel (GER) 98.45	Galina Alekseyeva (URS) 97.60
1968	Milena Duchková (TCH) 109.59	Natalia Lobanova (URS) 105.14	Ann Peterson (USA) 101.11
1972	Ulrika Knape (SWE) 390.00	Milena Duchková (TCH) 370.92	Marina Janicke (GDR) 360.54
1976	Elena Vaytsekhovskaya (URS) 406.59	Ulrika Knape (SWE) 402.60	Deborah Wilson (USA) 401.07
1980	Martina Jaschke (GDR) 596.250	Servard Emirzyan (URS) 576.465	Liana Tsotadze (URS) 575.925
1984	Jihong Zhou (CHN) 435.51	Michele Mitchell (USA) 431.19	Wendy Wyland (USA) 422.07

The following married medalists also won medals under their maiden names:

Eleanor Saville, formerly Gerratti

Lenore Wingard, formerly Kight

Marie-Louise Linssen, formerly Vaessen

Irma Heijting, formerly Schuhmacher

Paula Pope, formerly Myers

Dorothy Hill, formerly Poynton

Elizabeth Pinkston, formerly Becker

Zoe Ann Jensen, formerly Olsen

Ingrid Engel, formerly Krämer

Water Polo

Water Polo tournaments were held in 1900 and 1904 but entries were Clubs rather than International teams.

	GOLD	SILVER	BRONZE
1908	**GREAT BRITAIN**	**BELGIUM**	**SWEDEN**
	Charles S. Smith	Albert Michant	Thorsten Kumfeldt
	George Nevinson	Herman Meyboom	Axel Runström
	George Cornet	Victor Boin	Harald Julin
	Thomas Thould	Joseph Pletincx	Pontus Hansson
	George Wilkinson	Fernand Feyaerts	Gunnar Wennerström
	Paul Radmilovic	Oscar Grégoire	Robert Andersson
	Charles G. E. Forsyth	Herman Donners	Erik Bergvall
1912	**GREAT BRITAIN**	**SWEDEN**	**BELGIUM**
	Charles S. Smith	Thorsten Kumfeldt	Albert Durant
	George Cornet	Harald Julin	Herman Donners
	Charles Bugbee	Max Gumpel	Victor Boin
	Arthur Hill	Pontus Andersson	Joseph Pletincx
	George Wilkinson	Wilhelm Andersson	Oscar Grégoire
	Paul Radmilovic	Robert Andersson	Herman Meyboom
	Isaac Bentham	Eric Bergqvist	Félicien Courbet
			Jean Hoffman
			Pierre Nijs
1920	**GREAT BRITAIN**	**BELGIUM**	**SWEDEN**
	Charles S. Smith	Gérard Blitz	Harald Julin
	Paul Radmilovic	Maurice Blitz	Robert Andersson
	Charles Bugbee	Albert Durant	Wilhelm Andersson
	Noel M. Purcell	Joseph Pletincx	Eric Bergqvist
	Christopher Jones	Paul Gailly	Max Gumpel
	William Peacock	Pierre Nijs	Pontus Hansson
	William H. Dean	René Bauwens	Erik Andersson
		Pierre Dewin	Nils Backlund
			Theodor Nauman

	GOLD	SILVER	BRONZE
1924	**FRANCE** Paul Dujardin Henri Padou Georges Rigal Albert Deborgies Nöel Delberghe Robert Desmettre Albert Mayraud	**BELGIUM** Gérard Blitz Maurice Blitz Albert Durant Joseph Pletincx Joseph Cludts Joseph de Combe Pierre Dewin Georges Fleurix Paul Gailly Jules Thiry Pierre Vermetten	**UNITED STATES** Arthur Austin Oliver Horn Frederick Lauer Clarence Mitchell John Norton Wallace O'Connor George Schroth Herbert Vollmer Johnny Weissmuller
1928	**GERMANY** Erich Rademacher Fritz Gunst Otto Cordes Emil Benecke Joachim Rademacher Karl Bähre Max Amann Johann Blank	**HUNGARY** István Barta Sándor Ivády Márton Hommonay Alajos Keserü Olivér Halasy József Vértesy Ferenc Keserü	**FRANCE** Paul Dujardin Henri Padou Jules Keignaert Emile Bulteel Achille Tribouillet Henri Cuvelier Ernest Rogez Albert van de Plancke Albert Thévenon
1932	**HUNGARY** György Bródy Sándor Ivády Márton Hommonay Olivér Halasy József Vértesy János Németh Ferenc Keserü Alajos Keserü István Barta Miklós Sárkány	**GERMANY** Erich Rademacher Fritz Gunst Otto Cordes Emil Benecke Joachim Rademacher Heiko Schwartz Hans Schulze Hans Eckstein	**UNITED STATES** Herbert Wildman Wallace O'Connor Calvert Strong Philip Daubenspeck Harold McCallister Charles Finn Austin Clapp
1936	**HUNGARY** György Bródy Kálmán Hazai Márton Hommonay Olivér Halasy Jenő Brandi János Németh György Kutasi Mihály Bozsi István Molnár Sándor Tarics Miklós Sárkány	**GERMANY** Paul Klingenburg Bernhard Baier Gustav Schürger Fritz Gunst Josef Hauser Hans Schneider Hans Schulze Alfred Kienzle Heinrich Krug Helmuth Schwenn Fritz Stolze	**BELGIUM** Albert Castelens Gérard Blitz Pierre Coppieters Fernand Isselé Joseph de Combe Henry Stoelen Henry Disy Henri de Pauw Edmond Michiels
1948	**ITALY** Pasquale Buonocore Emilio Bulgarelli Cesare Rubini Geminio Ognio Ermenegildo Arena Aldo Ghira Tulio Pandolfini Mario Majoni Gianfranco Pandolfini	**HUNGARY** László Jenei Miklós Holop Dezsö Gyarmati Károly Szittya Oszkár Csuvik István Szivós Dezsö Lemhényi Jenő Brandi Dezsö Fábián Endre Györfi	**NETHERLANDS** Johannes J. Rohner Cornelius Korevaar Cor Braasem Hans Stam Alfred F. Ruimschotel Rudolph van Feggelen Frits Smol Hendrikus Z. Keetelaar Pieter J. Salomons

GOLD	SILVER	BRONZE
1952 HUNGARY	**YUGOSLAVIA**	**ITALY**
László Jenei	Zdravko Kovačić	Raffaello Gambino
György Vizvári	Veljiko Bakašun	Cesare Rubini
Dezsö Gyarmati	Ivo Štakula	Maurizio Mannelli
Kálmán Markovits	Ivo Kurtini	Geminio Ognio
Antal Bolvári	Boško Vuksanović	Ermenegildo Arena
István Szivós	Zdravko Ježić	Renato de Sanzuane
György Kárpáti	Lovro Radonić	Carlo Peretti
Róbert Antal	Vlado Ivković	Renato Traiola
Dezsö Fábián	Marko Brainović	Vincenzo Polito
Károly Szittya		Salvatore Gionta
Dezsö Lemhényi		
Miklós Martin		
István Hosznos		
1956 HUNGARY	**YUGOSLAVIA**	**U.S.S.R.**
Ottó Boros	Zdravko Kovačić	Boris Goikhman
Dezsö Gyarmati	Hrvoje Kačić	Vyacheslav Kurrenoy
Kálmán Markovits	Marijan Žužej	Yuriy Schlyapin
István Hevesi	Ivo Cipci	Valentin Prokopov
György Kárpáti	Tomislav Franjković	Boris Markarov
Mihály Mayer	Lovro Radonić	Petr Mchvenieradze
Antal Bolvári	Zdravko Ježić	Petr Breus
László Jenei	Vlado Ivković	Mikkhail Ryzhak
Tivadar Kanisza		Viktor Ageyev
István Szivós		Nodar Gvakharia
Ervin Zádor		
1960 ITALY	**U.S.S.R.**	**HUNGARY**
Danio Bardi	Vladimir Semyenov	Ottó Boros
Giuseppe d'Altrui	Anatoliy Kartashyov	István Hevesi
Franco Lavoratori	Vladimir Novikov	Mihály Mayer
Gianni Lonzi	Petr Mchvenieradze	Kálmán Markovits
Rosario Parmegiani	Yuriy Grigorovskiy	Tivadar Kanisza
Eraldo Pizzo	Viktor Ageyev	Zoltán Dömötör
Dante Rossi	Givi Chikvanaya	György Kárpáti
Amadeo Ambron	Leri Gogoladze	László Jenei
Salvatore Gionta	Vyacheslav Kurrenoy	Péter Rusorán II
Luigi Mannelli	Boris Goikhman	András Katona
Brunello Spinelli	Evgeniy Saltsyn	Dezsö Gyarmati
Giancario Guerrini		László Felkai
		János Konrád
		András Bodnár
1964 HUNGARY	**YUGOSLAVIA**	**U.S.S.R.**
Miklós Ambrus	Milan Muškatirović	Igor Grabovsky
László Felkai	Ivo Trumbić	Vladimir Kuznetsov
János Konrád	Vinco Rosić	Boris Grishin
Zoltán Dömötör	Slatco Šimenć	Boris Popov
Tivadar Kanisza	Božidor Stanišić	Nikolay Kalashnikov
Péter Rusorán II	Ante Nardeli	Zenon Bortevich
György Kárpáti	Zoran Janković	Nicolay Kuznetsov
Dezsö Gyarmati	Frane Nonković	Vladimir Semyenov
Dénes Pócsik	Karlo Stipanić	Viktor Ageyev
Mihály Mayer	Mirko Sandič	Leonid Ossipov
András Bodnár	Ozren Bonačic	Eduard Yegorov
Ottó Boros		

1968	YUGOSLAVIA	U.S.S.R.	HUNGARY
	Karlo Stipanić	Vadim Gulyaev	Endre Molnár
	Ivo Trumbić	Givi Chikvanaya	Mihály Mayer
	Ozren Bonačić	Boris Grishin	István Szivós
	Uroš Marović	Alexandr Dolgushin	János Konrád II
	Ronald Lopatny	Alexei Barkalov	László Sárosi
	Zoran Janković	Yuriy Grigorovskiy	László Felkai
	Miroslav Poljak	Vladimir Semyenov	Ferenc Konrád III
	Dejan Dabović	Alexandr Shidlovski	Dénes Pócsik
	Djordje Perišić	Vjacheslav Skok	András Bodnár
	Mirko Sandič	Leonid Ossipov	Zoltán Dömötör
	Zdravko Hebel	Oleg Bovin	János Steinmetz

1972	U.S.S.R.	HUNGARY	UNITED STATES
	Vadim Gulyaev	Endre Molnár	James Slatton
	Anatoli Akimov	András Bodnár	Stanley Cole
	Alexandr Dreval	István Goergenyi	Russell Webb
	Alexandr Dolgushin	Zoltán Kasas	Barry Weitzenberger
	Vladimir Shmudski	Tamás Fárágo	Gary Sheerer
	Alexandr Kabanov	László Sárosi	Bruce Bradley
	Alexei Barkalov	István Szivós	Peter Asch
	Alexandr Shidlovski	István Magas	James Ferguson
	Nikolai Melnikov	Dénes Pócsik	Steven Barnett
	Leonid Ossipov	Ferenc Konrád	John Parker
	Vyacheslav Sobchenko	Tibor Czervenyak	Eric Lindroth

1976	HUNGARY	ITALY	HOLLAND
	Endre Molnár	Alberto Alberani	Evert Kroon
	István Szivós	Roldano Simeoni	Nico Landeweerd
	Tamás Fárágo	Silvio Baracchini	Jan Evert Veer
	Laszló Sárosi	Sante Marsili	Hans van Zeeland
	Gyorgy Horkai	Marcello del Duca	Ton Buunk
	Gábor Csapó	Gianni de Magistris	Piet de Zwarte
	Attila Sudár	Alessandro Ghibellini	Hans Smit
	Gyorgy Kenéz	Luigi Castagnola	Rik Toonen
	Gyorgy Gerendás	Riccardo de Magistris	Gyze Stroboer
	Ferenc Konrád	Vincenzo d'Angelo	Andy Hoepelman
	Tibor Czervenyák	Umberto Panerai	Alex Boegschoten

1980	U.S.S.R.	YUGOSLAVIA	HUNGARY
	Yevgeniy Sharanov	Luka Vezilic	Endre Molnár
	Sergey Kotenko	Zoran Gopcevic	István Szivós Jr
	Vladimir Akimov	Damir Polić	Attila Sudár
	Yevgeniy Grischin	Ratko Rudić	Gyorgy Gerendás
	Mait Riisman	Zoran Mustur	Gyorgy Horkai
	Aleksandr Kabanov	Zoran Roje	Gábor Csapó
	Aleksey Barkalov	Milivoj Bebic	István Kiss
	Erkin Shagayev	Slobodan Trifunovic	István Udvardi
	Georgy Mshvenieradze	Bosko Lozica	László Kuncz
	Mikhail Ivanov	Predrag Manojlović	Tamás Fárágo
	Vyacheslav Sobchenko	Milorad Krivokapic	Károly Hauszler

1984	YUGOSLAVIA	USA	WEST GERMANY
	Milorad Krivokapic	Craig Wilson	Peter Rohle
	Deni Lusic	Kevin Robertson	Thomas Loebb
	Zoran Petrovic	Gary Figueroa	Frank Otto
	Bozo Vuletic	Peter Campbell	Rainer Hoppe
	Veselin Djuho	Douglas Burke	Armando Fernandez
	Zoran Roje	Joseph Vargas	Thomas Huber
	Milivoj Bebic	Jon Svendsen	Jurgen Schroeder
	Perica Bukic	John Siman	Rainer Osselmann
	Goran Sukno	Andrew McDonald	Hagen Stamm
	Tomislav Paskvalin	Terry Schroeder	Roland Freund
	Igor Milanovic	Jody Campbell	Dirk Theismann
	Dragan Andric	Timothy Shaw	Santiago Chalmovsky
	Andrija Popovic	Christopher Dorst	Werner Obschernikat

Tennis

MEN'S SINGLES

1896	John Boland (GBR)	Demis Kasdaglis (GRE)	— (GBR)
1900	Hugh Doherty (GBR)	Harold Mahony (GBR)	Reginald Doherty (GBR) A.B. Norris (GBR)
1904	Beals Wright (USA)	Robert LeRoy (USA)	Alonzo Bell (USA) Edgar Leonard (USA)
1906	Max Decugis (FRA)	Maurice Germot (FRA)	Zdenek Zemla (BOH)
1908	Josiah Ritchie (GBR)	Otto Froitzheim (GER)	Wilberforce Eves (GBR)
1908[1]	Wentworth Gore (GBR)	George Caridia (GBR)	Josiah Ritchie (GBR)
1912	Charles Winslow (SAF)	Harold Kitson (SAF)	Oscar Kreuzer (GER)
1912[1]	Andre Gobert (FRA)	Charles Dixon (GBR)	Anthony Wilding (NZL)
1920	Louis Raymond (SAF)	Ichiya Kumagae (JPN)	Charles Winslow (GBR)
1924	Vincent Richards (USA)	Henri Cochet (FRA)	Umberto De Morpurgo (ITA)
1928–1984 Event not held			

[1]Indoor tournaments

Jean Borotra (France), one of the leading players of his time, won the bronze with Reno Lacoste as his partner, in the 1924 doubles, when his career was just beginning. He made his 35th appearance at Wimbledon in 1964, just 40 years later.

MEN'S DOUBLES

1896	**GBR/GERMANY** John Boland Fritz Traun	**GREECE** Demis Kasdaglis Demetrios Petrokokkinos	**—**
1900	**GREAT BRITAIN** Reginald Doherty Hugh Doherty	**USA/FRANCE** Basil Spalding de Garmendia Max Decugis	**FRANCE** A. Prevost G. de la Chapelle **GREAT BRITAIN** Harold Mahony A.B. Norris
1904	**USA** Edgar Leonard Beals Wright	**USA** Alonzo Bell Robert LeRoy	**USA** Joseph Wear Allen West **USA** Clarence Gamble Arthur Wear
1906	**FRANCE** Max Decugis Maurice Germot	**GREECE** Xenophon Kasdaglis Ioannis Ballis	**BOHEMIA** Zdenek Zemla Ladislav Zemla
1908	**GREAT BRITAIN** George Hillyard Reginald Doherty	**GREAT BRITAIN** Josiah Ritchie James Parke	**GREAT BRITAIN** Charles Cazalet Charles Dixon
1908[1]	**GREAT BRITAIN** Wentworth Gore Herbert Barrett	**GREAT BRITAIN** George Simond George Caridia	**SWEDEN** Gunnar Setterwall Wollmar Bostrom
1912	**SOUTH AFRICA** Charles Winslow Harold Kitson	**AUSTRIA** Felix Pipes Arthur Zborzil	**FRANCE** Albert Canet Marc Meny de Marangue
1912[1]	**FRANCE** Andre Gobert Maurice Germot	**SWEDEN** Gunnar Setterwall Carl Kempe	**GREAT BRITAIN** Charles Dixon Arthur Beamish
1920	**GREAT BRITAIN** Noel Turnball Max Woosnam	**JAPAN** Ichiya Kumagae Seiichiro Kashio	**FRANCE** Max Decugis Pierre Albarran
1924	**USA** Vincent Richards Frank Hunter	**FRANCE** Jacques Brugnon Henri Cochet	**FRANCE** Jean Borotra Rene Lacoste
1928–1984	Event not held		

[1]Indoor tournaments

MIXED DOUBLES

1896	Event not held		
1900	**GREAT BRITAIN** Charlotte Cooper Reginald Doherty	**FRANCE/GBR** Helene Prevost Harold Mahony	**BOHEMIA/GBR** Hedwig Rosenbaum Archibald Walden **USA/GBR** Marion Jones Hugh Doherty
1904	Event not held		
1906	**FRANCE** Marie Decugis Max Decugis	**GREECE** Sophia Marinow Georgios Simiriotis	**GREECE** Aspasia Matsa Xenophon Kasdaglis
1908	Event not held		
1912	**GERMANY** Dora Koring Heinrich Schomburg	**SWEDEN** Sigrid Fick Gunnar Setterwall	**FRANCE** Marguerite Broquedis Albert Canet
1912[1]	**GREAT BRITAIN** Edith Hannam Charles Dixon	**GREAT BRITAIN** Helen Aitchison Herbert Barrett	**SWEDEN** Sigrid Fick Gunnar Setterwall
1920	**FRANCE** Suzanne Lenglen Max Decugis	**GREAT BRITAIN** Kathleen McKane Max Woosnam	**CZECHOSLOVAKIA** Milada Skrbova Ladislav Zemla
1924	**USA** Hazel Wightman Norris Williams	**USA** Marion Jessup Vincent Richards	**NETHERLANDS** Cornelia Bouman Hendrik Timmer
1928–1984	Event not held		

[1]Indoor tournament

Charlotte Cooper (GBR) was the first female Olympic gold medalist, when she won the women's tennis singles in 1900. She went on to 5 Wimbledon titles after that.

WOMEN'S SINGLES

1896	Event not held		
1900	Charlotte Cooper (GBR)	Helene Prevost (FRA)	Marion Jones (USA)
1904	Event not held		
1906	Esmee Simiriotou (GRE)	Sophia Marinou (GRE)	Euphrosine Paspati (GRE)
1908	Dorothea Chambers (GBR)	Dorothy Boothby (GBR)	Joan Winch (GBR)
1908[1]	Gwen Eastlake-Smith (GBR)	Angela Greene (GBR)	Martha Adlerstrahle (SWE)
1912	Marguerite Broquedis (FRA)	Dora Koring (GER)	Molla Bjurstedt (SWE)
1912[1]	Ethel Hannam (GBR)	Thora Castenschiold (DEN)	Mabel Parton (GBR)
1920	Suzanne Lenglen (FRA)	Dorothy Holman (GBR)	Kathleen McKane (GBR)
1924	Helen Wills (USA)	Julie Vlasto (FRA)	Kathleen McKane (GBR)
1928–1984	Event not held		

---

[1] Indoor tournaments

WOMEN'S DOUBLES

1896–1912	Event not held		
1920	**GREAT BRITAIN** Winifred McNair Kathleen McKane	**GREAT BRITAIN** Geraldine Beamish Dorothy Holman	**FRANCE** Suzanne Lenglen Elisabeth d'Ayen
1924	**USA** Hazel Wightman Helen Wills	**GREAT BRITAIN** Edith Covell Kathleen McKane	**GREAT BRITAIN** Dorothy Shepherd-Barron Evelyn Colyer
1928–1984	Event not held		

17. Track and Field Athletics (Men)

100 METERS (109 yd. 1 ft.)

	GOLD	SILVER	BRONZE
1896	Thomas E. Burke (USA) 12.0	Fritz Hofmann (GER) d.n.a.	Alajos Szokolyi (HUN) d.n.a.
1900	Francis W. Jarvis (USA) 11.0	J. Walter B. Tewksbury (USA) 1 ft.	Stanley Rowley (AUS/NZL) inches
1904	Archie Hahn (USA) 11.0	Nathaniel J. Cartmell (USA) d.n.a.	William Hogenson (USA) d.n.a.
1906	Archie Hahn (USA) 11.2	Fay R. Moulton (USA) 11.3	Nigel Barker (AUS) 11.3
1908	Reginald E. Walker (SAF) 10.8*	James A. Rector (USA) 2 ft.	Robert Kerr (CAN) inches
1912	Ralph C. Craig (USA) 10.8	Alvah Meyer (USA) 10.9	Donald F. Lippincott (USA) 10.9
1920	Charles W. Paddock (USA) 10.8	Morris M. Kirksey (USA) 1 ft.	Harry F. V. Edward (GBR) d.n.a.
1924	Harold M. Abrahams (GBR) 10.6*	Jackson V. Scholz (USA) 2 ft.	Arthur E. Porritt (NZL) d.n.a.
1928	Percy Williams (CAN) 10.8	Jack E. London (GBR) 2 ft.	Georg Lammers (GER) inches
1932	Eddie Tolan (USA) 10.3*	Ralph H. Metcalfe (USA) 10.3*	Arthur Jonath (GER) 10.4
1936	Jesse Owens (USA) 10.3	Ralph H. Metcalfe (USA) 10.4	Martinus B. Osendarp (HOL) 10.5
1948	W. Harrison Dillard (USA) 10.3	H. Norwood Ewell (USA) 10.4	Lloyd B. LaBeach (PAN) 10.4
1952	Lindy J. Remigino (USA) 10.4	Herbert H. McKenley (JAM) 10.4	Emmanuel McDonald Bailey (GBR) 10.4
1956	Bobby-Joe Morrow (USA) 10.5	W. Thane Baker (USA) 10.5	Hector D. Hogan (AUS) 10.6
1960	Armin Hary (GER) 10.2*	David W. Sime (USA) 10.2*	Peter F. Radford (GBR) 10.3
1964	Robert L. Hayes (USA) 10.0*	Enrique Figuerola (CUB) 10.2	Harry W. Jerome (CAN) 10.2
1968	James R. Hines (USA) 9.9*	Lennox Miller (JAM) 10.0	Charles E. Greene (USA) 10.0
1972	Valeriy Borzov (URS) 10.14	Robert Taylor (USA) 10.24	Lennox Miller (JAM) 10.33
1976	Hasely Crawford (TRI) 10.06	Donald Quarrie (JAM) 10.08	Valeriy Borzov (URS) 10.14
1980	Allan Wells (GBR) 10.25	Silvio Leonard (CUB) 10.25	Petar Petrov (BUL) 10.39
1984	Carl Lewis (USA) 9.99	Sam Graddy (USA) 10.19	Ben Johnson (CAN) 10.22

The performances listed below were Olympic Records set additionally in preliminaries.

11.8	Burke	1896	10.6	Williams	1928	10.3	Ira J. Murchison	
10.8	Jarvis	1900	10.6	Robert			(USA)	1956
10.8	Tewksbury	1900		MacAllister		10.3	Morrow	1956
10.8	Rector	1908		(USA)	1928	10.2	Hary	1960
10.8	Walker	1908	10.6	London	1928	10.0	Greene	1968
10.8	Rector	1908	10.4	Tolan	1932	10.0	Hermes Ramirez	
10.6	Lippincott	1912	10.3	Owens	1936		(CUB)	1968
10.6	(twice)		10.3	Morrow	1956	10.0	Greene	1968
	Abrahams	1924				10.0	Hines	1968

Performances of 10.2 and 10.3 (final) by Owens in 1936 and 9.9 by Hayes in 1964 were wind assisted.

Jim Hines (USA) won the 1968 Olympic 100 meters in the world record time of 9.9 seconds. High altitude helped sprinters because of reduced air resistance.

Jesse Owens (USA) captured public attention by winning 4 gold medals in the 1936 Games at Berlin. Owens was the top vote-getter in an election held to select 20 charter members of the U.S. Olympic Hall of Fame.

Carl Lewis (US) won 4 gold medals in the 1984 Olympics, emulating the feat of his hero, Jesse Owens, the star of the 1936 Olympics in Berlin. Lewis won in the 100 and 200 meters sprints, the long jump (28ft 0¼ in) and was anchor man in the 4 x 100 meters relay.

200 METERS (218 yd. 2 ft.)

	GOLD	SILVER	BRONZE
1896	Event not held		
1900	J. Walter B. Tewksbury (USA) 22.2*	Norman G. Pritchard (IND) 5 yd.	Stanley Rowley (AUS/NZL) 1 yd.
1904	Archie Hahn (USA) 21.6*[1]	Nathaniel J. Cartmell (USA) 2 yd.	William Hogenson (USA) d.n.a.
1906	Event not held		
1908	Robert Kerr (CAN) 22.6	Robert Cloughen (USA) 1 ft.	Nathaniel J. Cartmell (USA) 1 ft.
1912	Ralph C. Craig (USA) 21.7	Donald F. Lippincott (USA) 21.8	William R. Applegarth (GBR) 22.0
1920	Allen Woodring (USA) 22.0	Charles W. Paddock (USA) d.n.a.	Harry F. V. Edward (GBR) d.n.a.
1924	Jackson V. Scholz (USA) 21.6*	Charles W. Paddock (USA) ½ yd.	Eric H. Liddell (GBR) 1½ yd.
1928	Percy Williams (CAN) 21.8	Walter Rangeley (GBR) 2 ft.	Helmut Körnig[2] (GER) 1 ft.
1932	Eddie Tolan (USA) 21.2*	George Simpson (USA) 21.4	Ralph H. Metcalfe[3] (USA) 21.5
1936	Jesse Owens (USA) 20.7*	Mack M. Robinson (USA) 21.1	Martinus B. Osendarp (HOL) 21.3
1948	Melvin E. Patton (USA) 21.1	H. Norwood Ewell (USA) 21.1	Lloyd B. LaBeach (PAN) 21.2
1952	Andrew W. Stanfield (USA) 20.7*	W. Thane Baker (USA) 20.8	James Gathers (USA) 20.8
1956	Bobby-Joe Morrow (USA) 20.6*	Andrew W. Stanfield (USA) 20.7	W. Thane Baker (USA) 20.9
1960	Livio Berutti (ITA) 20.5*	Lester N. Carney (USA) 20.6	Abdoulaye Seye (FRA) 20.7

[1] Race run over straight course.
[2] Awarded bronze medal when Scholz refused to re-run after third place tie.
[3] Metcalfe's lane was later found to be 1½ meters too long.

	GOLD	SILVER	BRONZE
1964	Henry Carr (USA) 20.3*	O. Paul Drayton (USA) 20.5	Edwin Roberts (TRI) 20.6
1968	Tommie C. Smith (USA) 19.8*	Peter G. Norman (AUS) 20.0	John W. Carlos (USA) 20.0
1972	Valeriy Borzov (URS) 20.00	Larry J. Black (USA) 20.19	Pietro Mennea (ITA) 20.30
1976	Donald Quarrie (JAM) 20.23	Millard Hampton (USA) 20.29	Dwayne Evans (USA) 20.43
1980	Pietro Mennea (ITA) 20.19	Allan Wells (GBR) 20.21	Donald Quarrie (JAM) 20.29
1984	Carl Lewis (USA) 19.80*	Kirk Baptiste (USA) 19.96	Thomas Jefferson (USA) 20.26

The performances listed below were Olympic Records set additionally in preliminaries.

22.2	Hahn	1904	21.4	Arthur Jonath		20.3	Smith	1968
21.6	Körnig	1928		(GER)	1932	20.2	Norman	1968
21.5	Metcalfe	1932	21.1	(twice) Owens	1936	20.2	Smith	1968
21.5	Tolan	1932	21.1	Robinson	1936	20.1	Carlos	1968
21.4	Carlos B. Luti		20.5	Berutti	1960	20.1	Smith	1968
	(ARG)	1932	20.5	Drayton	1964			

400 METERS (437 yd. 1 ft.)

	GOLD	SILVER	BRONZE
1896	Thomas E. Burke (USA) 54.2*	Herbert Jamison (USA) 15 yd.	Fritz Hofmann (GER) d.n.a.
1900	Maxwell W. Long (USA) 49.4*	William J. Holland (USA) 1 yd.	Ernst Schultz (DEN) 15 yd.
1904	Harry L. Hillman (USA) 49.2*	Frank Waller (USA) 5 yd.	Herman C. Groman (USA) 1 yd.
1906	Paul H. Pilgrim (USA) 53.2	Wyndham Halswell (GBR) 53.8	Nigel Barker (AUS) 54.1
1908	Wyndham Halswell (GBR) 50.0	No other competitors[1]	
1912	Charles D. Reidpath (USA) 48.2*	Hanns Braun (GER) 48.3	Edward F. Lindberg (USA) 48.4
1920	Bevil G. d'U. Rudd (SAF) 49.6	Guy M. Butler (GBR) d.n.a.	Nils Engdahl (SWE) d.n.a.
1924	Eric H. Liddell (GBR) 47.6*	Horatio M. Fitch (USA) 48.4	Guy M. Butler (GBR) 48.6
1928	Raymond J. Barbuti (USA) 47.8	James Ball (CAN) 48.0	Joachim Büchner (GER) 48.2
1932	William A. Carr (USA) 46.2*	Benjamin B. Eastman (USA) 46.4	Alexander Wilson (CAN) 47.4
1936	Archie F. Williams (USA) 46.5	A. Godfrey K. Brown (GBR) 46.7	James E. LuValle (USA) 46.8
1948	Arthur S. Wint (JAM) 46.2*	Herbert H. McKenley (JAM) 46.4	Malvin G. Whitfield (USA) 46.6
1952	V. George Rhoden (JAM) 45.9*	Herbert H. McKenley (JAM) 45.9*	Ollie A. Matson (USA) 46.8
1956	Charles L. Jenkins (USA) 46.7	Karl-Friedrich Haas (GER) 46.8	Voitto V. Hellsten (FIN) 47.0 Ardalion V. Ignatyev (URS) 47.0
1960	Otis C. Davis (USA) 44.9*	Carl Kaufmann (GER) 44.9*	Malcolm C. Spence (SAF) 45.5
1964	Michael D. Larrabee (USA) 45.1	Wendell A. Mottley (TRI) 45.2	Andrzej Badenski (POL) 45.6
1968	Lee E. Evans (USA) 43.8*	G. Lawrence James (USA) 43.9	Ronald J. Freeman (USA) 44.4

[1] Re-run ordered after J. C. Carpenter (USA) disqualified in original final. Only Halswell showed up and "walked over" for the title.

GOLD	SILVER	BRONZE
1972 Vincent E. Matthews (USA) 44.66	Wayne C. Collett (USA) 44.80	Julius Sang (KEN) 44.92
1976 Alberto Juantorena (CUB) 44.26	Fred Newhouse (USA) 44.40	Herman Frazier (USA) 44.95
1980 Viktor Markin (URS) 44.60	Richard Mitchell (AUS) 44.84	Frank Schaffer (GDR) 44.87
1984 Alonzo Babers (USA) 44.27	Gabriel Tiacoh (CIV) 44.54	Antonio McKay (USA) 44.71

The performances listed below were Olympic Records set additionally in preliminaries.

50.4	Long	1900	47.8	Fitch	1924	45.5 Davis	1960
48.4	Halswell	1908	47.2	Carr	1932	44.8 Evans	1968
48.0	Josef Imbach (SUI)	1924					

800 METERS (874 yd. 2 ft.)

1896 Edwin H. Flack (AUS/NZL) 2:11.0	Nándor Dáni (HUN) 2:11.8	Demitrios Golemis (GRE) 100 yd.
1900 Alfred E. Tysoe (GBR) 2:01.2	John F. Cregan (USA) 1 yd.	David C. Hall (USA) d.n.a.
1904 James D. Lightbody (USA) 1:56.0*	Howard V. Valentine (USA) 2 yd.	Emil W. Breitkreutz (USA) d.n.a.
1906 Paul H. Pilgrim (USA) 2:01.5	James D. Lightbody (USA) 2:01.6	Wyndham Halswell (GBR) 2:03.0
1908 Melvin W. Sheppard (USA) 1:52.8*	Emilio Lunghi (ITA) 1:54.2	Hanns Braun (GER) 1:55.4
1912 James E. Meredith (USA) 1:51.9*	Melvin W. Sheppard (USA) 1:52.0	Ira N. Davenport (USA) 1:52.0
1920 Albert G. Hill (GBR) 1:53.4	Earl W. Eby (USA) 1 yd.	Bevil G. d'U. Rudd (SAF) d.n.a.

Alberto Juantorena (CUB), known as "The Horse," defeated 2 USA runners for the gold medal at 400 meters in 1976. He also won the gold at 800 meters.

GOLD	SILVER	BRONZE
1924 Douglas G. A. Lowe (GBR) 1:52.4	Paul Martin (SUI) 1:52.6	Schuyler C. Enck (USA) 1:53.0
1928 Douglas G. A. Lowe (GBR) 1:51.8*	Erik Byléhn (SWE) 1:52.8	Hermann Engelhardt (GER) 1:53.2
1932 Thomas Hampson (GBR) 1:49.7*	Alexander Wilson (CAN) 1:49.9	Philip A. Edwards (CAN) 1:51.5
1936 John Y. Woodruff (USA) 1:52.9	Mario Lanzi (ITA) 1:53.3	Philip A. Edwards (CAN) 1:53.6
1948 Malvin G. Whitfield (USA) 1:49.2*	Arthur S. Wint (JAM) 1:49.5	Marcel Hansenne (FRA) 1:49.8
1952 Malvin G. Whitfield (USA) 1:49.2*	Arthur S. Wint (JAM) 1:49.4	Heinz Ulzheimer (GER) 1:49.7
1956 Thomas W. Courtney (USA) 1:47.7*	Derek J. N. Johnson (GBR) 1:47.8	Audun Boysen (NOR) 1:48.1
1960 Peter G. Snell (NZL) 1:46.3*	Roger Moens (BEL) 1:46.5	George E. Kerr (BWI) 1:47.1
1964 Peter G. Snell (NZL) 1:45.1*	William Cothers (CAN) 1:45.6	Wilson Kiprugut (KEN) 1:45.9
1968 Ralph D. Doubell (AUS) 1:44.3*	Wilson Kiprugut (KEN) 1:44.5	Thomas F. Farrell (USA) 1:45.4
1972 David J. Wottle (USA) 1:45.9	Evgeni Arzhanov (URS) 1:45.9	Michael Boit (KEN) 1:46.0
1976 Alberto Juantorena (CUB) 1:43.5*	Ivo Van Damme (BEL) 1:43.9	Richard Wohlhuter (USA) 1:44.1
1980 Steven Ovett (GBR) 1:45.4	Sebastian Coe (GBR) 1:45.9	Nikolai Kirov (URS) 1:46.0
1984 Joaquim Cruz (BRA) 1:43.00*	Sebastian Coe (GBR) 1:43.64	Earl Jones (USA) 1:43.83

The performances listed below were Olympic Records set additionally in the preliminaries.

2:10.0	Flack	1896	1:47.1	Kerr	1960	1:46.1 Kiprugut	1964
1:59.0	Hall	1900	1:46.1	Kerr	1964		

1,500 METERS (1,640 yd. 1 ft.)

1896 Edwin H. Flack (AUS/NZL) 4:33.2*	Arthur Blake (USA) d.n.a.	Albin Lermusiaux (FRA) d.n.a.
1900 Charles Bennett (GBR) 4:06.2*	Henri Deloge (FRA) 2 yd.	John Bray (USA) d.n.a.
1904 James D. Lightbody (USA) 4:05.4*	W. Frank Verner (USA) d.n.a.	Lacey E. Hearn (USA) d.n.a.
1906 James D. Lightbody (USA) 4:12.0	John McGough (GBR/IRL) 4:12.6	Kristian Hellström (SWE) 4:13.4
1908 Melvin W. Sheppard (USA) 4:03.4*	Harold A. Wilson (GBR) 4:03.6	Norman F. Hallows[1] (GBR) 4:04.0
1912 Arnold N. S. Jackson[2] (GBR) 3:56.8*	Abel R. Kiviat (USA) 3:56.9	Norman S. Taber (USA) 3:56.9
1920 Albert G. Hill (GBR) 4:01.8	Philip J. Baker[2] (GBR) 4:02.4	M. Lawrence Shields (USA) d.n.a.
1924 Paavo J. Nurmi (FIN) 3:53.6*	Willy Schärer (SUI) 3:55.0	Henry B. Stallard (GBR) 3:55.6
1928 Harri E. Larva (FIN) 3:53.2*	Jules Ladoumègue (FRA) 3:53.8	Eino Purje (FIN) 3:56.4
1932 Luigi Beccali (ITA) 3:51.2*	John F. Cornes (GBR) 3:52.6	Philip A. Edwards (CAN) 3:52.8
1936 John E. Lovelock (NZL) 3:47.8*	Glenn Cunningham (USA) 3:48.4	Luigi Beccali (ITA) 3:49.2

---

[1] The Olympic record has only been set in those winning performances marked * with the exception of Hallows, who achieved 4:03.4 in the 1908 preliminaries.
[2] A. N. S. Jackson (1912) changed name to A. N. S. Strode-Jackson and P. J. Baker (1920) changed name to P. J. Noel-Baker.

LEFT: Lauri Lehtinen (FIN) (left) was rightly awarded the gold medal in 1932 for the 5,000 meters run, although both he and runner-up Ralph Hill were clocked at the same Olympic record time. RIGHT: Kip Keino (KEN) won the 1,500 meters by the remarkable margin of nearly 20 yards at Mexico City in 1968.

Lasse Viren of Finland (number 301) repeated his 1972 gold medal success at 5,000 meters in Montreal. Earlier that week he had won the gold medal at 10,000 meters for the second consecutive time.

GOLD	SILVER	BRONZE
1948 Henry Eriksson (SWE) 3:49.8	Lennart Strand (SWE) 3:50.4	Willem F. Slijkhuis (HOL) 3:50.4
1952 Josef Barthel (LUX) 3:45.1*	Robert E. McMillen (USA) 3:45.2	Werner Lueg (GER) 3:45.4
1956 Ron Delany (IRL) 3:41.2*	Klaus Richtzenhain (GER) 3:42.0	John M. Landy (AUS) 3:42.0
1960 Herbert J. Elliott (AUS) 3:35.6*	Michel Jazy (FRA) 3:38.4	István Rózsavölgyi (HUN) 3:39.2
1964 Peter G. Snell (NZL) 3:38.1	Josef Odložil (TCH) 3:39.6	John Davies (NZL) 3:39.6
1968 H. Kipchoge Keino (KEN) 3:34.9*	James R. Ryun (USA) 3:37.8	Bodo Tümmler (GER) 3:39.0
1972 Pekka Vasala (FIN) 3:36.3	H. Kipchoge Keino (KEN) 3:36.8	Rodney Dixon (NZL) 3:37.5
1976 John Walker (NZL) 3:39.2	Ivo Van Damme (BEL) 3:39.3	Paul Heinz Wellmann (GER) 3:39.3
1980 Sebastian Coe (GBR) 3:38.4	Jurgen Straub (GDR) 3:38.8	Steven Ovett (GBR) 3:39.0
1984 Sebastian Coe (GBR) 3:32.53*	Steve Cram (GBR) 3:33.40	Jose Abascal (ESP) 3:34.30

5,000 METERS (3 miles 188 yd.)

GOLD	SILVER	BRONZE
1896–1908 Event not held		
1912 Hannes Kolehmainen (FIN) 14:36.6*	Jean Bouin (FRA) 14:36.7	George W. Hutson (GBR) 15:07.6
1920 Joseph Guillemot (FRA) 14:55.6	Paavo J. Nurmi (FIN) 15:00.0	Erik Backman (SWE) 15:13.0
1924 Paavo J. Nurmi (FIN) 14:31.2*	Ville Ritola (FIN) 14:31.4	Edvin Wide (SWE) 15:01.8
1928 Ville Ritola (FIN) 14:38.0	Paavo J. Nurmi (FIN) 14:40.0	Edvin Wide (SWE) 14:41.2
1932 Lauri A. Lehtinen (FIN) 14:30.0*	Ralph Hill (USA) 14:30.0*	Lauri J. Virtanen (FIN) 14:44.0
1936 Gunnar Höckert (FIN) 14:22.2*	Lauri A. Lehtinen (FIN) 14:25.8	Henry Jonsson (SWE) 14:29.0
1948 Gaston E. G. Reiff (BEL) 14:17.6*	Emil Zátopek (TCH) 14:17.8	Willem F. Slijkhuis (HOL) 14:26.8
1952 Emil Zátopek (TCH) 14:06.6*	Allain Mimoun-o-Kacha (FRA) 14:07.4	Herbert Schade (GER) 14:08.6
1956 Vladimir P. Kuts (URS) 13:39.6*	D. A. Gordon Pirie (GBR) 13:50.6	G. Derek Ibbotson (GBR) 13:54.4
1960 Murray G. Halberg (NZL) 13:43.4	Hans Grodotzki (GER) 13:44.6	Kazimierz Zimny (POL) 13:44.8
1964 Robert K. Schul (USA) 13:48.8	Harald Norpoth (GER) 13:49.6	William Dellinger (USA) 13:49.8
1968 Mohamed Gammoudi (TUN) 14:05.0	H. Kipchoge Keino (KEN) 14:05.2	Naftali Temu (KEN) 14:06.4
1972 Lasse Viren (FIN) 13:26.4*	Mohamed Gammoudi (TUN) 13:27.4	Ian Stewart (GBR) 13:27.6
1976 Lasse Viren (FIN) 13:24.8	Dick Quax (NZL) 13:25.2	Klaus-Peter Hildenbrand (GER) 13:25.4
1980 Miruts Yifter (ETH) 13:21.0	Suleiman Nyambui (TAN) 13:21.6	Kaarlo Maaninka (FIN) 13:22.0
1984 Said Aouita (MAR) 13:05.59*	Markus Ryffel (SUI) 13:07.54	Antonio Leitao (POR) 13:09.20

The Olympic record has only been set in those medal-winning performances marked * with the exception of Emiel Puttemans (BEL), 13:31.8 in the 1972 preliminaries and Brendan Foster (GBR), 13:20.3 in the 1976 preliminaries.

Juan Carlos Zabala of Argentina, winner of the 1932 marathon, being helped off the track exhausted. He was 2 months short of his 21st birthday, the youngest Olympic champion ever at track.

Said Aouita of Morocco won the 5,000 meters run in the 1984 Olympics and now currently holds world records in the 1,500 and 5,000 meters races.

10,000 METERS (6 miles 376 yd.)

GOLD	SILVER	BRONZE
1896–1908 Event not held		
1912 Hannes Kolehmainen (FIN) 31:20.8*	Lewis Tewanima (USA) 32:06.6	Albin O. Stenroos (FIN) 32:21.8
1920 Paavo J. Nurmi (FIN) 31:45.8	Joseph Guillemot (FRA) 31:47.2	James Wilson (GBR) 31:50.8
1924 Ville Ritola (FIN) 30:23.2*	Edvin Wide (SWE) 30:55.2	Eero E. Berg (FIN) 31:43.0
1928 Paavo J. Nurmi (FIN) 30:18.8*	Ville Ritola (FIN) 30:19.4	Edvin Wide (SWE) 31:00.8
1932 Janusz Kusocinski (POL) 30:11.4*	Volmari Iso-Hollo (FIN) 30:12.6	Lauri J. Virtanen (FIN) 30:35.0
1936 Ilmari Salminen (FIN) 30:15.4	Arvo Askola (FIN) 30:15.6	Volmari Iso-Hollo (FIN) 30:20.2
1948 Emil Zátopek (TCH) 29:59.6*	Alain Mimoun-o-Kacha (FRA) 30:47.4	Bertil Albertsson (SWE) 30:53.6
1952 Emil Zátopek (TCH) 29:17.0*	Alain Mimoun-o-Kacha (FRA) 29:32.8	Aleksandr A. Anufriyev (URS) 29:48.2
1956 Vladimir P. Kuts (URS) 28:45.6*	József Kovács (HUN) 28:52.4	Allan Lawrence (AUS) 28:53.6
1960 Pyotr G. Bolotnikov (URS) 28:32.2*	Hans Grodotzki (GER) 28:37.0	W. David Power (AUS) 28:38.2
1964 William M. Mills (USA) 28:24.4*	Mohamed Gammoudi (TUN) 28:24.8	Ronald W. Clarke (AUS) 28:25.8
1968 Naftali Temu (KEN) 29:27.4	Mamo Wolde (ETH) 29:28.0	Mohamed Gammoudi (TUN) 29:34.2
1972 Lasse Viren (FIN) 27:38.4*	Emiel Puttemans (BEL) 27:39.6	Meruts Yifter (ETH) 27:41.0
1976 Lasse Viren (FIN) 27:40.4	Carlos Lopes (POR) 27:45.2	Brendan Foster (GBR) 27:54.9
1980 Miruts Yifter (ETH) 27:42.7	Kaarlo Maaninka (FIN) 27:44.3	Mohammed Kedir (ETH) 27:44.7
1984 Alberto Cova (ITA) 27:47.54	Mike McLeod (GBR) 28:06.22	Mike Musyoki (KEN) 28:06.46

The Olympic record has only been set in those medal-winning performances marked * with the exception of: 33:49.0 by Kolehmainen, and 32:30.8 by Len Richardson (SAF) both in 1912; and 27:53.4 by Puttemans in 1972.

MARATHON (42,195 meters—26 miles 385 yd.)

The length of a Marathon was standardized at the 1908 distance of 26 miles 385 yards (42 195 m) from 1924.

The distances run in other years were:

1896 & 1904	24 miles 1,503 yards 40 000 m		1912	24 miles 1,723 yards 40 200 m	
1900	25 miles	28 yards 40 260 m	1920	26 miles	991 yards 42 750 m
1906	26 miles	18 yards 41 860 m			

GOLD	SILVER	BRONZE
1896 Spyridon Louis (GRE) 2h 58:50.0	Charilaos Vasilakos (GRE) 3h 06:03.0	Gyula Kellner (HUN) 3h 09:35.0
1900 Michel Theato (FRA) 2h 59:45.0	Emile Champion (FRA) 3h 04:17.0	Ernst Fast (SWE) 3h 37:14.0
1904 Thomas J. Hicks (USA) 3h 28:35.0	Albert J. Coray (FRA) 3h 34:52.0	Arthur L. Newton (USA) 3h 47:33.0
1906 William J. Sherring (CAN) 2h 51:23.6	John Svanberg (SWE) 2h 58:20.8	William Frank (USA) 3h 00:46.8
1908 John J. Hayes[1] (USA) 2h 55:18.4*	Charles A. Hefferon (SAF) 2h 56:06.0	Joseph Foreshaw (USA) 2h 57:10.4
1912 Kenneth K. McArthur (SAF) 2h 36:54.8	Christian W. Gitsham (SAF) 2h 37:52.0	Gaston Strobino (USA) 2h 38:42.4

---

[1] Dorando Pietri (ITA) finished 1st but was disqualified for assistance by officials over the final few hundred yards.

	GOLD	SILVER	BRONZE
1920	Hannes Kolehmainen (FIN) 2h 32:35.8*	Jüri Lossman (EST) 2h 32:48.6	Valerio Arri (ITA) 2h 36:32.8
1924	Albin O. Stenroos (FIN) 2h 41:22.6	Romeo Bertini (ITA) 2h 47:19.6	Clarence H. DeMar (USA) 2h 48:14.0
1928	Mohamed El Ouafi (FRA) 2h 32:57.0	Miguel Plaza (CHI) 2h 33:23.0	Martti Marttelin (FIN) 2h 35:02.0
1932	Juan Carlos Zabala (ARG) 2h 31:36.0*	Samuel Ferris (GBR) 2h 31:55.0	Armas A. Toivonen (FIN) 2h 32:12.0
1936	Kitei Son (JPN) 2h 29:19.2*	Ernest Harper (GBR) 2h 31:23.2	Shoryu Nan (JPN) 2h 31:42.0
1948	Delfo Cabrera (ARG) 2h 34:51.6	Thomas Richards (GBR) 2h 35:07.6	Étienne Gailly (BEL) 2h 35:33.6
1952	Emil Zátopek (TCH) 2h 23:03.2*	Reinaldo B. Gorno (ARG) 2h 25:35.0	Gustaf N. Jansson (SWE) 2h 26:07.0
1956	Alain Mimoun-o-Kacha (FRA) 2h 25:00.0	Franjo Mihalič (YUG) 2h 26:32.0	Veikko Karvonen (FIN) 2h 27:47.0
1960	Abebe Bikila (ETH) 2h 15:16.2*	Rhadi Ben Abdesselem (MAR) 2h 15:41.6	A. Barry Magee (NZL) 2h 17:18.2
1964	Abebe Bikila (ETH) 2h 12:11.2*	Basil B. Heatley (GBR) 2h 16:19.2	Kokichi Tsuburaya (JPN) 2h 16:22.8
1968	Mamo Wolde (ETH) 2h 20:26.4	Kenji Kimihara (JPN) 2h 23:31.0	Michael Ryun (NZL) 2h 23:45.0
1972	Frank Shorter (USA) 2h 12:19.8	Karel Lismont (BEL) 2h 14:31.8	Mamo Wolde (ETH) 2h 15:08.4
1976	Waldemar Cierpinski (GDR) 2h 09:55.0*	Frank Shorter (USA) 2h 10:45.8	Karel Lismont (BEL) 2h 11:12.6
1980	Waldemar Cierpinski (GDR) 2h 11:03	Gerard Nijboer (HOL) 2h 11:20	Setymkul Dzhumanazarov (URS) 2h 11:35
1984	Carlos Lopes (POR) 2h 09:21*	John Treacy (IRL) 2h 09:56	Charles Spedding (GBR) 2h 09:58

4 × 100 METERS (109 yd. 1 ft.) RELAY

	GOLD	SILVER	BRONZE
1896–1908	Event not held		
1912	GREAT BRITAIN 42.4	SWEDEN 42.6	
	David H. Jacobs	Ivan Möller	
	Harold M. Macintosh	Charles Luther	
	Victor H. A. D'Arcy	Ture Persson	
	William R. Applegarth	Knut Lindberg	
1920	UNITED STATES 42.2*	FRANCE 42.6	SWEDEN d.n.a.
	Charles W. Paddock	René Tirard	Agne Holmström
	Jackson V. Scholz	René Lorain	William Pettersson
	Loren C. Murchison	René Mourlon	Sven Malm
	Morris M. Kirksey	Emile Ali Khan	Nils Sandström
1924	UNITED STATES 41.0*	GREAT BRITAIN 41.2	NETHERLANDS 41.8
	Francis Hussey	Harold M. Abrahams	Jakob, Boot
	Louis A. Clarke	Walter Rangeley	Henricus Broos
	Loren C. Murchison	Lancelot C. Royle	Jan de Vries
	J. Alfred Le Coney	William P. Nichol	Marinus van den Berge
1928	UNITED STATES 41.0*	GERMANY 41.2	GREAT BRITAIN 41.8
	Frank C. Wykoff	Georg Lammers	Cyril W. Gill
	James F. Quinn	Richard Corts	Eric R. Smouha
	Charles E. Borah	Hubert Houben	Walter Rangeley
	Henry A. Russell	Helmut Körnig	Jack E. London
1932	UNITED STATES 40.0*	GERMANY 40.9	ITALY 41.2
	Robert A. Kiesel	Helmut Körnig	Giuseppe Castelli
	Emmett Toppino	Walter Hendrix	Ruggero Maregatti
	Hector M. Dyer	Erich Borchmeyer	Gabriele Salviati
	Frank C. Wykoff	Arthur Jonath	Edgardo Toetti

GOLD	SILVER	BRONZE
1936 **UNITED STATES** 39.8*	**ITALY** 41.1	**GERMANY** 41.2
Jesse Owens	Orazio Mariani	Wilhelm Leichum
Ralph H. Metcalfe	Gianni Caldana	Erich Borchmeyer
Foy Draper	Elio Ragni	Erwin Gillmeister
Frank C. Wykoff	Tullio Gonnelli	Gerd Hornberger
1948 **UNITED STATES**[1] 40.6	**GREAT BRITAIN** 41.3	**ITALY** 41.5
H. Norwood Ewell	John Archer	Carlo Monti
Lorenzo C. Wright	John A. Gregory	Enrico Perucconi
W. Harrison Dillard	Alistair McCorquodale	Antonio Siddi
Melvin E. Patton	Kenneth J. Jones	Michele Tito
1952 **UNITED STATES** 40.1	**U.S.S.R.** 40.3	**HUNGARY** 40.5
F. Dean Smith	Boris Tokaryev	László Zarándi
W. Harrison Dillard	Levan Kalyayev	Géza Varasdi
Lindy J. Remigino	Levan Sanadze	György Csányi
Andrew W. Stanfield	Vladimir Sukharyev	Béla Goldoványi
1956 **UNITED STATES** 39.5	**U.S.S.R.** 39.8	**GERMANY** 40.3
Ira J. Murchison	Boris Tokaryev	Lothar Knörzer
Leamon King	Vladimir Sukharyev	Leonhard Pohl
W. Thane Baker	Leonid Bartenyev	Heinz Fütterer
Bobby-Joe Morrow	Yuriy Konovalov	Manfred Germar
1960 **GERMANY** 39.5*	**U.S.S.R.** 40.1	**GREAT BRITAIN** 40.2
Bernd Cullmann	Gusman Kosanov	Peter F. Radford
Armin Hary	Leonid Bartenyev	David H. Jones
Walter Mahlendorf	Yuriy Konovalov	David H. Segal
Martin Lauer	Edvin Ozolin	J. Neville Whitehead
1964 **UNITED STATES** 39.0*	**POLAND** 39.3	**FRANCE** 39.3
O. Paul Drayton	Andrzej Zielinski	Paul Genevay
Gerald A. Ashworth	Wieslaw Maniak	Bernard Laidebeur
Richard V. Stebbins	Marian Foik	Claude Piquemal
Robert L. Hayes	Marian Dudziak	Jocelyn Delecour
1968 **UNITED STATES** 38.2*	**CUBA** 38.3	**FRANCE** 38.4
Charles E. Greene	Hermes Ramirez	Gérard Fenouil
Melvin Pender	Juan Morales	Jocelyn Delecour
Ronnie Ray Smith	Pablo Montes	Claude Piquemal
James R. Hines	Enriques Figuerola	Roger Bambuck
1972 **UNITED STATES** 38.19*	**U.S.S.R.** 38.50	**WEST GERMANY** 38.79
Larry J. Black	Alexandr Korneliuk	Jobst Hirsch
Robert Taylor	Vladimir Lovetski	Karl-Heinz Klotz
Gerald Tinker	Yuri Silov	Gerhard Wucherer
Eddie J. Hart	Valeriy Borzov	Klaus Ehl
1976 **UNITED STATES** 38.33	**EAST GERMANY** 38.66	**U.S.S.R.** 38.78
Harvey Glance	Manfred Kokot	Alexandr Aksinin
John Jones	Jorg Pfeifer	Nikolai Kolesnikov
Millard Hampton	Klaus-Dieter Kurrat	Yuri Silov
Steven Riddick	Alexander Thieme	Valeriy Borzov
1980 **U.S.S.R.** 38.26	**POLAND** 38.33	**FRANCE** 38.53
Vladimir Muravyov	Krzysztof Zwolinski	Antoine Richard
Nikolai Sidorov	Zenon Licznerski	Pascal Barré
Aleksandr Aksinin	Leszek Dunecki	Patrick Barré
Andre Prokofiev	Marian Woronin	Hermann Panzo
1984 **USA** 37.83*	**JAMAICA** 38.62	**CANADA** 38.70
Sam Graddy	Al Lawrence	Ben Johnson
Ron Brown	Greg Meghoo	Tony Sharpe
Calvin Smith	Don Quarrie	Desai Williams
Carl Lewis	Ray Stewart	Sterling Hinds

[1] USA was disqualified but later reinstated.

The performances listed below were Olympic Records set additionally in preliminaries.

43.0	Great Britain 1912	42.0	Netherlands 1924	38.6	Jamaica 1968
42.5	Sweden 1912	41.2	United States 1924		(Errol Stewart,
42.3	Germany 1912	41.0	United States 1924		Michael Fray,
	(K. Halt,	40.6	United States 1932		Clifton Forbes,
	M. Hermann,	40.0	United States 1936		Lennox Miller)
	E. Kern,	39.5	Germany 1960	38.3	Jamaica 1968
	Richard Rau)	39.5	United States 1964		
42.0	Great Britain 1924	38.7	Cuba 1968		

4 × 400 METERS (437 yd. 1 ft.) RELAY

GOLD	SILVER	BRONZE
1896–1908 Event not held		
1912 UNITED STATES 3:16.6*	FRANCE 3:20.7	GREAT BRITAIN 3.23.2
Melvin W. Sheppard	Charles L. Lelong	George Nicol
Edward F. Lindberg	Robert Schurrer	Ernest J. Henley
James E. Meredith	Pierre Failliot	James T. Soutter
Charles D. Reidpath	Charles A. C. Poulenard	Cyril N. Seedhouse
1920 GREAT BRITAIN 3:22.2	S. AFRICA d.n.a.	FRANCE d.n.a.
Cecil R. Griffiths	Harry Davel	George André
Robert A. Lindsay	Clarence W. Oldfield	Gaston Féry
John C. Ainsworth-Davis	Jack K. Oosterlaak	Maurice Delvart
Guy M. Butler	Bevil G. d'U. Rudd	Jean Devaux
1924 UNITED STATES 3:16.0*	SWEDEN 3:17.0	GREAT BRITAIN 3:17.4
Con S. Cochrane	Artur Svensson	Edward J. Toms
Alan B. Helffrich	Erik Byléhn	George R. Renwick
James O. McDonald	Gustaf Wejnarth	Richard N. Ripley
William E. Stevenson	Nils Engdahl	Guy M. Butler
1928 UNITED STATES 3:14.2*	GERMANY 3:14.8	CANADA 3:15.4
George Baird	Otto Neumann	Alexander Wilson
Emerson Spencer	Richard Krebs	Philip A. Edwards
Frederick P. Alderman	Harry Storz	Stanley Glover
Raymond J. Barbuti	Hermann Engelhard	James Ball
1932 UNITED STATES 3:08.2*	GREAT BRITAIN 3:11.2	CANADA 3:12.8
Ivan Fuqua	Crew H. Stoneley	Raymond Lewis
Edgar A. Ablowich	Thomas Hampson	James Ball
Karl D. Warner	Lord Burghley	Philip A. Edwards
William A. Carr	Godfrey L. Rampling	Alexander Wilson
1936 GREAT BRITAIN 3:09.0	UNITED STATES 3:11.0	GERMANY 3:11.8
Frederick F. Wolff	Harold Cagle	Helmut Hamann
Godfrey L. Rampling	Robert C. Young	Friedrich von Stülpnagel
William Roberts	Edward T. O'Brien	Harry C. Voigt
A. Godfrey K. Brown	Alfred L. Fitch	Rudolf Harbig
1948 UNITED STATES 3:10.4	FRANCE 3:14.8	SWEDEN 3:16.3
Arthur H. Harnden	Jean Kerebel	Kurt Lundqvist
Clifford F. Bourland	Francis Schewetta	Lars-Enk Wolfbrandt
Roy B. Cochran	Robert C. Chef d'Hôtel	Folke Alnevik
Malvin G. Whitfield	Jacques J. Lunis	Rune Larsson
1952 JAMAICA 3:03.9*	UNITED STATES 3:04.0	GERMANY 3:06.6
Arthur S. Wint	Ollie A. Matson	Hans Geister
Leslie A. Laing	G. Eugene Cole	Günther Steines
Herbert H. McKenley	Charles H. Moore	Heinz Ulzheimer
V. George Rhoden	Malvin G. Whitfield	Karl-Friedrich Haas

GOLD	SILVER	BRONZE
1956 **UNITED STATES** 3:04.8	**AUSTRALIA** 3:06.2	**GREAT BRITAIN** 3:07.2
Lou Jones	Leslie S. Gregory	John E. Salisbury
Jesse W. Mashburn	David F. Lean	Michael K. V. Wheeler
Charles L. Jenkins	Graham Gipson	F. Peter Higgins
Thomas W. Courtney	Kevin V. Gosper	Derek J. N. Johnson
1960 **UNITED STATES** 3:02.2*	**GERMANY** 3:02.7	**BRITISH W.I.** 3:04.0
Jack L. Yerman	Hans-Joachim Reske	Malcolm Spence
Earl V. Young	Manfred Kinder	James Wedderburn
Glenn A. Davis	Johannes Kaiser	Keith A. St. H. Gardner
Otis C. Davis	Carl Kaufmann	George E. Kerr

Harry Hillman (US) had the unique distinction of winning the 400 meters foot race and the 400 meters hurdles in the 1904 Olympics.

GOLD	SILVER	BRONZE
1964 UNITED STATES 3:00.7*	GREAT BRITAIN 3:01.6	TRINIDAD 3:01.7
Ollan C. Cassell	Timothy J. M. Graham	Edwin Skinner
Michael D. Larrabee	Adrian P. Metcalfe	Kent Bernard
Ulis C. Williams	John H. Cooper	Edwin Roberts
Henry Carr	Robbie I. Brightwell	Wendell A. Mottley
1968 UNITED STATES 2:56.1*	KENYA 2:59.6	WEST GERMANY 3:00.5
Vincent E. Matthews	Daniel Rudisha	Helmar Müller
Ronald J. Freeman	Munyoro L. Nyamau	Manfred Kinder
G. Lawrence James	Naftali Bon	Gerhard Hennige
Lee E. Evans	Charles Asati	Martin Jellinghaus
1972 KENYA 2:59.8	GREAT BRITAIN 3:00.5	FRANCE 3:00.7
Charles Asati	Martin E. Reynolds	Gilles Bertould
Hezakiah Nyamau	Alan P. Pascoe	Daniel Velasques
Robert Ouko	David P. Hemery	Francis Kerbiriou
Julius Sang	David A. Jenkins	Jacques Carette

GOLD	SILVER	BRONZE
1976 **UNITED STATES** 2:58.7	**POLAND** 3:01.4	**WEST GERMANY** 3:02.0
Herman Frazier	Ryszard Podlas	Franz-Peter Hofmeiste
Benjamin Brown	Jan Werner	Lothar Krieg
Fred Newhouse	Zbigniew Jaremski	Harald Schmid
Maxie Parks	Jerzy Pietrzyk	Bernd Herrmann
1980 **U.S.S.R.** 3:01.1	**EAST GERMANY** 3:01.3	**ITALY** 3:04.3
Remigius Valyulis	Klaus Thiele	Stefano Malinverni
Michail Linge	Andreas Knebel	Mauro Zuliani
Nikolai Chernyetsky	Frank Schaffer	Roberto Tozzi
Viktor Markin	Volker Beck	Pietro Mennea
1984 **USA** 2:57.91	**GREAT BRITAIN** 2:59.13	**NIGERIA** 2:59.32
Sunder Nix	Kriss Akabusi	Sunday Uti
Ray Armstead	Gary Cook	Moses Ugbusie
Alonzo Babers	Todd Bennett	Rotimi Peters
Antonio McKay	Phil Brown	Innocent Egbunike

The Olympic record has only been set in those winning performances marked * with the exception of:

3:19.0	Great Britain	1912
3:11.8	United States	1932
3:00.7	United States	1968

110 METERS (120 yd. 1 ft.) HURDLES

	GOLD	SILVER	BRONZE
1896	Thomas P. Curtis (USA) 17.6	Grantley T. Goulding (GBR) 17.7	
1900	Alvin C. Kraenzlein (USA) 15.4*	John McLean (USA) 1½ ft.	Fred G. Moloney (USA) d.n.a.
1904	Frederick W. Schule (USA) 16.0	Thaddeus Shideler (USA) 2 yd.	L. Ashburner (USA) d.n.a.
1906	R. G. Leavitt (USA) 16.2	A. H. Healey (GBR) 16.2	Vincent DeV. Duncker (SAF) 16.3
1908	Forrest C. Smithson (USA) 15.0*	John C. Garrels (USA) 5 yd.	Arthur B. Shaw (USA) d.n.a.
1912	Frederick W. Kelly (USA) 15.1	James I. Wendell (USA) 15.2	Martin W. Hawkins (USA) 15.3
1920	Earl J. Thomson (CAN) 14.8*	Harold E. Barron (USA) 2½ yd.	Frederick S. Murray (USA) d.n.a.
1924	Daniel C. Kinsey (USA) 15.0	Sydney J. M. Atkinson (SAF) inches	Sten Pettersson (SWE) d.n.a.
1928	Sydney J. M. Atkinson (AF) 14.8	Stephen E. Anderson (USA) 14.8	John S. Collier (USA) 15.0
1932	George J. Saling (USA) 14.6	Percy M. Beard (USA) 14.7	Donald O. Finlay (GBR) 14.8
1936	Forrest G. Towns (USA) 14.2	Donald O. Finlay (GBR) 14.4	Frederick D. Pollard (USA) 14.4
1948	William F. Porter (USA) 13.9*	Clyde L. Scott (USA) 14.1	Craig K. Dixon (USA) 14.1
1952	W. Harrison Dillard (USA) 13.7*	Jack W. Davis (USA) 13.7*	Arthur Barnard (USA) 14.1
1956	Lee Q. Calhoun (USA) 13.5*	Jack W. Davis (USA) 13.5*	Joel W. Chankle (USA) 14.1

Willie Davenport, the 1968 hurdles champion, shows his strong form in Mexico City.

1960	Lee Q. Calhoun (USA) 13.8	Willie L. May (USA) 13.8	Hayes W. Jones (USA) 14.0
1964	Hayes W. Jones (USA) 13.6	H. Blaine Lindgren (USA) 13.7	Anatoly Mikhailov (URS) 13.7
1968	Willie Davenport (USA) 13.3*	Ervin Hall (USA) 13.4	Eddy Ottoz (ITA) 13.4
1972	Rodney Milburn (USA) 13.24*	Guy Drut (FRA) 13.34	Thomas L. Hill (USA) 13.48
1976	Guy Drut (FRA) 13.30	Alejandro Casanas (CUB) 13.33	Willie Davenport (USA) 13.38
1980	Thomas Munkelt (GDR) 13.39	Alejandro Casanas (CUB) 13.40	Aleksandr Puchkov (URS) 13.44
1984	Roger Kingdom (USA) 13.20*	Greg Foster (USA) 13.23	Arto Bryggare (FIN) 13.40

The performances listed below were Olympic records set additionally in preliminaries.

15.6	Kraenzlein	1900	14.8	Leighton Dye (USA)	1928	14.1	Towns	1936
15.4	Smithson	1908				14.1	Porter	1948
15.0	Barron	1920	14.8	Anderson	1928	13.9	Dillard	1952
15.0	Thomson	1920	14.6	Weightman-Smith		13.5	Ottoz	1968
14.8	George C. Weightman-Smith (SAF)	1928			1928	13.3	Hall	1968
			14.5	Jack Keller (USA)	1932	13.24	Foster	1984
			14.4	Saling	1932	13.24	Kingdom	1984

[1] Only two finalists.

400 METERS (437 yd. 1 ft.) HURDLES

	GOLD	SILVER	BRONZE
1896	Event not held		
1900	J. Walter B. Tewksbury (USA) 57.6*	Henri Tauzin (FRA) d.n.a.	George W. Orton (CAN) d.n.a.
1904[1]	Harry L. Hillman (USA) 53.0	Frank Waller (USA) 2 yd.	George Poage (USA) d.n.a.
1906	Event not held		
1908	Charles J. Bacon (USA) 55.0*	Harry L. Hillmann (USA) 1½ yd.	Leonard F. Tremeer (GBR) d.n.a.
1912	Event not held		
1920	Frank F. Loomis (USA) 54.0*	John K. Norton (USA) d.n.a.	August G. Desch (USA) d.n.a.
1924	F. Morgan Taylor (USA) 52.6[2]	Erik Vilén (FIN) 53.8*	Ivan H. Riley (USA) 54.2
1928	Lord Burghley (GBR) 53.4*	Frank J. Cuhel (USA) 53.6	F. Morgan Taylor (USA) 53.6
1932	Robert M. N. Tisdall (IRL) 51.7[2]	Glenn F. Hardin (USA) 51.9*	F. Morgan Taylor (USA) 52.0
1936	Glenn F. Hardin (USA) 52.4	John W. Loaring (CAN) 52.7	Miguel S. White (PHI) 52.8
1948	Roy B. Cochran (USA) 51.1*	Duncan White (CEY) 51.8	Rune Larsson (SWE) 52.2
1952	Charles H. Moore (USA) 50.8*	Yuriy N. Lituyev (URS) 51.3	John McF. Holland (NZL) 52.2
1956	Glenn A. Davis (USA) 50.1*	S. Eddie Southern (USA) 50.8	Joshua Culbreath (USA) 51.6
1960	Glenn A. Davis (USA) 49.3*	Clifton E. Cushman (USA) 49.6	Richard W. Howard (USA) 49.7
1964	Warren Cawley (USA) 49.6	John H. Cooper (GBR) 50.1	Salvadore Morale (ITA) 50.1
1968	David P. Hemery (GBR) 48.1*	Gerhard Hennige (GER) 49.0	John Sherwood (GBR) 49.0
1972	John Akii-bua (UGA) 47.82*	Ralph V. Mann (USA) 48.51	David P. Hemery (GBR) 48.52
1976	Edwin Moses (USA) 47.64*	Michael Shine (USA) 48.69	Evgeniy Gavrilenko (URS) 49.45
1980	Volker Beck (GDR) 48.70	Vasily Arkhipenko (URS) 48.86	Gary Oakes (GBR) 49.11
1984	Edwin Moses (USA) 47.75	Danny Harris (USA) 48.13	Harald Schmid (FRG) 48.19

The performances listed below were Olympic records set additionally in preliminaries.

57.0	Bacon	1908	52.8	Tisdall	1932	50.1	Southern	1956
56.4	Hillman	1908	51.9	Larsson	1948	49.0	Ronald Whitney	
53.4	Taylor	1928	51.9	Cochran	1948		(USA)	1968
52.8	Hardin	1932	50.8	Moore	1952			

[1] Hurdles only 2 ft. 6 in. *75,9 cm* high instead of more usual 3 ft. 0 in. *91,1 cm.*
[2] Record not allowed because a hurdle was knocked down.

Edwin Moses (US) won the 400 meters hurdles in the 1976 Olympics, and repeated in 1984. In fact Moses was undefeated in 121 consecutive races, and only met defeat in 1987 after 10 years of victories. He holds the world record at 47.02 sec.

3,000 METERS (1 mile 1,520 yd. 1 ft.) STEEPLECHASE

Steeplechases were held in 1900 (two races), 1904 and 1908 but none were over obstacles or at distances comparable with the existing event. No steeplechase event was held in 1896, 1906 or 1912.

	GOLD	SILVER	BRONZE
1920	Percy Hodge (GBR) 10:00.4*	Patrick J. Flynn (USA) 100 yd.	Ernesto Ambrosini (ITA) 40 yd.
1924	Ville Ritola (FIN) 9:33.6*	Elias Katz (FIN) 9:44.0	Paul Bontemps (FRA) 9:45.2
1928	Toivo A. Loukola (FIN) 9:21.8*	Paavo J. Nurmi (FIN) 9:31.2	Ove Andersen (FIN) 9:35.6
1932[1]	Volmari Iso-Hollo (FIN) 10:33.4	Thomas Evenson (GBR) 10:46.0	Joseph P. McCluskey (USA) 10:46.2
1936	Volmari Iso-Hollo (FIN) 9:03.8*	Kaarlo Tuominen (FIN) 9:06.8	Alfred Dompert (GER) 9:07.2
1948	Tore Sjöstrand (SWE) 9:04.6	Erik Elmsäter (SWE) 9:08.2	Göte Hagström (SWE) 9:11.8
1952	Horace Ashenfelter (USA) 8:45.4*	Vladimir V. Kazantsev (URS) 8:51.6	John I. Disley (GBR) 8:51.8
1956	Christopher W. Brasher (GBR) 8:41.2*	Sándor Rozsnyói (HUN) 8:43.6	Ernst Larsen (NOR) 8:44.0
1960	Zdzislaw Krzyszkowiak (POL) 8:34.2*	Nikolay Sokolov (URS) 8:36.4	Semyon Rzhishchin (URS) 8:42.2
1964	Gaston Roelants (BEL) 8:30.8*	Maurice Herriott (GBR) 8:32.4	Ivan Belyayev (URS) 8:33.8
1968	Amos Biwott (KEN) 8:51.0	Benjamin Kogo (KEN) 8:51.6	George Young (USA) 8:51.8
1972	H. Kipchoge Keino (KEN) 8:23.6*	Benjamin W. Jipcho (KEN) 8:24.6	Tapio Kantanen (FIN) 8:24.8
1976	Anders Garderud (SWE) 8:08.0*	Bronislaw Malinowski (POL) 8:09.1	Frank Baumgartl (GDR) 8:10.4
1980	Bronislaw Malinowski (POL) 8:09.7	Filbert Bayi (TAN) 8:12.5	Eshetu Tura (ETH) 8:13.6

1984	Julius Korir	Joseph Mahmoud	Brian Diemer
	(KEN) 8:11.80	(FRA) 8:13.31	(USA) 8:14.06

---

[1] Distance in final was 3,460 meters due to error on part of lap-scoring official.

The performances listed below were Olympic records set additionally in preliminaries.

10:17.4	Hodge	1920	8:51.0	Ashenfelter	8:24.8	Kantanen 1972
9:43.8	Katz	1924		1952	8:23.8	Biwott 1972
9:18.8	Evenson	1932	8:33.0	Herriott 1964	8:18.6	Bronislaw
9:14.6	Iso-Hollo	1932	8:31.8	Adolfas		Malinowski
8:58.0	Kazantsev			Aleksiejunas		1976
		1952		(URS) 1964		

20,000 METERS (12 miles 752 yd.) ROAD WALK

	GOLD	SILVER	BRONZE
1896–1952	Event not held		
1956	Leonid Spirin	Antonas Mikenas	Bruno Junk
	(URS) 1h 31:27.4*	(URS) 1h 32:03.0	(URS) 1 h 32.12.0
1960	Vladimir Golubnichiy	Noel F. Freeman	Stanley F. Vickers
	(URS) 1 h 34:07.2	(AUS) 1h 34:16.4	(GBR) 1h 34:56.4
1964	Kenneth J. Matthews	Dieter Lindner	Vladimir Golubnichiy
	(GBR) 1h 29:34.0*	(GER) 1h 31:13.2	(URS) 1h 31:59.4
1968	Vladimir Golubnichiy	José Pedraza	Nickolay Smaga
	(URS) 1h 33:58.4	(MEX) 1h 34:0.0	(URS) 1h 34:03.4
1972	Peter Frenkel	Vladimir Golubnichiy	Hans Reimann
	(GDR) 1h 26:42.4*	(URS) 1h 26:55.2	(GDR) 1h 27:16.6
1976	Daniel Bautista	Hans Reimann	Peter Frenkel
	(MEX) 1h 24:40.6*	(GDR) 1h 25:13.8	(GDR) 1h 25:29.4
1980	Maurizio Damilano	Pyotr Pochinchuk	Roland Wieser
	(ITA) 1h 23:35.5*	(URS) 1h 24:45.4	(GDR) 1h 25:58.2
1984	Ernesto Canto	Raul Gonzalez	Maurizio Damilano
	(MEX) 1h 23:13*	(MEX) 1h 23:20	(ITA) 1h 23:26

50,000 METERS (31 miles 120 yd.) ROAD WALK

1896–1928	Event not held		
1932	Thomas Green	Janis Dalinsh	Ugo Frigerio
	(GBR) 4h 50:10.0*	(LAT) 4h 47:20.0	(ITA) 4h 59:06.0
1936	Harold Whitlock	Arthur Schwab	Adalberts Bubenko
	(GBR) 4h 30:41.1*	(SUI) 4h 32:09.2	(LAT) 4h 32:42.2
1948	John Ljunggren	Gaston Godel	Tebbs Lloyd Johnson
	(SWE) 4h 41:52.0	(SUI) 4h 48:17.0	(GBR) 4h 48:31.0
1952	Guiseppe Dordoni	Josef Dolezal	Antal Roka
	(ITA) 4h 28:07.8*	(TCH) 4h 30:17.8	(HUN) 4h 31:27.2
1956	Norman Read	Yevgeniy Maskinskov	John Ljunggren
	(NZL) 4h 30:42.8	(URS) 4h 32:57.0	(SWE) 4h 35:02.0
1960	Don Thompson	John Ljunggren	Abdon Pamich
	(GBR) 4h 25:30.0*	(SWE) 4h 25:47.0	(ITA) 4h 27:55.4
1964	Abdon Pamich	Paul Nihill	Ingvar Pettersson
	(ITA) 4h 11:12.4*	(GBR) 4h 11:31.2	(SWE) 4h 14:17.4
1968	Christoph Höhne	Antal Kiss	Larry Young
	(GDR) 4h 20:13.6	(HUN) 4h 30:17.0	(USA) 4h 31:55.4
1972	Bernd Kannenberg	Veniamin Soldatenko	Larry Young
	(GER) 3h 56:11.6*	(URS) 3h 58:24.0	(USA) 4h 00:46.0
1976	Event not held		
1980	Hartwig Gauder	Jorge Liopart	Yevgeny Ivchenko
	(GDR) 3h 49:24.0*	(ESP) 3h 51:25.0	(URS) 3h 56:32.0
1984	Raul Gonzalez	Bo Gustafsson	Sandro Bellucci
	(MEX) 3h 47:26*	(SWE) 3h 53:19	(ITA) 3h 53:45

HIGH JUMP

	GOLD	SILVER	BRONZE
1896	Ellery H. Clark (USA) 5′11″ *1,81 m**	[1]	[1]
1900	Irving K. Baxter (USA) 6′2¾″ *1,90 m**	Patrick J. Leahy (GBR) 5′ 10″ *1,78 m*	Lajos Gönczy (HUN) 5′ 8¾″ *1,75 m*
1904	Samuel S. Jones (USA) 5′ 11″ *1,80 m*	Garrett P. Serviss (USA) 5′ 10″ *1,77 m*	Paul Weinstein (GER) 5′ 10″ *1,77 m*
1906	Con Leahy (GBR/IRL) 5′ 9¾″ *1,77 m*	Lajos Gönczy (HUN) 5′8¾″ *1,75 m*	[2]
1908	Harry F. Porter (USA) 6′ 3″ *1,905 m**	[3]	[3]
1912	Alma W. Richards (USA) 6′ 4″ *1,93 m**	Hans Liesche (GER) 6′ 3¼″ *1,91 m*	George L. Horine (USA) 6′ 2½″ *1,89 m*
1920	Richmond W. Landon (USA) 6′ 4¼″ *1,94 m**	Harold P. Muller (USA) 6′ 2¾″ *1,90 m*	Bo Ekelund (SWE) 6′ 2¾″ *1,90 m*
1924	Harold M. Osborn (USA) 6′ 6″ *1,98 m**	Leroy T. Brown (USA) 6′ 4¾″ *1,95 m*	Pierre Lewden (FRA) 6′ 3¼″ *1,92 m*
1928	Robert W. King (USA) 6′ 4¼″ *1,94 m*	Ben Van D. Hedges (USA) 6′ 3¼″ *1,91 m*	Claude Ménard (FRA) 6′ 3¼″ *1,91 m*
1932	Duncan McNaughton (CAN) 6′ 5½″ *1,97 m*	Robert L. Van Osdel (USA) 6′ 5½″ *1,97 m*	Simeon G. Toribio (PHI) 6′ 5½″ *1,97 m*

[1] Tie for second place between James B. Connolly (USA) and Robert S. Garrett (USA) at 5′ 4¾″ *1,65 m*.
[2] Tie for third place between Herbert Kerrigan (USA) and Themistoklis Diakidis (GRE) at 5′ 7½″ *1,72 m*.
[3] Con Leahy (GBR/IRL), István Somodi (HUN) and Geo André (FRA) tied for second place at 6′ 2″ *1,88 m*.

Dick Fosbury (USA), whose back flop style in winning the high jump in 1968 at 7 feet 4¼ inches caught the imagination of the stadium and television viewers all over the world.

	GOLD	SILVER	BRONZE
1936	Cornelius C. Johnson (USA) 6' 7¾" *2,03 m**	David D. Albritton (USA) 6' 6¾" *2,00 m*	Delos P. Thurber (USA) 6' 6¾" *2,00 m*
1948	John A. Winter (AUS) 6' 6" *1,98 m*	Björn Paulsen (NOR) 6' 4¾" *1,95 m*	George A. Stanich (USA) 6' 4¾" *1,95 m*
1952	Walter F. Davis (USA) 6' 8¼" *2,04 m**	Kenneth G. Wiesner (USA) 6' 7" *2,01 m*	Jose Telles da Conceicao (BRA) 6' 6" *1,98 m*
1956	Charles E. Dumas (USA) 6' 11½" *2,12 m**	Charles Porter (AUS) 6' 10½" *2,10 m*	Igor Kashkarov (URS) 6' 9¾" *2,08 m*
1960	Robert Shavlakadze (URS) 7' 1" *2,16 m**	Valeriy N. Brumel (URS) 7' 1" *2,16 m**	John C. Thomas (USA) 7' 0¼" *2,14 m*
1964	Valeriy N. Brumel (URS) 7' 1¾" *2,18 m**	John C. Thomas (USA) 7' 1¾" *2,18 m**	John Rambo (USA) 7' 1" *2,16 m*
1968	Richard Fosbury (USA) 7' 4¼" *2,24 m**	Edward J. Caruthers (USA) 7' 3½" *2,22 m*	Valentin Gavrilov (URS) 7' 2½" *2,20 m*
1972	Yuri Tarmak (URS) 7' 3¾" *2,23 m*	Stefan Junge (GDR) 7' 3" *2,21 m*	Dwight E. Stones (USA) 7' 3" *2,21 m*
1976	Jacek Wszola (POL) 7' 4½" *2,25 m**	Greg Joy (CAN) 7' 3¾" *2,23 m*	Dwight E. Stones (USA) 7' 3" *2,21 m*
1980	Gerd Wessig (GDR) 7' 8¾" *2,36 m**	Jacek Wszola (POL) 7' 7" *2,31 m*	Jorg Freimuth (GDR) 7' 7" *2,31 m*
1984	Dietmar Mogenburg (FRG) 7' 8½" *2.35m*	Patrik Sjoberg (SWE) 7' 7¾" *2.33m*	Zhu Jianbua (CHN) 7029 7" *2.31m*

POLE VAULT

	GOLD	SILVER	BRONZE
1896	William W. Hoyt (USA) 10' 9¾" *3,30 m**	Albert C. Tyler (USA) 10' 7¾" *3,25 m*	Evangelos Damaskos (GRE) 9' 4" *2,85 m*
1900	Irving K. Baxter (USA) 10' 9¾" *3,30 m**	M. B. Colkett (USA) 10' 7¾" *3,25 m*	Carl-Albert Andersen (NOR) 10' 5¾" *3,20 m*
1904	Charles E. Dvorak (USA) 11' 6" *3,50 m**	Leroy Samse (USA) 11' 3" *3,43 m*	L. Wilkins (USA) 11' 3" *3,43 m*
1906	Fernand Gonder (FRA) 11' 1¾" *3,40 m*	Bruno Söderström (SWE) 11' 1¾" *3,40 m*	Ernest C. Glover (USA) 10' 11¾" *3,35 m*
1908	Edward T. Cooke (USA) 12' 2" *3,70 m**	Alfred C. Gilbert[1] 12' 2" *3,70 m**	[2]
1912	Harry S. Babcock (USA) 12' 11½" *3,95 m**		
1920	Frank K. Foss (USA) 13' 5" *4,09 m**	Henry Petersen (DEN) 12' 1½" *3,70 m*	Edwin E. Meyers (USA) 11' 9½" *3,60 m*
1924	Lee S. Barnes (USA) 12' 11½" *3,95 m*	Glenn Graham (USA) 12' 11½" *3,95 m*	James K. Brooker (USA) 12' 9½" *3,90 m*
1928	Sabin W. Carr (USA) 13' 9¼" *4,20 m**	William Droegemuller (USA) 13' 5¼" *4,10 m*	Charles E. McGinnis (USA) 12' 11½" *3,95 m*
1932	William W. Miller (USA) 14' 1¾" *4,31 m**	Shuhei Nishida (JPN) 14'0" *4,26 m*	George G. Jefferson (USA) 13' 9" *4,19 m*
1936	Earle Meadows (USA) 14' 3¼" *4,35 m**	Shuhei Nishida (JPN) 13' 11¼" *4,25 m*	Sueo Oe (JPN) 13' 11¼" *4,25 m*
1948	O. Guinn Smith (USA) 14' 1¼" *4,30 m*	Erkki O. Kataja (FIN) 13' 9¼" *4,20 m*	Robert E. Richards (USA) 13' 9¼" *4,20 m*
1952	Robert E. Richards (USA) 14' 11" *4,55 m**	Donald D. R. Laz (USA) 14' 9" *4,50 m*	Ragnar T. Lundberg (SWE) 14' 5" *4,40 m*
1956	Robert E. Richards (USA) 14' 11½" *4,56 m**	Robert A. Gutowski (USA) 14' 10¼" *4,53 m*	Georgios Roubanis (GRE) 14' 9" *4,50 m*
1960	Donald G. Bragg (USA) 15' 5" *4,70 m**	Ronald H. Morris (USA) 15' 1" *4,60 m*	Eeles Landström (FIN) 14' 11" *4,55 m*
1964	Frederick M. Hansen (USA) 16' 8¾" *5,10 m**	Wolfgang Reinhardt (GER) 16' 6¾" *5,05 m*	Klaus Lehnertz (GER) 16' 4¾" *5,00 m*
1968	Robert L. Seagren (USA) 17' 8½" *5,40 m**	Claus Schiprowski (GER) 17' 8½" *5,40 m**	Wolfgant Nordwig (GDR) 17' 8½" *5,40 m**

---

[1] Tied for gold medal.
[2] Tie for bronze medal between Edward B. Archibald (CAN), Charles S. Jacobs (USA) and Bruno Söderström (SWE) at 11' 9" *3,58 m*.
[3] Tie for silver medal between Frank T. Nelson (USA) and Marcus S. Wright (USA) at 12' 7½" *3,85 m*.

GOLD	SILVER	BRONZE
1972 Wolfgang Nordwig (GDR) 18' 0½" 5,50 m*	Robert L. Seagren (USA) 17' 8½" 5,40 m	Jan E. Johnson (USA) 17' 6½" 5,35 m
1976 Tadeusz Slusarski (POL) 18' 0½" 5,50 m*	Antti Kalliomaki (FIN) 18' 0½" 5,50 m*	David Roberts (USA) 18' 0½" 5,50 m*
1980 Wladyslaw Kozakiewicz (POL) 18' 11½" 5,78 m*	Konstantin Volkov (URS) 18' 6½" 5,65 m	Tadeusz Slusarski (POL) 18' 6½" 5,65 m
1984 Pierre Quinon (FRA) 18' 10¼" 5.75m	Mike Tully (USA) 18' 6½" 5.65m	Earl Bell (USA) 18' 4½" 5.60m Thierry Vigneron (FRA) 18' 4½" 5.60m

Bob Seagren retained the USA unbeaten gold medal run in the pole vault, but only on the "count back" from two Germans who also cleared 17 feet 8½ inches in 1968.

BROAD JUMP (LONG JUMP)

1896 Ellery H. Clark (USA) 20' 10" 6,35 m*	Robert S. Garrett (USA) 20' 3¼" 6,18 m	James B. Connolly (USA) 20' 0½" 6,11 m
1900 Alvin C. Kraenzlein (USA) 23' 6¾" 7,18 m*	Myer Prinstein (USA) 23' 6¼" 7,17 m	Patrick J. Leahy (GBR) 22' 9½" 6,95 m
1904 Myer Prinstein (USA) 24' 1" 7,34 m*	Daniel Frank (USA) 22' 7¼" 6,89 m	Robert S. Stangland (USA) 22' 7" 6,88 m
1906 Myer Prinstein (USA) 23' 7¼" 7,20 m	Peter O'Connor (GBR/IRL) 23' 0½" 7,02 m	Hugo Friend (USA) 22' 10" 6,96 m
1908 Francis C. Irons (USA) 24' 6½" 7,48 m*	Daniel J. Kelly (USA) 23' 3¼" 7,09 m	Calvin D. Bricker (CAN) 23' 3" 7,08 m
1912 Albert L. Gutterson (USA) 24' 11" 7,60 m*	Calvin D. Bricker (CAN) 23' 7¾" 7,21 m	Georg Aberg (SWE) 23' 6½" 7,18 m
1920 William Petterson (SWE) 23' 5¼" 7,15 m	Carl E. Johnson (USA) 23' 3¼" 7,09 m	Erik Abrahamsson (SWE) 23' 2½" 7,08 m
1924[1] William De Hart Hubbard (USA) 24' 5" 7,44 m	Edward O. Gourdin (USA) 23' 10¼" 7,27 m	Sverre Hansen (NOR) 23' 9¾" 7,26 m
1928 Edward B. Hamm (USA) 25' 4¼" 7,73 m*	Silvio Cator (HAI) 24' 10¼" 7,58 m	Alfred H. Bates (USA) 24' 3¼" 7,40 m

---

[1] In the 1924 Pentathlon Robert LeGendre (US) had jumped 25' 5¾" 7,76 m but this was not classed as the Olympic broad jump record.

RIGHT: Bob Beamon (USA) achieving the star performance of the 1968 Olympics with a world-record-shattering long jump of 29 feet 2½ inches. This record is confidently predicted as one that will last into the 21st century.

	GOLD	SILVER	BRONZE
1932	Edward L. Gordon (USA) 25' 0¾" 7,63 m	C. Lambert Redd (USA) 24' 11¼" 7,60 m	Chuhei Nambu (JPN) 24' 5¼" 7,44 m
1936	Jesse Owens (USA) 26' 5¼" 8,06 m*	Luz Long (GER) 25' 9¾" 7,87 m	Naoto Tajima (JPN) 25' 4½" 7,74 m
1948	William S. Steele (USA) 25' 7¾" 7,82 m	Thomas Bruce (AUS) 24' 9" 7,55 m	Herbert P. Douglas (USA) 24' 8¾" 7,54 m
1952	Jerome C. Biffle (USA) 24' 10" 7,57 m	Meredith C. Gourdine (USA) 24' 8¼" 7,53 m	Ödön Földessy (HUN) 23' 11¼" 7,30 m
1956	Gregory C. Bell (USA) 25' 8¼" 7,83 m	John D. Bennett (USA) 25' 2¼" 7,68 m	Jorma Valkama (FIN) 24' 6¼" 7,48 m
1960	Ralph H. Boston (USA) 26' 7½" 8,12 m*	Irvin Roberson (USA) 26' 7¼" 8,11 m	Igor A. Ter-Ovanesyan (URS) 26' 4½" 8,04 m
1964	Lynn Davies (GBR) 26' 5½" 8,07 m	Ralph H. Boston (USA) 26' 4" 8,03 m	Igor A. Ter-Ovanesyan (URS) 26' 2½" 7,99 m
1968	Robert Beamon (USA) 29' 2½" 8,90 m*	Klaus Beer (GDR) 26' 10¼" 8,19 m	Ralph H. Boston[2] (USA) 26' 9¼" 8,16 m
1972	Randy L. Williams (USA) 27' 0¼" 8,24 m	Hans Baumgartner (GER) 26' 10" 8,18 m	Arnie Robinson (USA) 26' 4" 8,03 m
1976	Arnie Robinson (USA) 27' 4¾" 8,35 m	Randy L. Williams (USA) 26' 7¼" 8,11 m	Frank Wartenberg (GDR) 26' 3¾" 8,02 m
1980	Lutz Dombrowski (GDR) 28' 0¼" 8,54 m	Frank Paschek (GDR) 26' 11¼" 8,21 m	Valery Podluzhnyi (URS) 26' 10" 8,18 m
1984	Carl Lewis (USA) 28' 0¼" 8.54m	Gary Honey (AUS) 27' 0½" 8.24m	Giovanni Evangelisti (ITA) 27' 0½" 18.24m

---

* Set Olympic record of 27' 1¼" 8,27 m in qualifying round.

TRIPLE JUMP[1]

1896[2] James B. Connolly   Alexandre Tuffere   Joannis Persakis
     (USA) 44' 11¾" *13,71 m**(FRA) 41' 8" *12,70 m*   (GRE) 41' 0¾" *12,52 m*
1900   Myer Prinstein   James B. Connolly   Lewis P. Sheldon
     (USA) 47' 5½" *14,47 m**(USA) 45' 10" *13,97 m*   (USA) 44' 9" *13,64 m*
1904   Myer Prinstein   Frederick Englehardt   Robert S. Stangland
     (USA) 47' 1" *14,35 m*   (USA) 45' 7¼" *13,90 m*   (USA) 43' 10¼" *13,36 m*
1906   Peter O'Connor   Con Leahy   Thomas Cronan
     (GBR/IRL)   (GBR/IRL)   (USA) 44' 11¼" *13,70 m*
         46' 2" *14,07 m*   45' 10¼" *13,98 m*
1908   Timothy J. Ahearne   J. Garfield McDonald   Edvard Larsen
     (GBR) 48' 11¼" *14,91 m**(CAN) 48' 5¼" *14,76 m*   (NOR) 47' 2¾" *14,39 m*
1912   Gustaf Lindblom   Georg Åberg   Erik Almlöf
     (SWE) 48' 5" *14,76 m*   (SWE) 47' 7¼" *14,51 m*   (SWE) 46' 5¾" *14,17 m*
1920   Vilho Tuulos   Folke Jansson   Erik Almlöf
     (FIN) 47' 7" *14,50 m*   (SWE) 47' 6" *14,48 m*   (SWE) 46' 9¾" *14,27 m*
1924   Anthony W. Winter   Luis Brunetto   Vilho Tuulos
     (AUS) 50' 11¼" *15,52 m**(ARG) 50' 7¼" *15,42 m*   (FIN) 50' 5" *15,37 m*
1928   Mikio Oda   Levi Casey   Vilho Tuulos
     (JPN) 49' 10¾" *15,21 m*   (USA) 49' 9" *15,17 m*   (FIN) 49' 6¾" *15,11 m*
1932   Chuhei Nambu   Erik Svensson   Kenkichi Oshima
     (JPN) 51' 7" *15,72 m**   (SWE) 50' 3¼" *15,32 m*   (JPN) 49' 7¼" *15,12 m*
1936   Naoto Tajima   Masao Harada   John P. Metcalfe
     (JPN) 52' 5¾" *16,00 m** (JPN) 51' 4½" *15,66 m*   (AUS) 50' 10" *15,50 m*
1948   Arne Åhman   George G. Avery   Ruhi Sarialp
     (SWE) 50' 6¼" *15,40 m*   (AUS) 50' 4¾" *15,36 m*   (TUR) 49' 3½" *15,02 m*
1952   Adhemar Ferreira da   Leonid Shcherbakov   Arnoldo Devonish
               Silva   (URS) 52' 5" *15,98 m*   (VEN) 50' 11" *15,52 m*
     (BRA) 53' 2½" *16,22 m**
1956   Adhemar Ferreira da   Vilhjálmur Einarsson   Vitold Kreyer
               Silva   (ISL) 53'4" *16,26 m*   (URS) 52' 6½" *16,02 m*
     (BRA) 53' 7½" *16,35 m**
1960   Józef Schmidt   Vladimir Goryayev   Vitold Kreyer
     (POL) 55' 1¾" *16,81 m** (URS) 54' 6½" *16,63 m*   (URS) 53' 10¾" *16,43 m*

---

[1] Formerly known as the Hop, Step and Jump.
[2] Winner took two hops with his right foot, contrary to present rule.

Leo Sexton (USA), the 1932 gold
medal winner in the shot put, is one
of a long line of American champions
in this event.

	GOLD	SILVER	BRONZE
1964	Józef Schmidt (POL) 55' 3¼" 16,85 m*	Olyeg Fyedoseyev (URS) 54' 4¾" 16,58 m	Viktor Kravchenko (URS) 54' 4¼" 16,57 m
1968	Viktor Saneyev (URS) 57' 0¾" 17,39 m*	Nelson Prudencio (BRA) 56' 7¾" 17,27 m	Giuseppe Gentile (ITA) 56' 5¾" 17,22 m
1972	Viktor Saneyev (URS) 56' 11" 17,35 m	Joerg Drehmel (GDR) 56' 9¼" 17,31 m	Nelson Prudencio (BRA) 55' 11¼" 17,05 m
1976	Viktor Saneyev (URS) 56' 8¾" 17,29 m	James Butts (USA) 56' 8½" 17,18 m	Joao de Oliveira (BRA) 55' 5½" 16,90 m
1980	Jaak Uudmae (URS) 56' 11" 17,35 m	Viktor Saneyev (URS) 56' 6¾" 17,24 m	Joao de Oliveira (BRA) 56' 6" 17,22 m
1984	Al Joyner (USA) 56' 7½" 17.26m	Mike Conley (USA) 56' 4½" 17.18m	Keith Connor (GBR) 55' 4½" 16.87m

SHOT PUT

	GOLD	SILVER	BRONZE
1896[1]	Robert S. Garrett (USA) 36' 9½" 11,22 m*	Miltiades Gouskos (GRE) 36' 6¾" 11,15 m	Georgios Papasideris (GRE) 33' 11¾" 10,36 m
1900[1]	Richard Sheldon (USA) 46' 3" 14,10 m*	Josiah C. McCracken (USA) 42' 1¾" 12,85 m	Robert S. Garrett (USA) 40' 7" 12,37 m
1904[1]	Ralph W. Rose (USA) 48' 7" 14,80 m*	W. Wesley Coe (USA) 47' 3" 14,40 m	Leon E. J. Feuerbach (USA) 43' 10½" 13,37 m
1906	Martin Sheridan (USA) 40' 5" 12,32 m	Mihály Dávid (HUN) 38' 9½" 11,83 m	Erik V. Lemming (SWE) 36' 11¼" 11,26 m
1908	Ralph W. Rose (USA) 46' 7½" 14,21 m	Dennis Horgan (GBR) 44' 8¼" 13,61 m	John C. Garrels (USA) 43' 3" 13,18 m
1912	Patrick J. McDonald (USA) 50' 4" 15,34 m*	Ralph W. Rose (USA) 50' 0¼" 15,25 m	Lawrence A. Whitney (USA) 45' 5" 14,15 m
1920	Ville Pörhöla (FIN) 48' 7" 14,81 m	Elmer Niklander (FIN) 46' 5¼" 14,155 m	Harry B. Liversedge (USA) 46' 5" 14,15 m
1924	Clarence L. Houser (USA) 49' 2" 14,99 m	Glenn Hartranft (USA) 49' 1¾" 14,98 m	Ralph G. Hills (USA) 48' 0¼" 14,64 m
1928	John Kuck (USA) 52' 0¾" 15,87 m*	Herman H. Brix (USA) 51' 8" 15,75 m	Emil Hirschfeld (GER) 51' 6¾" 15,72 m
1932	Leo J. Sexton (USA) 52' 5¾" 16,00 m*	Harlow P. Rothert (USA) 51' 5" 15,67 m	František Douda (TCH) 51' 2½" 15,60 m
1936	Hans Woelke (GER) 53' 1¾" 16,20 m*	Sulo Bärlund (FIN) 52' 10½" 16,12 m	Gerhard Stöck (GER) 51' 4½" 15,66 m
1948	Wilbur M. Thompson (USA) 56' 2" 17,12 m*	F. James Delaney (USA) 54' 8½" 16,68 m	James E. Fuchs (USA) 53' 10¼" 16,42 m
1952	W. Parry O'Brien (USA) 57' 1¼" 17,41 m*	C. Darrow Hooper (USA) 57' 0½" 17,39 m	James E. Fuchs (USA) 55' 11½" 17,06 m
1956	W. Parry O'Brien (USA) 60' 11" 18,57 m*	William H. Nieder (USA) 59' 7½" 18,18 m	Jiří Skobla (TCH) 57' 10¾" 17,65 m
1960	William H. Nieder (USA) 64' 6¾" 19,68 m*	W. Parry O'Brien (USA) 62' 8¼" 19,11 m	Dallas C. Long (USA) 62' 4¼" 19,01 m
1964	Dallas C. Long (USA) 66' 8¼" 20,33 m*	J. Randel Matson (USA) 66' 3¼" 20,20 m	Vilmos Varju (HUN) 63' 7¼" 19,39 m
1968	J. Randel Matson[2] (USA) 67' 4½" 20,54 m	George R. Woods (USA) 66' 0" 20,12 m	Eduard Gushchin (URS) 65' 10¾" 20,09 m
1972	Wladyslaw Komar (POL) 69' 6" 21,18 m*	George R. Woods (USA) 69' 5½" 21,17 m	Hartmut Briesenick (GDR) 69' 4¼" 21,14 m
1976	Udo Beyer (GDR) 69' 0¾" 21,05 m	Evgeniy Mironov (URS) 69' 0" 21,03 m	Alexandr Baryshnikov[3] (URS) 68' 10¾" 21,00 m
1980	Vladimir Kiselyov (URS) 70' 0½" 21, 35 m*	Alexandr Baryshnikov (URS) 69' 2" 21,08 m	Udo Beyer (GDR) 69' 1¼" 21,06 m
1984	Alessandro Andrei (ITA) 69' 9" 21.16m	Michael Carter (USA) 69' 2½" 21.09m	Dave Laut (USA) 68' 9¾" 20.97m

[1] The shot was put from a 7 foot 2,13 m square.
[2] Set Olympic record of 67' 10¼" 20,68 m in qualifying round.
[3] Set Olympic record of 69' 11½" 21,32 m in qualifying round.

DISCUS THROW

Year	Gold	Silver	Bronze
1896	Robert S. Garrett (USA) 95' 7½" 29,15 m*	Panagiotis Paraskeyopoulos (GRE) 94' 11½" 28,95 m	Sotirios Versis (GRE) 94' 5" 28,78 m
1900	Rudolf Bauer (HUN) 118' 2½" 36,04 m*	František Janda-Suk (BOH) 115' 7½" 35,25 m	Richard Sheldon (USA) 113' 6" 34,60 m
1904	Martin J. Sheridan[1] (USA) 128' 10½" 39,28 m*	Ralph W. Rose (USA) 128' 10½" 39,28 m*	Nicolaos Georgantas (GRE) 123' 7½" 37,68 m
1906	Martin J. Sheridan (USA) 136' 0" 41,46 m	Nicolaos Georgantas (GRE) 124' 10" 38,06 m	Werner Järvinen (FIN) 120' 9½" 36,82 m
1908	Martin J. Sheridan (USA) 134' 2" 40,89 m	Merritt H. Giffin (USA) 133' 6½" 40,70 m	Marquis F. Horr (USA) 129' 5" 39,44 m
1912	Armas R. Taipale (FIN) 148' 3½" 45,21 m*	Richard L. Byrd (USA) 138' 10" 42,32 m	James H. Duncan (USA) 138' 8½" 42,28 m
1920	Elmer Niklander (FIN) 146' 7" 44,68 m	Armas R. Taipale (FIN) 144' 11½" 44,19 m	Augustus R. Pope (USA) 138' 2½" 42,13 m
1924	Clarence L. Houser (USA) 151' 5" 46,15 m*	Vilho A. Niittymaa (FIN) 147' 5½" 44,95 m	Thomas J. Lieb (USA) 147' 0½" 44,83 m
1928	Clarence L. Houser (USA) 155' 2½" 47,32 m*	Antero Kivi (FIN) 154' 11" · 7,23 m	James Corson (USA) 154' 6" 47,10 m
1932	John F. Anderson (USA) 162' 4½" 49,49 m*	Henri J. Laborde (FRA) 159' 0½" 48,47 m	Paul Winter (FRA) 157' 0" 47,85 m
1936	Kenneth K. Carpenter (USA) 165' 7" 50,48 m*	Gordon G. Dunn (USA) 161' 11" 49,36 m	Giorgio Oberweger (ITA) 161' 6" 49,23 m
1948	Adolfo Consolini (ITA) 173' 1½" 52,78 m*	Giuseppe Tosi (ITA) 169' 10½" 51,78 m	Fortune E. Gordien (USA) 166' 6½" 50,77 m
1952	Sim G. Iness (USA) 180' 6½" 55,03 m*	Adolfo Consolini (ITA) 176' 5" 53,78 m	James L. Dillion (USA) 174' 9½" 53,28 m
1956	Alfred A. Oerter (USA) 184' 10½" 56,36 m*	Fortune E. Gordien (USA) 179' 9½" 54,81 m	Desmond Koch (USA) 178' 5½" 54,40 m
1960	Alfred A. Oerter (USA) 194' 1½" 59,18 m*	Richard A. Babka (USA) 190' 4" 58,02 m	Richard L. Cochran (USA) 187' 6" 57,16 m
1964	Alfred A. Oerter (USA) 200' 1½" 61,00 m*	Ludvik Danek (TCH) 198' 6½" 60,52 m	David Weill (USA) 195' 2" 59,49 m
1968	Alfred A. Oerter (USA) 212' 6" 64,78 m*	Lothar Milde (GDR) 206' 11" 63,08 m	Ludvik Danek (TCH) 206' 5" 62,92 m
1972	Ludvik Danek (TCH) 211' 3" 64,40 m	L. Jay Silvester (USA) 208' 4" 63,50 m	Rickard Bruch (SWE) 208' 0" 63,40 m
1972	Ludvik Danek (TCH) 211' 3" 64.40 m	L. Jay Silvester (USA) 208' 4" 63.50 m	Rickard Bruch (SWE) 208' 0" 63,40 m
1976	Maurice MacWilkins (USA) 221' 5" 67,50 m[2]	Wolfgang Schmidt (GDR) 217' 3" 66,22 m	John Powell (USA) 215' 7" 65,70 m
1980	Viktor Rasshchupkin (URS) 218' 7" 66,64 m	Imrich Bugar (TCH) 217' 9" 66,38 m	Luis Delis (CUB) 217' 7" 66,32 m
1984	Rolf Danneberg (FRG) 218' 6" 66.60m	Mac Wilkins (USA) 217' 6" 66.30m	John Powell (USA) 214' 9" 65.46m

[1] First place decided by a throw-off.
[2] Set Olympic record of 224' 0" 68,28 m in qualifying round.

HAMMER THROW

	GOLD	SILVER	BRONZE
1896	Event not held		
1900[1]	John J. Flanagan (USA) 163' 1½" 49,73 m	Truxton T. Hare (USA) 161' 2" 49,13 m	Josiah C. McCracken (USA) 139' 3½" 42,46 m
1904	John J. Flanagan (USA) 168' 0½" 51,23 m*	John R. DeWitt (USA) 164' 10½" 50,26 m	Ralph W. Rose (USA) 150' 0" 45,73 m
1906	Event not held		
1908	John J. Flanagan (USA) 170' 4" 51,92 m*	Matthew J. McGrath (USA) 167' 11" 51,18 m	Cornelius Walsh (CAN) 159' 1½" 48,50 m

LEFT: Hal Connolly (USA) won the hammer throw in Melbourne in 1956 with a throw of 207 feet 3½ inches.

ABOVE: Al Oerter (USA) dominated the discus competition for 4 consecutive meetings (1956 to 1968), a unique achievement in Olympic track and field.

1912	Matthew J. McGrath (USA) 179' 7" 54,74 m*	Duncan Gillis (CAN) 158' 9" 48,39 m	Clarence C. Childs (USA) 158' 0" 48,17 m
1920	Patrick J. Ryan (USA) 173' 5½" 52,87 m	Carl Johan Lind (SWE) 158' 10½" 48,43 m	Basil Bennet (USA) 158' 3½" 48,25 m
1924	Frederick D. Tootell (USA) 174' 10" 53,29 m	Matthew J. McGrath (USA) 166' 9½" 50,84 m	Malcolm C. Nokes (GBR) 160' 4" 48,87 m
1928	Patrick O'Callaghan (IRL) 168' 7" 51,39 m	Ossian Skiöld (SWE) 168' 3" 51,29 m	Edmund F. Black (USA) 160' 10" 49,03 m
1932	Patrick O'Callaghan (IRL) 176' 11" 53,92 m	Ville Pörhölä (FIN) 171' 6" 52,27 m	Peter E. Zaremba (USA) 165' 1½" 50,33 m
1936	Karl Hein (GER) 185' 4" 56,49 m*	Erwin Blask (GER) 180' 6½" 55,04 m	Fred Warngård (SWE) 179' 10½" 54,83 m
1948	Imre Németh (HUN) 183' 11" 56,07 m	Ivan Gubijan (YUG) 178' 0½" 54,27 m	Robert H. Bennett (USA) 176' 3" 53,73 m
1952	József Csermák (HUN) 197' 11½" 60,34 m*	Karl Storch (GER) 193' 1" 58,86 m	Imre Németh (HUN) 189' 5" 57,74 m
1956	Harold V. Connolly (USA) 207' 3½" 63,19 m*	Mikhail P. Krivonosov (URS) 206' 9" 63,03 m	Anatoliy Samotsvetov (URS) 205' 2½" 62,56 m
1960	Vasiliy Rudenkov (URS) 220' 1½" 67,10 m*	Gyula Zsivótzky (HUN) 215' 10" 65,79 m	Tadeusz Rut (POL) 215' 4" 65,64 m
1964	Romuald Klim (URS) 228' 9½" 69,74 m*	Gyula Zsivótzky (HUN) 226' 8" 69,09 m	Uwe Beyer (GER) 223' 4½" 68,09 m
1968	Gyula Zsivótzky (HUN) 240' 8" 73,36 m*	Romuald Klim (URS) 240' 5" 73,28 m	Lázár Lovász (HUN) 228' 11" 69,78 m
1972	Anatoli Bondarchuk (URS) 247' 8" 75,50 m*	Jochen Sachse (GDR) 245' 11" 74,96 m*	Vasili Khmelevski (URS) 242' 10½" 74,04 m
1976	Yuri Sedykh (URS) 254' 4" 77,52 m*	Alexei Spiridonov (URS) 249' 7" 76,08 m	Anatoli Bondarchuk (URS) 247' 8" 75,48 m
1980	Yuri Sedykh (URS) 268' 4" 81,80 m*	Sergei Litvinov (URS) 264' 6" 80,64 m	Yuri Tamm 259' 0" 78,96 m
1984	Juha Tiainen (FIN) 256' 2" 78.08m	Karl-Hans Riehm (FRG) 255' 10" 77.98m	Klaus Ploghaus (FRG) 251' 7" 76.68m

[1] Thrown from a 9 foot 2,74 m instead of the now regular 7 foot 2,135 m circle.

JAVELIN THROW

GOLD	SILVER	BRONZE

1896–1904 Event not held

1906 Erik V. Lemming (SWE) 176' 10" *53,90 m**
      Knut Lindberg (SWE) 148' 2" *45,17 m*
      Bruno Söerström (SWE) 147' 10½" *44,92 m*

1908 Erik V. Lemming (SWE) 179' 10½" *54,82 m**
      Arne Halse (NOR) 165' 11" *50,57 m*
      Otto Nilsson (SWE) 154' 6" *47,09 m*

1912 Erik V. Lemming (SWE) 198' 11" *60,64 m**
      Juho Saaristo (FIN) 192' 5" *58,66 m*
      Mór Kóczán (HUN) 182' 1" *55,50 m*

1920 Jonni Myyrä (FIN) 215' 9½" *65,78 m**
      Urho Peltonen (FIN) 208' 4" *63,50 m*
      Pekka Johansson (FIN) 207' 0" *63,09 m*

1924 Jonni Myyrä (FIN) 206' 6½" *62,96 m*
      Gunnar Lindström (SWE) 199' 10" *60,92 m*
      Eugene G. Oberst (USA) 191' 5" *58,35 m*

1928 Erik Lundkvist (SWE) 218' 6" *66,60 m**
      Béla Szepes (HUN) 214' 1" *65,26 m*
      Olav Sunde (NOR) 209' 10½" *63,97 m*

1932 Matti Järvinen (FIN) 238' 6½" *72,71 m**
      Matti Sippala (FIN) 229' 0" *69,79 m*
      Eino Penttila (FIN) 225' 4½" *68,69 m*

1936 Gerhard Stöck (GER) 235' 8" *71,84 m*
      Yrjö Nikkanen (FIN) 232' 2" *70,77 m*
      Kalervo Toivonen (FIN) 232' 0" *70,72 m*

1948 K. Tapio Rautavaara (FIN) 228' 10½" *69,77 m*
      Steve A. Seymour (USA) 221' 7½" *67,56 m*
      József Várszegi (HUN) 219' 10½" *67,03 m*

1952 Cyrus C. Young (USA) 242' 0½" *73,78 m**
      William Miller (USA) 237' 8½" *72,46 m*
      Toivo Hyytiäinen (FIN) 235' 10" *71,89 m*

1956 Egil Danielsen (NOR) 281' 2" *85,71 m**
      Janusz Sidlo (POL) 262' 4½" *79,98 m*
      Viktor Tsibulenko (URS) 260' 9½" *79,50 m*

1960 Viktor Tsibulenko (URS) 277' 8" *84,64 m*
      Walter Krüger (GER) 260' 4" *79,36 m*
      Gergely Kulcsár (HUN) 257' 9" *78,57 m*

1964 Pauli Nevala (FIN) 271' 2" *82,66 m*
      Gergely Kulcsár (HUN) 270' 0½" *82,32 m*
      Janis Lusis (URS) 264' 2" *80,57 m*

Bruce Jenner (USA) acknowledges the cheers of the crowd after shattering Olympic and world records in the 1976 decathlon.

Daley Thompson (GBR) won the decathlon in 1980 and repeated in 1984 with an Olympic record of 8,797 points under a new scoring system.

	GOLD	SILVER	BRONZE
1968	Janis Lusis (URS) 295' 7" *90,10 m**	Jorma V. P. Kinnunen (FIN) 290' 7" *88,58 m*	Gergely Kulcsár (HUN) 285' 7½" *87,06 m*
1972	Klaus Wolfermann (GER) 296' 10" *90.48 m**	Janis Lusis (URS) 296' 9" *90,46 m*	William Schmidt (USA) 276' 11½" *84,42 m*
1976	Miklos Nemeth (HUN) 310' 4" *94,58 m**	Hannu Siitonen (FIN) 288' 5" *87,92 m*	Gheorghe Megelea (ROM) 285' 11" *87,16 m*
1980	Dainis Kula (URS) 299' 2" *91,20 m*	Aleksandr Makarov (URS) 294' 1" *89,64 m*	Wolfgang Hanisch (GDR) 284' 6" *86,72 m*
1984	Arto Härkonen (FIN) 284' 8" *86.76m*	David Ottley (GBR) 281' 3" *85.74m*	Kenth Eldebrink (SWE) 274' 8" *83.72m*

DECATHLON[1]

(Figures refer to points scored)

	GOLD	SILVER	BRONZE
1896–1908	Event not held		
1912	Hugo Wieslander[2] (SWE) 6,162	Charles Lomberg (SWE) 5,943	Gösta Holmér (SWE) 5,956
1920	Helge Løvland (NOR) 5,970	Brutus Hamilton (USA) 5,912	Bertil Ohlson (SWE) 5,825
1924	Harold M. Osborn (USA) 6,668	Emerson Norton (USA) 6,360	Aleksander Klumberg (EST) 6,260
1928	Paavo Yrjölä (FIN) 6,774	Akilles Järvinen (FIN) 6,815	J. Kenneth Doherty (USA) 6,593
1932	James A. B. Bausch (USA) 6,986	Akilles Järvinen (FIN) 7,038	Wolrad Eberle (GER) 6,830
1936	Glenn E. Morris (USA) 7,421	Robert H. Clark (USA) 7,226	Jack Parker (USA) 6,918
1948	Robert B. Mathias (USA) 6,826	Ignace Heinrich (FRA) 6,740	Floyd M. Simmons (USA) 6,711
1952	Robert B. Mathias (USA) 7,731	Milton G. Campbell (USA) 7,132	Floyd M. Simmons (USA) 7,069

		GOLD	SILVER	BRONZE
1956	Milton G. Campbell (USA) 7,708	Rafer L. Johnson (USA) 7,568	Vasiliy Kuznetsov (URS) 7,461
1960	Rafer L. Johnson (USA) 8,001	Yang Chuan-kwang (TAI) 7,930	Vasiliy Kuznetsov (URS) 7,624
1964	Willi Holdorf (GER) 7,887	Rein Aun (URS) 7,842	Hans-Joachim Walde (GER) 7,809
1968	William A. Toomey (USA) 8,193*	Hans-Joachim Walde (FRG) 8,111	Kurt Bendlin (FRG) 8,064
1972	Nikolai Avilov (URS) 8,454*	Leonid Litvinenko (URS) 8,035	Ryszard Katus (POL) 7,984
1976	Bruce Jenner (USA) 8,618*	Guido Kratschmer (FRG) 8,411	Nikolai Avilov (URS) 8,369
1980	Daley Thompson (GBR) 8,495	Yuri Kutsenko (URS) 8,331	Sergei Zhelanov (URS) 8,135
1984	Daley Thompson (GBR) 8,798 pts*[2]	Jürgen Hingsen (FRG) 8,673	Siegfried Wentz (FRG) 8,412

[1] The decathlon consists of 100 m, long jump, shot put, high jump, 400 m, 110 m hurdles, discus, pole vault, javelin and 1500 m. The competition occupies 2 days (but 3 days in 1912). Scores given above are all recalculated on the 1962 tables. 1912 scores were based on the then Olympic record; the 1920–1932 scores on the Olympic records standing after the 1912 Games; the 1936 and 1948 Games were scored on the tables published in 1934; 1952–1960 Games on tables published in 1952, since then on tables published in 1962. It is noted that in 3 years (1912, 1928 and 1932) the original medal order would have been different had the 1962 values then prevailed.
[2] Jim Thorpe (USA) finished first with 6,845 pts but was later disqualified for a breach of the then amateur rules. He was reinstated posthumously by the IOC in 1982, but only as joint first.

[2] Olympic record 8,847 pts under new 1986 tables

Track and Field Athletics (Women)

MARRIED NAMES
  The following won medals under both their maiden and their married names:

Becker—Mickler	Kirszenstein—Szewinska	Schaller—Klier
Brehmer—Lathan	Kohler—Birkemeyer	Schlaak—Jahl
Eckert—Wockel	Manning—Jackson	Smallwood—Cook
Foulds—Paul	Odam—Tyler	Strickland—Delahunty
Goddard—Callender	Oelsner—Gohr	Vergova—Petkova
Hunte—Oakes	Richter—Górecka	Wieczorek—Ciepla
Khnykina—Dvalishvili	Romashkova—Ponomaryeva	Zharkova—Maslakova

100 METERS (109 yd. 1 ft.)

	GOLD	SILVER	BRONZE
1928	Elizabeth Robinson (USA) 12.2*	Fanny Rosenfeld (CAN) inches	Ethel Smith (CAN) inches
1932	Stanislawa Walasiewicz (POL) 11.9*	Hilda Strike (CAN) 11.9*	Wilhelmina von Bremen (USA) 12.0
1936	Helen H. Stephens (USA) 11.5	Stanislawa Walasiewicz (POL) 11.7	Kathe Krauss (GER) 11.9
1948	Francina E. Blankers-Koen (HOL) 11.9	Dorothy G. Manley (GBR) 12.2	Shirley B. Strickland (AUS) 12.2
1952	Marjorie Jackson (AUS) 11.5	Daphne L. E. Hasenjager (SAF) 11.8	Shirley B. Strickland (AUS) 11.9
1956	Betty Cuthbert (AUS) 11.5	Christa Stubnick (GER) 11.7	Marlene J. Mathews (AUS) 11.7

Wyomia Tyus (USA) successfully defends her 100 meters title in 1968 in the world record of 11.0 seconds.

Renate Stecher (No. 147) edges Raelene Boyle of Australia to become the fifth woman ever to win the 100 meters/200 meters double.

	GOLD	SILVER	BRONZE
1960	Wilma G. Rudolph (USA) 11.0*	Dorothy Hyman (GBR) 11.3	Giuseppina Leone (ITA) 11.3
1964	Wyomia Tyus (USA) 11.4	Edith Maguire (USA) 11.6	Ewa Kobukowska (POL) 11.6
1968	Wyomia Tyus (USA) 11.0*	Barbara A. Ferrell (USA) 11.1	Irena Szewińska (POL) 11.1
1972	Renate Stecher (GDR) 11.07	Raelene A. Boyle (AUS) 11.23	Silvia Chivas (CUB) 11.24
1976	Annegret Richter (GER) 11.08	Renate Stecher (GDR) 11.13	Inge Helten (GER) 11.17
1980	Ludmila Kondrateva (URS) 11.06	Marlies Gohr (GDR) 11.07	Ingrid Auerswald (GDR) 11.14
1984	Evelyn Ashford (USA) 10.97*	Alice Brown (USA) 11.13	Merlene Ottey-Page (JAM) 11.16

The performances listed below were Olympic records set additionally in preliminaries.

(Nine records were established prior to the 1928 final.)

12.2	Marie Dollinger (GER)	1932	11.4	Cuthbert	1956
11.9	Walasiewicz (twice)	1932	11.3	Rudolph	1960
			11.01	Richter	1976

Performances of 11.4 and 11.5 (final) by Stephens in 1936; 11.5 (final) by Cuthbert 1956; 11.0 (final) by Rudolph 1960; 11.3 by Tyus in 1964; 11.1 by Ferrell and 11.0 by Tyus in 1968 were wind assisted.

200 METERS (218 yd. 2 ft.)

	GOLD	SILVER	BRONZE
1928–1936	Event not held		
1948	Francina E. Blankers-Koen (HOL) 24.4	Audrey D. Williamson (GBR) 25.1	Audrey Patterson[1] (USA) 25.2
1952	Marjorie Jackson (AUS) 23.7	Bertha Brouwer (HOL) 24.2	Nadyezhda Khnykina (URS) 24.2
1956	Betty Cuthbert (AUS) 23.4*	Christa Stubnick (GER) 23.7	Marlene J. Mathews (AUS) 23.8
1960	Wilma G. Rudolph (USA) 24.0	Jutta Heine (GER) 24.4	Dorothy Hyman (GBR) 24.7
1964	Edith Maguire (USA) 23.0*	Irena Kirszenstein (POL) 23.1	Marilyn M. Black (AUS) 23.1
1968	Irena Szewinska (POL) 22.5*	Raelene A. Boyle (AUS) 22.7	Jennifer Lamy (AUS) 22.8
1972	Renate Stecher (GDR) 22.40*	Raelene A. Boyle (AUS) 22.45	Irena Szewinska (POL) 22.74
1976	Barbel Eckert (GDR) 22.37*	Annegret Richter (GER) 22.39	Renate Stecher (GDR) 22.47
1980	Barbel Wockel (GDR) 22.03*	Natalya Bochina (URS) 22.19	Merlene Ottey (JAM) 22.20
1984	Valerie Brisco-Hooks (USA) 21.81*	Florence Griffith (USA) 22.04	Merlene Ottey-Page (JAM) 22.09

---

[1] A recently discovered photo-finish indicates that Shirley Strickland (AUS) was third.

The performances listed below were Olympic records set additionally in preliminaries.

25.7	Blankers-Koen 1948	24.3	Blankers-Koen 1948	22.9	Barbara A. Ferrell (USA)	1968
25.6	Cynthia A. Thompson (JAM) 1948	24.3	Khnykina	1952	22.9	Boyle	1968
		23.6	Jackson	1952	22.8	Ferrell	1968
		23.4	Jackson	1952			
25.3	Daphne L. E. Robb (SAF) 1948	23.2	Rudolph	1960			
		23.0	Boyle	1968			

400 METERS (437 yd. 1 ft.)

1928–1960 Event not held

1964	Betty Cuthbert (AUS) 52.0*	Ann E. Packer (GBR) 52.2	Judith F. Amoore (AUS) 53.4
1968	Colette Besson (FRA) 52.0*	Lillian B. Board (GBR) 52.1	Natalya Pyechenkina (URS) 52.2
1972	Monika Zehrt (GDR) 51.08*	Rita Wilden (GER) 51.21	Kathy Hammond (USA) 51.64
1976	Irena Szewinska (POL) 49.29*	Christina Brehmer (GDR) 50.51	Ellen Streidt (GDR) 50.55
1980	Marita Koch (GDR) 48.88*	Jarmila Kratochvilova (TCH) 49.46	Christina Lathan (GDR) 49.66
1984	Valerie Brisco-Hooks (USA) 48.83*	Chandra Cheeseborough (USA) 49.05	Kathy Cook (GBR) 49.43

The performances listed below were Olympic records set additionally in preliminaries.

54.4	Antonia Munkácsi (HUN)	1964	51.94	Charlene Rendina (AUS) 1972	51.68	Helga Seidler (GDR)	1972
53.1	Packer	1964	51.71	Györgyi Balogh (HUN) 1972	51.47	Zehrt	1972
52.7	Packer	1964			50.48	Szewinska	1976

Valerie Brisco-Hooks (US) is the first woman to win gold medals in 2 Olympic events in the same Games. She broke Olympic records in the 200 and 400 meters.

The 200 meters final in 1960 with Wilma Rudolph (USA) (far right), the gold medal winner of the 100 meters dash as well, wearing No. 117; Jutta Heine (GER), the silver medal winner wearing No. 77; and Dorothy Hyman (GBR), the bronze medal winner wearing No. 100. Also in the photo is Giuseppina Leone (ITA), No. 181, bronze medal winner in the 100 meters dash.

At the 1980 Games, Barbel Wockel (née Eckert) (GDR) successfully defended her Olympic titles at 200 meters and the 4 × 100 meters relay, thus becoming only the third woman athlete to win 4 gold medals in track and field.

800 METERS (874 yd. 2 ft.)

	GOLD	SILVER	BRONZE
1928	Lina Radke (GER) 2:16.8*	Kinuye Hitomi (JPN) 2:17.6	Inga Gentzel (SWE) 2:17.8
1932–1956	Event not held		
1960	Ludmila I. Shevtsova (URS) 2:04.3*	Brenda Jones (AUS) 2:04.4	Ursula Donath (GER) 2:05.6
1964	Ann E. Packer (GBR) 2:01.1*	Maryvonne Dupureur (FRA) 2:01.9	M. Ann M. Chamberlain (NZL) 2:02.8
1968	Madeline Manning (USA) 2:00.9*	Ilona Silai (ROM) 2:02.5	Maria F. Gommers (HOL) 2:02.6

GOLD	SILVER	BRONZE
1972 Hildegard Falck (GER) 1:58.6*	Niole Sabaite (URS) 1:58.7	Gunhild Hoffmeister (GDR) 1:59.2
1976 Tatyana Kazankina (URS) 1:54.9*	Nikolina Chtereva (BUL) 1:55.4	Elfi Zinn (GDR) 1:55.6
1980 Nadezhda Olizarenko (URS) 1:53.5*	Olga Mineyeva (URS) 1:54.9	Tatyana Providokhina (URS) 1:55.5
1984 Doina Melinte (ROM) 1:57.60	Kim Gallagher (USA) 1:58.63	Fita Lovin (ROM) 1:58.83

The performances listed below were Olympic records set additionally in preliminaries.

2:10.9 Antje Gleichfeld (GER) 1960	2:07.8	Donath 1960	2:04.1	Dupureur 1964	
2:05.9	Dixie I. Willis (AUS) 1960	1:58.9	Svetla Zlateva (BUL) 1972	
			1:56.5	Anita Weiss (GDR) 1976	

1,500 METERS (1640 yd. 1 ft.)

1928–68 Event not held		
1972 Lyudmila Bragina[1] (URS) 4:01.4*	Gunhild Hoffmeister (GDR) 4:02.8	Paola Cacchi-Pigni (ITA) 4:02.9
1976 Tatyana Kazankina (URS) 4:05.5	Gunhild Hoffmeister (GDR) 4:06.0	Ulrike Klapezynski (GDR) 4:06.1
1980 Tatyana Kazankina (URS) 3:56.6*	Christiane Wartenberg (GDR) 3:57.8	Nadezhda Olizarenko (URS) 3:59.6
1984 Gabriella Dorio (ITA) 4:03.25	Doina Melinte (ROM) 4:03.76	Maricica Puica (ROM) 4:04.15

[1] Set Olympic Records of 4:06.5 and 4:05.1 in preliminaries.

3000 METERS (3,280 yd. 2 ft.)

1984 Maricica Puica (ROM) 8:35.96*	Wendy Sly (GBR) 8:39.47	Lynn Williams (CAN) 8:42.14

MARATHON

1984 Joan Benoit (USA) 2h 24:52*	Grete Waitz (NOR) 2h 26:18	Rosa Mota (POR) 2h 26:57

4 × 100 METERS (109 yd. 1 ft.) RELAY

1928 CANADA 48.4*	UNITED STATES 48.8	GERMANY 49.2
Fanny Rosenfeld	Mary Washburn	Rosa Kellner
Ethel Smith	Jessie Gross	Leni Schmidt
Florence Bell	Loretta McNeil	Anni Holdmann
Myrtle Cook	Elizabeth Robinson	Leni Junker
1932 UNITED STATES 47.0*	CANADA 47.0*	GREAT BRITAIN 47.6
Mary L. Carew	Mildred Frizell	Eileen M. Hiscock
Evelyn Furtsch	Lilian Palmer	Gwendoline A. Porter
Annette J. Rogers	Mary Frizell	Violet R. Webb
Wilhelmina Von Bremen	Hilda Strike	Nellie Halstead
1936 UNITED STATES 46.9	GREAT BRITAIN 47.6	CANADA 47.8
Harriet C. Bland	Eileen M. Hiscock	Dorothy E. Brookshaw
Annette J. Rogers	Violet Olney	Mildred J. Dolson
Elizabeth Robinson	Audrey K. Brown	Hilda M. Cameron
Helen H. Stephens	Barbara H. A. Burke	Aileen A. Meagher

	GOLD	SILVER	BRONZE
1948	**NETHERLANDS** 47.5 Xenia Stad-de-Jong Jeanette J. M. Witziers- Timmers Gerda J. M. Van der Kade Koudijs Francina E. Blankers-Koen	**AUSTRALIA** 47.6 Shirley B. Strickland Joy E. Maston Betty L. McKinnon Joyce A. King	**CANADA** 47.8 Viola Myers Nancy Mackay Doris P. Foster Patricia Jones
1952	**UNITED STATES** 45.9* Mae Faggs Barbara P. Jones Janet T. Moreau Catherine Hardy	**GERMANY** 45.9* Ursula Knab Maria Sander Helga Klein Marga Peterson	**GREAT BRITAIN** 46.2 Sylvia Cheeseman June F. Foulds Jean C. Desforges Heather J. Armitage
1956	**AUSTRALIA** 44.5* Shirley B. Delahunty Norma Crocker Fleur Mellor Betty Cuthbert	**GREAT BRITAIN** 44.7 Anne Pashley Jean E. Scrivens June F. Paul Heather J. Armitage	**UNITED STATES** 44.9 Mae Faggs Margaret Matthews Wilma G. Rudolph Isabelle Daniels
1960	**UNITED STATES** 44.5 Martha Hudson Lucinda Williams Barbara P. Jones Wilma G. Rudolph	**GERMANY** 44.8 Martha Langbein Anni Biechl Brunhilde Hendrix Jutta Heine	**POLAND** 45.0 Tereza B. Wieczorek Barabara Janiszewska Celina Jesionowska Halina Richter
1964	**POLAND** 43.6* Tereza B. Ciepla Irena Kirzsenstein Halina Górecka Ewa Klobukowska	**UNITED STATES** 43.9 Willye D. White Wyomia Tyus Marilyn White Edith Maguire	**GREAT BRITAIN** 44.0 Janet M. Simpson Mary D. Rand Daphne Arden Dorothy Hyman
1968	**UNITED STATES** 42.8* Barbara A. Ferrell Margaret A. Bailes Mildrette Netter Wyomia Tyus	**CUBA** 43.3 Marlene Elejarde Fulgencia Romay Violeta Quesada Miguelina Cobián	**U.S.S.R.** 43.4 Ludmila Zharkova Galina Bukharina Vyera Popkova Ludmila Samotyesova
1972	**WEST GERMANY** 42.81* Christine Krause Ingrid Mickler Annegret Richter Heidemarie Rosendahl	**EAST GERMANY** 42.95 Evelyn Kaufer Christina Heinich Barbel Struppert Renate Stecher	**CUBA** 43.36 Marlene Elejarde Carmen Valdes Fulgencia Romay Silvia Chivas

1976	**EAST GERMANY**
	     42.55*
	Marlies Oelsner
	Renate Stecher
	Carla Bodendorf
	Barbel Eckert
		WEST GERMANY
		     42.59
		Elvira Possekel
		Inge Helten
		Annegret Richter
		Annegret Kroniger
			U.S.S.R. 43.09
			Tatyana Prorochenko
			Ludmila Maslakova
			Nadezda Besfamilnaya
			Vera Anisimova

1980	**EAST GERMANY** 41.60* Romy Muller Barbel Wockel Ingrid Auerswald Marlies Gohr	**U.S.S.R.** 42.10 Vera Komissova Ludmila Maslakova Vera Anissimova Natalya Bochina	**GREAT BRITAIN** 42.43 Heather Hunte Kathryn Smallwood Beverley Goddard Sonia Lannaman
1984	**USA** 41.65 Alice Brown Jeanette Bolden Chandra Cheeseborough Evelyn Ashford	**CANADA** 42.77 Angela Bailey Marita Payne Angella Taylor France Gareau	**GREAT BRITAIN** 43.11 Simone Jacobs Kathy Cook Bev Callender Heather Oakes

Close finish in the 4 × 100 meters relay in 1956, which produced a world record and gold medals for Australia, with Betty Cuthbert (middle) the winner over Great Britain's anchor runner Heather Armitage.

The performances listed below were Olympic records set additionally in preliminaries.

49.4	Canada	1928	44.9	Australia	1956	43.4	United States 1968
46.4	Germany	1936	44.9	Germany	1956	43.4	Netherlands 1968
46.1	Australia	1952	44.4	United States	1960	42.61	West Germany 1976

4 × 400 METERS (437 yd. 1 ft.) RELAY

GOLD	SILVER	BRONZE
1928–68 Event not held		
1972 EAST GERMANY 3:23.0*	**UNITED STATES** 3:25.2	**WEST GERMANY** 3:26.5
Dagmar Kasling	Mable Fergerson	Annette Ruckes
Rita Kuhne	Madeline Jackson	Inge Bödding
Helga Seidler	Cheryl Toussaint	Hildegard Falck
Monika Zehrt	Kathy Hammond	Rita Wilden
1976 EAST GERMANY 3:19.2*	**UNITED STATES** 3:22.8	**U.S.S.R.** 3:24.2
Doris Maletzki	Debra Sapenter	Inta Klimovicha
Brigitte Rohde	Sheila Ingram	Ludmila Aksenova
Ellen Streidt	Pam Jiles	Natalia Sokolova
Christina Brehmer	Rosalyn Bryant	Nadezda Ilina
1980 U.S.S.R. 3:20.2	**EAST GERMANY** 3:20.4	**GREAT BRITAIN** 3:27.5
Tatyana Prorochenko	Gabriele Lowe	Linsey MacDonald
Tatyana Goichik	Barbara Krug	Michelle Probert
Nina Zuskova	Christina Lathan	Joslyn Hoyte-Smith
Irina Nazarova	Marita Koch	Janine MacGregor
1984 USA 3:18.29*	**CANADA 3:21.21**	**WEST GERMANY** 3:22.98
Lillie Leatherwood	Charmaine Crooks	Heike Schulte-Mattler
Sherri Howard	Jillian Richardson	Ute Thimm
Valerie Brisco-Hooks	Molly Killingbeck	Heide Gaugel
Chandra Cheeseborough	Marita Payne	Gaby Bussmann

The following record times were set in the preliminaries of the 1972 Games: 3:29.3 West Germany, 3:28.5 East Germany.

100 METERS (109 yd.1 ft.) HURDLES

GOLD	SILVER	BRONZE
1928–68 Event not held		
1972 Annelie Ehrhardt (GDR) 12.59*	Valeria Bufanu (ROM) 12.84	Karin Balzer (GDR) 12.90
1976 Johanna Schaller (GDR) 12.77	Tatyana Anisimova (URS) 12.78	Natalia Lebedeva (URS) 12.80
1980 Vera Komisova (URS) 12.56*	Johanna Klier (GDR) 12.63	Lucyna Langer (POL) 12.65

The following record times were set in the preliminaries of the 1972 Games: 12.0 and 12.73 by Ehrhardt.

1984 Benita Fitzgerald-Brown (USA) 12.84	Shirley Strong (GBR) 12.88	Kim Turner (USA) 13.06 Michele Chardonnet (FRA) 13.06

400 METERS HURDLES

1928–1980 Event not held		
1984 Nawal El Mouthwa-Kel (MAR) 54.61*	Judi Brown (USA) 55.20	Cristina Cojocaru (ROM) 55.41

HIGH JUMP

1928 Ethel Catherwood (CAN) 5' 2½" 1,59 m*	Carolina A. Gisolf (HOL) 5' 1¼" 1,56 m	Mildred Wiley (USA) 5' 1¼" 1,56 m
1932 Jean M. Shiley (USA) 5' 5" 1,65 m*	Mildred Didrikson (USA) 5' 5" 1,65 m*	Eva Dawes (CAN) 5' 3" 1,60 m
1936 Ibolya Csák (HUN) 5' 3" 1,60 m	Dorothy J.B. Odam (GBR) 5' 3" 1,60 m	Elfriede Kaun (GER) 5' 3" 1,60 m
1948 Alice Coachman (USA) 5' 6" 1,68 m*	Dorothy J.B. Tyler (GBR) 5' 6" 1,68 m*	Micheline O. M. Ostermeyer (FRA) 5'3¼" 1,61 m
1952 Esther C. Brand (SAF) 5' 5½" 1,67 m	Sheila W. Lerwill (GBR) 5' 5" 1,65 m	Alexandra G. Chudina (URS) 5' 4" 1,63m
1956 Mildred McDaniel (USA) 5' 9¼" 1,76 m*		
1960 Iolanda Balas (ROM) 6' 0¾" 1,85 m*	[2]	[2]
1964 Iolanda Balas (ROM) 6' 2¾" 1,90 m*	Michele Brown (AUS) 5' 10¾" 1,80 m	Taisia Chenchik (URS) 5' 10" 1,78 m
1968 Miloslava Rezkova (TCH) 5' 11½" 1,82 m	Antonina Okorokova (URS) 5' 10¾" 1,80 m	Valentina Kozyr (URS) 5' 10¾" 1,80 m
1972 Ulrike Meyfarth (GER) 6' 3½" 1,92 m*	Yordanka Blagoyeva (BUL) 6' 2" 1,88 m	Ilona Gusenbauer (AUT) 6' 2" 1,88 m
1976 Rosemarie Ackermann (GDR) 6' 4" 1,93 m*	Sara Simeoni (ITA) 6' 3¼" 1,91 m	Yordanka Blagoyeva (BUL) 6' 3¼" 1,91 m
1980 Sara Simeoni (ITA) 6' 5½" 1,97 m*	Urszula Kielan (POL) 6' 4½" 1,94 m	Jutta Kirst (GDR) 6' 4½" 1,94 m
1984 Ulrike Meyfarth (FRG) 6' 7½" 2.02m*	Sara Simeoni (ITA) 6' 6¾" 2.00m	Joni Huntley (USA) 6' 5½" 1.97m

[1] Tie for second place by Thelma E. Hopkins (GBR) and Maria Pissrayeva (URS) at 5' 5½" 1,67 m.
[2] Tie for second place by Jaroslawa Józwiakowska (POL) and Dorothy A. Shirley (GBR) at 5' 7¼" 1,71 m.

LONG JUMP

GOLD	SILVER	BRONZE
1928–1936 Event not held		
1948 V. Olga Gyarmati (HUN) 18' 8" *5,69 m**	Noemi Simonetto de Portela (ARG) 18' 4¼" *5,60 m*	B. Ann-Britt Leyman (SWE) 18' 3¼" *5,57 m*
1952 Yvette W. Williams (NZL) 20' 5½" *6,24 m**	Alexandra G. Chudina (URS) 20' 1½" *6,14 m*	Shirley Cawley (GBR) 19' 5" *5,92 m*
1956 Elzbieta Krzesinska (POL) 20' 10" *6,35 m**	Willye D. White (USA) 19' 11¾" *6,09 m*	Nadyezhda Dvalishvili (URS) 19' 10¾" *6,07 m*
1960 Vyera Krepkina (URS) 20' 10¾" *6,37 m**	Elzbieta Krzesinska (POL) 20' 6¾" *6,27 m*	Hildrun Claus (GER) 20' 4¼" *6,21 m*
1964 Mary D. Rand (GBR) 22' 2¼" *6,76 m**	Irena Kirszenstein (POL) 21' 7¾" *6,60 m*	Tatyana S. Schelkanova (URS) 21' 0¾" *6,42 m*
1968 Viorica Viscopoleanu (ROM) 22' 4½" *6,82 m**	Sheila Sherwood (GBR) 21' 10¾" *6,68 m*	Tatyana Talysheva (URS) 21' 10" *6,66 m*
1972 Heidemarie Rosendahl[1] (GER) 22' 3" *6,78 m*	Diana Yorgova (BUL) 22' 2½" *6,77 m*	Eva Suranova (TCH) 21' 10¾" *6,67 m*
1976 Angela Voigt (GDR) 22' 0¾" *6,72 m*	Kathy McMillan (USA) 21' 10¼" *6,66 m*	Lidia Alfeyeva (URS) 21' 8" *6,60 m*
1980 Tatiana Kolpakova (URS) 23' 2" *7,06 m**	Brigitte Wujak (GDR) 23' 1¼" *7,04 m*	Tatiana Skachko (URS) 23' 0" *7,01 m*
1984 Anisoara Stanciu (ROM) 22' 10" *6.96m*	Vali Ionescu (ROM) 22' 4¼" *6.81m*	Susan Hearnshaw (GBR) 22' 3¾" *6.80m*

[1]Set Olympic record of 22' 5" *6,83 m* in Pentathlon.

SHOT PUT

GOLD	SILVER	BRONZE
1928–1936 Event not held		
1948 Micheline O. M. Ostermeyer (FRA) 45' 1¼" *13,75 m**	Amelia Piccinini (ITA) 42' 11½" *13,09 m*	Ina Schäffer (AUT) 42' 10¾" *13,08 m*
1952 Galina I. Zybina (URS) 50' 1½" *15,28 m**	Marianne Werner (GER) 47' 9½" *14,57 m*	Klavdia Tochenova (URS) 47' 6¾" *14,50 m*
1956 Tamara Tyshkyevich (URS) 54' 5" *16,59 m**	Galina I. Zybina (URS) 54' 2¾" *16,53 m*	Marianne Werner (GER) 51' 2½" *15,61 m*
1960 Tamara N. Press (URS) 56' 9¾" *17,32 m**	Johanna Lüttge (GER) 54' 5¾" *16,61 m*	Earlene I. Brown (USA) 53' 10¼" *16,42 m*
1964 Tamara N. Press (URS) 59' 6" *18,14 m**	Renate Garisch (GER) 57' 9¼" *17,61 m*	Galina I. Zybina (URS) 57' 3" *17,45 m*
1968 Margitta Gummel (GDR) 64' 4" *19,61 m**	Marita Lange (GDR) 61' 7¼" *18,78 m*	Nadyezhda Chizhova *(URS)* 59' 8" *18,19 m*
1972 Nadyezhda Chizhova (URS) 69' 0" *21,03 m**	Margitta Gummel (GDR) 66' 4¼" *20,22 m*	Ivanka Khristova (BUL) 63' 6" *19,35 m*
1976 Ivanka Khristova (BUL) 69' 5¼" *21,16 m**	Nadyezhda Chizhova (URS) 68' 9¼" *20,96 m*	Helena Fibingerova (TCH) 67' 9¾" *20,67 m*
1980 Ilona Slupianek (GDR) 73' 6¼" *22,41m**	Svetlana Krachevskaya (URS) 70' 3¼" *21,42 m*	Margitta Pufe (GDR) 69' 6¾" *21,20 m*
1984 Claudia Losch (FRG) 67' 2¼" *20.48m*	Mihaela Loghin (ROM) 67' 2" *20.47m*	Gael Martin (AUS) 62' 11½" *19.19m*

Tamara Andreyevna Tyschkyevich,
the Russians' 244-lb. gold medal
winner in the shot put in 1956.

DISCUS THROW

	GOLD	SILVER	BRONZE
1928	Helena Konopacka (POL) 129' 11½" 39,62m*	Lillian Copeland (USA) 121' 7½" 37,08 m	Ruth Svedberg (SWE) 117' 10" 35,92 m
1932	Lillian Copeland (USA) 133' 1½" 40,58 m*	Ruth Osburn (USA) 131' 7½" 40,11 m	Jadwiga Wajsówna (POL) 127' 1" 38,73 m
1936	Gisela Mauermayer (GER) 156' 3" 47,63 m*	Jadwiga Wajsówna (POL) 151' 7½" 46,22 m	Paula Mollenhauer (GER) 130' 6½" 39,80 m
1948	Micheline O. M. Ostermeyer (FRA) 137' 6" 41,92 m	Edera C. Gentile (ITA) 135' 0½" 41,17 m	Jacqueline Mazeas (FRA) 132' 9" 40,47 m
1952	Nina Romashkova (URS) 168' 8" 51,42 m*	Yelizaveta Bagryantseva (URS) 154' 5½" 47,08 m	Nina Dumbadze (URS) 151' 10" 46,29 m
1956	Olga Fikotová (TCH) 176' 1½" 53,69 m*	Irina Beglyakova (URS) 172' 4½" 52,54 m	Nina Ponomaryeva (URS) 170' 8" 52,02 m
1960	Nina Ponomaryeva (URS) 180' 9" 55,10 m*	Tamara N. Press (URS) 172' 6" 52,59 m	Lia Manoliu (ROM) 171' 9" 52,36 m
1964	Tamara N. Press (URS) 187' 10½" 57,27 m*	Ingrid Lotz (GER) 187' 8" 57,21 m	Lia Manoliu (ROM) 186' 10½" 56,97 m
1968	Lia Manoliu (ROM) 191' 2" 58,28 m*	Liesel Westermann (GER) 189' 6" 57,76 m	Jolán Kleiber (HUN) 180' 1" 54,90 m
1972	Faina Melnik (URS) 218' 7" 66,62 m*	Argentina Menis (ROM) 213' 5" 65,06 m	Vassilka Stoyeva (BUL) 211' 1" 64,34 m
1976	Evelin Schlaak (GDR) 226' 4" 69,00 m*	Maria Vergova (BUL) 220' 9" 67,30 m	Gabriele Hinzmann (GDR) 219' 3" 66,84 m
1980	Evelin Jahl (GDR) 229' 6" 69,96 m*	Maria Petkova (BUL) 222' 9" 67,90 m	Tatyana Lesovaya (URS) 221' 1" 67,40 m
1984	Ria Stalman (HOL) 214' 5" 65.36m	Leslie Deniz (USA) 212' 9" 64.86m	Florenta Craciunescu (ROM) 208' 9" 63.64m

JAVELIN THROW

1928	Event not held		
1932	Mildred Didrikson (USA) 143' 4" *43,68 m**	Ellen Braumüller (GER) 142' 8½" *43,49 m*	Tilly Fleischer (GER) 142' 1¼" *43,40 m*
1936	Tilly Fleischer (GER) 148' 2½" *45,18 m**	Luise Krüger (GER) 142' 0" *43,29 m*	Marja Kwasniewska (POL) 137' 1½" *41,80 m*
1948	Herma Bauma (AUT) 149' 6" *45,57 m**	Kaisa V. Parviainen (FIN) 143' 8" *43,79 m*	Lily M. L. Carlstedt (DEN) 140' 6½" *42,08 m*
1952	Dana Zátopková (TCH) 165' 7" *50,47 m**	Alexandra G. Chudina (URS) 164' 0½" *50,01 m*	Yelena Y. Gorchakova (URS) 163' 3" *49,76 m*
1956	Inese Jaunzeme (URS) 176' 8" *53,86 m**	Marlene Ahrens (CHI) 165' 3" *50,38 m*	Nadyezhda E. Konyayeva (URS) 164' 11½" *50,28 m*
1960	Elvira A. Ozolina (URS) 183' 7½" *55,98 m**	Dana Zátopková (TCH) 176' 5" *53,78 m*	Birute Kalediene (URS) 175' 4" *53,45 m*
1964	Mihaela Penes (ROM) 198' 7" *60,54 m*	Martá Rudase (HUN) 191' 2" *58,27 m*	Yelena Y. Gorchakova (URS) 187' 2" *57,06 m*[1]
1968	Angéla Németh (HUN) 198' 0" *60,36 m*	Mihaela Penes (ROM) 196' 7" *59,92 m*	Eva Janko (AUT) 190' 5" *58,04 m*
1972	Ruth Fuchs (GDR) 209' 7" *63,88m**	Jacqueline Todten (GDR) 205' 2" *62,54 m*	Kathy Schmidt (USA) 196' 8" *59,94 m*
1976	Ruth Fuchs (GDR) 216' 4" *65,94 m**	Marion Becker (GDR) 212' 3" *64,70 m*[2]	Kathy Schmidt (USA) 209' 10" *63,96 m*
1980[3]	Maria Colon (CUB) 224' 5" *68,40 m**	Saida Gunba (URS) 222' 2" *67,76 m*	Ute Hommola (GDR) 218' 4" *66,56 m*
1984	Tessa Sanderson (GBR) 228' 2" *69.56m**	Tiina Lillak (FIN) 226' 4" *69.00m*	Fatima Whitbread (GBR) 220' 3" *67.14m*

---

[1] Set Olympic record of 204' 8½" *62,40 m* in qualifying round.
[2] Set Olympic record of 213' 8" *65,14 m* in qualifying round.
[3] Ute Richter (GDR) set Olympic record of 218' 8" *66,67 m* in qualifying round.

ABOVE: Ruth Fuchs (GDR) was a convincing winner in the 1972 javelin throw, beating the previous Olympic record by nearly 5 feet.

ABOVE: Dana Zatopkova (Czechoslovakia), whose husband won 4 gold medals, won a gold medal in the javelin throw herself in the 1952 Olympics.

RIGHT: Powerful Nadezhda Tkachenko (URS) turned in a world record performance in capturing the women's pentathlon gold medal in 1980.

PENTATHLON[1]
(Figures refer to points scored)

	GOLD	SILVER	BRONZE
1928–1960	Event not held		
1964	Trina R. Press (URS) 5,246*	Mary D. Rand (GBR) 5,035	Galina Bystrova (URS) 4,956
1968	Ingrid Becker (GER) 5,098	Liese Prokop (AUT) 4,966	Annamária Tóth (HUN) 4,959
1972	Mary E. Peters (GBR) 4,801*[2]	Heidemarie Rosendahl (GER) 4,791	Burglinde Pollak (GDR) 4,768
1976	Sigrun Siegl (GDR) 4,745[3]	Christine Laser (GDR) 4,745	Burglinde Pollak (GDR) 4,740
1980	Nadezhda Tkachenko (URS) 5,083*	Olga Rukavishnikova (URS) 4,937	Olga Kuragina (URS) 4,875

---

[1] The Pentathlon consisted of 100 m hurdles, shot put, high jump, long jump and 200 m from 1964 to 1976. In 1980 the 200 m was replaced by 800 m.
[2] New scoring tables introduced in May 1971.
[3] Siegl finished ahead of Laser in three events.

(Figures refer to points scored)

1984	Glynis Nunn (AUS) 6390 pts[*2]	Jackie Joyner (USA) 6385	Sabine Everts (FRG) 6363

[1] The heptathlon consists of 100m hurdles, high jump, shot put, 200m on the first day; long jump, javeling and 800m on the second day.
[2] Olympic record 6387 pts under new 1986 tables

---

18. Volleyball (Men)

1896–1960 Event not held

1964	U.S.S.R.	CZECHOSLOVAKIA	JAPAN
	Yury Chesnokov	Václav Šmidl	Yataka Demachi
	Yury Vengerovsky	Josef Labuda	Tsutomu Koyama
	Eduard Sibiryakov	Josef Musil	Sadatoshi Sugahara
	Dmitry Voskoboynikov	Petr Kop	Naohiro Ikeda
	Vazha Kacharava	Milan Čuda	Yasutaka Sato
	Stanislaw Ljugailo	Karel Paulus	Toshiaki Kosedo
	Vitaly Kovalenko	Bohumil Golián	Tokiłiko Higuchi
	Yury Poyarkov	Boris Perušič	Masayuki Minami
	Ivan Bugaenkov	Pavel Schenk	Takeshi Tokutomi
	Nikolay Burobin	Ladislav Toman	Teruhisa Moriyama
	Valery Kalachikhin	Zdenek Humhal	Yuzo Nakamura
	Georgy Mondzolevsky	Josef Šorim	Katsutoshi Nekoda
1968	U.S.S.R.	JAPAN	CZECHOSLOVAKIA
	Eduard Sibiryakov	Naohiro Ikeda	Antonin Procházka
	Valery Kravchenko	Masayuki Minami	Jiri Svoboda
	Vladimir Belyaev	Katsutoshi Nekoda	Lubomir Zajiček
	Evgeny Lapinsky	Mamoru Shiragami	Josef Musil
	Oleg Antropov	Isao Koizumi	Josef Smolka
	Vasilijus Matushevas	Kenji Kimura	Vladimir Petlak
	Victor Mikhalchuk	Yasuaki Mitsumori	Petr Kop
	Yury Poyarkov	Jungo Morita	František Sokol
	Boris Tereshuk	Tadayoshi Yokota	Bohumil Golián
	Vladimir Ivanov	Seiji Oko	Zdenek Groessl
	Ivan Bugaenkov	Tetsuo Sato	Pavel Schenk
	Georgy Mondzolevsky	Kenji Shimaoka	Drahomir Koudelka
1972	JAPAN	EAST GERMANY	U.S.S.R.
	Katsutoshi Nekoda	Arnold Schulz	Valery Kravchenko
	Kenji Kimura	Wolfgang Webner	Efim Tchulak
	Yoshihide Fukao	Siegfried Schneider	Vladimir Poutiatov
	Jungo Morita	Wolfgang Weise	Vladimir Patkin
	Tadayoshi Yokota	Rudi Schumann	Leonid Zaiko
	Seiji Oko	Eckehard Pietzsch	Yuri Starunski
	Kenji Shimaoka	Wolfgang Löwe	Vladimir Kondra
	Yuzo Nakamura	Wolfgang Maibohm	Viatcheslav Domani
	Masayuki Minami	Rainer Tscharke	Victor Borsch
	Tetsuo Sato	Jürgen Maune	Alexandre Saprykine
	Yasuhiro Noguchi	Horse Peter	Evgeny Lapinsky
	Tetsuo Nishimoto	Horse Hagen	Yury Poyarkov

GOLD	SILVER	BRONZE
1976 POLAND	**U.S.S.R.**	**CUBA**
Wlodzimierz Stefanski	Anatoli Polishuk	Leonel Marshall
Bronislaw Bebel	Viacheslav Zaitsev	Victoriano Sarmientos
Lech Lasko	Efim Tchulak	Ernesto Martinez
Tomasz Wojtowicz	Vladimir Dorohov	Victor Garcia
Edward Skorek	Aleksandr Ermilov	Carlos Salas
Wieslaw Gawlowski	Pavel Selivanov	Raul Vilches
Miroslaw Rybaczewski	Oleg Moliboga	Jesus Savigne
Zbigniew Lubiejewski	Vladimir Kondra	Lorenzo Martinez
Ryszard Bosek	Yuri Starunski	Diego Lapera
Wlodzimierz Sadalski	Vladimir Chernyshov	Antonio Rodriguez
Zbigniew Zarzycki	Vladimir Ulanov	Alfredo Figueredo
Marek Karbarz	Aleksandr Savin	Jorge Perez
1980 U.S.S.R.	**BULGARIA**	**RUMANIA**
Yuriy Panchenko	Stoyan Guntchev	Corneliu Oros
Viacheslav Zaitsev	Kristo Stoyanov	Laurentiu Dumanoiu
Aleksandr Savin	Dimitar Zlatanov	Dan Girleanu
Vladimir Dorohov	Stefan Dimitrov	Nicu Stoian
Aleksandr Ermilov	Tzano Tzanov	Sorin Macavei
Pavel Selivanov	Petko Petkov	Constantin Sterea
Oleg Moliboga	Mitko Todorov	Neculae Vasile Pop
Vladimir Kondra	Emil Valchev	Gunter Enescu
Vladimir Chernyshov	Kristo Iliyev	Valter-Corneliu Chifu
Feodor Lashchenov	Yordan Anghelov	Marius Cata-Chitiga
Vilyar Loor	Dimitar Dimitrov	Florin Mina
Valeriy Krivov	Kaspar Simeonov	Viorel Manole
1984 USA	**BRAZIL**	**ITALY**
Dusty Dvorak	Bernardo Rezende	Marco Negri
Dave Saunders	Mario Oliveira Neto	Pier Paolo Lucchetta
Steve Salmons	Antonio Ribiero	Gian Carlo Dametto
Paul Sunderland	Jose Montanaro Jr	Franco Bertoli
Rich Duwelius	Ruy Campos Nascimento	Francesco Dall'Olio
Steve Timmons	Renan Dal Zotto	Piero Rebaudengo
Craig Buck	William Silva	Giovanni Errichiello
Marc Waldie	Amauri Ribiero	Guido De Luigi
Chris Marlowe	Marcus Freire	Fabio Vullo
Aldis Berzins	Domingo Lampariello	Giovanni Lanfranco
Pat Powers	Neto	Paolo Vecchi
Karch Kiraly	Bernard Rajzman	Andrea Lucchetta
	Fernando D'Avila	

Volleyball (Women)

1896–1960 Event not held		
1964 JAPAN	**U.S.S.R.**	**POLAND**
Masae Kasai	Antonina Ryzhova	Krystyna Czajkowska
Emiko Miyamoto	Astra Biltauer	Jozefa Ledwigowa
Kinuko Tanida	Ninel Lukanina	Maria Golimowska
Yuriko Handa	Ljudmila Buldakova	Jadwiga Rutkowska
Yoshiko Matsumara	Nelly Abramova	Danuta Kordaczuk
Sata Isobe	Tamara Tikhonina	Krystyna Jakobowska
Masako Kondo	Valentina Kamenek	Jadwiga Marko
Ayano Shibuki	Inna Ryskal	Maria Sliwkowa
Katsumi Matsumara	Marita Katusheva	Zofia Szczesniewska
Yoko Shinozaki	Tatyana Roschina	Krystyna Krupowa
Yuko Fujimoto	Valentina Mishak	
Setsuko Sasaki	Ludmila Gureeva	

	GOLD	SILVER	BRONZE
1968	**U.S.S.R.**	**JAPAN**	**POLAND**
	Ljudmila Buldakova	Setsuko Yoshika	Krystyna Czajkowska
	Ljudmila Mikhailovskaya	Suzue Takayama	Jozefa Ledwigowa
	Vera Lantratova	Toyoko Iwahara	Elzbieta Porzec
	Vera Galushka	Yukiyo Kojima	Wanda Wiecha
	Tatyana Sarycheva	Sachiko Fukunaka	Zofia Szczesniewska
	Tatyana Ponyaeva	Kunie Shiskikura	Krystyna Jakobowska
	Nina Smoleeva	Setsuko Inoue	Lidia Chmielnicka
	Inna Ryskal	Sumie Oinuma	Barbara Niemczyk
	Galina Leantieva	Keiko Hama	Krystyna Krupowa
	Roza Salikhova		Halina Aszkielowicz
	Valentina Vinogradova		Jadwiga Ksiazek
			Krystyna Ostromecka
1972	**U.S.S.R.**	**JAPAN**	**N. KOREA**
	Inna Ryskal	Sumie Oinuma	Chun Ok Ri
	Vera Douiounova	Noriko Yamashita	Myong Suk Kim
	Tatyana Tretiakova	Seiko Shimakage	Zung Bok Kim
	Nina Smoleeva	Makiko Furukawa	Ok Sun Kang
	Roza Salikhova	Takako Iida	Yeun Ja Kim
	Ljudmila Buldakova	Katsumi Matsumura	He Suk Hwang
	Tatyana Gonobobleva	Michiko Shiokawa	Ok Rim Jang
	Lubov Turina	Takako Shirai	Myong Suk Paek
	Galina Leontieva	Mariko Okamoto	Chun Ja Ryom
	Tatyana Sarycheva	Keiko Hama	Su Dae Kim
	Ludmila Borozna	Yaeko Yamazaki	Ok Jin Jong
	Natalia Koudreva	Toyoko Iwahara	
1976	**JAPAN**	**U.S.S.R.**	**KOREA**
	Takako Iida	Anna Rostova	Soonbok Lee
	Mariko Okamoto	Ludmila Shetinina	Junghye Yu
	Echiko Maeda	Lilia Osadchaya	Kyungja Byon
	Noriko Matsuda	Natalia Kushnir	Soonok Lee
	Takako Shirai	Olga Kozakova	Myungsun Baik
	Kiyomi Kato	Nina Smoleeva	Heesook Chang
	Yuko Arakida	Lubov Rudovskaya	Kumja Ma
	Katsuko Kanesaka	Larisa Bergen	Youngnae Yun
	Mariko Yoshida	Inna Ryskal	Kyunghwa Yu
	Shoko Takayanagi	Ludmila Chernysheva	Mikum Park
	Hiromi Yano	Zoya Iusova	Soonok Jung
	Juri Yokoyamma	Nina Muradian	Heajung Jo
1980	**U.S.S.R.**	**EAST GERMANY**	**BULGARIA**
	Nadyezda Radzevich	Ute Kostrzeva	Tania Dimitrova
	Natalya Razumova	Andrea Heim	Silva Petrunova
	Olga Solovova	Annette Schultz	Anka Khristolova
	Yelena Akhaminova	Christine Mummhardt	Verka Borissova
	Irina Makagonova	Heike Lehmann	Roumiana Kaicheva
	Lubov Kozyreva	Barbara Czekalla	Maya Gheorghieva
	Svetlana Nikishina	Karla Roffeis	Tania Gogova
	Ludmila Chernysheva	Martina Schmidt	Tzvetana Bojourina
	Svetlana Badulina	Anke Westendorf	Valentina Iliyeva
	Lidiya Loginova	Karin Puschel	Galina Stantcheva
	Larisa Pavlova	Brigitte Fetzer	Margarita Gerasimova
	Yelena Andreyuk	Katharina Bullin	Rossitza Dimitrova
1984	**CHINA**	**USA**	**JAPAN**
	Ping Lang	Paula Weishoff	Yumi Egami
	Yan Liang	Susan Woodstra	Kimie Morita
	Ling Zhu	Rita Crockett	Yuko Mitsuya
	Yuzhu Hou	Laurie Flachmeier	Miyoko Hirose
	Xiaolan Zhou	Carolyn Becker	Kyoko Ishida
	Xilan Yang	Flo Hyman	Yoko Kagabu
	Huijuan Su	Rosie Magers	Norie Hiro
	Ying Jiang	Julie Vollertsen	Kayoko Sugiyama
	Yanjun Li	Debbie Green	Sachiko Otani
	Xiaojun Yang	Kimberley Ruddins	Keiko Miyajima
	Meizhu Zheng	Jeanne Beauprey	Emiko Odaka
	Rongfang Zhang	Linda Chisholm	Kumi Nakada

19. Weightlifting

This sport became standardized in 1928 with the result depending on the aggregate weight of three two-handed overhead lifts: the Press, the Snatch and Jerk. But from 1976 the competition is decided by the aggregate of the Snatch and the Jerk only. The present Middleweight, Light-Heavyweight and Middle Heavyweight were previously called Welterweight, Middleweight, and Light-Heavyweight respectively.

FLYWEIGHT

(Weight up to *52 kg* 114½ lb)

GOLD	SILVER	BRONZE
1928–1968 Event not held		
1972 Zygmunt Smalcerz (POL) 744 lb *337,5 kg**	Lajos Szuecs (HUN) 727½ lb *330 kg*	Sandor Holczreiter (HUN) 722 lb *327,5 kg*
1976 Alexandr Voronin (URS) 534½ lb *242,5 kg*	Gyorgy Koszegi (HUN) 523½ lb *237,5 kg*	Mohammad Nassiri (IRN) 518 lb *235,0 kg*
1980 Kanybek Osmanoliev (URS) 540 lb *245 kg*	Bong Chol Ho (PRK) 540 lb *245 kg*	Gyong Si Han (PRK) 540 lb *245 kg*
1984 Zeng Guoqiang (CHN) 518 lb *235 kg*	Zhou Peishun (CHN) 518 lb *235 kg*	Kazushito Manabe (JPN) 512½ lb *232.5 kg*

BANTAMWEIGHT

(Weight up to *56 kg* 123½ lb)

GOLD	SILVER	BRONZE
1928–1936 Event not held		
1948 Joseph de Pietro (USA) 678 lb *307,5 kg*	Julian Creus (GBR) 655¾ lb *297,5 kg*	Richard Tom (USA) 650¼ lb *295 kg*
1952 Ivan Udodov (URS) 694¼ lb *315 kg*	Mahmoud Namdjou (IRN) 678 lb *307,5 kg*	Ali Mirzai (IRN) 661¼ lb *300 kg*
1956 Charles Vinci (USA) 755 lb *342,5 kg*	Vladimir Stogov (URS) 744 lb *337,5 kg*	Mahmoud Namdjou (IRN) 733 lb *332,5 kg*
1960 Charles Vinci (USA) 760½ lb *345 kg*	Yoshinobu Miyake (JPN) 744 lb *337,5 kg*	Esmail E. Khan (IRN) 727½ lb *330 kg*
1964 Alexey Vakhonin (URS) 788 lb *357,5 kg*	Imre Földi (HUN) 782½ lb *355 kg*	Shiro Ichinoseki (JPN) 766 lb *347,5 kg*
1968 Mohammad Nassiri (IRN) 810 lb *367,5 kg*	Imre Földi (HUN) 810 lb *367,5 kg*	Henryk Trebicki (POL) 788 lb *357,5 kg*
1972 Imre Földi (HUN) 832 lb *377,5 kg*	Mohammad Nassiri (IRN) 815½ lb *370 kg*	Gennadi Chetin (URS) 810 lb *367,5 kg*
1976 Norair Nurikyan (BUL) 578½ lb *262,5 kg*	Grzegorz Cziura (POL) 556½ lb *252,5 kg*	Kenkichi Ando (JPN) 551 lb *250 kg*
1980 Daniel Nunez (CUB) 606¼ lb *275 kg*	Yurik Sarkisian (URS) 595 lb *270 kg*	Tadeusz Dembonczyk (POL) 584 lb *265 kg*
1984 Wu Shude (CHN) 589½ lb *267.5 kg*	Lai Runming (CHN) 584 lb *265 kg*	Masahito Kotaka (JPN) 556½ lb *252.5 kg*

FEATHERWEIGHT
(Weight up to *60 kg* 132 lb)

1928	Franz Andrysek (AUT) 633¾ lb *287,5 kg*	Pierino Gabetti (ITA) 622¾ lb *282,5 kg*	Hans Wölpert (GER) 622¾ lb *282,5 kg*
1932	Raymond Suvigny (FRA) 633¾ lb *287,5 kg*	Hans Wölpert (GER) 622¾ lb *282,5 kg*	Anthony Terlazzo (USA) 617¼ lb *280 kg*
1936	Anthony Terlazzo (USA) 688¾ lb *312,5 kg*	Saleh Moh Soliman (EGY) 672¼ lb *305 kg*	Ibrahim H. Shams (EGY) 661¼ lb *300 kg*
1948	Mahmoud Fayad (EGY) 733 lb *332,5 kg*	Rodney Wilkes (TRI) 699¾ lb *317,5 kg*	Jaffar Salmassi (IRN) 688¾ lb *312,5 kg*
1952	Rafael Chimishkyan (URS) 774 lb *337,5 kg*	Nikolay Saksonov (URS) 733 lb *332,5 kg*	Rodney Wilkes (TRI) 711 lb *322,5 kg*
1956	Isaac Berger (USA) 777 lb *352,5 kg*	Evgeniy Minayev (URS) 755 lb *342,5 kg*	Marian Zielinski (POL) 738½ lb *355 kg*
1960	Evgeniy Minayev (URS) 821 lb *372,5 kg*	Isaac Berger (USA) 799 lb *362,5 kg*	Sebastiano Mannironi (ITA) 777 lb *352,5 kg*
1964	Yoshinobu Miyake (JPN) 876¼ lb *397,5 kg*	Isaac Berger (USA) 843¼ lb *382,5 kg*	Mieczyslaw Nowak (POL) 832 lb *377,5 kg*
1968	Yoshinobu Miyake (JPN) 865¼ lb *392,5 kg*	Dito Shanidze (URS) 854¼ lb *387,5 kg*	Yoshiyuki Miyake (JPN) 848¾ lb *385 kg*
1972	Norair Nurikyan (BUL) 887¼ lb *402,5 kg*	Dito Shanidze (URS) 881¾ lb *400 kg*	Janos Benedek (HUN) 859¾ lb *390 kg*
1976	Nikolai Kolesnikov (URS) 628¼ lb *285 kg*	Georgi Todorov (BUL) 617¼ lb *280 kg*	Kuzumasa Hirai (JPN) 606¼ lb *275 kg*
1980	Viktor Mazin (URS) 639¼ lb *290 kg*	Stefan Dimitrov (BUL) 633¾ lb *287,5 kg*	Marek Seweryn (POL) 622¾ lb *282,5 kg*
1984	Chen Weiqiang (CHN) 622¾ lb *282,5 kg*	Gelu Radu (ROM) 617¼ lb *280 kg*	Wen-Yee Tsai (TPE) 600¾ lb *272.5 kg*

LIGHTWEIGHT
(Weight up to *67,5 kg* 149 lb)

	GOLD	SILVER	BRONZE
1928[1]	Kurt Helbig (GER) 711 lb *322,5 kg* Hans Haas (AUT) 711 lb *322,5 kg*	—	Fernand Arnout (FRA) 666¾ lb *302,5 kg*
1932	René Duverger (FRA) 716½ lb *325 kg*	Hans Haas (AUT) 678 lb *307,5 kg*	Gastone Pierini (ITA) 666¾ lb *302,5 kg*
1936[1]	Anwar Mohammed Mesbah (EGY) 755 lb *342,5 kg* Robert Fein (AUT) 755 lb *342,5 kg*		Karl Jansen (GER) 722 lb *327,5 kg*
1948	Ibrahim H. Shams (EGY) 793½ lb *360 kg*	Attia Hamouda (EGY) 793½ lb *360 kg*	James Halliday (GBR) 749½ lb *340 kg*
1952	Thomas Kono (USA) 799 lb *365,5 kg*	Yevgeniy Lopatin (URS) 771½ lb *350 kg*	Verne Barberis (AUS) 771½ lb *350 kg*
1956	Igor Rybak (URS) 837¾ lb *380 kg*	Ravil Khabutdinov (URS) 821 lb *372,5 kg*	Chang-Hee Kim (KOR) 815½ lb *370 kg*
1960	Viktor Bushuyev (URS) 876¼ lb *397,5 kg*	Howe-Liang Tan (SIN) 837¾ lb *380 kg*	Abdul Wahid Aziz (IRQ) 837¾ lb *380 kg*
1964	Waldemar Baszanowski (POL) 953¼ lb *432,5 kg*	Vladimir Kaplunov (URS) 953¼ lb *432,5 kg*	Marian Zielinski (POL) 925¾ lb *420 kg*
1968	Waldemar Baszanowski (POL) 964½ lb *437,5 kg*	Parviz Jalayer (IRN) 931¼ lb *422,5 kg*	Marian Zielinski (POL) 925¾ lb *420 kg*
1972	Mukharbi Kirzhinov (URS) 1,014 lb *460 kg*	Mladen Koutchev (BUL) 992 lb *450 kg*	Zbigniew Kaczmarek (POL) 964½ lb *437,5 kg*
1976[2]	Piotr Korol (URS) 672¼ lb *305 kg*	Daniel Senet (FRA) 661¼ lb *300 kg*	Kazimierz Czarnecki (POL) 650¼ lb *295 kg*
1980	Yanko Roussev (URS) 755 lb *342,5 kg*	Joachim Kunz (GDR) 738½ lb *335 kg*	Mintcho Pachov (BUL) 716 lb *325 kg*

1984	Yao Jingyuan (CHN) 705¼ lb *320 kg*	Andrei Socaci (ROM) 688¾ lb *312.5 kg*	Jouni Grenman (FIN) 688¾ lb *312.5 kg*

---

[1] Results and bodyweights being equal both were declared champions.
[2] Zbigniew Kaczmarek (POL) finished in first place with 677¾ lb *307,5 kg* but was subsequently disqualified.

MIDDLEWEIGHT

(Weight up to *75 kg* 165¼ lb)

1928	Roger François (FRA) 738½ lb *335 kg*	Carlo Galimberti (ITA) 733 lb *332,5 kg*	August Scheffer (HOL) 722 lb *327,5 kg*
1932	Rudolf Ismayr (GER) 760½ lb *345 kg*	Carlo Galimberti (ITA) 749½ lb *340 kg*	Karl Hipfinger (AUT) 744 lb *337,5 kg*
1936	Khadr S. El Touni (EGY) 854¼ lb *387,5 kg*	Rudolf Ismayr (GER) 777 lb *352,5 kg*	Adolf Wagner (GER) 777 lb *352,5 kg*
1948	Frank Spellman (USA) 859¾ lb *390 kg*	Peter George (USA) 843¾ lb *382,5 kg*	Sung-Jip Kim (KOR) 837¾ lb *380 kg*
1952	Peter George (USA) 881¾ lb *400 kg*	Gérard Gratton (CAN) 859¾ lb *390 kg*	Sung-Jip Kim (KOR) 843¼ lb *382,5 kg*
1956	Fyodor Bogdanovskiy (URS) 925¾ lb *420 kg*	Peter George (USA) 909¼ lb *412,5 kg*	Ermanno Pignatti (ITA) 843¼ lb *382,5 kg*
1960	Aleksandr Kurynov (URS) 964½ lb *437,5 kg*	Thomas Kono (USA) 942¼ lb *427,5 kg*	Győző Veres (HUN) 892¾ lb *405 kg*
1964	Hans Zdražila (TCH) 981 lb *445 kg*	Viktor Kurentsov (URS) 970 lb *440 kg*	Masashi Ouchi (JPN) 964½ lb *437,5 kg*
1968	Viktor Kurentsov (URS) 1,047 lb *475 kg*	Masashi Ouchi (JPN) 1,003 lb *455 kg*	Károly Bakos (HUN) 970 lb *440 kg*
1972	Yordan Bikov (BUL) 1,069 lb *485 kg*	Mohamed Trabulsi (LIB) 1,041½ lb *472,5 kg*	Anselmo Silvino (ITA) 1,036 lb *470 kg*
1976	Yordan Mitkov (BUL) 738½ lb *335 kg*	Vartan Militosyan (URS) 727½ lb *330 kg*	Peter Wenzel (GDR) 722 lb *327,5 kg*
1980	Assen Zlatev (BUL) 793½ lb *360 kg*	Alexandr Pervy (URS) 788 lb *357,5 kg*	Nedeltcho Kolev (BUL) 760½ lb *345 kg*
1984	Karl-Heinz Radschinsky (FRG) 749½ lb *340 kg*	Jacques Demers (CAN) 738½ lb *335 kg*	Dragomir Cioroslan (ROM) 733 lb *332.5 kg*

LIGHT-HEAVYWEIGHT

(Weight up to *82,5 kg* 182 lb)

	GOLD	SILVER	BRONZE
1928	Said Nosseir (EGY) 782½ lb *355 kg*	Louis Hostin (FRA) 777 lb *352,5 kg*	Johannes Verheijen (HOL) 744 lb *337,5 kg*
1932	Louis Hostin (FRA) 804½ lb *365 kg*	Svend Olsen (DEN) 793½ lb *360 kg*	Henry Duey (USA) 727½ lb *330 kg*
1936	Louis Hostin (FRA) 821 lb *372,5 kg*	Eugen Deutsch (GER) 804½ lb *365 kg*	Ibrahim Wasif (EGY) 793½ lb *360 kg*
1948	Stanley Stanczyk (USA) 920¼ lb *417,5 kg*	Harold Sakata (USA) 837¾ lb *380 kg*	Gösta Magnusson (SWE) 826½ lb *375 kg*
1952	Trofim Lomakin (URS) 920¼ lb *417,5 kg*	Stanley Stanczyk (USA) 914¾ lb *415 kg*	Arkhadiy Vorobyov (URS) 898¼ lb *407,5 kg*
1956	Thomas Kono (USA) 986½ lb *447,5 kg*	Vasiliy Stepanov (URS) 942¼ lb *427,5 kg*	James George (USA) 920¼ lb *417,5 kg*
1960	Ireneusz Palinski (POL) 975½ lb *442,5 kg*	James George (USA) 947¾ lb *430 kg*	Jan Bochenek (POL) 925¾ lb *420 kg*
1964	Rudolf Plukfelder (URS) 1,047 lb *475 kg*	Géza Tóth (HUN) 1,030½ lb *467,5 kg*	Győző Veres (HUN) 1,030½ lb *467,5 kg*

	GOLD	SILVER	BRONZE
1968	Boris Selitsky (URS) 1,069 lb *485 kg*	Vladimir Belyaev (URS) 1,069 lb *485 kg*	Norbert Ozimek (POL) 1,041½ lb *472,5 kg*
1972	Leif Jenssen (NOR) 1,118¾ lb *507,5 kg*	Norbert Ozimek (POL) 1,096¾ lb *497,5 kg*	György Horvath (HUN) 1,091¼ lb *495 kg*
1976[1]	Valeri Schary (URS) 804½ lb *365 kg*	Trendachil Stoichev (BUL) 793½ lb *360 kg*	Peter Baczako (HUN) 760½ lb *345 kg*
1980	Yurik Vardanyan (URS) 881¾ lb *400 kg*	Blagoi Blagoev (BUL) 821 lb *372,5 kg*	Dusan Poliacik (TCH) 810 lb *367,5 kg*
1984	Petre Becheru (ROM) 782½ lb *355 kg*	Robert Kabbas (AUS) 755 lb *342.5 kg*	Ryoji Isaoka (JPN) 749½ *340 kg*

[1] Blagoi Blagoev (BUL) finished in second place with 799 lb *362,5 kg* but was subsequently disqualified.

MIDDLE-HEAVYWEIGHT
(Weight up to *90 kg* 198¼ lb)

	GOLD	SILVER	BRONZE
1928–1948	Event not held		
1952	Norbert Shemansky (USA) 981 lb *445 kg*	Grigoriy Novak (URS) 903¾ lb *410 kg*	Lennox Kilgour (TRI) 887¼ lb *402,5 kg*
1956	Arkhadiy Vorobyov (URS) 1,019½ lb *462,5 kg*	David Sheppard (USA) 975½ lb *442,5 kg*	Jean Debuf (FRA) 936¾ lb *425 kg*
1960	Arkhadiy Vorobyov (URS) 1,041½ lb *472,5 kg*	Trofim Lomakin (URS) 1,008½ lb *457,5 kg*	Louis Martin (GBR) 981 lb *445 kg*
1964	Vladimir Golovanov (URS) 1,074¾ lb *487,5 kg*	Louis Martin (GBR) 1,047 lb *475 kg*	Ireneusz Palinski (POL) 1,030½ lb *467,5 kg*
1968	Kaarlo Kangasniemi (FIN) 1,140¾ lb *517,5 kg*	Jan Talts (URS) 1,118¾ lb *507,5 kg*	Marek Golab (POL) 1,091¼ lb *495 kg*
1972	Andon Nikolav (BUL) 1,157¼ lb *525 kg*	Atanas Shopov (BUL) 1,140¾ lb *517,5 kg*	Hans Bettembourg (SWE) 1,129¾ lb *512,5 kg*
1976	David Rigert (URS) 843¼ lb *382,5 kg*	Lee James (USA) 799 lb *362,5 kg*	Atanas Shopov (BUL) 793½ lb *360 kg*
1980	Peter Baczako (URS) 832 lb *377,5 kg*	Roumen Alexandrov (BUL) 826½ lb *375 kg*	Frank Mantek (GDR) 815½ lb *370 kg*
1984	Nicu Vlad (ROM) 865¼ lb *392.5 kg**	Dumitru Petre (ROM) 793½ lb *360 kg*	David Mercer (GBR) 771 lb *352.5 kg*

90 kg.

	GOLD	SILVER	BRONZE
1984	Niou Vlad (ROM) 865¼ lb *392.5 kg*		

100 kg.
(Weight up to *100 kg* 220½ lb)

	GOLD	SILVER	BRONZE
1928–1976	Event not held		
1980	Ota Zaremba (TCH) 870¾ lb *395 kg*	Igor Nikitin (URS) 865¼ lb *392,5 kg*	Alberto Blanco (CUB) 848¾ lb *385 kg*
1984	Rolf Milser (FRG) 848¾ lb *385 kg*	Vasile Gropa (ROM) 843¼ lb *382.5 kg*	Pekka Niemi (FIN) 810 lb *367.5 kg*

HEAVYWEIGHT

From 1928 to 1952 Heavyweight had to be over *82,5 kg* 182 lb. From 1956 to 1968 the limit was *90,0 kg* 198¼ lb. Since 1972 the top weight has been *110 kg* 242 lb.

	GOLD	SILVER	BRONZE
1928	Josef Strassberger (GER) 821 lb *372,5 kg*	Arnold Luhaäär (EST) 793½ lb *360 kg*	Jaroslav Skobla (TCH) 788 lb *357,5 kg*
1932	Jaroslav Skobla (TCH) 837¾ lb *380 kg*	Václav Pšenička (TCH) 832 lb *377,5 kg*	Josef Strassberger (GER) 832 lb *377,5 kg*

1936	Josef Manger	Václav Pšenička	Arnold Luhaäär
	(AUT) 903¾ lb *410 kg*	(TCH) 887¼ lb *402,5 kg*	(EST) 881¾ lb *400 kg*
1948	John Davis	Norbert Schemansky	Abraham Charité
	(USA) 997½ lb *452,5 kg*	(USA) 936¾ lb *425 kg*	(HOL) 909¼ lb *412,5 kg*
1952	John Davis	James Bradford	Humberto Selvetti
	(USA) 1,014 lb *460 kg*	(USA) 964½ lb *437,5 kg*	(ARG) 953¼ lb *432,5 kg*
1956	Paul Anderson	Humberto Selvetti	Alberto Pigaiani
	(USA) 1,102 lb *500 kg*	(ARG) 1,102 lb *500 kg*	(ITA) 997½ lb *452,5 kg*
1960	Yuriy Vlassov	James Bradford	Norbert Schemansky
	(URS) 1,262 lb *537,5 kg*	(USA) 1,129¾ lb *512,5 kg*	(USA) 1,102 lb *500 kg*
1964	Leonid Zhabotinsky	Yuriy Vlassov	Norbert Schemansky
	(URS) 1,262 lb *572,5 kg*	(URS) 1,256½ lb *570 kg*	(USA) 1,184¾ lb *537,5 kg*
1968	Leonid Zhabotinsky	Serge Reding	Joseph Dube
	(URS) 1,262 lb *572,5 kg*	(BEL) 1,223½ lb *555 kg*	(USA) 1,223½ lb *555 kg*
1972	Jan Talts	Alexandre Kraitchev	Stefan Gruetzner
	(URS) 1,278½ lb *580 kg*	(BUL) 1,240 lb *562,5 kg*	(GDR) 1,223½ lb *555 kg*
1976[1]	Yuri Zaitsev	Krastio Semerdjiev	Tadeusz Rutkowski
	(URS) 848¾ lb *385 kg*	(BUL) 848¾ lb *385 kg*	(POL) 832 lb *377,5 kg*
1980	Leonid Taranenko	Valentin Khristov	Gyorgy Szlai
	(URS) 931¼ lb *422,5 kg*	(BUL) 892¾ lb *405 kg*	(HUN) 859 ¾ lb *390 kg*
1984	Norberto Oberburger	Stefan Tasnadi	Guy Carlton
	(ITA) 859¾ lb *390 kg*	(ROM) 837¾ lb *380 kg*	(USA) 832 lb *377.5 kg*

[1] Valentin Khristov (BUL) finished in first place with 881¾ lb *400 kg*, but was subsequently disqualified.

SUPER-HEAVYWEIGHT
(Weight limit over *110 kg* 242½ lb)

	GOLD	SILVER	BRONZE
1928–1968	Event not held		
1972	Vassili Alexeev	Rudolf Mang	Gerd Bonk
	(URS) 1,410¾ lb *640 kg*	(GER) 1,344¾ lb *610 kg*	(GDR) 1,262 lb *572,5 kg*
1976	Vassili Alexeev	Gerd Bonk	Helmut Losch
	(URS) 970 lb *440 kg*	(GDR) 892¾ lb *405 kg*	(GDR) 854¼ lb *387,5 kg*
1980	Sultan Rakhmanov	Jurgen Heuser	Tadeusz Rutkowski
	(URS) 970 lb *440 kg*	(GDR) 903¾ lb *410 kg*	(POL) 898¼ lb *407,5 kg*
1984	Dinko Lukin	Mario Martinez	Manfred Nerlinger
	(AUS) 909¼ lb *412.5 kg*	(USA) 903¾ lb *410 kg*	(FRG) 876¼ lb *397.5 kg*

LEFT: In 1980, Sultan Rakhmanov (URS) earned the super-heavyweight gold medal, succeeding the famous former two-time champion, Vassili Alexeev.

Paul Anderson (USA) set an Olympic record in winning the heavyweight class gold medal in 1956. A year later he raised 6,270 lb. on his back.

20. Wrestling

The contemporary descriptions of some bodyweight classes have varied during the history of the Games. Current descriptions are used in the lists below.

FREE-STYLE—LIGHT FLYWEIGHT
(Weight up to *48 kg* 105¾ lb.)

	GOLD	SILVER	BRONZE
1896–1900	Event not held		
1904	Robert Curry (USA)	John Heim (USA)	Gustav Thiefenthaler (USA)
1906–1968	Event not held		
1972	Roman Dmitriev (URS)	Ognian Nikolov (BUL)	Ebrahim Javadpour (IRN)
1976	Khassan Issaev (BUL)	Roman Dmitriev (URS)	Akira Kudo (JPN)
1980	Claudio Pollio (ITA)	Se Hong Jang (PRK)	Sergei Kornilaev (URS)
1984	Robert Weaver (USA)	Takashi Irie (JPN)	Gab-Do Son (KOR)

FREE-STYLE—FLYWEIGHT

Note: 1904 weight up to 115 lb *52,16 kg*. From 1948 weight up to *52 kg* 114½ lb.

1896–1900	Event not held		
1904	George Mehnert (USA)	Gustave Bauers (USA)	William Nelson (USA)
1906–1936	Event not held		
1948	Lennart Viitala (FIN)	Halit Balamir (TUR)	Thure Johansson (SWE)
1952	Hasan Gemici (TUR)	Yushu Kitano-Ali (JPN)	Mahmoud Mollaghassemi (IRN)
1956	Mirian Tsalkalamanidze (URS)	Mohamad-Ali Khojastehpour (IRN)	Hüseyin Akbas (TUR)
1960	Ahmet Bilek (TUR)	Masayuki Matsubara (JPN)	Mohamad Saifpour Saidabadi (IRN)
1964	Yoshikatsu Yoshida (JPN)	Chang-sun Chang (KOR)	Said Aliaakbar Haydari (IRN)
1968	Shigeo Nakata (JPN)	Richard Sanders (USA)	Surenjav Sukhbaatar (MGL)
1972	Kiyomi Kato (JPN)	Arsen Alakhverdiev (URS)	Hyong Kim Gwong (PRK)
1976	Yuji Takada (JPN)	Alexandr Ivanov (URS)	Hae-Sup Jeon (KOR)
1980	Anatoly Beloglazov (URS)	Wladyslaw Stecyk (POL)	Nermedin Selimov (BUL)
1984	Saban Trstena (YUG)	Jong-Kyu Kim (KOR)	Yuji Takada (JPN)

FREE-STYLE—BANTAMWEIGHT

Note: The weight limit for this event has been: 1908, 125 lb *56,70 kg*; 1980, 119 lb *54 kg*; 1924–1936, *56 kg* 123½ lb and from 1948, *57 kg* 125¾ lb.

1896–1900	Event not held		
1904	Isaac Niflot (USA)	August Wester (USA)	Z. B. Strebler (USA)
1906	Event not held		
1908	George Mehnert (USA)	William Press (GBR)	Aubert Côté (CAN)

GOLD	SILVER	BRONZE
1912–1920 Event not held		
1924 Kustaa Pihlajamäki (FIN)	Kaarlo Mäkinen (FIN)	Bryant Hines (USA)
1928 Kaarlo Mäkinen (FIN)	Edmond Spapen (BEL)	James Trifunov (CAN)
1932 Robert Pearce (USA)	Ödön Zombori (HUN)	Aatos Jaskari (FIN)
1936 Ödön Zombori (HUN)	Ross Flood (USA)	Johannes Herbert (GER)
1948 Nasuk Akar (TUR)	Gerald Leeman (USA)	Charles Kouyos (FRA)
1952 Shohachi Ishii (JPN)	Rashid Mamedbekov (URS)	Kha-Shaba Jadav (IND)
1956 Mustafa Dagistanli (TUR)	Mohamad Yaghoubi (IRN)	Mikhail Chakhov (URS)
1960 Terrence McCann (USA)	Nejdet Zalev (BUL)	Tadeusz Trojanowski (POL)
1964 Yojiro Uetake (JPN)	Hüseyin Akbas (TUR)	Aidyn Ibragimov (URS)
1968 Yojiro Uetake (JPN)	Donald Behm (USA)	Abutaleb Gorgori (IRN)
1972 Hideaki Yanagide (JPN)	Richard Sanders (USA)	László Klinga (HUN)
1976 Vladimir Umin (URS)	Hans-Dieter Bruchert (GDR)	Masao Arai (JPN)
1980 Sergei Beloglazov (URS)	Ho Pyong Li (PRK)	Dugarsuren Quinbold (MGL)
1984 Hideyaki Tomiyama (JPN)	Barry Davis (USA)	Eui-Kon Kim (KOR)

A free-style bout between bantamweights at Empress Hall, Earls Court, London in the 1948 Olympics. Nasuk Akar (TUR), the eventual gold medal winner, is on top of Charles Kouyos (FRA), who won the bronze medal.

FREE-STYLE—FEATHERWEIGHT

Note: The weight limit for this event has been: 1904, 135 lb *61,24 kg*; 1908, 133 lb *60,30 kg*; 1920, 132¼ lb *60 kg*; 1924–1936, 134½ lb *61 kg*; 1948–1960, and 1972, 62 *kg* 136½ lb; 1964–1968, *63 kg* 138¾ lb.

	GOLD	SILVER	BRONZE
1896–1900	Event not held		
1904	Benjamin Bradshaw (USA)	Theodore McLear (USA)	Charles Clapper (USA)
1906	Event not held		
1908	George Dole (USA)	James P. Slim (GBR)	William McKie (GBR)
1912	Event not held		
1920	Charles E. Ackerly (USA)	Samuel Gerson (USA)	P. W. Bernard (GBR)
1924	Robin Reed (USA)	Chester Newton (USA)	Katsutoshi Naito (JPN)
1928	Allie Morrison (USA)	Kustaa Pihlajamäki (FIN)	Hans Minder (SUI)
1932	Hermanni Pihlajamäki (FIN)	Edgar Nemir (USA)	Einar Karlsson (SWE)
1936	Kustaa Pihlajamäki (FIN)	Francis Millard (USA)	Gösta Jönsson (SWE)
1948	Gazanfer Bilge (TUR)	Ivar Sjölin (SWE)	Adolf Müller (SUI)
1952	Bayram Sit (TUR)	Nasser Guivehtchi (IRN)	Josiah Henson (USA)
1956	Shozo Sasahara (JPN)	Joseph Mewis (BEL)	Erkki Penttilä (FIN)
1960	Mustafa Dagistanli (TUR)	Stantcho Ivanov (BUL)	Vladimir Rubashvili (URS)
1964	Osamu Watanabe (JPN)	Stantcho Ivanov (BUL)	Nodar Khokhashvili (URS)
1968	Masaaki Kaneko (JPN)	Enyu Todorov (BUL)	Shamseddin Seyed-Abbassi (IRN)
1972	Zagalav Abdulbekov (URS)	Vehbi Akdag (TUR)	Ivan Krastev (BUL)
1976	Jung-Mo Yang (KOR)	Zeveg Oidov (MGL)	Gene Davis (USA)
1980	Magomedgasan Abushev (URS)	Mikho Doukov (BUL)	Georges Hadjioannidis (GRE)
1984	Randy Lewis (USA)	Kosei Akaishi (JPN)	Jung-Keun Lee (KOR)

FREE-STYLE—LIGHTWEIGHT

Note: The weight limit for this event has been: 1904, 145 lb *65,77 kg*; 1908, 146¾ lb *66,60 kg*; 1920, 148¾ lb *67,50 kg*; 1924 to 1936, 145½ lb *66 kg*; 1948 to 1960, *67 kg* 147½ lb; 1964 and 1968, *70 kg* 154 lb; and from 1972, *68 kg* 149¾ lb.

1896–1900	Event not held		
1904	Otto Roehm (USA)	R. Tesing (USA)	Albert Zirkel (USA)
1906	Event not held		
1908	G. de Relwyskow (GBR)	William Wood (GBR)	Albert Gingell (GBR)
1912	Event not held		
1920	Kalle Anttila (FIN)	Gottfrid Svensson (SWE)	Peter Wright (GBR)
1924	Russell Vis (USA)	Volmart Wickström (FIN)	Arvo Haavisto (FIN)
1928	Osvald Käpp (EST)	Charles Pacôme (FRA)	Eino Leino (FIN)

GOLD	SILVER	BRONZE
1932 Charles Pacôme (FRA)	Károly Kárpáti (HUN)	Gustaf Klarén (SWE)
1936 Károly Kárpáti (HUN)	Wolfgang Ehrl (GER)	Hermanni Pihlajamäki (FIN)
1948 Celal Atik (TUR)	Gösta Frändfors (SWE)	Hermann Baumann (SUI)
1952 Olle Anderberg (SWE)	J. Thomas Evans (USA)	Djahanbakte Tovfighe (IRN)
1956 Emamali Habibi (IRN)	Shigeru Kasahara (JPN)	Alimberg Bestayev (URS)
1960 Shelby Wilson (USA)	Viktor Sinyavskiy (URS)	Enyu Dimov (BUL)
1964 Enyu Valtschev[1] (BUL)	Klaus-Jürgen Rost (GER)	Iwao Horiuchi (JPN)
1968 Abdollah Movahed (IRN) Ardabili	Enyu Valtschev[1] (BUL)	Sereeter Danzandarjaa (MGL)
1972 Dan Gable (USA)	Kikuo Wada (JPN)	Ruslan Ashuraliev (URS)
1976 Pavel Pinigin (URS)	Lloyd Keaser (USA)	Yasaburo Sagawara (JPN)
1980 Saipulla Absaidov (URS)	Ivan Yankov (BUL)	Saban Sejdi (YUG)
1984 In-Tak You (KOR)	Andrew Rein (USA)	Jukka Rauhala (FIN)

---

[1] Valtschev competed as Dimov in 1960.

FREE-STYLE—WELTERWEIGHT

Note: The weight limit for this event has been: 1904, 158 lb *71,67 kg*; 1924 to 1936, 158½ lb *72 kg*; 1948 to 1960, *73 kg* 160¾ lb; from 1972, *74 kg* 163 lb.

1896–1900 Event not held		
1904 Charles Erickson (USA)	William Beckmann (USA)	Jerry Winholtz (USA)
1906–1920 Event not held		
1924 Hermann Gehri (SUI)	Eino Leino (FIN)	Otto Müller (SUI)
1928 Arvo Haavisto (FIN)	Lloyd Appleton (USA)	Maurice Letchford (CAN)
1932 Jack van Bebber (USA)	Daniel MacDonald (CAN)	Eino Leino (FIN)
1936 Frank Lewis (USA)	Ture Andersson (SWE)	Joseph Schleimer (CAN)
1948 Yasar Dogu (TUR)	Richard Garrard (AUS)	Leland Merrill (USA)
1952 William Smith (USA)	Per Berlin (SWE)	Abdullah Modjtabavi (IRN)
1956 Mitsuo Ikeda (JPN)	Ibrahim Zengin (TUR)	Vakhtang Balavadze (URS)
1960 Douglas Blubaugh (USA)	Ismail Ogan (TUR)	Mohammad Bashir (PAK)
1964 Ismail Ogan (TUR)	Guliko Sagaradze (URS)	Mohamad-Ali (IRN) Sanatkaran
1968 Mahmut Atalay (TUR)	Daniel Robin (FRA)	Dagvasuren Purev (MGL)
1972 Wayne Wells (USA)	Jan Karlsson (SWE)	Adolf Seger (GER)
1976 Jiichiro Date (JPN)	Mansour Barzegar (IRN)	Stanley Dziedzic (USA)
1980 Valentin Raitchev (BUL)	Jamtsying Davaajav (MGL)	Dan Karabin (TCH)
1984 David Schultz (USA)	Martin Knosp (FRG)	Saban Sejdi (YUG)

FREE-STYLE—MIDDLEWEIGHT

Note: The weight limit for this event has been: 1908, 161 lb *73 kg*; 1920, 165¼ lb *75 kg*; 1924 to 1960, 174 lb *79 kg*; 1964 and 1968, *87 kg* 191¾ lb; from 1972, *82 kg* 180¾ lb.

GOLD	SILVER	BRONZE
1896–1906 Event not held		
1908 Stanley Bacon (GBR)	George de Relwyskow (GBR)	Frederick Beck (GBR)
1912 Event not held		
1920 Eino Leino (FIN)	Väinö Penttala (FIN)	Charles Johnson (USA)
1924 Fritz Hagmann (SUI)	Pierre Ollivier (BEL)	Vilho Pekkala (FIN)
1928 Ernst Kyburz (SUI)	Donald P. Stockton (CAN)	Samuel Rabin (GBR)
1932 Ivar Johansson (SWE)	Kyösti Luukko (FIN)	József Tunyogi (HUN)
1936 Emile Poilvé (FRA)	Richard Voliva (USA)	Ahmet Kireiçci (TUR)
1948 Glen Brand (USA)	Adil Candemir (TUR)	Erik Lindén (SWE)
1952 David Tsimakuridze (URS)	Gholamheza Takhti (IRN)	György Gurics (HUN)
1956 Nikola Stautscher (BUL)	Daniel Hodge (USA)	Georgiy Skhirtladze (URS)
1960 Hasan Güngör (TUR)	Georgiy Skhirtladze (URS)	Hans Y. Antonsson (SWE)
1964 Prodan Gardschev (BUL)	Hasan Güngör (TUR)	Daniel Brand (USA)
1968 Boris Gurevitch (URS)	Munkbat Jigjid (MGL)	Prodan Gardschev (BUL)
1972 Levan Tediashvili (URS)	John Peterson (USA)	Vasile Jorga (ROM)
1976 John Peterson (USA)	Viktor Novojilov (URS)	Adolf Seger (GER)
1980 Ismail Abilov (BUL)	Magomedhan Aratsilov (URS)	Istvan Kovacs (HUN)
1984 Mark Schultz (USA)	Hideyuki Nagashima (JPN)	Chris Rinke (CAN)

FREE-STYLE—LIGHT-HEAVYWEIGHT

Note: The weight limit for this event has been: 1920, 181¾ lb *82,5 kg*; 1924 to 1960, *87 kg* 191¾ lb; 1964 and 1968, *97 kg* 213¾ lb; from 1972, *90 kg* 198¼ lb.

1896–1912 Event not held		
1920 Anders Larsson (SWE)	Charles Courant (SUI)	Walter Maurer (USA)
1924 John Spellman (USA)	Rudolf Svensson (SWE)	Charles Courant (SUI)
1928 Thure Sjöstedt (SWE)	Anton Bögli (SUI)	Henri Lefèbre (FRA)
1932 Peter Mehringer (USA)	Thure Sjöstedt (SWE)	Eddie Scarf (AUS)
1936 Knut Fridell (SWE)	August Neo (EST)	Erich Siebert (GER)
1948 Henry Wittenberg (USA)	Fritz Stöckli (SUI)	Bengt Fahlkvist (SWE)
1952 Wiking Palm (SWE)	Henry Wittenberg (USA)	Adil Atan (TUR)
1956 Gholam Reza Tahkti (IRN)	Boris Kulayev (URS)	Peter S. Blair (USA)
1960 Ismet Atli (TUR)	Gholam Reza Tahkti (IRN)	Anatoliy Albul (URS)

John Peterson (right side up), the only American wrestler to win a gold medal at the 1976 Games, here defeats Mehmet Uzun (TUR) in a semi-final bout.

	GOLD	SILVER	BRONZE
1964	Alexander Medved (URS)	Ahmet Ayik (TUR)	Said Mustafafov (BUL)
1968	Ahmet Ayik (TUR)	Shota Lomidze (URS)	József Csatári (HUN)
1972	Ben Peterson (USA)	Gennadi Strakhov (URS)	Karoly Bajko (HUN)
1976	Levan Tediashvili (URS)	Ben Peterson (USA)	Stelica Morcov (ROM)
1980	Sanasar Oganesyan (URS)	Uwe Neupert (GDR)	Aleksander Cichon (POL)
1984	Ed Banach (USA)	Akira Ohta (JPN)	Noel Loban (GBR)

FREE-STYLE—HEAVYWEIGHT

Note: The weight limit for this event has been: 1904, over 158 lb *71,6 kg*; 1908, over 161 lb *73 kg*; 1920, over 181¾ lb *82,5 kg*; 1924 to 1960, over 87 *kg* 191¾ lb; 1964 and 1968, over 97 *kg* 213¾ lb; from 1972, up to *100 kg* 220¼ lb.

1896–1900	Event not held		
1904	B. Hansen (USA)	Frank Kungler (USA)	F. C. Warmbold (USA)
1906	Event not held		
1908	George C. O'Kelly (GBR/IRL)	Jacob Gundersen (NOR)	Edmond Barrett (GBR/IRL)
1912	Event not held		
1920	Robert Roth (SUI)	Nathan Pendleton (USA)	Ernst Nilsson (SWE) Frederick Meyer (USA)

	GOLD	SILVER	BRONZE
1924	Harry Steele (USA)	Henry Wernli (SUI)	Andrew McDonald (GBR)
1928	Johan Richthoff (SWE)	Aukusti Sihovla (FIN)	Edmond Dame (FRA)
1932	Johan Richthoff (SWE)	John Riley (USA)	Nikolaus Hirschl (AUT)
1936	Kristjan Palusalu (EST)	Josef Klapuch (TCH)	Hjalmar Nyström (FIN)
1948	Gyula Bóbis (HUN)	Bertil Antonsson (SWE)	Joseph Armstrong (AUS)
1952	Arsen Mekokishvili (URS)	Bertil Antonsson (SWE)	Kenneth Richmond (GBR)
1956	Hamit Kaplan (TUR)	Hussein Mekhmedov (BUL)	Taisto Kangasniemi (FIN)
1960	Wilfried Dietrich (GER)	Hamit Kaplan (TUR)	Savkus Dzarassov (URS)
1964	Alexandr Ivanitsky (URS)	Liutvi Djiber (BUL)	Hamit Kaplan (TUR)
1968	Alexander Medved (URS)	Osman Duraliev (BUL)	Wilfried Dietrich (GER)
1972	Ivan Yarygin (URS)	Khorloo Baianmunkh (MGL)	József Csatáti (HUN)
1976	Ivan Yarygin (URS)	Russell Hellickson (USA)	Dimo Kostov (BUL)
1980	Ilya Mate (URS)	Slavtcho Tchervenkov (BUL)	Julius Strnisko (TCH)
1984	Lou Banach (USA)	Joseph Atiyeh (SYR)	Vasile Pascasu (ROM)

FREE-STYLE—SUPER-HEAVYWEIGHT
(Weight over 220¼ lb *100 kg*)

	GOLD	SILVER	BRONZE
1896–1968	Event not held		
1972	Alexander Medved (URS)	Osman Duraliev (BUL)	Chris Taylor (USA)
1976	Soslan Andiev (URS)	Jozsef Balla (HUN)	Ladislau Simon (ROM)
1980	Soslan Andiev (URS)	Jozsef Balla (HUN)	Adam Sandruski (POL)
1984	Bruce Baumgartner (USA)	Bob Molle (CAN)	Ayhan Taskin (TUR)

GRECO-ROMAN—LIGHT-FLYWEIGHT
(Weight up to *48 kg* 105¾ lb)

	GOLD	SILVER	BRONZE
1896–1968	Event not held		
1972	Gheorghe Berceanu (ROM)	Rahim Ahabadi (IRN)	Stefan Anghelov (BUL)
1976	Alexei Shumakov (URS)	Gheorghe Berceanu (ROM)	Stefan Anghelov (BUL)
1980	Zaksylik Ushkempirov (URS)	Constantin Alexandru (ROM)	Ferenc Seres (HUN)
1984	Vincenzo Maenza (ITA)	Markus Scherer (FRG)	Ikazo Saito (JPN)

GRECO-ROMAN—FLYWEIGHT
(Weight up to 114½ lb *52 kg*)

GOLD	SILVER	BRONZE
1896–1936 Event not held		
1948 Pietro Lombardi (ITA)	Kenan Olcay (TUR)	Reino Kangasmäki (FIN)
1952 Boris Gurevich (URS)	Ignazio Fabra (ITA)	Leo Honkala (FIN)
1956 Nikolay Solovyov (URS)	Ignazio Fabra (ITA)	Durum Ali Egribas (TUR)
1960 Dumitru Pirvulescu (ROM)	Osman Sayed (UAR)	Mohamad Paziraye (IRAN)
1964 Tsutomu Hanahara (JPN)	Angel Kerezov (BUL)	Dumitru Pirvulescu (ROM)
1968 Petar Kirov (BUL)	Vladimir Bakulin (URS)	Miroslav Zeman (TCH)
1972 Petar Kirov (BUL)	Koichiro Hirayama (JPN)	Giuseppe Bognanni (ITA)
1976 Vitali Konstantinov (URS)	Nicu Ginga (ROM)	Koichiro Hirayama (JPN)
1980 Vakhtang Blagidze (URS)	Lajos Racz (HUN)	Mladen Mladenov (BUL)
1984 Atsuji Miyahara (JPN)	Daniel Aceves (MEX)	Dae-Du Bang (KOR)

GRECO-ROMAN—BANTAMWEIGHT

Note: The weight limit for this event has been: 1924 to 1928, 127¾ lb. *58 kg.*; 1932 to 1936, 123¼ lb. *56 kg.*; since 1948, 125½ lb. *57 kg.*

GOLD	SILVER	BRONZE
1896–1920 Event not held		
1924 Eduard Pütsep (EST)	Anselm Ahlfors (FIN)	Väinö Ikonen (FIN)
1928 Kurt Leucht (GER)	Jindrich Maudr (TCH)	Giovanni Gozzi (ITA)
1932 Jakob Brendel (GER)	Marcello Nizzola (ITA)	Louis François (FRA)
1936 Márton Lörincz (HUN)	Egon Svensson (SWE)	Jakob Brendel (GER)
1948 Kurt Pettersén (SWE)	Aly Mahmoud Hassan (EGY)	Habil Kaya (TUR)
1952 Imre Hódos (HUN)	Zakaria Chihab (LIB)	Artem Teryan (URS)
1956 Konstantin Vyrupayev (URS)	Evdin Veseterby (SWE)	Francisc Horvat (ROM)
1960 Olyeg Karavayev (URS)	Ion Cernea (ROM)	Petrov Dinko (BUL)
1964 Masamitsu Ichiguchi (JPN)	Vladlen Trostiansky (URS)	Ion Cernea (ROM)
1968 János Varga (HUN)	Ion Baciu (ROM)	Ivan Kochergin (URS)
1972 Rustem Kazakov (URS)	Hans-Jürgen Veil (GER)	Risto Björlin (FIN)
1976 Pertti Ukkola (FIN)	Ivan Frgic (YUG)	Farhat Mustafin (URS)
1980 Shamil Serikov (URS)	Josef Lipien (POL)	Benni Ljungbeck (SWE)
1984 Pasquale Passarelli (FRG)	Masaki Eto (JPN)	Haralambos Holidis (GRE)

GRECO-ROMAN—FEATHERWEIGHT

GOLD	SILVER	BRONZE

Note: The weight limit for this event has been: 1912 to 1920, 132¼ lb. *60 kg.;* 1924 to 1928, 1948 to 1960 and since 1972, *62 kg.* 136½ lb.; 1932 to 1936, *61 kg.* 134¼ lb.; 1964 to 1968, *63 kg.* 138¾ lb.

	GOLD	SILVER	BRONZE
1896–1908	Event not held		
1912	Kaarlo Koskelo (FIN)	Georg Gerstacker (GER)	Otto Lasanen (FIN)
1920	Oskari Friman (FIN)	Hekki Kähkönen (FIN)	Fridtjof Svensson (SWE)
1924	Kalle Antila (FIN)	Aleksanteri Toivola (FIN)	Erik Malmberg (SWE)
1928	Voldemar Väli (EST)	Erik Malmberg (SWE)	Giacomo Quaglia (ITA)
1932	Giovanni Gozzi (ITA)	Wolfgang Ehrl (GER)	Lauri Koskela (FIN)
1936	Yasar Erkan (TUR)	Aarne Reiní (FIN)	Einar Karlsson (SWE)
1948	Mehmet Oktav (TUR)	Olle Anderberg (SWE)	Ferenc Tóth (HUN)
1952	Yakov Punkin (URS)	Imre Polyák (HUN)	Abdel Rashed (EGY)
1956	Rauno Mäkinen (FIN)	Imre Polyák (HUN)	Roman Dzneladze (URS)
1960	Müzahir Sille (TUR)	Imre Polyák (HUN)	Konstantin Vyrupayev (URS)
1964	Imre Polyák (HUN)	Roman Rurua (URS)	Branko Martinovič (YUG)
1968	Roman Rurua (URS)	Hideo Fujimoto (JPN)	Simeon Popescu (ROM)
1972	Gheorghi Markov (BUL)	Heinz-Helmut Wehling (GDR)	Kazimierz Lipien (POL)
1976	Kazimierz Lipien (POL)	Nelson Davidian (URS)	Laszlo Reczi (HUN)
1980	Stilianos Migiakis (GRE)	Istvan Toth (HUN)	Boris Kramorenko (URS)
1984	Weon-Kee Kim (KOR)	Kentolle Johansson (SWE)	Hugo Dietsche (SUI)

GRECO-ROMAN—LIGHTWEIGHT

Note: The weight limit for this event has been: 1906, 165¼ lb, *75 kg.;* 1908, 146¾ lb. *66,6 kg.;* 1912 to 1928, 148¾ lb. *67.5 kg.;* 1932 to 1936, 145½ lb. *66 kg.;* 1948 to 1960, 147½ lb. *67 kg.;* 1964 to 1968, 154¼ lb. *70 kg.;* since 1972, 149¾ lb. *68 kg.*

	GOLD	SILVER	BRONZE
1896–1904	Event not held		
1906	Rudolf Watzl (AUT)	Karl Karlsen (DEN)	Ferenc Holuban (HUN)
1908	Enrico Porro (ITA)	Nikolay Orlov (URS)	Avid Lindén-Linko (FIN)
1912	Eemil Wäre (FIN)	Gustaf Malmström (SWE)	Edvin Matiasson (SWE)
1920	Eemil Wäre (FIN)	Taavi Tamminen (FIN)	Fritjof Andersen (NOR)
1924	Oskari Friman (FIN)	Lajos Keresztes (HUN)	Kalle Westerlund (FIN)
1928	Lajos Keresztes (HUN)	Eduard Sperling (GER)	Eduard Westerlund (FIN)

1932	Erik Malmberg (SWE)	Abraham Kurland (DEN)	Eduard Sperling (GER)
1936	Lauri Koskela (FIN)	Josef Herda (TCH)	Voldemar Väli (EST)
1948	Gustaf Freij (SWE)	Aage Eriksen (NOR)	Károly Ferencz (HUN)
1952	Shazam Safin (URS)	Gustaf Freij (SWE)	Mikuláš Athanasov (TCH)
1956	Kyösti Lehtonen (FIN)	Riza Dogan (TUR)	Gyul Tóth (HUN)
1960	Avtandil Koridze (URS)	Branislav Martinovič (YUG)	Gustaf Freij (SWE)
1964	Kazim Ayvaz (TUR)	Valeriu Bularca (ROM)	David Gvantseladze (URS)
1968	Munji Mumemura (JPN)	Stevan Horvat (YUG)	Petros Galaktopoulos (GRE)
1972	Shamil Khisamutdinov (URS)	Stoyan Apostolov (BUL)	Gian Matteo Ranzi (ITA)
1976	Suren Nalbandyan (URS)	Stefan Rusu (ROM)	Heinz-Helmut Wehling (GDR)
1980	Stefan Rusu (ROM)	Andrzej Supron (POL)	Lars-Erik Skiold (SWE)
1984	Vlado Lisjak (YUG)	Tapio Sipila (FIN)	James Martinez (USA)

GRECO-ROMAN—WELTERWEIGHT

Note: The weight limit for this event has been: 1932 to 1936, 158½ lb. *72 kg.*; 1948 to 1960, 160¾ lb. *73 kg.*; 1964 to 1968, 171¾ lb. *78 kg.*; since 1972, 163 lb. *74 kg.*

	GOLD	SILVER	BRONZE
1896–1928	Event not held		
1932	Ivar Johansson (SWE)	Väinö Kajander (FIN)	Ercole Gallegatti (ITA)
1936	Rudolf Svedberg (SWE)	Frit Schäfer (GER)	Eino Virtanen (FIN)
1948	Gösta Andersson (SWE)	Miklós Szilvási (HUN)	Henrik Hansen (DEN)
1952	Miklós Szilvási (HUN)	Gösta Andersson (SWE)	Khalil Taha (LIB)
1956	Mithat Bayrak (TUR)	Vladimir Maneyev (URS)	Per Berlin (SWE)
1960	Mithat Bayrak (TUR)	Günther Maritschnigg (GER)	René Schiermeyer (FRA)
1964	Anatoly Kolesov (URS)	Cyril Todorov (BUL)	Bertil Nyström (SWE)
1968	Rudolf Vesper (GDR)	Daniel Robin (FRA)	Károly Bajkó (HUN)
1972	Vitezslav Mache (TCH)	Petros Galaktopoulos (GRE)	Jan Karlsson (SWE)
1976	Alexandr Bykov (URS)	Vitezslav Macha (TCH)	Karlheinz Helbing (GER)
1980	Ferenc Kocsis (HUN)	Anatoly Bykov (URS)	Mikko Huntala (FIN)
1984	Jouko Salomaki (FIN)	Roger Tallroth (SWE)	Stefan Rusu (ROM)

GRECO-ROMAN—MIDDLEWEIGHT

Note: The weight limit for this event has been: 1906, 187¼ lb. *85 kg.;* 1908, 160¾ lb. *73 kg.;* 1912 to 1928, 165¼ lb. *75 kg.;* 1932 to 1960, 174 lb. *79 kg.;* 1964 to 1968, 191¾ lb. *87 kg.;* since 1972, 180¾ lb. *82 kg.*

1896–1904	Event not held		
1906	Verner Weckman (FIN)	Rudolf Lindmayer (AUT)	Robert Bebrens (DEN)
1908	Frithiof Mårtensson (SWE)	Mauritz Andersson (SWE)	Anders Andersen (DEN)
1912	Claes Johansson (SWE)	Martin Klein[1] (URS)	Alfred Asikainen (FIN)
1920	Carl Westergren (SWE)	Artur Lindfors (FIN)	Matti Perttila (FIN)
1924	Eduard Westerlund (FIN)	Artur Lindfors (FIN)	Roman Steinberg (EST)
1928	Väinö Kokkinen (FIN)	László Papp (HUN)	Albert Kusnetz (EST)
1932	Väinö Kokkinen (FIN)	Jean Földeák (GER)	Axel Cadier (SWE)
1936	Ivar Johansson (SWE)	Ludwig Schweikert (GER)	József Palotás (HUN)
1948	Axel Grönberg (SWE)	Muhlis Tayfur (TUR)	Ercole Gallegatti (ITA)
1952	Axel Grönberg (SWE)	Kalervo Rauhala (FIN)	Nikolay Byelov (URS)
1956	Guivi Kartozia (URS)	Dimiter Dobrev (BUL)	Rune Jansson (SWE)
1960	Dimiter Dobrev (BUL)	Lothar Metz (GER)	Ion Taranu (ROM)
1964	Branislav Simic (YUG)	Jiri Kormanik (TCH)	Lothar Metz (GER)
1968	Lothar Metz (GDR)	Valentin Olenik (URS)	Bransislav Simič (YUG)
1972	Csaba Hegedus (HUN)	Anatoli Nazarenko (URS)	Milan Nenadic (YUG)
1976	Momir Petkovic (YUG)	Vladimir Cheboksarov (URS)	Ivan Kolev (BUL)
1980	Gennady Korban (URS)	Jan Dolgowicz (POL)	Pavel Pavlov (BUL)
1984	Ion Draica (ROM)	Dimitrios Thanapoulos (GRE)	Soren Claeson (SWE)

[1] In fact an Estonian.

GRECO-ROMAN—LIGHT-HEAVYWEIGHT

Note: The weight limit in this event has been: 1908, 205 lb. *93 kg.;* 1912 to 1928, 181¾ lb. *82.5 kg.;* 1932 to 1960, 191¾ lb. *87 kg.;* 1964 to 1968, 213¾ lb. *97 kg.;* since 1972, 198¼ lb. *90 kg.*

1896–1906	Event not held		
1908	Verner Weckman (FIN)	Yrjö Saarela (FIN)	Carl Jensen (DEN)
1912	—	Anders Ahlgren† (SWE)	Béla Varga (HUN)
		Ivar Böhling (FIN)	

† Declared equal second after 9 hours of wrestling—no gold medal awarded.

Verner Weckman and Yrjo Saarela, both of Finland, battled out the final match of the 1908 light-heavyweight Greco-Roman competition.

	GOLD	SILVER	BRONZE
1920	Claes Johansson (SWE)	Edil Rosenqvist (FIN)	Johannes Eriksen (DEN)
1924	Carl Westergren (SWE)	Rudolf Svensson (SWE)	Onni Pellinen (FIN)
1928	Ibrahim Moustafa (EGY)	Adolf Rieger (GER)	Onni Pellinen (FIN)
1932	Rudolf Svensson (SWE)	Onni Pellinen (FIN)	Mario Gruppioni (ITA)
1936	Axel Cadier (SWE)	Edwins Bietags (LITH)	August Néo (EST)
1948	Karl-Erik Nilsson (SWE)	Kaelpo Gröndahl (FIN)	Ibrahim Orabi (EGY)
1952	Kaelpo Gröndahl (FIN)	Shalva Shikhladze (URS)	Karl-Erik Nilsson (SWE)
1956	Valentin Nikolayev (URS)	Petko Sirakov (BUL)	Karl-Erik Nilsson (SWE)
1960	Tevfik Kis (TUR)	Krali Bimbalov (BUL)	Givy Kartozlya (URS)
1964	Boyan Radev (BUL)	Pev Sfensson (SWE)	Heinz Kiehl (GER)
1968	Boyan Radev (BUL)	Nikolai Yakovenko (URS)	Nicolae Martinescu (ROM)
1972	Valeri Rezantsev (URS)	Josip Corak (YUG)	Czeslaw Kwiecinski (POL)
1976	Valeri Rezantsev (URS)	Stoyan Ivanov (BUL)	Czeslaw Kwiecinski (POL)
1980	Norbert Nottny (HUN)	Igor Kanygin (URS)	Petre Dicu (ROM)
1984	Steven Fraser (USA)	Ilie Matei (ROM)	Frank Andersson (SWE)

GRECO-ROMAN—HEAVYWEIGHT

Note: The weight limit for this event has been: 1896, open: 1906, over 187¼ lb. *85 kg;* 1908, over 205 lb. *93 kg.;* 1912 to 1928, over 181¾ lb. *82.5 kg.;* 1932 to 1960, over 191¾ lb. *87 kg.;* 1964 to 1968, over 213¾ lb. *97 kg.;* since 1972, up to 202¼ lb. *100 kg.*

1896	Carl Schuhmann (GER)	Georgios Tsitas (GRE)	Stephanos Christopoulos (GRE)

1900–1904   Event not held

1906	Sören M. Jensen (DEN)	Heari Baur (AUT)	Marcel Dubois (BEL)
1908	Richard Weisz (HUN)	Aliksandr Petrov (URS)	Sören M. Jensen (DEN)
1912	Yrjö Saarela (FIN)	Johan Olin (FIN)	Sören M. Jensen (DEN)
1920	Adolf Lindfors (FIN)	Poul Hansen (DEN)	Martti Nieminen (FIN)
1924	Henri Deglane (FRA)	Edil Rosenqvist (FIN)	Raymund Badó (HUN)
1928	Rudolf Svensson (SWE)	Hjalmar E. Nyström (FIN)	Georg Gehring (GER)
1932	Carl Westergren (SWE)	Josef Urban (TCH)	Nikolaus Hirschl (AUT)
1936	Kirstjan Palusalu (EST)	John Nyman (SWE)	Kurt Hornfischer (GER)
1948	Ahmet Kireççi (TUR)	Tor Nilsson (SWE)	Guido Fantoni (ITA)
1952	Johannes Kotkas (URS)	Josef Ružička (TCH)	Tauno Kovanen (FIN)
1956	Anatoliy Parfenov (URS)	Wilfried Dietrich (GER)	Adelmo Bulgarelli (ITA)
1960	Ivan Bogdan (URS)	Wilfried Dietrich (GER)	Bohumil Kubat (TCH)
1964	István Kozma (HUN)	Anatoly Roshin (URS)	Wilfried Dietrich (GER)
1968	István Kozma (HUN)	Anatoly Roshin (URS)	Petr Kment (TCH)
1972	Nicolae Martinescu (ROM)	Nikolai Yakovenko (URS)	Ferenc Kiss (HUN)
1976	Nikolai Bolboshin (URS)	Kamen Goranov (BUL)	Andrzej Skrzylewski (POL)
1980	Gheorgi Raikov (BUL)	Roman Bierla (POL)	Vasile Andrei (ROM)
1984	Vasile Andrei (ROM)	Greg Gibson (USA)	Jozef Tertelje (YUG)

GRECO-ROMAN—SUPER-HEAVYWEIGHT
(Weight over *100 kg.* 202¼ lb.)

	GOLD	SILVER	BRONZE
1896–1968 Event not held			
1972	Anatoly Roshin (URS)	Alexandre Tomov (BUL)	Victor Dolipschi (ROM)
1976	Alexandr Kolchinski (URS)	Alexandre Tomov (BUL)	Roman Codreanu (ROM)
1980	Alexandr Kolchinski (URS)	Alexandre Tomov (BUL)	Hassan Bchara (LIB)
1984	Jeffrey Blatnick (USA)	Refik Memisevic (YUG)	Victor Dolipschi (ROM)

21. Yachting

1896–1968   Event not held

1972 **UNITED STATES**	**SWEDEN**	**CANADA**
Harry Melges, Jr.	Stig Wennerstroem	David Miller
William Bentsen	Bo Knape	John Ekels
William Allen	Stefan Krook	Paul Cote
1976 **DENMARK**	**UNITED STATES**	**EAST GERMANY**
Paul Jensen	John Kolius	Dieter Below
Vald Bandolowski	Walter Glasgow	Michael Zachries
Erik Hansen	Richard Hoepfner	Olaf Engelhardt
1980 **DENMARK**	**U.S.S.R**	**GREECE**
Paul Jensen	Boris Budnikov	Anastassios Boudouris
Vald Bandolowski	Aleksandr Budnikov	Anastassios Gavrilis
Erik Hansen	Nikolai Polyakov	Aristidis Rapanakis
1984 **USA**	**BRAZIL**	**CANADA**
Robert Haines Jr	Torben Grael	Hans Fogh
Edward Trevelyan	Daniel Adler	John Kerr
Roderick Davis	Ronaldo Senfft	Steve Calder

INTERNATIONAL STAR CLASS

1896–1928   Event not held

1932 **UNITED STATES**	**GREAT BRITAIN**	**SWEDEN**
Gilbert Gray	Colin Ratsey	Gunnar Asther
Andrew Libano, Jr.	Peter Jaffe	Daniel Sunden-Cullberg
1936 **GERMANY**	**SWEDEN**	**NETHERLANDS**
Peter Bischoff	Arved Laurin	Adriaan Maas
Hans-Joachim Weise	Uno Wallentin	Willem de Vries Lentsch
1948 **UNITED STATES**	**CUBA**	**NETHERLANDS**
Hilary Smart	Carlos de Cardenas	Adriaan Maas
Paul Smart	Carlos de Cardenas, Jr.	Edward Stutterheim
1952 **ITALY**	**UNITED STATES**	**PORTUGAL**
Agostino Straulino	John Reid	Francisco de Andrade
Nicolo Rode	John Price	Joaquim Fiuza
1956 **UNITED STATES**	**ITALY**	**BAHAMAS**
Herbert Williams	Agostino Straulino	Durward Knowles
Lawrence Low	Nicolo Rode	Sloan Farrington
1960 **U.S.S.R.**	**PORTUGAL**	**UNITED STATES**
Timir Pinegin	Mario Quina	William Parks
Fyedor Shutkov	José Quina	Robert Halperin
1964 **BAHAMAS**	**UNITED STATES**	**SWEDEN**
Durward Knowles	Richard Stearns	Pelle Pettersson
Cecil Cooke	Lynn Williams	Holger Sundstrom
1968 **UNITED STATES**	**NORWAY**	**ITALY**
Lowell North	Peder Lunde	Franco Cavallo
Peter Barrett	Per Olav Wiken	Camillo Gargano
1972 **AUSTRALIA**	**SWEDEN**	**WEST GERMANY**
David Forbes	Pelle Pettersson	Willi Kuhweide
John Anderson	Stellan Westerdahl	Karsten Meyer
1976 Event not held		
1980 **U.S.S.R.**	**AUSTRIA**	**ITALY**
Valentin Mankin	Hubert Raudaschl	Giorgio Gorla
Aleksandr Muzychenko	Karl Ferstl	Alfio Peraboni
1984 **USA**	**WEST GERMANY**	**ITALY**
William E. Buchan	Joachim Griese	Giorgio Gorla
Stephen Erikson	Michael Marcour	Alfio Peraboni

INTERNATIONAL FLYING DUTCHMAN CLASS

GOLD	SILVER	BRONZE
1896–1956 Event not held		
1960 **NORWAY**	**DENMARK**	**GERMANY**
Peder Lunde Jr.	Hans Fogh	Rolf Mulka
Björn Bergvall	Ole Erik Petersen	Ingo von Bredow
1964 **NEW ZEALAND**	**GREAT BRITAIN**	**UNITED STATES**
Helmer Pedersen	Franklyn Musto Jr.	Harry Melges Jr.
Earle Wells	Arthur Morgan	William Bentsen
1968 **GREAT BRITAIN**	**WEST GERMANY**	**BRAZIL**
Rodney Pattisson	Ullrich Libor	Reinaldo Conrad
Iain Macdonald-Smith	Peter Naumann	Burkhard Cordes
1972 **GREAT BRITAIN**	**FRANCE**	**WEST GERMANY**
Rodney Pattisson	Yves Pajot	Ullrich Libor
Christopher Davies	Marc Pajot	Peter Naumann
1976 **WEST GERMANY**	**GREAT BRITAIN**	**BRAZIL**
Jorg Diesch	Rodney Pattisson	Reinaldo Conrad
Eckart Diesch	Julian Brooke Houghton	Peter Ficker
1980 **SPAIN**	**IRELAND**	**HUNGARY**
Alejandro Abascal	David Wilkins	Szabolcs Detre
Miguel Noguer	James Wilkinson	Zsolt Detre
1984 **USA**	**CANADA**	**GREAT BRITAIN**
Jonathan McKee	Terry McLaughlin	Jonathan Richards
William C. Buchan	Evert Bastet	Peter Allam

INTERNATIONAL 470 CLASS

GOLD	SILVER	BRONZE
1896–1972 Event not held		
1976 **WEST GERMANY**	**SPAIN**	**AUSTRALIA**
Frank Huebner	Antonio Gorostegui	Ian Brown
Harro Bode	Pedro Millet	Ian Ruff
1980 **BRAZIL**	**EAST GERMANY**	**FINLAND**
Marcos Soares	Jorn Borowski	Jouko Lindgren
Eduardo Penido	Egbert Swensson	Georg Tallberg
1984 **SPAIN**	**USA**	**FRANCE**
Luis Doreste	Stephen Benjamin	Thierry Peponnet
Roberto Molina	Christopher Steinfeld	Luc Pillot

INTERNATIONAL FINN CLASS

GOLD	SILVER	BRONZE
1896–1948 Event not held		
1952 Paul Elvström (DEN)	Charles Currey (GBR)	Rickard Sarby (SWE)
1956 Paul Elvström (DEN)	André Nelis (BEL)	John Marvin (USA)
1960 Paul Elvström (DEN)	Aleksandr Chuchelov (URS)	André Nelis (BEL)
1964 Willi Kuhweide (GER)	Peter Barrett (USA)	Henning Wind (DEN)
1968 Valentin Mankin (URS)	Hubert Raudaschl (AUT)	Fabio Albarelli (ITA)
1972 Serge Maury (FRA)	Ilias Hatzipavlis (GRE)	Victor Potapov (URS)
1976 Jochen Schumann (GDR)	Andrei Balashov (URS)	John Bertrand (AUS)
1980 Esko Rechardt (FIN)	Wolfgang Mayrhofer (AUT)	Andrei Balashov (URS)
1984 Russell Coutts (NZL)	John Bertrand (USA)	Terry Neilson (CAN)

INTERNATIONAL TORNADO CLASS

1896–1972   Event not held

1976	**GREAT BRITAIN** Reginald White John Osborn	**UNITED STATES** David McFaull Michael Rothwell	**WEST GERMANY** Jorg Spengler Jorg Schmall
1980	**BRAZIL** Alexandre Welter Lars Bjorkstrom	**DENMARK** Peter Due Per Kjergard	**SWEDEN** Goran Marstrom Jorgen Ragnarsson
1984	**NEW ZEALAND** Rex Sellers Christopher Timms	**USA** Randy Smyth Jay Glaser	**AUSTRALIA** Chris Cairns John Anderson

WINDGLIDER CLASS

1984	Steve Van Den Berg (HOL)	Randall Steele (USA)	Bruce Kendall (NZL)

WINTER OLYMPIC GAMES
TABLE OF MEDAL WINNERS
BY NATIONS 1908–1980

(including ice events in 1908 and 1920)

Note: These totals include all first, second and third places including those in events no longer on the current schedule. Results of demonstration events are not included.

		GOLD	SILVER	BRONZE	TOTAL
1.	USSR	68	48	50	166
2.	Norway	54	57	52	163
3.	USA	40	46	31	117
4.	Sweden	32	25	29	86
5.	East Germany	30	26	29	85
6.	Finland	29	42	32	103
7.	Austria	25	33	30	88
8.	Germany	24	22	21	67
9.	Switzerland	18	20	20	58
10.	Canada	14	10	15	39
11.	France	12	10	15	37
12.	Italy	12	9	7	28
13.	Netherlands	10	15	10	35
14.	Great Britain	7	4	10	21
15.	Czechoslovakia	2	7	11	20

[1] Germany 1908–1964, West Germany from 1968
[2] East Germany (GDR) from 1968

DEVELOPMENT OF THE
WINTER OLYMPIC GAMES

These figures relate to the Winter Games, and Ice Events in 1908 and 1920.

GAMES	NO. OF COUNTRIES	NO. OF SPORTS	NO. OF COMPETITORS	
			Male	Female
London (IVth Summer)	6	1	14	7
Antwerp (VIIth Summer)	10	2	73	12
I Chamonix	16	5	281	13
II St. Moritz	25	6	468	27
III Lake Placid	17	5	274	32
IV Garmisch	28	6	675	80
V St. Moritz	28	7	636	77
VI Oslo	30	6	623	109
VII Cortina	32	6	687	132
VIII Squaw Valley	30	5	521	144
IX Innsbruck	36	7	986	200
X Grenoble	37	7	1,081	228
XI Sapporo	35	7	1,015	217
XII Innsbruck	37	7	900	228
XIII Lake Placid	37	7	833	234
XIV Sarajevo	49	7	1,002	276

THE WINTER OLYMPICS

Although the Winter Games were not inaugurated until 1924—28 years after the Modern Olympics were first held in Athens in 1896—there were ice rink events held in both the IVth Games in 1908 and the VIIth Games in 1920. Indeed ice skating was on the draft program for the IInd 1900 Games at Paris.

In London in 1908 there were four ice skating events to which six nations—Argentina, Germany, Great Britain, Russia, Sweden and the United States—sent competitors. The Swedes dominated the men's competition with the great Ulrich Salchow showing why he was 10 times world champion. Britain's Madge Syers won the ladies championships. In a special figure contest Nikolai Panin of Russia won the gold medal.

In 1920 at Antwerp there were individual figure skating events won by Sweden and the pairs by Finland. An ice hockey tournament was won by Canada. Ten countries sent competitors.

Nikolai Panin, winner of a special figure skating title of 1908, was the only Russian to win an Olympic gold medal prior to the 1952 Games.

1924—Ist Winter Games, Chamonix-Mont Blanc, France

The success of the 1920 events assisted the advocates of a separate Winter Games against Nordic opposition. Sixteen nations sent teams to the Games which were only retrospectively recognized as the Ist Winter Olympics. The heroes were the Finnish speed skater Clas Thunberg who won 3 gold, 1 silver and 1 bronze medal and Thorleif Haug (Norway) who won 3 gold and a bronze medal for Nordic skiing. Little noticed was a tiny 11-year-old Norwegian figure skater who came last—Sonja Henie. The Canadians trounced all ice hockey opposition, scoring 85 goals in three games.

1928—IInd Winter Games, St. Mortiz, Switzerland

All real opposition to a series of Winter Olympics was subdued by the success of the Chamonix celebration. This time 25 countries including, for example, Japan and Mexico, appeared. The unwelcome warm weather nearly spoiled the Games—one speed skating event was cancelled and the bobsleigh program curtailed. The top skiier proved to be the Norwegian Johan Gröttumsbraaten while Thunberg collected two more speed skating golds. In figure skating the Swede Grafström won his third gold medal and the 15-year-old Sonja Henie opened her massive account.

North America dominated the bobsleigh with two USA crews and the ice hockey with the Canadians harvesting 38 goals to nil in three games.

1932—IIIrd Winter Games, Lake Placid, New York, USA

The world economic recession coupled with the long trans-Atlantic travelling time that would be necessary for Europeans, who have always numerically predominated, depleted the competitors from 495 to 306.

Again the weather spoiled some events: snow had to be transported to repair the cross-country skiing courses. The Nordic skiiers maintained their Olympic monopoly as the inevitable introduction of Alpine skiing was still four years away but Norway's stranglehold was broken by the Swedes and Finns. In the speed skating North Americans predominated because of their successful insistence on imposing their bunched start rules which invited bodily contact instead of the more clinical European pair starts. The figure skating saw the eclipse of Grafström by Austria's Karl Schäfer and the high noon of Sonja Henie's talent.

1936—IVth Winter Games, Garmisch-Partenkirchen, Germany

The Winter Olympics hit the "big time" in 1936 with half a million paying spectators, which was more than the first three Games in aggregate. Twenty-eight countries, now including, for example, Australia and Turkey, sent 755 competitors. The weather smiled on this prestige exercise by the Nazi State and the level of competition hit new heights. The introduction of Alpine skiing events was sensational as two Nordics, the Norwegians Birger Ruud, the great ski jumper, and Laila Schou Nilsen, a sixteen-year-old girl who held all five speed skating records, won the downhill races. These remarkable performances only earned them a fourth place and a bronze medal respectively because the only Alpine championship was a combined event with a slalom section (watched by a record 70,000 people) in which the Central Europeans recovered their lost ground. The Norwegian speed skater Ivan Ballangrud dominated the rink with 3 golds; in figure skating Schäfer (Austria) and Sonja Henie (Norway) gained their final Olympic laurels; and a British team sensationally won the ice hockey tournament largely thanks to recruiting a number of Anglo-Canadians.

ABOVE: Canada, in white, won the 1932 ice hockey gold medal.

LEFT: Sonja Henie, a Norwegian who later became wealthy from professional ice shows, won the second of her 3 gold medals at Lake Placid in 1932

1948—Vth Winter Games, St. Mortiz, Switzerland

The Games in 1940 were originally intended for Sapporo, Japan, but the Sino-Japanese war put an end to that. The situtation then became highly confused because of the open hostilities between the International Skiing Federation (F.I.S.), who wanted to allow ski instructors to appear in the Games, and the International Olympic Committee (I.O.C.), who regarded them as professionals. In the context of this battle, Oslo, Helsinki, St. Mortiz and Garmisch all in turn offered to host the Games. The war clouds overshadowed this conflict and also eclipsed thoughts as to the best site for 1944. On a postal vote the I.O.C. granted the Vth Winter Games of 1948 to St. Mortiz and twenty-eight countries sent 713 competitors.

Alpine skiing with six championships now attracted a far wider entry than the five Nordic skiing titles.

The most successful Alpine skier was Henri Oreiller (France) with two golds and a bronze. Gretchen Fraser (USA) by winning the slalom achieved the first ever non-European skiing success. North America grabbed both individual figure skating titles through Richard Button (USA) and the glamorous Barbara Ann Scott (Canada). The Norwegians dominated the speed skating as did the Americans and Swiss the bob races. The ice hockey tournament was marred by a blazing row over which of two US teams should represent their country. The Canadians won very narrowly over the Czechs.

1952—VIth Winter Games, Oslo, Norway

It is perhaps extraordinary that the Games of 1952 are the only ones to be held in a Nordic country. Norway is the top medal-winning nation and Finland and Sweden are also in the top six countries as regards successes in these Games.

There was a record number of 30 countries present—with Germany and Japan being allowed back into the fold—and a new attendance record of 541,407 paying spectators.

The Norwegians excelled on their home ground with Stein Erikson even winning the less familiar Alpine skiing event, the giant slalom. Hjalmar Andersen with 3 golds was the most successful speed skater in the packed Bislet Stadium. Figure skating saw the master, Richard Button (USA), retain his crown while Britain's Jeanette Altwegg's impeccable compulsory figures survived the onslaught of several more dramatic free skaters.

The two winning German bob teams were so grotesquely heavy (they averaged over 260 lb. a man) that the International Federation legislated for a maximum weight limit in future contests. The Canadians again won the ice hockey but the quality of their opposition was rising steadily.

1956—VIIth Winter Games, Cortina d'Ampezzo, Italy

These Games were paradoxically largely financed by Italian soccer, via pools. New ground was broken in the first appearance since 1908 of Russians who promptly won the men's 4 × 10 km relay and took three out of the first four places in the women's 10 km race, harvested many speed skating successes and sensationally won the ice hockey tournament. The hero of the Games was Toni Sailer (Austria), who won a grand slam in the three Alpine skiing events—all by an imperious margin.

The USA triumphed in both the men's and the women's individual figure skating. These Winter Games were the first to be televised and so enjoyed by record numbers of people, but the price for spreading the interest in this way was some loss in the gate money from spectators actually attending the Games.

1960—VIIIth Winter Games, Squaw Valley, California, USA

In 1955 these Games were awarded by two votes to this then virtually non-existent ski resort in preference to the famous established center of Innsbrück. In the end, despite furious objections from the bobsleighers who were not provided for any by the Nordic skiers, because they disliked the great altitude of their courses (2,000 meters or over 6,500 ft.), the Games were a remarkable success. One strong feature was the compactness of the sites, which made it possible for spectators to see a large variety of the competitions.

The program was extended by the addition of speed skating for women and the Winter Biathlon (cross-country skiing and shooting). The Swedish iron man Sixten Jernberg added to his Cortina successes by winning the tough 30 km Nordic race. The Russian women's four entrants in the 10 km event took the first four places. For the first time ever a non-Scandinavian, Georg Thoma (Germany), won the combined event, while another German, Helmut Recknagel, decisively won the special ski jump.

No one skier established personal ascendancy in the very tightly contested Alpine events. The speed skating times were sensational especially in the 10,000 meters in which Knut Johannesen (Norway) beat the world's record by some 46 seconds.

David Jenkins (USA), extracting a rare six points (the maximum possible) from one judge, won the gold medal for figure skating. The USA and Canada shunted the USSR, the winners at Cortina, to third place in the ice hockey tournament.

Jean-Claude Killy (FRA) achieved the triple in Alpine skiing of downhill, slalom, and giant slalom before a home crowd at Grenoble in 1968.

1964—IXth Winter Games, Innsbrück, Austria

These Games hit new high water marks regarding the number of competitors present, the number of nations represented and the number of paying spectators—nearly a million.

The USSR collected 25 medals, the USA, with the largest team, only 6, and neighboring Switzerland an embarrassing nil.

The heroine of the Games was a Russian lady, Lydia Skoblikova, who won a Winter Games record of four golds. She was a speed skater with a superb style, who had already won two previous golds in 1960.

To the French contingent the Goitschel sisters Christine, 19 (slalom gold) and Marielle, 18 (giant slalom gold) were goddesses, especially as each was a runner-up to the other in these events. Austria and France were 3-all over the six Alpine titles. The Scandinavians allowed not one trespasser in the men's Nordic events but the Russians monopolized the women's cross-country program and the Russian men recaptured the ice hockey title which they had won in 1956 and lost in 1960.

Two lowland nations, the Netherlands and Britain, each had a popular success. Sjoukje Dijkstra, in front of her Queen, won the women's figure skating and so Netherlands' first gold. Britain's Tony Nash and the Hon. Robin Dixon won the boblet gold.

1968—Xth Winter Games, Grenoble, France

These Games were Jean-Claude Killy's. The handsome hotelier's rather disputatious Alpine skiing grand slam was hard fought with winning margins for the downhill, slalom and giant slalom being 8/100th, 9/100th and 2.3 seconds respectively. The outstanding Nordic skiier was a Swedish lady—Toini Gustafsson—who collected two individual golds and a relay silver. The East German ladies were disqualified from the Luge event for secretly heating their runners.

The speed skating, despite pessimistic forecasts, produced fast times and three golds for the Netherlands, but only one out of eight for the Russians. The Soviets, however, retained their ice hockey title despite losing a very tense match 4-5 to the Czechs.

1972—XIth Winter Games, Sapporo, Japan

These Games, which cost the Japanese $61 million to stage, reflected the mounting strain that international sport suffers as the competitive screw turns. The magic of the Japanese-style opening ceremony seemed however to quell the endless behind-the-scenes rows about the alleged professionalism of full-time skiiers who are inevitably regarded as commercial models by equipment and clothing manufacturers. Austria's hero, Karl Schranz, was sent home by the Committee before the Games opened.

The Alpine nations were stunned when the slalom title went to a Spaniard—"Paquito" Fernandez Ochoa. There was an unexpected but popular double gold by a seventeen-year-old Swiss miss—Marie Therese Nadig—leaving the slalom for Barbara Cochran, the United States' first skiing gold medalist for twenty years.

The Russians won 4 out of the 6 Nordic cross-country titles includ

Ard Schenk (HOL) was the hero of the Sapporo Games in 1972, winning 3 out of the 4 speed-skating events.

ing an individual double by Galina Kulakova, who won a third gold in the relay. The Japanese by dint of endless practice were able to achieve a grand slam in the 70 meter hill ski jumping. Individual star of Asia's first Winter Games was Ard Schenk, the Dutch speed skater, who outclassed the world and won three gold medals.

1976—XIIth Winter Games, Innsbrück, Austria

The citizens of Colorado, USA, by referendum, forced the Denver organizing committee to withdraw its application for the allocation of the XIIth Games to that city. Innsbrück, host for the second time, kept it "simple." An influenza epidemic could not stop Germany's Rosi Mittermaier becoming the personality of these Games, with only 13/100ths of a second in the giant slalom between her and an unprecedented Alpine skiing grand slam by a woman.

1980—XIIIth Winter Games, Lake Placid, New York, U.S.A.

Lake Placid had been applying for the Games unsuccessfully since 1962 and finally was rewarded in 1974. With remarkable foresight speed skater Eric Heiden was selected to take the oath. Mainland China and Cyprus made their Winter Games debuts. There were many complaints about the organization of the Games, the prime one being in the field of transportation. Spectators in particular found it very difficult to get to sites.

Eric Heiden (USA) won the most medals at the Games with an unprecedented sweep of all five speed skating gold medals, all in Olympic record times. His sister Beth also won a bronze in the women's events.

Galina Kulakova (URS) won a silver in the Nordic relay to bring her total to a women's Winter Games record of eight medals, comprising four golds, two silvers and two bronze, in the four Games since 1968.

At the end of the Lake Placid Games only Great Britain, Sweden and the United States could claim to have been represented in all Winter events of the Modern Olympics, including those of 1908 and 1920.

1984—XIVth Winter Games, Sarajevo, Yugoslavia

The first Winter Games held in Eastern Europe was awarded to Sarajevo, which previously was famous as the site of the assassination of Archduke Ferdinand in 1914—an act which historians argue caused World War I. A record 49 countries attended and though the weather was not good, the enthusiasm of the organizers and local populace overcame most difficulties.

The outstanding competitor was Marja Liisa Hamalainen of Finland, who won all three ladies' individual events as well as a team bronze in Nordic skiing. However, Britain's Jayne Torvill and Christopher Dean gained most media attention with their superb ice dancing routines—their artistic interpretation of Ravel's *Bolero* was awarded nine perfect sixes. American Alpine skiers made a major impact with Bill Johnson winning the downhill with a record average speed. Twin teammates Phil and Steve Mahre won gold and silver medals in the slalom, while Italy's Michela Figini became the youngest-ever Alpine skiing gold medalist, and the Soviet Union equaled Canada's record of six hockey titles. Just prior to the Games two defending champions, Ingemar Stenmark of Sweden and Hanni Wenzel of Liechtenstein were banned as "professionals."

1988—XVth Winter Games, Calgary, Canada

After three previous unsuccessful bids, Calgary was finally awarded these Games in 1981. Most venues are close together except for Mount Allan and Kenmore, some 90 km away, where the Alpine and Nordic skiing take place. The program has been stretched to 16 days to include three weekends, particularly favorable for television coverage—for which ABC paid $309 million for the North American rights, over three times the sum for Sarajevo. There are a number of new events; Nordic Combination, Team Jumping, Alpine Combination, Super Giant Slalom, and a 5000m speed skating event for women. Demonstration sports will be curling, short track speed skating, and freestyle skiing.

Gunde Swan of Sweden set an Olympic record for the 15-km cross-country Nordic ski race in the 1984 Winter Games.

ROLL OF OLYMPIC MEDAL WINNERS IN THE WINTER EVENTS SINCE 1908

1. Nordic Skiing (Men)

15 KM. (9.3 miles) CROSS-COUNTRY

GOLD	SILVER	BRONZE
1908–1920 Event not held		
1924[1] Thorleif Haug (NOR) 1h 14:31.0	Johan Gröttumsbraaten (NOR) 1h 15:51.0	Tipani Niku (FIN) 1h 26:26.0
1928[2] Johan Gröttumsbraaten (NOR) 1h 37:01.0	Ole Hegge (NOR) 1h 39:01.0	Reidar Ödegaard (NOR) 1h 40:11.0
1932[3] Sven Utterström (SWE) 1h 23:07.0	Axel T. Wikström (SWE) 1h 25:07.0	Veli Saarinen (FIN) 1h 25:24.0
1936[1] Erik-August Larsson (SWE) 1h 14:38.0	Oddbjörn Hagen (NOR) 1h 15:33.0	Pekka Niemi (FIN) 1h 16:59.0
1948[1] Martin Lundström (SWE) 1h 13:50.0	Nils Östensson (SWE) 1h 14:22.0	Gunnar Eriksson (SWE) 1h 16:06.0
1952[1] Hallgeir Brenden (NOR) 1h 1:34.0	Tapio Mäkelä (FIN) 1h 2:09.0	Paavo Lonkila (FIN) 1h 2:20.0
1956 Hallgeir Brenden (NOR) 49:39.0	Sixten Jernberg (SWE) 50:14.0	Pavel Koltschin (URS) 50:17.0
1960 Haakon Brusveen (NOR) 51:55.5	Sixten Jernberg (SWE) 51:58.6	Veikko Hakulinen (FIN) 52:03.0
1964 Eero Mäntyranta (FIN) 50:54.1	Harald Grönningen (NOR) 51:34.8	Sixten Jernberg (SWE) 51:42.2
1968 Harald Grönningen (NOR) 47:54.2	Eero Mäntyranta (FIN) 47:56.1	Gunnar Larsson (SWE) 48:33.7
1972 Sven-Ake Lundback (SWE) 45:28.24	Fedor Simaschov (URS) 46:00.84	Ivar Formo (NOR) 46:02.86
1976 Nikolay Bajukov (URS) 43:58.47	Evgeniy Beliayev (URS) 44:01.10	Arto Koivisto (FIN) 44:19.25
1980 Thomas Wassberg (SWE) 41:57.63	Juha Mieto (FIN) 41:57.64	Ove Aunli (NOR) 42:28.62
1984 Gunde Swan (SWE) 41:25.6	Aki Karvonen (FIN) 41:34.9	Harri Kirvesniemi (FIN) 41:45.6

[1] The distance was 18 km.
[2] The distance was 19,7 km.
[3] The distance was 18,2 km.

30 KM. (18.6 miles) CROSS-COUNTRY

1908–1952 Event not held		
1956 Veikko Hakulinen (FIN) 1h 44:06.0	Sixten Jernberg (SWE) 1h 44:30.0	Pavel Koltschin (URS) 1h 45:45.0
1960 Sixten Jernberg (SWE) 1h 51:03.9	Rolf Rämgård (SWE) 1h 51:61.9	Nikolay Anikin (URS) 1h 52:28.2
1964 Eero Mäntyranta (FIN) 1h 30:50.7	Harald Grönningen (NOR) 1h 32:02.3	Igor Voronchikin (URS) 1h 32:15.8
1968 Franco Nones (ITA) 1h 35:39.2	Odd Martinsen (NOR) 1h 36:28.9	Eero Mäntyranta (FIN) 1h 36:55.3

	GOLD	SILVER	BRONZE
1972	Viaceslav Vedenine (URS) 1h 36:31.2	Paal Tyldum (NOR) 1h 37:25.3	Johs Harviken (NOR) 1h 37:32.4
1976	Sergei Savelyev (URS) 1h 30:29.38	William Koch (USA) 1h 30:57.84	Ivan Garanin (URS) 1h 31:09.29
1980	Nikolai Simyatov (URS) 1h 27:02.80	Vasiliy Rochev (URS) 1h 27:34.22	Ivan Lebanov (BUL) 1h 28:03.87
1984	Nikolai Simyatov (URS) 1h 28:56.3	Aleksdandr Savyalov (URS) 1h 29:23.3	Gunde Swan (SWE) 1h 29:35.7

50 KM. (31 miles) CROSS-COUNTRY

	GOLD	SILVER	BRONZE
1908–1920	Event not held		
1924	Thorleif Haug (NOR) 3h 44:32.0	Thoralf Strömstad (NOR) 3h 46:23.0	Johan Gröttumsbraaten (NOR) 3h 47:46.0
1928	Per Erik Hedlund (SWE) 4h 52:03.0	Gustaf Jonsson (SWE) 5h 05:30.0	Volger Andersson (SWE) 5h 05:46.0
1932	Veli Saarinen (FIN) 4h 28:00.0	Väinö Likkanen (FIN) 4h 28:20.0	Arne Rustadstuen (NOR) 4h 31:53.0
1936	Elis Wiklund (SWE) 3h 30:11.0	Axel Wikström (SWE) 3h 33:20.0	Nils-Joel Englund (SWE) 3h 34:10.0
1948	Nils Karlsson (SWE) 3h 47:48.0	Harald Eriksson (SWE) 3h 52:20.0	Benjamin Vanninen (FIN) 3h 57:28.0
1952	Veikko Hakulinen (FIN) 3h 33:33.0	Eero Kolehmainen (FIN) 3h 38:11.0	Magnar Estenstad (NOR) 3h 38:28.0
1956	Sixten Jernberg (SWE) 2h 50:27.0	Veikko Hakulinen (FIN) 2h 51:45.0	Fyedor Terentyeve (URS) 2h 53:32.0
1960	Kalevi Hämäläinen (FIN) 2h 59:06.3	Veikko Hakulinen (FIN) 2h 59:26.7	Rolf Rämgård (SWE) 3h 02:46.7
1964	Sixten Jernberg (SWE) 2h 43:52.6	Assar Roennlund (SWE) 2h 44:58.2	Arto Tiainen (FIN) 2h 45:30.4
1968	Olle Ellefsaeter (NOR) 2h 28:45.8	Viaceslav Vedenine (URS) 2h 29:02.5	Josef Haas (SUI) 2h 29:14.8
1972	Paal Tyldrum (NOR) 2h 43:14.75	Magne Myrmo (NOR) 2h 43:29.45	Viaceslav Vedenine (URS) 2h 44:00.19
1976	Ivar Formo (NOR) 2h 37:30.50	Gert-Dietmar Klause (GDR) 2h 38:13.21	Benny Soedergren (SWE) 2h 39:39.21
1980	Nikolai Simyatov (URS) 2h 27:24.60	Juha Mieto (FIN) 2h 30:20.52	Aleksandr Savyalov (URS) 2h 30:51.52
1984	Thomas Wassberg (SWE) 2h 15:55.8	Gunde Swan (SWE) 2h 16:00.7	Aki Karvonen (FIN) 2h 17:04.7

RELAY RACE 4 x 10 KM. (6 miles 376 yd.)

	GOLD	SILVER	BRONZE
1908–1932	Event not held		
1936	FINLAND 2h 41:33.0	NORWAY 2h 41:39.0	SWEDEN 2h 43:03.0
	Sulo Nurmela	Oddbjörn Hagen	John Berger
	Klaes Karppinen	Olaf Hoffsbakken	Erik-August Larsson
	Matti Lahde	Sverre Brodahl	Artur Häggblad
	Kalle Jalkanen	Bjarne Iversen	Martin J. Matsbo
1948	SWEDEN 2h 32:08.0	FINLAND 2h 41:06.6	NORWAY 2h 44:33.0
	Nils Östensson	Lauri Silvennoinen	Erling Evensen
	Nils Täpp	Teuvo Laukkanen	Olav Ökern
	Gunnar Eriksson	Sauli Rytky	Reidar Nyborg
	Martin Lundström	August Kiuru	Olav Hagen
1952	FINLAND 2h 20:16.0	NORWAY 2h 23:13.0	SWEDEN 2h 24:13.0
	Heikki Hasu	Magnar Estenstad	Nils Täpp
	Paavon Lonkila	Mikal Kirkholt	Sigurd Andersson
	Urho Korhonen	Martin Stokken	Enar Josefsson
	Tapio Mäkelä	Hallgeir Brenden	Martin Lundström
1956	U.S.S.R. 2h 15:30.0	FINLAND 2h 16:31.0	SWEDEN 2h 17:42.0
	Fhedor Terentyev	August Kiuru	Lennart Larsson
	Pavel Koltschin	Jorma Kortelainen	Gunnar Samuelsson
	Nikolay Anikin	Arvo Viitanen	Per-Erik Larsson
	Vladimir Kusin	Veikko Hakulinen	Sixten Jernberg

GOLD	SILVER	BRONZE
1960 **FINLAND** 2h 18:45.6	**NORWAY** 2h 18:46.4	**U.S.S.R.** 2h 21:21.6
Toimi Alatalo	Harald Grönningen	Anatoliy Schelyuchin
Eero Mäntyranta	Hallgeir Brenden	Gennadiy Vaganov
Vaino Huhtala	Einar Ostby	Aleksey Kusnetsov
Veikko Hakulinen	Haakon Brusveen	Nikolay Anikin
1964 **SWEDEN** 2h 18:34.6	**FINLAND** 2h 18:42.4	**U.S.S.R.** 2h 18:46.9
Karl-Ake Asph	Vaino Huhtala	Ivan Utrobin
Sixten Jernberg	Arto Tiainen	Gennadiy Vaganov
Janne Stefansson	Kalevi Laurila	Igor Voronchikin
Assar Roennlund	Eero Mäntyranta	Pavel Koltschin
1968 **NORWAY** 2h 08:33.5	**SWEDEN** 2h 10:13.2	**FINLAND** 2h 10:56.7
Odd Martinsen	Jan Halvarsson	Kalevi Oikarainen
Paal Tyldrum	Bjarne Andersson	Hannu Taipale
Harald Grönningen	Gunnar Larsson	Kalevi Laurila
Olle Ellefsaeter	Assar Roennlund	Eero Mäntyranta
1972 **U.S.S.R.** 2h 04:47.94	**NORWAY** 2h 04:57.06	**SWITZERLAND** 2h 07:00.06
Vladimir Voronkov	Oddvar Braa	Alfred Kaflin
Yuri Skobov	Paal Tyldrum	Albert Giger
Fedor Simaschov	Ivor Formo	Alois Kaelin
Viaceslav Vedenine	Johs Harviken	Edi Hauser
1976 **FINLAND** 2h 07:59.72	**NORWAY** 2h 09:58.36	**U.S.S.R.** 2h 10:51.46
Matti Pitkaenen	Paal Tyldrum	Eveniy Beliayev
Juha Mieto	Einar Sagstuen	Nikolay Bajukov
Pertti Teurajaervi	Ivar Formo	Sergei Savelyev
Arto Koivisto	Odd Martinsen	Ivan Garanin
1980 **U.S.S.R.** 1h 57:03.46	**NORWAY** 1h 58:45.77	**FINLAND** 2h 00:00.18
Vasiliy Rochev	Lars Erik Eriksen	Harri Kirvesniemi
Nikolai Bajukov	Per Knut Aalund	Pertti Teurajaervi
Eveniy Beliayev	Ove Aunli	Matti Pitkaenen
Nikolai Simyatov	Oddvar Bra	Juha Mieto
1984 **SWEDEN** 1h 55:06.3	**USSR** 1h 55:16.5	**FINLAND** 1h 56:31.4
Thomas Wassberg	Aleksandr Batuk	Kari Ristanen
Benny Kohlberg	Aleksandr Savyalov	Juha Mieto
Jan Bo Ottosson	Vladimir Nikitin	Harri Kirvesniemi
Gunde Swan	Nikolai Zimyatov	Aki Karvonen

Ski Jumping

1924–1960   Held on one hill only

BIG HILL (90 meters)

GOLD	SILVER	BRONZE
1964 Toralf Engan (NOR) 230.70	Veikko Kankkonen (FIN) 228.90	Torgeir Brandtzaeg (NOR) 227.20
1968 Vladimir Beloussov (URS) 231.3	Jiri Raska (TCH) 229.4	Lars Grini (NOR) 214.3
1972 Wojciech Fortuna (POL) 219.9	Walter Steiner (SUI) 219.8	Rainer Schmidt (GDR) 219.3
1976 Karl Schnabl (AUT) 234.8	Anton Innauer (AUT) 232.9	Henry Glass (GDR) 221.7
1980 Jouko Tormanen (FIN) 271.0	Hubert Neuper (AUT) 262.4	Jari Puikkonen (FIN) 248.5
1984 Matti Nykaenen (FIN) 231.2	Jens Weissflog (GDR) 213.7	Pavel Ploc (TCH) 202.9

Sixten Jernberg of Sweden has won more medals in winter Olympic competition than any other athlete—4 gold, 3 silver, and 2 bronze.

SMALL HILL (70 meters)

1964	Veikko Kankkonen (FIN) 229.90	Toralf Engan (NOR) 226.30	Torgeil Brandtzaeg (NOR) 222.90
1968	Jiri Raska (TCH) 216.5	Reinhold Bachler (AUT) 214.2	Baldur Preiml (AUT) 212.6
1972	Yukio Kasaya (JPN) 244.2	Akitsugo Konno (JPN) 234.8	Seiji Aochi (JPN) 229.5
1976	Hans-Georg Aschenbach (GDR) 252.0	Jochen Danneberg (GDR) 246.2	Karl Schnabl (AUT) 242.0
1980	Toni Innauer (AUT) 266.3	Manfred Deckert (GDR) 249.2 Hirokazu Yagi (JPN) 249.2	—
1984	Jens Weissflog (GDR) 215.2	Matti Nykaenen (FIN) 214.0	Jari Puikkonen (FIN) 212.8

Karl Schnabl of Austria won a gold medal on the 90 meter hill at Innsbruck in 1976, and a bronze medal on the 70 meter hill.

NORDIC COMBINED (15 km.[2] and jumping)

	GOLD	SILVER	BRONZE
1908–1920	Event not held		
1924[1]	Thorleif Haug (NOR)	Thoralf Strömstad (NOR)	Johan Gröttumsbraaten (NOR)
1928[1]	Johan Gröttumsbraaten (NOR)	Hans Vinjarengen (NOR)	John Snersrud (NOR)
1932	Johan Gröttumsbraaten (NOR) 446.0	Ole Stenen (NOR) 436.05	Hans Vinjarengen (NOR) 434.60
1936	Oddbjörn Hagen (NOR) 430.30	Olaf Hoffsbakken (NOR) 419.80	Sverre Brodahl (NOR) 408.10
1948	Heikki Hasu (FIN) 448.80	Martti Huhtala (FIN) 433.65	Sfen Israelsson (SWE) 433.40
1952	Simon Slåttvik (NOR) 451.621	Heikki Hasu (FIN) 447.5	Sverre Stenersen (NOR) 436.335
1956	Sverre Stenersen (NOR) 455.0	Bengt Eriksson (SWE) 473.4	Franciszek Gron-Gasienica (POL) 436.8
1960	Georg Thoma (GER) 457.952	Tormod Knutsen (NOR) 453.0	Nikolay Gusakow (URS) 452.0
1964	Tormod Knutsen (NOR) 469.28	Nikolai Kiselev (URS) 453.04	Georg Thoma (GER) 452.88
1968	Frantz Keller (GER) 449.04	Alois Kaelin (SUI) 447.94	Andreas Kunz (GDR) 444.10
1972	Ulrich Wehling (GDR) 413.34	Rauno Mittinen (FIN) 405.55	Karl-Heinz Luck (GDR) 398.80
1976	Ulrich Wehling (GDR) 423.39	Urban Hettich (GR) 418.90	Konrad Winkler (GDR) 417.47
1980	Ulrich Wehling (GDR) 432.20	Jouko Karjalainen (FIN) 429.50	Konrad Winkler (GDR) 425.32
1984	Tom Sandberg (NOR) 422.595	Kuoko Karjalainen (FIN) 416.900	Jukka Ylipulli (FIN) 410.825

[1] In 1924 and 1928, the scoring was decided upon a different basis from that used from 1932 onwards.
[2] From 1924–1952 distance was 18 km.

Biathlon

10 KM.

1908–1976   Event not held
1980	Frank Ullrich	Vladimir Alikin	Anatoliy Alyabiev
	(GDR) 32:10.69	(URS) 32:53.10	(URS) 33:09.16
1984	Eirik Kvalfoss	Peter Angerer	Matthias Jacob
	(NOR) 30:53.8	(FRG) 31:02.4	(GDR) 31:10.5

20 KM.

1908–1956   Event not held
1960	Klas Lestander	Antti Tyrväinen	Aleksandr Privalov
	(SWE) 1h 33:21.6	(FIN) 1h 33:57.7	(URS) 1h 34:54.2
1964	Vladimir Melyanin	Aleksandr Privalov	Olav Jordet
	(URS) 1h 20:26.8	(URS) 1h 23:42.5	(NOR) 1h 24:38.8
1968	Magnar Solberg	Alexander Tikhonov	Vladimir Goundartsev
	(NOR) 1h 13:45.9	(URS) 1h 14:40.4	(URS) 1h 18:27.4
1972	Magnar Solberg	Hans-Jürg Knauthe	Lars Arvidson
	(NOR) 1h 15:55.5	(GDR) 1h 16:07.6	(SWE) 1h 16:27.03
1976	Nikolay Kruglov	Heikki Ikola	Alexander Elizarov
	(URS) 1h 14:12.26	(FIN) 1h 15:54.10	(URS) 1h 16:05.57
1980	Anatoliy Alyabiev	Frank Ullrich	Eberhard Rosch
	(URS) 1h 08:16.31	(GDR) 1h 08:27.79	(GDR) 1h 11:11.73
1984	Peter Angerer	Frank-Peter Roetsch	Eirik Kvalfoss
	(FRG) 1h 11:52.7	(GDR) 1h 13:21.4	(NOR) 1h 14:02.4

BIATHLON RELAY (4 × 7.5 km.)

1908–1964   Event not held

1968	**U.S.S.R.**	**NORWAY**	**SWEDEN**
	Alexander Tikhonov	Ola Waerhaug	Lars Arvidson
	Nikolai Pousanov	Olav Jordet	Tore Eriksson
	Victor Mamatov	Magnar Solberg	Olle Petrusson
	Vladimir Groundartsev	Jon Istad	Holmfrid Olsson
	2h 13:02.4	2h 14:50.2	2h 17:26.3
1972	**U.S.S.R**	**FINLAND**	**EAST GERMANY**
	Rinnat Safine	Esko Saira	Hans-Jürg Knauthe
	Ivan Biakov	Juhani Suutarinen	Joachim Mischner
	Victor Mamatov	Heikki Ikola	Heinz Dieter Speer
	Alexander Tikhonov	Mauri Röppänen	Horst Koschla
	1h 51:44.92	1h 54:37.22	1h 54:57.67
1976	**U.S.S.R.**	**FINLAND**	**EAST GERMANY**
	Alexander Elizarov	Henrik Floejt	Karl-Heinz Menz
	Ivan Biakov	Esko Saira	Frank Ullrich
	Nikolay Kruglov	Juhani Suutarinen	Manfred Beer
	Alexander Tikhonov	Heikki Ikola	Manfred Geyer
	1h 57:55.64	2h 01:45.58	2h 04:08.61
1980	**U.S.S.R.**	**EAST GERMANY**	**GERMANY**
	Vladimir Alikin	Mathias Jung	Franz Bernreiter
	Alexandr Tikhonov	Klaus Siebert	Hans Estner
	Vladimir Barnashov	Frank Ullrich	Peter Angerer
	Anatoliy Alyabiev	Eberhard Rosch	Gerhard Winkler
	1h 34:03.27	1h 34:56.99	1h 37:30.26
1984	**U.S.S.R.**	**NORWAY**	**GERMANY**
	Dmitri Vassilyev	Odd Lirhus	Ernst Reiter
	Yuri Kachkarov	Eirik Kvalfoss	Walter Pichler
	Alguimantas Shalna	Rolf Storsveen	Peter Angerer
	Sergey Buliguin	Kjell Soebak	Fritz Fischer
	1h 38:51.7	1h 39:03.9	1h 39:05.1

The 4 × 7.5 kilometer biathlon relay has been contested four times since its insertion in the 1968 program, and Soviet biathlete Alexander Tikhinov has been on the gold medal team at each Celebration.

Galina Kulakova (URS) set a women's Winter Games record with 8 total medals (4 gold, 2 silver and 2 bronze) in the 4 Games since 1968.

Nordic Skiing (Women)

5 KM. CROSS-COUNTRY (3 miles 188 yd.)

GOLD	SILVER	BRONZE
1908–1960 Event not held		
1964 Klaudia Boyarskikh (URS) 17:50.5	Mirja Lehtonen (FIN) 17:52.9	Alevtina Koltschina (URS) 18:08.4
1968 Toini Gustafsson (SWE) 16:45.2	Galina Kulakova (URS) 16:48.4	Alevtina Koltschina (URS) 16:51.6
1972 Galina Kulakova (URS) 17:00.50	Marjatta Kajosmaa (FIN) 17:05.50	Helena Sikolova (TCH) 17:07.32
1976 Helena Takalo (FIN) 15:48.69	Raisa Smetanina (URS) 15:49.73	Nina Baldicheva[1] (URS) 16:12.82
1980 Raisa Smetanina (URS) 15:06.92	Hilkka Riihivuori (FIN) 15:11.96	Kvetslava Jeriova (TCH) 15:23.44
1984 Marja-Liisa Hamalainen (FIN) 17:04.0	Berit Aunli (NOR) 17:14.1	Kvetoslava Jeriova (TCH) 17:18.3

[1] Third finisher Galina Kulakova (URS) disqualified.

10 KM. CROSS-COUNTRY (6.2 miles)

GOLD	SILVER	BRONZE
1908–1948 Event not held		
1952 Lydia Widemen (FIN) 41:40.0	Mirja Hietamies (FIN) 42:39.0	Siiri Rantanen (FIN) 42:50.0
1956 Lyubov Kosyryeva (URS) 38:11.0	Radya Yeroschina (URS) 38:16.0	Sonja Edström (SWE) 38:23.0
1960 Maria Gusakova (URS) 39:46.6	Lyubov Baranova-Kosyryeva (URS) 40:04.2	Radya Yeroschina (URS) 40:06.0
1964 Klaudia Boyarskikh (URS) 40:24.3	Eudokia Mekshilo (URS) 40:26.6	Maria Gusakova (URS) 40:46.6
1968 Toini Gustafsson (SWE) 36:46.5	Berit Moerdre (NOR) 37:54.6	Inger Aufles (NOR) 37:59.9
1972 Galina Kulakova (URS) 34:17.8	Alevtina Olunina (URS) 34:54.1	Marjatta Kajosmaa (FIN) 34:56.5
1976 Rafsa Smetanina (URS) 30:13.41	Helena Takalo (FIN) 30:14.28	Galina Kulakova (URS) 30:38.61
1980 Barbara Petzold (GDR) 30:31.54	Hilkka Riihivuori (FIN) 30:35.05	Helena Takalo (FIN) 30:45.25
1984 Marja-Liisa Hamalainen (FIN) 31:442.	Raisa Smetanina (URS) 32:02.9	Brit Pettersen (NOR) 32:12.7

20 KM. CROSS-COUNTRY

GOLD	SILVER	BRONZE
1984 Marja-Liisa Hamalainen (FIN) 1h 01:45.0	Raisa Smetanina (URS) 1h 02:26.7	Anne Jahren (NOR) 1h 03:13.6

Marja-Liisa Haemaelainen (Fin) dominated the women's skiing events, taking all three individual gold medals in the 1984 Olympics.

4 × 5 KM. RELAY[1]

1908–1952 Event not held

1956 **FINLAND** 1:9:01.0	**U.S.S.R.** 1h 9:28.0	**SWEDEN** 1h 9:48.0
Sirkka Polkunen	Lyubov Kosyryeva	Irma Johansson
Mirja Hietamies	Alevtina Koltschina	Anna-Lisa Eriksson
Siiri Rantanen	Radya Yeroschina	Sonja Edström
1960 **SWEDEN** 1h 4:21.4	**U.S.S.R.** 1h 5:2.6	**FINLAND** 1h 6:27.5
Irma Johansson	Radya Yeroschina	Siiri Rantanen
Britt Strandberg	Maria Gusakova	Eeva Ruoppa
Sonja Ruthström-Edström	Lyubov Baranova-Kosyryeva	Toini Pöysti
1964 **U.S.S.R.** 59:20.2	**SWEDEN** 1h 1:27.0	**FINLAND** 1h 2:45.1
Alevtina Koltschina	Barbo Martinsson	Senja Pusula
Eudokia Mekshilo	Britt Strandberg	Toini Pöysti
Klaudia Boyarskikh	Toini Gustafsson	Mirja Lehtonen
1968 **NORWAY** 57:30.0	**SWEDEN** 57:51.0	**U.S.S.R.** 58:13.6
Inger Aufles	Britt Strandberg	Alevtina Koltschina
Babben Enger Damon	Toini Gustafsson	Rita Achkina
Berit Moerdre	Barbo Martinsson	Galina Kulakova
1972 **U.S.S.R.** 48:46.15	**FINLAND** 49:19.37	**NORWAY** 49:51.49
Lyubov Moukhateva	Helena Takalo	Inger Aufles
Alevtina Olunina	Hilkka Kuntola	Aslaug Dahl
Galina Kulakova	Marjatta Kajosmaa	Berit Lammedal
1976 **U.S.S.R.** 1h 07:49.75	**FINLAND** 1h 08:36.57	**EAST GERMANY** 1h 09:57.95
Nina Baldicheva	Liisa Suihkonen	Monika Debertshaeuser
Zinaida Amosova	Marjatta Kajosmaa	Sigrun Krause
Raisa Smetanina	Hilkka Kuntola	Barbara Petzold
Galina Kulakova	Helena Takalo	Veronika Schmid
1980 **EAST GERMANY** 1h 02:11.10	**U.S.S.R.** 1h 03:18.30	**NORWAY** 1h 04:13.50
Marlies Rostock	Nina Baldicheva	Brit Pettersen
Carola Anding	Nina Rocheva	Anette Boe
Veronika Hesse	Galina Kulakova	Marit Myrmael
Barbara Petzold	Raisa Smetanina	Berit Aunli
1984 **NORWAY** 1h 06:49.7	**CZECHOSLOVAKIA** 1h 07:34.7	**FINLAND** 1h 07:36.7
Inger Nygraaten	Dagmar Schvubova	Pirkko Maatta
Anne Jahren	Blanka Paulu	Eija Hyytiainen
Brit Pettersen	Gabriela Svobodova	Marjo Matikainen
Berit Aunli	Kvetoslava Jeriova	Marja-Liisa Hämäläinen

[1] Race over three stages before 1976.

2. Alpine Skiing (Men)

GIANT SLALOM

1908–1948 Event not held

1952 Stein Erikson (NOR) 2:25.0	Christian Pravda (AUT) 2:26.9	Toni Spiss (AUT) 2:28.8

Alpine Skiing ■ 243

GOLD	SILVER	BRONZE
1956 Anton Sailer (AUT) 3:00.1	Andreas Molterer (AUT) 3:06.3	Walter Schuster (AUT) 3:07.2
1960 Roger Staub (SUI) 1:48.3	Josef Stiegler (AUT) 1:48.7	Ernst Hinterseer (AUT) 1:49.1
1964 Francois Boulieu (FRA) 1:46.71	Karl Schranz (AUT) 1:47.09	Josef Stiegler (AUT) 1:48.05
1968 Jean-Claude Killy (FRA) 3:29.28	Willy Favre (SUI) 3:31.50	Heinrich Messner (AUT) 3:31.83
1972 Gustavo Thoeni (ITA) 3:09.62	Edmund Bruggmann (SUI) 3:10.75	Werner Mattle (SUI) 3:10.99
1976 Heini Hemmi (SUI) 3:26.97	Ernst Good (SUI) 3:27.17	Ingemar Stenmark (SWE) 3:27.41
1980 Ingemar Stenmark (SWE) 2:40.74	Andreas Wenzel (LIE) 2:41.49	Hans Enn (AUT) 2:42.51
1984 Max Julen (SUI) 2:41.18	Juriy Franko (YUG) 2:41.41	Andreas Wenzel (LIE) 2:41.75

SLALOM

GOLD	SILVER	BRONZE
1908–1936 Event not held		
1948 Edi Reinalter (SUI) 2:10.3	James Couttet (FRA) 2:10.8	Henri Oreiller (FRA) 2:12.8
1952 Othmar Schneider (AUT) 2:00.0	Stein Eriksen (NOR) 2:01.2	Guttorm Berge (NOR) 2:01.7
1956 Anton Sailer (AUT) 3:14.7	Chiharu Igaya (JPN) 3:18.7	Stig Sollander (SWE) 3:20.2
1960 Ernst Hinterseer (AUT) 2:08.9	Matthias Lietner (AUT) 2:10.3	Charles Bozon (FRA) 2:10.4
1964 Josef Stiegler (AUT) 2:21.13	William Kidd (USA) 2:21.27	James Heuga (USA) 2:21.52
1968 Jean-Claude Killy (FRA) 1:39.73	Herbert Huber (AUT) 1:39.82	Alfred Matt (AUT) 1:40.09
1972 Francisco Fernandez Ochoa (ESP) 1:49.27	Gustavo Thoeni (ITA) 1:50.28	Rolando Thoeni (ITA) 1:50.30
1976 Piero Gros (ITA) 2:03.29	Gustavo Thoeni (ITA) 2:03.73	Willy Frommelt (LIE) 2:04.28
1980 Ingemar Stenmark (SWE) 1:44.26	Phil Mahre (USA) 1:44.76	Jacques Luethy (SUI) 1:45.06
1984 Phil Mahre (USA) 1:39.21	Steve Mahre (USA) 1:39.62	Didier Bouvet (FRA) 1:40.20

DOWNHILL

GOLD	SILVER	BRONZE
1908–1936 Event not held		
1948 Henri Oreiller (FRA) 2:55.0	Franz Gabl (AUT) 2:59.1	Karl Molitor (SUI) 3:00.3 Rolf Olinger (SUI) 3:00.3
1952 Zeno Colo (ITA) 2:30.8	Othmar Schneider (AUT) 2:32.0	Christian Pravda (AUT) 2:32.4
1956 Anton Sailer (AUT) 2:52.2	Raymond Fellay (SUI) 2:55.7	Andreas Molterer (AUT) 2:56.2
1960 Jean Vuarnet (FRA) 2:06.0	Hans-Peter Lanig (GER) 2:06.5	Guy Perillat (FRA) 2:06.9
1964 Egon Zimmermann (AUT) 2:18.16	Leo Lacroix (FRA) 2:18.90	Wolfgang Bartels (GER) 2:19.48
1968 Jean-Claude Killy (FRA) 1:59.85	Guy Périllat (FRA) 1:59.93	J. Daniel Daetwyler (SUI) 2:00.32
1972 Bernhard Russi (SUI) 1:51.43	Roland Collombin (SUI) 1:52.07	Heinrich Messner (AUT) 1:52.40

Toni Sailer (AUT) dominated the Alpine skiing in the 1956 Games at Cortina, winning all 3 gold medals.

Although he regularly dominated the Alpine World Cup competition, Ingemar Stenmark (SWE) was frustrated in his desire for an Olympic gold medal until he swept the slalom and giant slalom events at Lake Placid in 1980.

Phil Mahre (US) beat his twin brother Steve by 21/100ths of a second in the Giant Slalom in the 1984 Olympics, to win the gold and silver medals between them.

1976	Franz Klammer (AUT) 1:45.73	Bernhard Russi (SUI) 1:46.06	Herbert Plank (ITA) 1:46.59
1980	Leonhard Stock (AUT) 1:45.50	Peter Wirnsberger (AUT) 1:46.12	Stephen Podborski (CAN) 1:46.62
1984	Bill Johnson (USA) 1:45.59	Peter Mueller (SUI) 1:45.86	Anton Steiner (AUT) 1:45.95

ALPINE COMBINATION (Downhill and Slalom)

1908–1932	Event not held		
1936	Franz Pfnür (GER) 99.25pts	Gustav Lantschner (GER) 96.26	Emile Allais (FRA) 94.69
1948	Henri Oreiller (FRA) 3.27pts	Karl Molitor (SUI) 6.44	James Couttet (FRA) 6.95
1952–1984	Event not held		

Alpine Skiing (Women)

GIANT SLALOM

	GOLD	SILVER	BRONZE
1908–1948	Event not held		
1952	Andrea Lawrence-Mead (USA) 2:06.8	Dagmar Rom (AUT) 2:09.0	Annemarie Buchner (GER) 2:10.0
1956	Ossi Reichert (GER) 1:56.5	Josefine Frandl (AUT) 1:57.8	Dorothea Hochleitner (AUT) 1:58.2
1960	Yvonne Rüegg (SUI) 1:39.9	Penelope Pitou (USA) 1:40.0	Giuliana Chenal-Minuzzo (ITA) 1:40.2
1964	Marielle Goitschel (FRA) 1:52.24	Christine Goitschel (FRA) 1:53.11	Jean Saubert (USA) 1:53.11
1968	Nancy Greene (CAN) 1:51.97	Annie Famose (FRA) 1:54.61	Fernande Bochatay (SUI) 1:54.74
1972	Marie-Therese Nadig (SUI) 1:29.90	Annemarie Pröll (AUT) 1:30.75	Wiltrud Drexel (AUT) 1:32.35
1976	Kathy Kreiner (CAN) 1:29.13	Rosi Mittermaier (GER) 1:29.25	Danielle Debernard (FRA) 1:29.95
1980	Hanni Wenzel (LIE) 2:41.66	Irene Epple (GER) 2:42.12	Perrine Pelen (FRA) 2:42.41
1984	Debbie Armstrong (USA) 2:20.98	Christin Cooper (USA) 2:21.38	Perrine Pelen (FRA) 2:21.40

Gretchen Fraser (USA) won the women's slalom race the first time it was contested, in 1948 at St. Mortiz.

Rosi Mittermaier of West Germany won 2 golds and one silver in women's Alpine skiing events at Innsbruck in 1976.

SLALOM

	GOLD	SILVER	BRONZE
1908–1936	Event not held		
1948	Gretchen Fraser (USA) 1:57.2	Antoinette Meyer (SUI) 1:57.7	Erika Mahringer (AUT) 1:58.0
1952	Andrea Lawrence-Mead (USA) 2:10.6	Ossi Reichert (GER) 2:11.4	Annemarie Buchner (GER) 2:13.3
1956	Renée Colliard (SUI) 1:52.3	Regina Schöpf (AUT) 1:55.4	Jevginija Sidorova (URS) 1:56.7
1960	Anne Heggtveit (CAN) 1:49.6	Betsy Snite (USA) 1:52.9	Barbi Henneberger (GER) 1:56.6
1964	Christine Goitschel (FRA) 1:29.86	Marielle Goitschel (FRA) 1:30.77	Jean Saubert (USA) 1:31.36

	GOLD	SILVER	BRONZE
1968	Marielle Goitschel (FRA) 1:25.86	Nancy Greene (CAN) 1:26.15	Annie Famose (FRA) 1:27.89
1972	Barbara Cochran (USA) 1:31.24	Danielle Debernard (FRA) 1:31.26	Florence Steurer (FRA) 1:32.69
1976	Rosi Mittermaier (GER) 1:30.54	Claudia Giordani (ITA) 1:30.87	Hanny Wenzel (LIE) 1:32.20
1980	Hanni Wenzel (LIE) 1:25.09	Christa Kinshofer (GER) 1:26.50	Erika Hess (SUI) 1:27.89
1984	Paolette Magoni (ITA) 1:36.47	Perrine Pelen (FRA) 1:37.38	Ursula Konsett (LIE) 1:37.50

DOWNHILL

	GOLD	SILVER	BRONZE
1908–1936	Event not held		
1948	Hedy Schlunegger (SUI) 2:28.3	Trude Beiser (AUT) 2:29.1	Resi Hammerer (AUT) 2:30.2
1952	Trude Jochum-Beiser (AUT) 1:47.1	Annemarie Buchner (GER) 1:48.0	Giuliana Minuzzo (ITA) 1:49.0
1956	Madeleine Berthod (SUI) 1:40.7	Frieda Dänzer (SUI) 1:45.4	Lucile Wheeler (CAN) 1:45.9
1960	Heidi Biebl (GER) 1:37.6	Penelope Pitou (USA) 1:38.6	Traudl Hecher (AUT) 1:38.9
1964	Christl Haas (AUT) 1:55.39	Edith Zimmerman (AUT) 1:56.42	Traudl Hecher (AUT) 1:56.66
1968	Olga Pall (AUT) 1:40.87	Isabelle Mir (FRA) 1:41.33	Christl Haas (AUT) 1:41.41
1972	Marie-Therese Nadig (SUI) 1:36.68	Annemarie Pröll (AUT) 1:37.00	Susan Corrock (USA) 1:37.68
1976	Rosi Mittermaier (GER) 1:46.16	Brigitte Totschnig (AUT) 1:46.68	Cindy Nelson (USA) 1:47.50
1980	Annemarie Moser-Pröll (AUT) 1:37.52	Hanni Wenzel (LIE) 1:38.22	Marie-Therese Nadig (SUI) 1:38.36
1984	Michela Figini (SUI) 1:13.36	Maria Walliser (SUI) 1:13.41	Olga Chartova (TCH) 1:13.53

ALPINE COMBINATION

	GOLD	SILVER	BRONZE
1908–1932	Event not held		
1936	Christel Cranz (GER) 97.06pts	Kathe Grasegger (GER) 95.26	Laila Schou Nilsen (NOR) 93.48
1948	Trude Beiser (AUT) 6.58pts	Gretchen Fraser (USA) 6.95	Erika Mahringer (AUT) 7.04
1952–1984	Event not held		

RIGHT: Hanni Wenzel, from the tiny Principality of Liechtenstein (66 sq. miles), won gold medals in the slalom and giant slalom, as well as the silver medal in the downhill, at the 1980 Winter Games.

3. Figure Skating (Men)

	GOLD	SILVER	BRONZE
1908	Ulrich Salchow (SWE) 1,886.5 pts.	Richard Johansson (SWE) 1,826.0 pts.	Per Thorén (SWE) 1,787.0 pts.
1920	Gillis Grafström (SWE) 2,838.5 pts.	Andreas Krogh (NOR) 2,634 pts.	Martin Stixrud (NOR) 2,561.5 pts.
1924	Gillis Grafström (SWE) 2,575.25 pts.	Willy Böckl (AUT) 2,518.75 pts.	Georges Gautschi (SUI) 2,233.5 pts.
1928	Gillis Grafström (SWE) 2,698.25 pts.	Willy Böckl (AUT) 2,682.50 pts.	Robert v. Zeebroeck (BEL) 2,578.75 pts.
1932	Karl Schäfer (AUT) 2,602.0 pts.	Gillis Grafström (SWE) 2,514.5 pts.	Montgomery Wilson (CAN) 2,448.3 pts.
1936	Karl Schäfer (AUT) 2,959.0 pts.	Ernst Baier (GER) 2,805.3 pts.	Felix Kaspar (AUT) 2,801.0 pts.
1948	Richard Button (USA) 1,720.6 pts.	Hans Gerschwiler (SUI) 1,630.1 pts.	Edi Rada (AUT) 1,603.2 pts.
1952	Richard Button (USA) 1,730.3 pts.	Helmut Seibt (AUT) 1,621.3 pts.	James Grogan (USA) 1,627.4 pts.
1956	Hayes Alan Jenkins (USA) 1,497.95 pts.	Ronald Robertson (USA) 1,492.15 pts.	David Jenkins (USA) 1,465.41 pts.
1960	David Jenkins (USA) 1,440.2 pts.	Jarol Divin (TCH) 1,414.3 pts.	Donald Jackson (CAN) 1,401.0 pts.
1964	Manfred Schnelldorfer (GER) 1,916.9 pts.	Alain Calmat (FRA) 1,876.5 pts.	Scott Allen (USA) 1,873.6 pts.
1968	Wolfgang Schwartz (AUT) 1,094.1 pts.	Timothy Wood (USA) 1,891.6 pts.	Patrick Péra (FRA) 1,864.5 pts.
1972	Ondrej Nepela (TCH) 2,739.1 pts.	Sergei Chetverukhin (URS) 2,672.4 pts.	Patrick Péra (FRA) 2,653.1 pts.
1976	John Curry (GBR) 192.74 pts.	Vladimir Kovalev (URS) 187.64 pts.	Toller Cranston (CAN) 187.38 pts.
1980	Robin Cousins (GBR) 189.48 pts.	Jan Hoffmann (GDR) 189.72 pts.	Charles Tickner (USA) 187.06 pts.
1984	Scott Hamilton (USA) 3.4pl	Brian Orser (CAN) 5.6	Jozef Sabovtchik (TCH) 7.4

Figure Skating (Women)

1908	E. Madge Syers (GBR) 1,262.5 pts.	Elsa Rendschmidt (GER) 1,055.0 pts.	Dorothy Greenhough-Smith (GBR) 960.5 pts.
1920	Magda Julin-Mauroy (SWE) 913.5 pts.	Svea Norén (SWE) 887.75 pts.	Theresa Weld (USA) 898.0 pts.
1924	Herma Planck-Szabo (AUT) 2,094.25 pts.	Beatrix Loughran (USA) 1,959.0 pts.	Ethel Muckelt (GBR) 1,750.50 pts.
1928	Sonja Henie (NOR) 2,452.25 pts.	Fritzi Burger (AUT) 2,248.50 pts.	Beatrix Loughran (USA) 2,254.50 pts.
1932	Sonja Henie (NOR) 2,302.5 pts.	Fritzi Burger (AUT) 2,167.1 pts.	Maribel Vinson (USA) 2,158.5 pts.
1936	Sonja Henie (NOR) 2,971.4 pts.	Cecilia Colledge (GBR) 2,926.8 pts.	Vivi-Anne Hultén (SWE) 2,763.2 pts.
1948	Barbara Scott (CAN) 1,467.7 pts.	Efa Pawlik (AUT) 1,418.3 pts.	Jeanette Altwegg (GBR) 1,405.5 pts.

GOLD	SILVER	BRONZE
1952 Jeanette Altwegg (GBR) 1,455.8 pts.	Tenley Albright (USA) 1,432.2 pts.	Jacqueline du Bief (FRA) 1,422.0 pts.
1956 Tenley Albright (USA) 1,866.39 pts.	Carol Heiss (USA) 1,848.24 pts.	Ingrid Wendl (AUT) 1,753.91 pts.
1960 Carol Heiss (USA) 1,490.1 pts.	Sjoukje Dijkstra (HOL) 1,424.8 pts.	Barbara Roles (USA) 1,414.8 pts.
1964 Sjoukje Dijkstra (HOL) 2,018.5 pts.	Regine Heitzer (AUT) 1,945.5 pts.	Petra Burka (CAN) 1,940.0 pts.
1968 Peggy Fleming (USA) 1,970.5 pts.	Gabrielle Seyfert (GDR) 1,882.3 pts.	Hana Maskova (TCH) 1,828.8 pts.
1972 Beatrix Schuba (AUT) 2,751.5 pts.	Karen Magnussen (CAN) 2,673.2 pts.	Janet Lynn (USA) 2,663.1 pts.
1976 Dorothy Hamill (USA) 193.80 pts.	Dianne De Leeuw (HOL) 190.24 pts.	Christine Errath (GDR) 188.16 pts.
1980 Anett Poetzsch (GDR) 189.00 pts.	Linda Fratianne (USA) 188.30 pts.	Dagmar Lurz (GER) 183.04 pts.
1984 Katarina Witt (GDR) 3.2pl	Rosalyn Sumners (USA) 4.6	Kira Ivanova (URS) 9.2

PAIRS

GOLD	SILVER	BRONZE
1908 Anna Hübler Heinrich Burger (GER) 56.0 pts.	Phyllis W. Johnson James H. Johnson (GBR) 51.5 pts.	Madge Syers Edgar Syers (GBR) 48.0 pts.
1920 Ludovika Jakobsson Walter Jakobsson (FIN) 80.75 pts.	Alexia Bryn Yngvar Bryn (NOR) 72.75 pts.	Phyllis W. Johnson Basi Williams (GBR) 66.25 pts.
1924 Helene Engelmann Alfred Berger (AUT) 74.50 pts.	Ludovika Jakobsson Walter Jakobsson (FIN) 71.75 pts.	Andrée Joly Pierre Brunet (FRA) 69.25 pts.
1928 Andrée Joly Pierre Brunet (FRA) 100.50 pts.	Lilly Scholz Otto Kaiser (AUT) 99.25 pts.	Melitta Brunner Ludwig Wrede (AUT) 93.25 pts.
1932 Andrée Brunet Pierre Brunet (FRA) 76.7 pts.	Beatrix Loughran Sherwin Badger (USA) 77.5 pts.	Emilia Rotter László Szollás (HUN) 76.4 pts.
1936 Maxi Herber Ernst Baier (GER) 103.3 pts.	Ilse Pausin Erik Pausin (AUT) 102.7 pts.	Emilia Rotter László Szollás (HUN) 97.6 pts.
1948 Micheline Lannoy Pierre Baugniet (BEL) 123.5 pts.	Andrea Kékessy Ede Király (HUN) 122.2 pts.	Suzanne Morrow Wallace Diestelmeyer (CAN) 121.0 pts.
1952 Ria Falk Paul Falk (GER) 102.6 pts.	Karol Estelle Kennedy Michael Kennedy (USA) 100.6 pts.	Marianna Nagy László Nagy (HUN) 97.4 pts.
1956 Elisabeth Schwarz Kurt Oppelt (AUT) 101.8 pts.	Frances Dafoe Norris Bowden (CAN) 101.9 pts	Marianna Nagy László Nagy (HUN) 99.3 pts.
1960 Barbara Wagner Robert Paul (CAN) 80.4 pts.	Marika Kilius Hansjürgen Bäumler (GER) 76.8 pts.	Nancy Ludington Ronald Ludington (USA) 76.2 pts.
1964[1] Ludmilla Belousova Oleg Protopopov (URS) 104.4 pts.	Debbie Wilkes Guy Revell (CAN) 98.5 pts.	Vivian Joseph Ronald Joseph (USA) 98.2 pts.
1968 Ludmilla Belousova Oleg Protopopov (URS) 315.2 pts.	Tatiana Chesternyava Alexander Gorelik (URS) 312.3 pts.	Margo Glockshuber Wolfgang Danne (GER) 304.4 pts.

1972	Irina Rodnina Alexei Ulanov (URS) 420.4 pts.	Ludmila Smirnova Andrei Suraikin (URS) 419.4 pts.	Manuela Gross Uwe Kagelmann (GDR) 411.8 pts.
1976	Irina Rodnina Aleksander Zaitsev (URS) 140.54 pts.	Romy Kermer Rolf Oesterreich (GDR) 136.35 pts.	Manuela Grosse Uwe Kagelmann (GDR) 134.57 pts.
1980	Irina Rodina Aleksander Zaitsev (URS) 147.26 pts.	Marina Tcherkosova Sergey Shakrai (URS) 143.80 pts.	Manuela Mager Uwe Bewersdorff (GDR) 140.52 pts.
1984	Elena Valova Oleg Vassilyev (URS) 1.4pl	Kitty Carruthers Peter Carruthers (USA) 2.8	Larissa Selezneyva Oleg Makarov (URS) 3.8

---

[1] Marika Kilius and Hansjürgen Bäumler (GER) finished second but were subsequently disqualified.

Scott Hamilton (US) dazzled the 1984 Olympic spectators with his performance in figure skating, and won the gold medal.

ICE DANCE

1908–1972	Event not held		
1976	Ludmila Pakhomova Aleksander Gorshkov (URS) 209.92 pts.	Irina Moiseyeva Andrei Minenkov (URS) 204.88 pts.	Colleen O'Connor James Millns (USA) 202.64 pts.
1980	Natalya Linichuk Gennadiy Karponosov (URS) 205.48 pts.	Krisztina Regoczy Andras Sallay (HUN) 204.52 pts.	Irina Moiseyeva Andrei Minenkov (URS) 201.86 pts.
1984	Jayne Torvill Christopher Dean (GBR) 2.0pl	Natalya Bestemyanova Andrei Bukin (URS) 4.0	Marina Klimova Sergey Ponomarenko (URS) 7.0

4. Speed Skating (Men)

500 METERS

1908–1920 Event not held		
1924 Charles Jewtraw (USA) 44.0*	Oskar Olsen (NOR) 44.2	Roald Larsen (NOR) 44.8 Clas Thunberg (FIN) 44.8
1928 Clas Thunberg (FIN) 43.4* Bernt Evensen (NOR) 43.4*		John O'Neil Farrell (USA) 43.6 Roald Larsen (NOR 43.6 Jaako Friman (FIN) 43.6
1932 John Amos Shea (USA) 43.4*	Bernt Evensen (NOR) d.n.a.	Alexander Hurd (CAN) d.n.a.
1936 Ivar Ballangrud (NOR) 43.4*	Georg Krog (NOR) 43.5	Leo Freisinger (USA) 44.0
1948 Finn Helgesen (NOR) 43.1*	Kenneth Bartholomew (USA) 43.2 Thomas Byberg (NOR) 43.2 Robert Fitzgerald (USA) 43.2	
1952 Kenneth Henry (USA) 43.2	Donald McDermott (USA) 43.9	Arne Johansen (NOR) 44.0 Gordon Audley (CAN) 44.0
1956 Yevgeniy Grischin (URS) 40.2*	Rafael Gratsch (URS) 40.8	Alv Gjestvang (NOR) 41.0
1960 Yevgeniy Grischin (URS) 40.2*	William Disney (USA) 40.3	Rafael Gratsch (URS) 40.4
1964 Richard McDermott (USA) 40.1*	Yevgeniy Grischin (URS) 40.6 Vladimir Orlov (URS) 40.6 Alv Gjestvang (NOR) 40.6	
1968 Erhard Keller (GER) 40.3	Richard McDermott (USA) 40.5 Magne Thomassen (NOR) 40.5	
1972 Erhard Keller (GER) 39.44*	Hasse Borjes (SWE) 39.69	Valeriy Muratov (URS) 39.80
1976 Evgeniy Kulikov (URS) 39.17*	Valeriy Muratov (URS) 39.25	Daniel Immerfall (USA) 39.54
1980 Eric Heiden (USA) 38.03*	Yevgeniy Kulikov (URS) 38.37	Lieuwe de Boer (HOL) 38.48
1984 Sergey Fokitchev (URS) 38.19	Yoshihiro Kitazawa (JPN) 38.30	Gaetan Boucher (CAN) 38.39

1,000 METERS

GOLD	SILVER	BRONZE
1909–1972 Event not held		
1976 Peter Mueller (USA) 1:19.32*	Jorn Didriksen (NOR) 1:20.45	Valeriy Muratov (URS) 1:20.57
1980 Eric Heiden (USA) 1:15.18*	Gaetan Boucher (CAN) 1:16.68	Frode Ronning (NOR) 1:16.91 Vladimir Lobanov (URS) 1:16.91

| 1984 | Gaetan Boucher (CAN) 1:15.80 | Sergey Khlebnikov (URS) 1:16.63 | Kai Arne Engelstad (NOR) 1:16.75 |

1,500 METERS

1908–1920	Event not held		
1924	Clas Thunberg (FIN) 2:20.8*	Roald Larsen (NOR) 2:22.0	Sigurd Moen (NOR) 2:25.6
1928	Clas Thunberg (FIN) 2:21.1	Bernt Evensen (NOR) 2:21.9	Ivar Ballangrud (NOR) 2:22.6
1932	John Amos Shea (USA) 2:57.5	Alexander Hurd (CAN) d.n.a.	William F. Logan (CAN) d.n.a.
1936	Charles Mathiesen (NOR) 2:19.2*	Ivar Ballangrud (NOR) 2:20.2	Birger Wasenius (FIN) 2:20.9
1948	Sverre Farstad (NOR) 2:17.6*	Ake Seyffarth (SWE) 2:18.1	Odd Lundberg (NOR) 2:18.9
1952	Hjalmar Andersen (NOR) 2:20.4	Willem van der Voort (HOL) 2:20.6	Roald Aas (NOR) 2:21.6
1956	Yevgeniy Grischin (URS) 2:08.6 Yuriy Michailov (URS) 2:08.6		Toivo Salonen (FIN) 2:09.4
1960	Roald Aas (NOR) 2:10.4 Yevgeniy Grischin (URS) 2:10.4		Boris Stenin (URS) 2:11.5
1964	Ants Antson (URS) 2:10.3	Cornelis Verkerk (HOL) 2:10.6	Villy Haugen (NOR) 2:11.25
1968	Cornelis Verkerk (HOL) 2:03.4*	Ard Schenk (HOL) 2:05.0 Ivar Eriksen (NOR) 2:05.0	
1972	Ard Schenk (HOL) 2:02.96*	Roar Gronvold (NOR) 2:04.26	Goran Clässon (SWE) 2:05.89
1976	Jan Egil Storholt (NOR) 1:59.38*	Yuriy Kondakov (URS) 1:59.97	Hans Van Helden (HOL) 2:00.87
1980	Eric Heiden (USA) 1:53.44*	Kai Stenshjemmet (NOR) 1:56.81	Terje Andersen (NOR) 1:56.92
1984	Gaetan Boucher (CAN) 1:58.36	Sergey Khlebnikov (URS) 1:58.83	Oleg Bogiev (URS) 1:58.89

5,000 METERS

1908–1920	Event not held		
1924	Clas Thunberg (FIN) 8:39.0*	Julius Skutnabb (FIN) 8:48.4	Roald Larsen (NOR) 8:50.2
1928	Ivar Ballangrud (NOR) 8:50.5	Julius Skutnabb (FIN) 8:59.1	Bernt Evensen (NOR) 9:01.1
1932	Irving Jaffee (USA) 9:40.8	Edward S. Murphy (USA) d.n.a.	William F. Logan (CAN) d.n.a.
1936	Ivar Ballangrud (NOR) 8:19.6*	Birger Wasenius (FIN) 8:23.3	Antero Ojala (FIN) 8:30.1
1948	Reidar Liaklev (NOR) 8:29.4	Odd Lundberg (NOR) 8:32.7	Göthe Hedlund (SWE) 8:34.8
1952	Hjalmar Andersen (NOR) 8:10.6*	Kees Broekman (HOL) 8:21.6	Sverre Haugli (NOR) 8:22.4
1956	Boris Schilkov (URS) 7:48.7*	Sigvard Ericsson (SWE) 7:56.7	Oleg Gontscharenko (URS) 7:57.5
1960	Viktor Kositschkin (URS) 7:51.3	Knut Johannesen (NOR) 8:00.8	Jan Pesman (HOL) 8:05.1
1964	Knut Johannesen (NOR) 7:38.4*	P. Moe (NOR) 7:38.6	F. Anton Maier (NOR) 7:42.0

GOLD	SILVER	BRONZE
1968 F. Anton Maier (NOR) 7:22.4*	Cornelis Verkerk (HOL) 7:23.2	Petrus Nottet (HOL) 7:25.5
1972 Ard Schenk (HOL) 7:23.6	Roar Gronvold (NOR) 7:28.18	Sten Stensen (NOR) 7:33.39
1976 Sten Stensen (NOR) 7:24.48	Piet Kleine (HOL) 7:26.47	Hans Van Helden (HOL) 7:26.54
1980 Eric Heiden (USA) 7:02.29*	Kai Stenshjemmet (NOR) 7:03.28	Tom Oxholm (NOR) 7:05.59
1984 Tomas Gustafsson (SWE) 7:12.28	Igor Malkov (URS) 7:12.30	Rene Schoefisch (GDR) 7:17.49

10,000 METERS

GOLD	SILVER	BRONZE
1908–1920 Event not held		
1924 Julius Sknutnabb (FIN) 18:04.8*	Clas Thunberg (FIN) 18:07.8	Roald Larsen (NOR) 18:12.2
1928 Event abandoned		
1932 Irving Jaffee (USA) 19:13.6	Ivar Ballangrud (NOR) d.n.a.	Frank Stack (CAN) d.n.a.
1936 Ivar Ballangrud (NOR) 17:24.3*	Birger Wasenius (FIN) 17:28.2	Max Stiepl (AUT) 17:30.0
1948 Ake Seyffarth (SWE) 17:26.3	Lauri Parkkinen (FIN) 17:36.0	Pentti Lammio (FIN) 17:42.7
1952 Hjalmar Andersen (NOR) 16:45.8*	Kees Broekman (HOL) 17:10.6	Carl-Erik Asplund (SWE) 17:16.6
1956 Sigvard Ericsson (SWE) 16:35.9*	Knut Johannesen (NOR) 16:36.9	Oleg Gontscharenko (URS) 16:42.3

Eric Heiden (USA) earned an unprecedented sweep of all five speed skating gold medals at Lake Placid, setting an Olympic record in each event.

	GOLD	SILVER	BRONZE
1960	Knut Johannesen (NOR) 15:46.6*	Viktor Kositschkin (URS) 15:49.2	Kjell Bäckman (SWE) 16:14.2
1964	Johnny Nilsson (SWE) 15:50.1	F. Anton Maier (NOR) 16:06.0	Knut Johannesen (Nor) 16:06.3
1968	Johnny Hoeglin (SWE) 15:23.6*	F. Anton Maier (NOR) 15:23.9	Orejan Sandler (SWE) 15:31.8
1972	Ard Schenk (HOL) 15:01.35*	Cornelis Verkerk (HOL) 15:04.70	Sten Stensen (NOR) 15:07.08
1976	Piet Kleine (HOL) 14:50.59*	Sten Stensen (NOR) 14:53.30	Hans Van Helden (HOL) 15:02.02
1980	Eric Heiden (USA) 14:28.13*	Piet Kleine (HOL) 14:36.03	Tom Oxholm (NOR) 14:36.60
1984	Igor Malkov (URS) 14:39.90	Tomas Gustafsson (SWE) 14:39.95	Rene Schoefisch (GDR) 14:46.91

Former world cycling champion Sheila Young (USA) won gold, silver and bronze medals in the 1976 speed skating competition.

Speed Skating (Women)

1908–1956 Events not held, but in 1932 there were three demonstration events for women speed skaters.

500 METERS

1960	Helga Hasse (GER) 45.9*	Natalie Dontschenko (URS) 46.0	Jeanne Ashworth (USA) 46.1
1964	Lydia Skoblikova (URS) 45.0*	Irina Yegorova (URS) 45.4	Tatyana Sidorova (URS) 45.5
1968	Ludmila Titova (URS) 46.1	Mary Meyers (USA) 46.3 Dianne Holum (USA) 46.3 Jennifer Fish (USA) 46.3	No bronze award

The Russian speed skater Lydia Skoblikova won a record 6 Olympic gold medals in the 1960 and 1964 Games.

	GOLD	SILVER	BRONZE
1972	Anne Henning (USA) 43.33*	Vera Krasnova (URS) 44.01	Ludmila Titova (URS) 44.45
1976	Sheila Young (USA) 42.76*	Catherine Priestner (CAN) 43.12	Tatyana Averina (URS) 43.17
1980	Karin Enke (GDR) 41.78*	Leah Mueller (USA) 42.26	Natalya Petruseva (URS) 42.42
1984	Christa Rothenburger (GDR) 41.02*	Karin Enke (GDR) 41.28	Natalya Chive (URS) 41.50

1,000 METERS

	GOLD	SILVER	BRONZE
1960	Klala Guseva (URS) 1:34.1*	Helga Haase (GER) 1:34.3	Tamara Rylova (URS) 1:34.8
1964	Lydia Skoblikova (URS) 1:33.2*	Irina Yegorova (URS) 1:34.3	Kaija Mustonen (FIN) 1:34.8
1968	Carolina Geijssen (HOL) 1:32.6	Ludmila Titova (URS) 1:32.9	Dianne Holum (USA) 1:33.4
1972	Monika Pflug (GER) 1:31.40*	Atje Keulen-Deelstra (HOL) 1:31.61	Anne Henning (USA) 1:31.62
1976	Tatyana Averina (URS) 1:28.43*	Leah Poulos (USA) 1:28.57	Sheila Young (USA) 1:29.14
1980	Natalya Petruseva (URS) 1:24.10*	Leah Mueller (USA) 1:25.41	Sylvia Albrecht (GDR) 1:26.46
1984	Karin Enke (GDR) 1:21.61*	Andrea Schoene (GDR) 1:22.83	Natalya Petruseva (URS) 1:23.21

Karin Enke Kania of East Germany, after winning her first Olympic gold at 500 meters in 1980, won 2 more golds in 1984 at 1,000 and 1,500 meters and silvers at 500 and 2,000 meters.

1,500 METERS

	GOLD	SILVER	BRONZE
1960	Lydia Skoblikova (URS) 2:25.2*	Elvira Seroczynska (POL) 2:25.7	Helena Pilejeyk (POL) 2:27.1
1964	Lydia Skoblikova (URS) 2:22.6*	Kaija Mustonen (FIN) 2:25.5	Berta Kolokoltseva (URS) 2:27.1
1968	Kaija Mustonen (FIN) 2:22.4*	Carolina Geijssen (HOL) 2:22.7	Christina Kaiser (HOL) 2:24.5
1972	Dianne Holum (USA) 2:20.85*	Christina Baas-Kaiser (HOL) 2:21.05	Atje Keulen-Deelstra (HOL) 2:22.05
1976	Galina Stepanskaya (URS) 2:16.58*	Sheila Young (USA) 2:17.06	Tatyana Averina (URS) 2:17.96
1980	Annie Borckink (HOL) 2:10.95*	Ria Visser (HOL) 2:12.35	Sabine Becker (GDR) 2:12.38
1984	Karin Enke (GDR) 2:03.42*	Andrea Schoene (GDR) 2:05.29	Natalya Petruseva (URS) 2:05.78

3,000 METERS

	GOLD	SILVER	BRONZE
1960	Lydia Skoblikova (URS) 5:14.3*	Valentina Stenina (URS) 5:16.9	Eevi Huttunen (FIN) 5:21.0
1964	Lydia Skoblikova (URS) 5:14.9	Valentina Stenina (URS) 5:18.5 Pil-Hwa Han (PRK) 5:18,5	
1968	Johanna Schut (HOL) 4:56.2*	Kaija Mustonen (FIN) 5:01.0	Christina Kaiser (HOL) 5:01.3
1972	Christina Baas-Kaiser (HOL) 4:52.14*	Dianne Holum (USA) 4:58.67	Atje Keulen-Deelstra (HOL) 4:59.91
1976	Tatyana Averina (URS) 4:45.19*	Andrea Mitscherlich (GDR) 4:45.23	Lisbeth Korsmo (NOR) 4:45.24
1980	Bjorg Eva Jensen (NOR) 4:32.13*	Sabine Becker (GDR) 4:32.79	Beth Heiden (USA) 4:33.77
1984	Andrea Schoene (GDR) 4:24.79*	Karin Enke (GDR) 4:26.33	Gabi Schoenbrunn (GDR) 4:33.13

5. Bobsleigh

2-MAN BOB

1908–1928 Event not held		
1932 **UNITED STATES I**	**SWITZERLAND II**	**UNITED STATES II**
8:14.74	8:16.28	8:29.15
J. Hubert Stevens	R. Capadrutt	J. R. Heaton
Curtis P. Stevens	O. Geier	R. Minton
1936 **UNITED STATES I**	**SWITZERLAND II**	**UNITED STATES II**
5:29.29	5:30.64	5:33.96
Ivan Brown	F. Feierabend	G. Colgate
Alan Washbond	J. Beerli	R. Lawrence
1948 **SWITZERLAND II**	**SWITZERLAND I**	**UNITED STATES II**
5:29.2	5:30.4	5:35.3
Felix Endrich	F. Feierabend	F. Fortune
Friedrich Waller	P. Eberhard	S. Carron
1952 **GERMANY I**	**UNITED STATES I**	**SWITZERLAND I**
5:24.54	5:26.89	5:27.71
Andreas Ostler	S. Benham	F. Feierabend
Lorenz Nieberl	P. Martin	S. Waser
1956 **ITALY I**	**ITALY II**	**SWITZERLAND I**
5:30.14	5:31.45	5:37.46
Lamberto Dall Costa	Eugenio Monti	M. Angst
Giacomo Conti	R. Alvera	H. Warburton
1960 Event not held		
1964 **GREAT BRITAIN**	**ITALY II**	**ITALY I**
4:21.90	4:22.02	4:22.63
Anthony J. D. Nash	S. Zardini	Eugenio Monti
The Hon. Robin Dixon	R. Bonagura	S. Siorpaes
1968 **ITALY I**	**WEST GERMANY I**	**RUMANIA I**
4:41.54	4:41.54	4:44.46
Eugenio Monti	Horst Floth	Ion Panturu
Luciano de Paolis	Pepi Bader	Nicolae Neagoe
1972 **WEST GERMANY II**	**WEST GERMANY I**	**SWITZERLAND I**
4:57.07	4:58.84	4:59.33
Wolfgang Zimmerer	Horst Floth	Jean Wicki
Peter Utzschneider	Pepi Bader	Egy Hubacher
1976 **EAST GERMANY II**	**GERMANY I**	**SWITZERLAND I**
3:44.42	3:44.99	3:45.70
Meinhard Nehmer	Wolfgang Zimmerer	Erich Schaerer
Bernard Germeshausen	Manfred Schumann	Josef Benz

The winning US 4-man bobsled team of 1932, with Eddie Eagen in second position. Eagen, later head of the NY State Boxing Commission, is the only athlete to win gold medals in both Summer and Winter Games—his other medal being as light-heavyweight boxing champion in 1920.

GOLD	SILVER	BRONZE
1980 SWITZERLAND II 4:09.36	EAST GERMANY II 4:10.93	EAST GERMANY I 4:11.08
Erich Shaerer	Bernhard	Meinhard Nehmer
Josef Benz	Germeshausen	Bogdan Musiol
	Hans-Jurgen Gerhardt	
1984 GDR II 3:25.56	GDR I 3:26.04	USSR II 3:26.16
Wolfgang Hoppe	Bernhard Lehmann	Zintis Ekmanis
Dietmar Schauerhammer	Bogdan Musiol	Vladimir Aleksandrov

4-MAN BOB

GOLD	SILVER	BRONZE
1908–1920 Event not held		
1924 SWITZERLAND I 5:45.54	GREAT BRITAIN II 5:48.83	BELGIUM I 6:02.29
Eduard Scherrer	R. H. Broome	C. Mulder
Alfred Neveu	T. A. Arnold	R. Mortiaux
Alfred Schläppi	H. A. W. Richardson	P. v. d. Broeck
Heinrich Schläppi	R. E. Soher	V. A. Verschueren or
		H. P. Willems
1928 UNITED STATES II 3:20.5	UNITED STATES I 3:21.0	GERMANY II 3:21.9
(5-man event)		
William Fiske	J. Heaton	H. Kilian
Nion Tocker	D. Granger	V. Krempl
Charles Mason	L. Hine	H. Hess
Clifford Gray	T. Doe	S. Huber
Richard Parke	J. O'Brien	H. Nägle
1932 UNITED STATES I 7:53.68	UNITED STATES I 7:55.70	GERMANY I 8:00.04
William Fiske	H. Homburger	H. Kilian
Edward Eagen	P. Bryant	M. Ludwig
Clifford Gray	F. P. Stevens	Dr. H. Mehlhorn
Jay O'Brien	E. Horton	S. Huber
1936 SWITZERLAND II 5:19.85	SWITZERLAND II 5:22.73	GREAT BRITAIN 5:23.41
Pierre Mussy	R. Capadrutt	F. McEvoy
Arnold Gartmann	H. Aichele	J. Cardno
Charles Bouvier	F. Feierabend	G. Dugdale
Joseph Beerli	H. Bütikofer	C. Green
1948 UNITED STATES II 5:20.1	BELGIUM 5:21.3	UNITED STATES I 5:21.5
Francis Tyler	M. Houben	J. Bickford
Patrick Martin	F. Mansveld	T. Hicks
Edward Rimkus	G. Niels	D. Dupree
William D'Amico	J. Mouvet	W. Dupree
1952 GERMANY 5:07.84	UNITED STATES I 5:10.48	SWITZERLAND I 5:11.70
Andreas Ostler	S. Benham	F. Feierabend
Friedrich Kuhn	P. Martin	A. Madörin
Lorenz Nieberl	H. Crossett	A. Filippini
Franz Kemser	J. Atkinson	S. Waser
1956 SWITZERLAND I 5:10.44	ITALY II 5:12.10	UNITED STATES 5:12.39
Franz Kapus	Eugenio Monti	A. Tyler
Gottfried Diener	U. Girardi	W. Dodge
Robert Alt	R. Alvera	C. Butler
Heinrich Angst	R. Mocellini	J. Lamy
1960 Event not held		
1964 CANADA I 4:14.46	AUSTRIA I 4:15.48	ITALY II 4:15.60
Victor Emery	Erwin Thaler	Eugenio Monti
Peter Kirby	A. Knoxeder	S. Siorpaes
Douglas Anakin	J. Nairz	B. Rigoni
John Emery	Reinhold Durnthaler	G. Siorpaes

GOLD	SILVER	BRONZE
1968 **ITALY I** 2:17.39	**AUSTRAIA I** 2:17.48	**SWITZERLAND** 2:18.04
Eugenio Monti	Erwin Thaler	Jean Wicki
Luciano De Paolis	Reinhold Durnthaler	Hans Candrian
Roberto Zandonella	Herbert Gruber	Willi Hofmann
Mario Armano	Josef Eder	Walter Graf
1972 **SWITZERLAND I** 4:43.07	**ITALY I** 4:43.83	**WEST GERMANY I** 4:43.92
Jean Wicki	Nevio de Zordo	Wolfgang Zimmerer
Edy Hubacher	G. Bonichon	Peter Utzschneider
Hans Leutenegger	Adriano Frassinelli	Stefan Gaisreister
Werner Camichel	C. dal Fabbo	Walter Steinbauer
1976 **EAST GERMANY I** 3:40.43	**SWITZERLAND II** 3:40.89	**GERMANY I** 3:41.37
Meinhard Nehmer	Erich Schaerer	Wolfgang Zimmerer
Jochen Babok	Ulrich Baechli	Peter Utzschneider
Bernhard Germeshausen	Rudolf Marti	Bodo Bittner
Bernhard Lehmann	Josef Benz	Manfred Schumann
1980 **EAST GERMANY I** 3:59.92	**SWITZERLAND I** 4:00.87	**EAST GERMANY II** 4:00.97
Meinhard Nehmer	Erich Shaerer	Horst Schonau
Bogdan Musiol	Ulrich Baechli	Roland Wetzig
Bernhard Germeshausen	Rudolf Marti	Detlef Richter
Hans-Jurgen Gerhardt	Josef Benz	Andreas Kirchner
1984 **GDR I** 3:20.22	**GDR II** 3:20.78	**SWITZERLAND I** 3:21.39
Wolfgang Hoppe	Bernhard Lehmann	Silvio Giobellina
Roland Wetzig	Bogdan Musiol	Heinz Stettler
Dietmar Schauerhammer	Ingo Voge	Urs Salzmann
Andreas Kirchner	Eberhard Weise	Rico Freiermuth

6. Tobogganing (Lugeing)

SINGLE SEATER—MEN

1908–1960 Event not held		
1964 Thomas Koehler (GER) 3:26.77	Klaus Bonsack (GER) 3:27.04	Hans Plenk (GER) 3:30.15
1968 Manfred Schmid (AUT) 2:52.48	Thomas Koehler (GDR) 2:52.66	Klaus Bonsack (GDR) 2:53.33
1972 Wolfgang Scheidel (GDR) 3:27.58	Harald Ehrig (GDR) 3:28.39	Wolfram Fiedler (GDR) 3:28.73
1976 Detlef Guenther (GDR) 3:27.688	Josef Fendt (GER) 3:28.196	Hans Rinn (GER) 3:28.574
1980 Bernhard Glass (GDR) 2:54.796	Paul Hildgartner (ITA) 2:55.372	Anton Winkler (GER) 2:56.545
1984 Paul Hildgartner (ITA) 3:04.258	Sergey Danilin (URS) 3:04.962	Valeriy Dudin (URS) 3:05.012

TWO-SEATER—MEN

GOLD	SILVER	BRONZE
1908–1960 Event not held		
1964 **AUSTRIA** 1:41.62	**AUSTRIA** 1:41.91	**ITALY** 1:42.87
Josef Feistmantl	Reinhold Senn	W. Aussendorfer
Manfred Stengl	H. Thaler	S. Mair
1968 **EAST GERMANY** 1:35.85	**AUSTRIA** 1:36.34	**GERMANY** 1:37.29
Klaus Bonsack	Manfred Schmid	Wolfgang Winkler
Thomas Koehler	Ewald Walch	Fritz Nachmann
1972 **ITALY** 1:28.35		**EAST GERMANY** 1:29.16
Paul Hildgartner		Klaus Bonsack
Walter Plaikner		Wolfram Fiedler
EAST GERMANY 1:28.35		
Horst Hornlein		
Reinhard Bredow		
1976 **EAST GERMANY** 1:25.604	**GERMANY** 1:25.889	**AUSTRIA** 1:25.919
Hans Rinn	Hans Brandner	Rudolf Schmid
Norbert Hahn	Balthasar Schwarm	Franz Schachner
1980 **EAST GERMANY** 1:19.331	**ITALY** 1:19.606	**AUSTRIA** 1:19.795
Hans Rinn	Peter Gschitzer	Georg Fluckinger
Norbert Hahn	Karl Brunner	Karl Schrott
1984 **WEST GERMANY** 1:23.620	**USSR** 1:23.660	**EAST GERMANY** 1:23.887
Hans Stangassinger	Evgeni Beloussov	Jörg Hoffmann
Franz Wembacher	Aleksandr Belyakov	Jochen Pietzsch

SINGLE-SEATER—WOMEN

1908–1960 Event not held		
1964 Otrun Enderlein (GER) 3:24.67	Ilse Geisler (GER) 3:27.42	Helene Thurner (AUT) 3:29.06
1968 Erica Lechner (ITA) 2:28.66	Christa Schmuck (GER) 2:29.37	Angelika Duenhaupt (GER) 2:29.56
1972 Anna-Maria Muller (GDR) 2:59.18	Ute Ruehrold (GDR) 2:59.49	Margit Schumann (GDR) 2:59.54
1976 Margit Schumann (GDR) 2:50.621	Ute Ruehrold (GDR) 2:50.846	Elisabeth Demleitner (GER) 2:51.056
1980 Vera Sosulya (URS) 2:36.537	Melitta Sollmann (GDR) 2:37.657	Ingrida Amantova (URS) 2:37.817
1984 Steffi Martin (GDR) 2:46.570	Bettine Schmidt (GDR) 2:46.873	Ute Weiss (GDR) 2:47.248

7. Ice Hockey

1908 Event not held

1920	CANADA	UNITED STATES	CZECHOSLOVAKIA
	Robert J. Benson	Raymond L. Bonney	Dr. Adolf Dusek
	Wally Byron	Anthony J. Conroy	Dr. Karel Hartmann
	Frank Frederickson	Herbert L. Drury	Vilém Loos
	Chris Fridfinnson	J. Edward Fitzgerald	Jan Pallausch
	Mike Goodman	George P. Geran	Jan Peka
	Haldor Halderson	Frank X. Goheen	Dr. Karel Pesek
	Konrad Johannesson	Joseph McCormick	Josef Sroubek
	A. "Huck" Woodman	Lawrence J. McCormick	Otakar Vindyš
		Frank A. Synott	
		Leon P. Tuck	
		Cyril Weidenborner	

1924	CANADA	UNITED STATES	GREAT BRITAIN
	Jack A. Cameron	Clarence J. Abel	W. H. Anderson
	Ernest J. Collett	Herbert L. Drury	Lorne H. Carr-Harris
	Albert J. McCaffery	Alphonse A. Lacroix	Colin G. Carruthers
	Harold E. McMunn	John A. Langley	Eric D. Carruthers
	Duncan B. Munro	John J. Lyons	Guy E. Clarkson
	W. Beattie Ramsay	Justin J. McCarthy	Ross Cuthbert
	Cyril S. Slater	Willard W. Rice	George Holmes
	Reginald J. Smith	Irving W. Small	Hamilton D. Jukes
	Harry E. Watson	Frank A. Synott	Edward B. Pitblado
			Blane N. Sexton

1928	CANADA	SWEDEN	SWITZERLAND
	Charles Delahay	Carl Abrahamsson	Giannin Andreossi
	Frank Fisher	Emil Bergman	Mezzi Andreossi
	Dr. Louis Hudson	Birger Holmqvist	Robert Breiter
	Norbert Mueller	Gustaf Johansson	Louis Dufour
	Herbert Plaxton	Henry Johansson	Charles Fasel
	Hugh Plaxton	Nils Johansson	Albert Geromini
	Roger Plaxton	Ernst Karlberg	Fritz Kraatz
	John G. Porter	Erik Larsson	Arnold Martignoni
	Frank Sullivan	Bertil Linde	Heini Meng
	Dr. Joseph Sullivan	Sigurd Oberg	Anton Morosani
	Ross Taylor	Vilhelm Petersen	Dr. Luzius Rüedi
	David Trottier	Kurt Sucksdorff	Richard Torriani

1932	CANADA	UNITED STATES	GERMANY
	William H. Cockburn	Osborn Anderson	Rudi Ball
	Clifford T. Crowley	John B. Bent	Alfred Heinrich
	Albert G. Duncanson	John Chase	Erich Herker
	George F. Garbutt	John E. Cookman	Gustav Jaenecke
	Roy Hinkel	Douglas N. Everett	Werner Korff
	C. Victor Lindquist	Franklin Farrell	Walter Leinwever
	Norman J. Malloy	Joseph F. Fitzgerald	Erich Römer
	Walter Monson	Edward M. Frazier	F. Marquardt Slevogt
	Kenneth S. Moore	John B. Garrison	Martin Schröttle
	N. Romeo Rivers	Gerard Hallock III	Georg Strobl
	Harold A. Simpson	Robert C. Livingston	
	Hugh R. Sutherland	Francis A. Nelson	
	W. Stanley Wagner	Winthrop H. Palmer	
	J. Aliston Wise	Gordon Smith	

1936	GREAT BRITAIN	CANADA	UNITED STATES
	Alexander Archer	Maxwell Deacon	John B. Garrison
	James Borland	Hugh Farquharson	August F. Kammer
	Edgar Brenchley	Kenneth Farmer	Philip W. LaBatte
	James Chappell	James Haggarty	John C. Lax
	John Coward	Walter Kitchen	Thomas H. Moone
	Gordon Dailley	Raymond Milton	Eldridge B. Ross
	John Davey	Francis W. Moore	Paul E. Rowe
	Carl Erhardt	Herman Murray	Francis J. Shaugnessy
	James Foster	Arthur Nash	Gordon Smith
	John Kilpatrick	David Neville	Francis J. Spain
	Archibald Stinchcombe	Ralph St. Germain	Frank R. Stubbs
	Robert Wyman	Alexander Sinclair	
		William Thomson	
1948	CANADA	CZECHOSLOVAKIA	SWITZERLAND
	Murray-Alb Dowey	Vladimir Bouzek	Hans Bänninger
	Bernard Dunster	Augustin Bubnik	Alfred Bieler
	Orval Gravelle	Jaroslav Drobny	Heinrich Boller
	Patrick Guzzo	Premsyl Hajny	Ferdinand Cattini
	Walter Halder	Zdenek Jarkovsky	Hans Cattini
	Thomas Hibbert	Stanislav Konopásek	Hans Dürst
	Ross King	Bohumil Modry	Walter Dürst
	Henri-André Laperrire	Miloslav Pokorny	Emil Handschin
	John Lecompte	Vaclay Rozinak	Heini Lohrer
	George A. Mara	Dr. Mirosláv Sláma	Werner Lohrer
	Albert Renaud	Karel Stibor	Reto Perl
	Reginald Schroeter	Vilém Stovik	Gebhard Poltera
		Ladislav Troják	Ulrich Poltera
		Josef Trousilek	Beat Ruedi
		Oldrich Zábrodsky	Otto Schubinger
		Vladimir Zábrodsky	Richard Torriani
			Hans Trepp
1952	CANADA	UNITED STATES	SWEDEN
	George G. Able	Ruben E. Bjorkman	Gote Almqvist
	John F. Davies	Leonard S. Ceglarski	Hans Andersson
	William Dawe	Joseph J. Czarnota	S. "Tvilling" Andersson
	Robert B. Dickson	Richard J. Desmond	Ake Andersson
	Donald V. Gauf	Andre P. Gambucci	Lars Bjorn
	William J. Gibson	Clifford N. Harrison	Gote Blomqvist
	Ralph L. Hansch	Gerald W. Kilmartin	Thord Flodqvist
	Robert R. Meyers	John F. Mulhern	Erik Johansson
	David E. Miller	Joyn M. Noah	Gosta Johansson
	Eric E. Paterson	Arnold C. Oss, Jr.	Rune Johansson
	Thomas A. Pollock	Robert E. Rompre	Sven Johansson
	Allan R. Purvis	James W. Sedin	Ake Lassas
	Gordon Robertson	Allen A. Van	Holger Nurmela
	Louis J. Secco	Donald F. Whiston	Hans Oberg
	Francis C. Sullivan	Kenneth J. Yackel	Lars Pettersson
	Robert Watt		Lars Svensson
			Sven Thunman

	GOLD	SILVER	BRONZE
1956	**U.S.S.R.**	**UNITED STATES**	**CANADA**
	Yevgeniy Babitsch	Wendell Anderson	Denis Brodeur
	Usevolod Bobrov	Wellington Burnett	Charles Brooker
	Nikolay Chlystov	Eugene Campbell	William Colvin
	Aleksey Guryschev	Gordon Christian	Alfred J. Horne
	Juriy Krylov	William Cleary	Arthur Hurst
	Alfred Kutschewskiy	Richard Dougherty	Byrle Klinck
	Vlanetin Kusin	Willard Ikola	Paul Knox
	Grigoriy Mkrttschan	John Matchefts	Kenneth Laufman
	Viktor Nikiforov	John Mayasich	Howard Lee
	Juriy Pantjuchov	Daniel McKinnon	James Logan
	Nikolay Putschkov	Richard Meredith	Floyd Martin
	Viktor Schuwalov	Weldon Olson	Jack McKenzie
	Genrich Sidorenkov	John E. Petroske	Donald Rope
	Nikolay Sologubov	Kenneth Purpur	Georges Scholes
	Ivan Tregubov	Ronald Rigazio	Gerald Theberge
	Dmitriy Ukolov	Richard Rodenhiser	Robert White
	Aleksandr Uwarov	Edward Sampson	Keith Woodall
1960	**UNITED STATES**	**CANADA**	**U.S.S.R.**
	Roger A. Christian	Bob Attersley	Veniamin Aleksandrov
	William Christian	Moe Benoit	Aleksandr Aljimetov
	Robert B. Cleary	Jim Connelly	Juriy Baulin
	William J. Cleary	Jack Douglas	Michail Bytschkov
	Eygene Grazia	Fred Etcher	Vladimir Grebennikov
	Paul Johnson	Bob Forhan	Yevgeniy Groschev
	John Kirrane	Don Head	Viktor Jakuschev
	John Mayasich	Harold Hurley	Yevgeniy Jerkin
	Jack McCartan	Kenneth Laufman	Nikolay Karpov
	Robert McVey	Floyd Martin	Alfred Kutschewskiy
	Richard Meredith	Bob McKnight	Konstantin Loktev
	Weldon Olson	Clifford Pennington	Stanislav Petuchov
	Edwyn Owen	Donald Rope	V. Prjaschtschnikov
	Rodney Paavola	Bob Rousseau	Nikolay Putschkov
	Lawrence Palmer	George Samolenko	Genrich Sidorenkov
	Richard Rodenhiser	Harry Sinden	Nikolay Sologybov
	Thomas Williams	Darryl Sly	Juriy Tsitsinov
1964	**U.S.S.R.**	**SWEDEN**	**CZECHOSLOVAKIA**
	Viktor Konovalenko	K. Svensson	Vlado Dzurila
	Boris Zaitsev	L. Haeggroth	Vlado Nadrchal
	Viktor Kuzkin	G. Blome	F. Gregor
	Eduard Ivanov	R. Stoltz	R. Potsch
	Vitaliy Davidov	N. Johansson	F. Tikal
	Aleksandr Ragulin	B. Nordlander	S. Sventek
	Olyeg Zatisev	N. Nilsson	L. Smid
	Aleksandr Almetov	U. Sterner	J. Walter
	Viktor Yakushev	T. Johansson	Josef Golonka
	Vyacheslav Starchinov	R. Pettersson	Jiri Holik
	Konstantin Loktev	E. Macaettae	V. Bubnik
	Boris Mayorov	L. Johansson	Jan Klapac
	Anatoliy Firsov	L. Lundvall	J. Dolana
	Stanislav Petuchov	C. Oeberg	S. Pryl
	Veniamin Aleksandrov	A. Andersson	M. Vlach
	Evgeniy Maiorov	U. Oehrlund	Jaroslav Jirik
	Leonid Volkov	H. Mild	Josef Cerny

GOLD	SILVER	BRONZE
1968 **U.S.S.R.**	**CZECHOSLOVAKIA**	**CANADA**
Viktor Zinger	Vladimir Nadrchal	Wayne Stephenson
Viktor Konovalenko	Vlado Dzurila	Kenneth Broderick
Vitaliy Davidov	Oldrich Machac	Marshall Johnston
Viktor Blinov	Jan Suchy	Brian Glennie
Igor Romishevskiy	Josef Horesovsky	Barry Mckenzie
Olyeg Zaitsev	Frantisek Pospisil	Paul Conlin
Aleksandr Ragulin	Karel Masopust	Edward Hargreaves
Viktor Kuzkin	Frantisek Sevcik	Terence O'Malley
Boris Mayorov	Jan Havel	Raymond Cadieux
Anatoliy Firsov	Jan Hrbaty	Stephen Monteith
Evgeniy Zymin	Vaclav Nedomansky	William Macmillan
Viktor Polupanov	Josef Golonka	Francis Huck
Anatoliy Ionov	Petr Hejma	Garry Dineen
Vyacheslav Starchinov	Jiri Kochta	Danny O'Shea
Evgeniy Michakov	Jaroslav Jirik	Morris Mott
Vladimir Vikulov	Jiri Holik	Herbert Pinder
Yuriy Moiseyev	Josef Cerny	Rogert Bourbonnais
Venyamin Aleksandrov	Jan Klapac	Gerry Pinder
1972 **U.S.S.R.**	**UNITED STATES**	**CZECHOSLOVAKIA**
Vladislav Tretiak	Michael Curran	Vado Dzurila
Aleksandr Pachkov	Peter Sears	Jiri Holocek
Viktor Kuzkin	James McElmury	Rudolf Tajcnar
Vitaliy Davidov	Thomas Mellor	Jaroslav Holik
Yevgeniy Michalkov	Frank Sanders	Vaclav Nedomansky
Aleksandr Maltsev	Charles Brown	Vladimir Bednar
Aleksandr Iakuchev	Richard McGlynn	Frantisek Pospisil
Vladimir Lutchenko	Walter Old	Jiri Holik
Aleksandr Ragulin	Kenneth Ahearn	Karal Vohralik
Igor Romichevskiy	Stuart Irving	Josef Horesovsky
Gennadiy Tsygankov	Mark Howe	Oldrich Machac
Valeri Kharlamov	Henry Bucha	Josef Cerny
Yuriy Blinov	Keith Christiansen	Bohuslav Stastny
Vladimir Petrov	Robbie Ftorek	Richard Farda
Anatoliy Firsov	Ronald Marsland	Ivan Hlinka
Boris Mikhailov	Craig Farmer	Jiri Kochta
Vladimir Vikulov	Timothy Sheehy	Vladimir Martinec
1976 **U.S.S.R.**	**CZECHOSLOVAKIA**	**GERMANY**[1]
Alexandr Sidelnikov	Jiri Holecek	Erich Weishaupt
Vladislav Tretiak	Pavel Svitana	Anton Kehle
Alexiandr Gusev	Oldrich Machac	Rudolf Thanner
Vladimir Lutchenko	Milan Chalupa	Josef Voelk
Sergei Babinov	Frantisek Pospisil	Udo Kiessling
Yuriy Liapkin	Miroslav Dvorak	Stefan Metz
Valeriy Vasilyev	Milan Kajkl	Klans Auhuber
Gennadiy Tsygankov	Jiri Bubla	Ignaz Berndaner
Sergei Kapustin	Milan Novy	Rainer Philipp
Victor Shalimov	Vladimir Martinec	Lorenz Funk
Alexandr Maltsev	Jiri Novak	Wolfgang Boos
Boris Alexandrov	Bohuslav Stastny	Ernst Koepf
Boris Mikhailov	Jiri Holik	Ferenc Vozar
Alexandr Iakuchev	Ivan Hlinka	Walter Koeberle
Vladimir Petrov	Eduard Novak	Erich Kuehnhackl
Valeriy Kharlamov	Jaroslav Pouzar	Alois Schloder
Vladimir Shadrin	Bohuslav Ebermann	Martin Hinterstocker
Victor Jlutkov	Josef Augusta	Franz Reindl

---

[1] Three-way tie for bronze with USA and Finland decided on goal average.

	GOLD	SILVER	BRONZE
1980	**UNITED STATES**	**U.S.S.R.**	**SWEDEN**
	Steven Janaszak	Vladimir Mischkin	Pelle Lindbergh
	James Craig	Vladislav Tretiak	William Lofqvist
	Kenneth Morrow	Vyacheslav Fetissov	Tomas Jonsson
	Michael Ramsey	Vasiliy Pervuchin	Sture Andersson
	William Baker	Valeriy Vassilyev	Ulf Weinstock
	John O'Callahan	Aleksey Kasanotov	Jan Eriksson
	Bob Suter	Sergey Starikov	Tommy Samuelsson
	David Silk	Zinetula Bilyaletdinov	Mats Waltin
	Neal Broten	Vladimir Krutov	Thomas Eriksson
	Mark Johnson	Alexandr Maltsev	Per Lundqvist
	Steven Christoff	Yuriy Lebedyev	Mats Ahlberg
	Mark Wells	Boris Mikhailov	Hakan Eriksson
	Mark Pavelich	Vladimir Petrov	Mats Naslund
	Eric Strobel	Valeriy Kharlamov	Lennart Norberg
	Michael Eruzione	Helmut Balderis	Bengt Lundholm
	David Christain	Victor Jlutkov	Leif Holmgren
	Robert McLanahan	Aleksandr Golikov	Bo Berglund
	William Schneider	Sergey Makarov	Harald Luckner
	Philip Verchota	Vladimir Golikov	Dan Soderstrom
	John Harrington	Aleksandr Skvortzov	Lars Molin
1984	**USSR**	**CZECHOSLOVAKIA**	**SWEDEN**
	Vyatcheslav Fetissov	Milan Chalupa	Arne Michael Thelven
	Aleksey Kassatonov	Jaroslav Benak	Bo Ericsson
	Sergey Makarov	Jiri Lala	Jens Erik Ohling
	Igor Larionov	Vladimir Kyhos	Per-Erik Eklung
	Vladimir Kroutov	Franticheck Tchernik	Peter Gradin
	Vassili Pervukhin	Arnold Kadlec	Thomas Ahlen
	Zenetoula Bilyatletdinov	Miloslav Horava	Mats Thelin
	Sergey Chepelev	Igor Liba	Karl Soedergren
	Aleksandr Guerasimov	Darius Rusnak	Mats Waltin
	Andrei Khomoutov	Vincent Lukatch	Tommy Motrh
	Igor Stelnov	Radoslav Svoboda	Goeran Lindblom
	Sergey Starikov	Eduard Uvira	Leif Nordin
	Nikolai Drozdetsky	Pavel Richter	Tomas Sandstroem
	Viktor Tumenyev	Vladimir Ruzsitchka	Lars Eriksson
	Aleksandr Kozhevnikov	Vladimir Cladr	Thom Eklund
	Aleksandr Skvortsov	Jiri Hrdina	Peter Hjalm
	Vladimir Kovin	Duschan Paschek	Thomas Rundquist
	Mikhail Vasilyev	Jaroslav Korbela	Mats Hessel
	Valdimir Zoubkov		

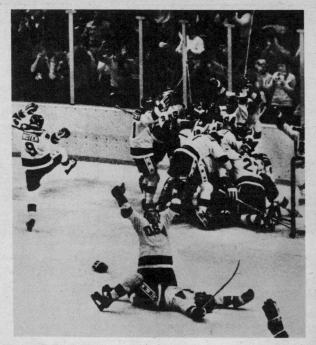

The U.S.A. hockey team celebrated wildly after its 4-3 upset victory in the semi-finals against the heavily favored Soviet team in 1980. A 4-2 victory over Finland in the final game secured the gold medal for the American skaters.

OLYMPIC RECORDS

ARCHERY

EVENT	POINTS	NAME & COUNTRY	YEAR
Men's Double FITA	2616	Darrell Pace (USA)	1984
Women's Double FITA	2568	Hyang-Soon Seo (KOR)	1984

CYCLING

EVENT	MIN/SEC.	NAME & COUNTRY	YEAR
1000 meters time trial	1 02.955	Lothar Thoms (GDR)	1980
4000 meters individual pursuit	4 34.92	Robert Dill-Bundi (SWI)	1980
4000 meters team pursuit	4 14.64	U.S.S.R.	1980

SHOOTING

EVENT	POINTS	NAME & COUNTRY	YEAR
Small-bore (3 pos) equals	1173	Malcolm Cooper (GBR)	1984
Small bore rifle (prone)	599	Ho Jun Li (PRK)	1972
	599	Karl-Heinz Smieszek (GER)	1976
	599	Karoly Varga (HUN)	1980
	599	Hellfried Heilfort (GDR)	1980
Small-bore (prone) equals	599	Edward Etzel (USA)	1984
Free pistol	581	Aleksandr Melentev (URS)	1980
Rapid fire pistol	597	Norbert Klaar (GDR)	1976
Running game	589	Igor Sokolov (URS)	1980
	589	Thomas Pfeffer (GDR)	1980
Trap	199	Angelo Scalzone (ITA)	1972
Skeet	198	Evgeny Petrov (URS)	1968
	198	Romano Garagnani (ITA)	1968
	198	Konrad Wirnhier (GER)	1968
	198	Josef Panacek (TCH)	1976
	198	Eric Swinkels (HOL)	1976
	198	Luciano Giovannetti (ITA)	1980
Skeet equals	198	Matthew Dryke (USA)	1984
Air Rifle	589	Philippe Herberle (FRA)	1984

WOMEN

EVENT	POINTS	NAME & COUNTRY	YEAR
Sport Pistol	585	Linda Thom (CAN)	1984
	585	Ruby Fox (USA)	1984
Standard Rifle	581	Xiaoxuan Wu (CHN)	1984
Air Rifle	393	Pat Spurgin (USA)	1984

SWIMMING

EVENT	MIN./SEC.	NAME & COUNTRY	YEAR
100 meters freestyle	49.80	Ambrose Gaines (USA)	1984
200 meters freestyle	1 47.44	Michael Gross (FRG)	1984
400 meters freestyle	3 50.91	Thomas Fahrner (FRG)	1984
4 × 100 meters freestyle relay	3 19.03	USA	1984
4 × 200 meters freestyle relay	7 15.69	USA	1984
100 meters breaststroke	1 01.65	Steve Lundquist (USA)	1984
200 meters breaststroke	2 13.34	Victor Davis (CAN)	1984
100 meters butterfly	53.08	Michael Gross (FRG)	1984
200 meters butterfly	1 57.04	Jon Sieben (AUS)	1984
100 meters backstroke	1 58.99	Rick Carey (USA)	1984
200 meters medley	2 01.42	Alex Baumann (CAN)	1984
400 meters medley	4 17.41	Alex Baumann (CAN)	1984
4 × 100 meters medley relay	3 39.30	USA	1984

MEN
EVENT

WOMEN

100 meters freestyle	54.79	Barbara Krause (GDR)	1980
200 meters freestyle	1 58.33	Barbara Krause (GDR)	1980
400 meters freestyle	4 07.10	Tiffany Cohen (USA)	1984
800 meters freestyle	8 24.95	Tiffany Cohen (USA)	1984
4 × 100 meters freestyle relay	3 42.71	East Germany	1980
100 meters breaststroke	1 09.88	Petra Van Staveren (HOL)	1984
200 meters breaststroke	2 29.54	Lina Kachushite (URS)	1980
100 meters butterfly	59.05	Mary Meagher (USA)	1984
200 meters butterfly	2 06.90	Mary Meagher (USA)	1984
100 meters backstroke	1 00.86	Rica Reinisch (GDR)	1980
200 meters backstroke	2 11.77	Rica Reinisch (GDR)	1980
200 meters medley	2 12.64	Tracy Caulkins (USA)	1984
400 meters medley	4 36.29	Petra Schneider (GDR)	1980
4 × 100 meters medley relay	4 06.67	East Germany	1980

TRACK & FIELD ATHLETICS

MEN
EVENT

EVENT	HR	MIN	SEC	NAME & COUNTRY	YEAR
100 meters			9.95	Jim Hines (USA)	1968
200 meters			19.80	Carl Lewis (USA)	1984
400 meters			43.86	Lee Evans (USA)	1968
800 meters		1	43.00	Joaquim Cruz (BRA)	1984
1500 meters		3	32.53	Sebastian Coe (GBR)	1984
5000 meters		13	05.59	Said Aouita (MAR)	1984
10000 meters		27	38.35	Lasse Viren (FIN)	1972
Marathon	2	09	21.0	Carlos Lopes (POR)	1984
20 km walk	1	23	13.0	Ernesto Canto (MEX)	1984
50 km walk	3	47	26.0	Raul Gonzalez (MEX)	1984
110 meters hurdles			13.20	Roger Kingdom (USA)	1984
400 meters hurdles			47.64	Ed Moses (USA)	1976
3000 meters steeplechase		8	08.02	Anders Garderud (SWE)	1976
4 × 100 meters relay			37.83	USA	1984
			38.19	U.S.A.	1972
4 × 400 meters relay		2	56.16	U.S.A.	1968
			meters		

High jump	2.36	Gerd Wessig (GDR)	1980
Pole vault	5.78	Wladyslaw Kozakiewics (POL)	1980
Long jump	8.90	Bob Beamon (USA)	1968
Triple jump	17.39	Viktor Saneyev (URS)	1968
Shot put	21.35	Vladimir Kiselyev (URS)	1980
Discus throw	68.28	Mac Wilkins (USA)	1976
Hammer throw	81.80	Yuriy Sedykh (URS)	1980
Javelin throw	94.58	Miklos Nemeth (HUN)	1976
Decathlon	8847 points*	Daley Thompson (GBR)	1984

*New tables

WOMEN	MIN SEC		
100 meters	10.97	Evelyn Ashford (USA)	1984
200 meters	21.81	Valerie Brisco-Hooks (USA)	1984
400 meters	48.83	Valerie Brisco-Hooks (USA)	1984
800 meters	1 53.43	Nadezda Olizarenko (URS)	1980
1500 meters	3 56.56	Tatyana Kazankina (URS)	1980
3000 meters	8 35.96	Maricica Puica (ROM)	1984
Marathon	2 24 52.0	Joan Benoit (USA)	1984
100 meters hurdles	12.56	Vera Komissova (URS)	1980
400 meters hurdles	Not previously held		
4 × 100 meters relay	41.60	East Germany	1980
4 × 400 meters relay	3 18.29	USA	1984
	meters		
High jump	2.02	Ulrike Meyfarth (FRG)	1984
Long jump	7.06	Tatyana Kolpakova (URS)	1980
Shot put	22.41	Ilona Slupianek (GDR)	1980
Discus throw	69.96	Evelin Jahl (GDR)	1980
Javelin throw	69.56	Tessa Sanderson (GBR)	1984
Heptathlon	6387 points*	Glynis Nunn (AUS)	1984

*New Tables

WEIGHTLIFTING

EVENT	TOTAL WEIGHT (KG)	NAME & COUNTRY	YEAR
52 kg class	245.0	Kanykek Osmonoliev (URS)	1980
	245.0	Ho Bong Chol (PRK)	1980
	245.0	Han Gyong Si (PRK)	1980
	245.0	Bela Olah (HUN)	1980
56 kg class	275.0	Daniel Nunez (CUB)	1980
60 kg class	290.0	Viktor Mazin (URS)	1980
67.5 kg class	342.5	Yanko Rusev (BUL)	1980
75 kg class	360.0	Asen Zlatev (BUL)	1980
82.5 kg class	400.0	Yurik Vardanyan (URS)	1980
90 kg class	382.5	David Rigert (URS)	1976
100 kg class	395.0	Ota Zaremba (TCH)	1980
110 kg class	422.5	Leonid Taranenko (URS)	1980
100+ kg class	440.0	Vasiliy Alexeyev (URS)	1976
	440.0	Sultan Rachmanov (URS)	1980

SPEED SKATING

EVENT	MIN	SEC	NAME & COUNTRY	YEAR
500 meters		38.03	Eric Heiden (USA)	1980
1000 meters	1	15.18	Eric Heiden (USA)	1980
1500 meters	1	55.44	Eric Heiden (USA)	1980
3000 meters	7	02.29	Eric Heiden (USA)	1980
5000 meters	14	28.13	Eric Heiden (USA)	1980

WOMEN

EVENT	MIN	SEC	NAME & COUNTRY	YEAR
500 meters		41.02	Christa Rothenburger (GDR)	1984
1000 meters	1	21.61	Karin Enke (GDR)	1984
1500 meters	2	03.42	Karin Enke (GDR)	1984
3000 meters	4	24.79	Andrea Schoene (GDR)	1984

VENUES FOR OLYMPIC GAMES SPORTS AT SEOUL 1988

Sport   *Venue*

Track & Field   Olympic Stadium, Seoul Sports Complex
Archery   Hwarang Archery Field
Basketball   Chamshil Gymnasium, Seoul Sports Complex
Boxing   Chamshil Students' Gymnasium, Seoul Sports Complex
Canoeing   Han River Regatta Course
Cycling   Velodrome, Olympic Park
Equestrianism
    General   Seoul Equestrian Park
    Endurance Test   Wondang Ranch
    Grand Prix   Olympic Stadium, Seoul Sports Complex
Fencing   Fencing Gymnasium, Olympic Park
Football
    Preliminaries   Pusan, Tongdaemun, Taejon, Kwangju, Taegu stadiums
    Semi-finals   Pusan Stadium, Olympic Stadium
    Final   Olympic Stadium, Seoul Sports Complex
Gymnastics   Gymnastics Hall, Olympic Park
Handball   Suwon Gymnasium
Handball—Men's Final   Gymnastics Hall, Olympic Park
Hockey (Field)   Songnam Stadium
Judo   Changchoog Gymnasium
Modern Pentathlon
    Riding   Seoul Equestrian Park
    Fencing   Fencing Gymnasium, Olympic Park
    Swimming   Indoor Swimming Pool, Olympic Park
    Shooting   Taenung International Shooting Range
    Cross-country   Taenung Country Club
Rowing   Han River Regatta Course
Shooting   Taenung International Shooting Range
Swimming
    Swimming   Indoor Swimming Pool, Olympic Park
    Diving   Chamshil Indoor Pool, Seoul Sports Complex
    Synchronized   Indoor Swimming Pool, Olympic Park
    Water Polo
      Preliminaries   Chamshil Indoor Pool, Seoul Sports Complex
      Finals   Indoor Swimming Pool, Olympic Park
Table Tennis   Seoul National University Gymnasium
Tennis   Tennis Courts, Olympic Park
Volleyball   Hanyang University Gymnasium & Saemaul Sports Hall
Weightlifting   Weightlifting Gymnasium, Olympic Park
Wrestling   Sangmu Gymnasium
Yachting   Pusan Yachting Centre

Demonstrations

Baseball   Chamshil Baseball Stadium, Seoul Sports Comlex
Judo, Women   Changchoong Gymnasium
Taekwondo   Changchoong Gymnasium

PICTURE CREDITS

The editors and publisher wish to thank the following for pictures used in this book:
Aitken Ltd.; Allsport Photographic; Associated Press; Canoeing Magazine; Central
Press; Gerry Cranham; Tony Duffy; European Picture Union; Mary Evans;
International News Photo; Keystone Press Agency; E.D. Lacey; London & Wide
World Photos; Don Morley; Planet News; Radio Times Hulton Picture Library;
Popperfoto; Sports and General Press Agency; United Press International; World
Sports; Dave Terry.

BANTAM
SHOP-AT-HOME
C·A·T·A·L·O·G

Special Offer,
Buy a Bantam Book
for only 50¢.

Now you can have Bantam's catalog filled with hundreds of titles plus take advantage of our unique and exciting bonus book offer. A special offer which gives you the opportunity to purchase a Bantam book for only 50¢. Here's how!

By ordering any five books at the regular price per order, you can also choose any other single book listed (up to a $5.95 value) for just 50¢. Some restrictions do apply, but for further details why not send for Bantam's catalog of titles today!

Just send us your name and address and we will send you a catalog!

BANTAM BOOKS, INC.
P.O. Box 1006, South Holland, Ill. 60473

Mr./Mrs./Ms. _____
(please print)

Address _____

City _____ State _____ Zip _____
FC(A)—10/87

Please allow four to six weeks for delivery.